CW01637789

Escaping Alienation

A Philosophy of Alienation and Dealienation

Warren Frederick Morris

University Press of America,® Inc.
Lanham · New York · Oxford

University Press of America,® Inc.
4720 Boston Way
Lanham, Maryland 20706
UPA Acquisitions Department (301) 459-3366

12 Hid's Copse Rd.
Cumnor Hill, Oxford OX2 9JJ

Printed in the United States of America
British Library Cataloging in Publication Information Available

Library of Congress Cataloging-in-Publication Data

Morris, Warren Frederick.
Escaping alienation : a philosopy of alienation and dealienation /
Warren Frederick Morris.
p. cm
Includes bibliographical references and index.
l. Alienation (Philosophy) I. Title.

B808.2 .M68 2002
128—dc21 2002020142 CIP

ISBN 0-7618-2220-8 (paperback : alk. ppr.)

The paper used in this publication meets the minimum requirements of American National Standard for Information Sciences—Permanence of Paper for Printed Library Materials, ANSI Z39.48—1984

This work is dedicated to my wife
and all those like her who express
their love by nurturing others.

Fred Morris
October, 2002

Table of Contents

Preface

The philosophy of alienation expressed herein is motivated by and flows from my own life experience and the effort to understand it. Alienation, a universal phenomenon, is highly personal in that everyone confronts it in one form or another. I have confronted it with slow maturation resulting from poor childhood physical health, incomplete parental nurturing, academic under-achievement and an absence of satisfaction in making a living in a governmental bureaucracy. Retired life has liberated me from all but the physical form of alienation common to anyone my age. These vintage years of retirement have turned out to be the happiest.

Leisure has given me the opportunity to develop a deeper philosophical understanding of alienation. It is based upon over forty years of study culminating in a synthesis of various philosophical perspectives. From this and from pondering various philosophical questions relating to alienation, I have established what I believe to be an original contribution to a modern understanding of alienation and dealienation. Much is owed to philosophers of negativity from Parmenides to Hegel and Heidegger. The same is also to be said of naturalism, as expressed by pragmatism, that original philosophy of American culture. Freudian psychoanalytic theory has contributed much as has the critiques of modern culture from social psychologists, notably Fromm, Reisman and White. With the assistance of such keen intellects, and from pondering my personal experience of alienation, its philosophical meaning has been revealed. The intellectual journey of writing this philosophy has been a great pleasure in this closing phase of life.

This work seeks the wisdom of life in the tradition of the great Socrates. The intellectual journey has provided me with the insight of knowing why the alienation and dealienation of my life had to be the way it turned out to be. I believe and hope that it offers some insight that would be beneficial to those curious enough to tackle some very compact thinking, possibly difficult for those uninitiated to philosophy. Recognizing this possibility, I have striven for clear expression, providing assistance to any bemused reader with a glossary defining some psychological and philosophical terminology, including my own. An index has also been constructed to assist those with special scholarly interests. My thanks to the following three individuals for supporting this work. It was enhanced with a glossary suggested by Dr. Andrew Schwartz. Dr. Nelson Wikstrom provided incisive questioning of my philosophy and made helpful suggestions relating to publication. My son, Jefferson Morris, provided manuscript editing, formatting, and book cover design.

June 18, 2001
Alexandria, Virginia

Introduction

Purpose, Structure and Method

This work is an ontologically based philosophical anthropology providing a comprehensive theory of alienation and dealienation. What it means to be human is answered from diverse perspectives provided by naturalism, pragmatism, existentialism, psychoanalysis and social psychology. Ontological negativity discussed by thinkers such as Parmenides, Hegel, Heidegger and Freud is the conceptual core of this philosophy. The ontological question of the meaning of being is answered existentially. But the perspective is also naturalistic in that an essential human nature is postulated. The implications of this essential nature are drawn out to exhibit the universal significance of alienation and dealienation. Finally, this essential nature provides a normative basis for self-existence thus making possible a prescription for dealienation.

This philosophy progressively provides concepts for understanding alienation and dealienation. Beginning with a general ontological conception of negativity, there follows a definition of the essential nature of the self. It is defined by what it needs, desires and by its capacity for rationality and freedom. But the self is also most importantly a social being. This dimension of its being requires a conception of the process of socialization. Its aim is to enable dealienation by constructing a self-concept. This is accomplished by identifications that can be formed non-rationally, irrationally or rationally. A self-concept is then projected through the work of self-objectification. When socialization is defective, the outcome is alienation and evil. If, however, socialization is successful, the capacity for dealienation is maximized. An analysis of rationality and freedom coupled with an analysis of socialization answers the question, "What are the conditions for successful dealienation?" An ontological theory of negativity logically integrated with a conception of self and socialization provide the foundation for understanding culture, religion and formulating a modern philosophical prescription for successful dealienation.

The purpose of this work is to understand alienation and to provide a philosophical prescription for dealienation. The structure of the work reflects its purpose. Each chapter logically builds upon those preceding it, thereby forming an extended argument. Development proceeds by first explaining alienation with a general conception of negativity. Upon this basis, the self is defined and the phases of its development are described. The process of socialization is then analyzed with its contributing components defined. This foundation of philosophical concepts is applied to understanding social institutions and phenomena, particularly of religion and culture. Alienation and socialization is then related to personal freedom and its contemporary cultural experimentation with extending its scope and limits. Along the way in these analyses, the roots of evil and the role of traditional authority are dealt with. Finally, the argument concludes with a prescription for dealienation. The requirements for maximizing the human capacity for successful dealienation are specified in terms of socialization and the development of freedom and rationality for every individual.

Although this work would obviously appeal to academic philosophers, it is also intended to reach the general public. The reader need not learn an idiosyncratic philosophical language of the author to acquire an understanding of the text. That is not to say there is no technical language provided herein. However, it is sparingly used and only to convey key concepts, often repeated. Whenever the terminology of other philosophers or psychologists is employed, it is defined for the reader in an extensive glossary citing the founder of it. This, it is hoped, will make the text less arcane to the general reader. For this author's intention is to communicate as clearly and simply as possible. If some wisdom is contained herein, so much the better. More importantly, if the reader is stimulated to think deeply about the issues raised, that result would be even more satisfactory.

One can become philosophical when asking fundamentally important questions with very general implications. For example: what or who is the Other, self, or God? The answer to such a question often leads to others. Moreover, the result of answering a series of logically interrelated questions organizes thought and the behavioral consequences of it into a coherent system of concepts. This result is a philosophy. A philosophy of alienation was developed from a personal interest in answering certain fundamental questions with broad import. Answering one question logically led to others. This questioning and answering endeavor amounted to a process of discovery. What was discovered was coherence among the questions considered and answers forthcoming. After a time it became clear that a philosophy was being constructed focused upon an intellectual attempt to achieve a general understand of alienation and dealienation.

No doubt that the emerging coherence among concepts is embedded in language. Nevertheless, the process of discovery was not simply a trivial linguistic exercise. For what is signified, the facts of experience and generalizations about them were fully operative in philosophizing. At the completion of the inquiry, an attempt was made to ask what questions were asked and answered. In fact, it was thought possible to structure the whole work as a coherent series of questions with answers supplied in each successive chapter. If the work were rewritten in this manner, it would be logically very neat and tight. However, this would only have been a result of reflecting logically upon the whole intellectual endeavor; not how the process of research and thinking in fact proceeded.

Language has existential signification. Philosophical discourse can discover hidden meaning among signifiers with existential import embedded in the structure of language itself. The thought of being and being of thought reside within the structure of language. And, the meaning of being is revealed through discourse based upon self-existence and human experience in general. Philosophical discourse is about answering questions of fundamental importance to understanding the world and how we ought to live. From Socrates onward, classical philosophy has sought the wisdom to live rightly in order to achieve a measure of happiness from a melancholy life marked by human suffering, loss, and death. This work maintains a classical focus, although the philosophical questions may be somewhat differently phrased. Still, they reappear with the same urgency for every generation. The following questions, many of which have been addressed by great philosophers of the past, are again addressed herein:

Chapter	Question
1	What conditions constitute meaning?
1	How are thought and being related?
1	What is the relationship of truth to value?
1	What is the meaning of being?
1, 2, 5	What or who is the Other, self, and God?
1, 2, 3	What is the theoretical basis of alienation?
2	What is the psychological and sociological basis of evil?
2	Can a sense of obligation be derived from human need and desire?
2	Is there an essential human nature?

3	How can work alienate or dealienate?
3	Is so-called *necessary connection* derivable from work?
3	Is socialization sufficient to effect successful dealienation?
3	Can the self creates social norms and roles?
3	How is desire modified by changing its original object?
4	Can the self be the locus of truth and value?
4	How is freedom related to rationality?
2, 4	How is a sense of obligation related to rational freedom?
4	Can freedom be trusted?
4	Why escape freedom?
4	Can freedom be normative?
4	How does a democratic society facilitate dealienation?
5	What does religion signify psychologically and sociologically?
6	Is the process of self-identification lifelong?
6	How is culture conceived relative to alienation and dealienation?
6	What is the alienating or dealienating effect of subordinating self to culture or vice versa?
3, 6	How can the process of identification be alienating?
3, 6, 7	How are authenticity and autonomy related, and are they necessary for dealienation?
7	Can alienation be overcome?
7	Can naturalism provide a philosophical prescription for dealienation?

Any philosophy with a synoptic purpose must be to some extent speculative. This invariably follows from the nature of signification. For to use universal concepts and to generalize with them moves thought beyond actuality. Ontological negativity, the basis of signification and logical implication suggests a reality and knowledge yet unexperienced, but potentially realizable by future experience. This philosophy of alienation and dealienation is synoptic and therefor necessarily speculative to some degree, particularly with regard to its theoretical basis in ontological negativity. The roots of this perspective are of ancient origin in western philosophy, but peculiarly relevant to the contemporary development of science, both speculative and applied, whether dealing with macro or micro level phenomena. Yet, although this philosophy attempts an explanation from the slime to God, so to speak, it is not metaphysics. Science is left to the scientists with their amazing discoveries. What is attempted herein is to answer some fundamental questions which, when integrated, present a synoptic vision of what is most real to everyone. In this, there is a *gestalt* or *Weltanschauung*, as the Germans call it.

Tribute to Hegel

Great thinkers stand on the shoulders of their predecessors, as did Aristotle upon those of Plato and Hegel upon those of both philosophers. The greatness of Hegel's thought lies partly in the reactions it stimulates centuries after its original expression. We continue to learn from it. Moreover, to know why we disagree with it is to make an advance in philosophy. Great intellectual rewards can be reaped from the brilliant insights and suggestibility of great philosophers such as Georg Wilhelm Fredrich Hegel. What makes him such a great thinker is that he was so wrong about the fundamentals. This is not as paradoxical as it might at first seem. Working out the reasons for disagreement with him often enough suggested a very different philosophical perspective. Explicating it has hopefully led to a modest advance toward philosophical wisdom. The research for this work began with a comprehensive study of Hegelian philosophy. It was aimed at discovering an adequate view of alienation; recognizing the fact that Hegel was a seminal thinker on the subject. Although his philosophy reflected the orthodox Judeo-Christian view of alienation, his ontology has hidden in it a more modern explanation of alienation than that provided by the ancients.

Hegel did not systematically explicate alienation. The term is found only occasionally, for example, in scattered discourse on property rights and culture. Even so, the thrust of his whole philosophical outlook can be considered an implicit general treatment of the subject. Hegel's Absolute Idealism and Christian interpretation of alienation has become untenable by the subsequent intellectual history of western civilization. Extensive modifications to Hegelian thought on the subject is warranted by subsequent thinkers such as Marx, Freud, existentialists, pragmatists, structuralists and contemporary social psychologists. Hegelian philosophy is frequently employed as a base to be integrated with the additional insights of subsequent thinkers to formulate a more adequate treatment of the subject. The inevitable result is in some sense eclectic, yet an original treatment. The outcome of this endeavor is then, in effect, a tribute to Hegel: indeed one of the greats of philosophy, whose originality and suggestiveness on the subject of alienation echoes to posterity centuries later.

Hegel's philosophy is all about alienation. He provided an excellent theoretical basis for understanding the subject. My task is to contribute toward developing a complete philosophy of alienation. Hegel was *the thinker* from which to make a start toward this goal. Of course, other thinkers both before and after him have dealt with the subject, so pervasive is it in personal life and human history. But Hegel was the first philosopher to provide an ontological foundation for understanding alienation in a generalized sense. His analyses of being and the finitude of determinate being form the basis for understanding alienation and dealienation in its vast array of particular forms. His key philosophical concepts explain dealienation as a developmental process operative at every level of being, with a natural interest intensely focused upon personal life and cultural history.

Hegelian ontology suggested that a negative dialectic drives alienation and dealienation in thought and living history. Yet, Hegel never systematically developed a comprehensive explanation of alienation. This was precluded by his religious and cultural authoritarianism buttressed by a narrow conception of rationality borrowed from Aristotelian deductive logic. In addition, his authoritarian orientation projected a distrust of the very freedom he so highly prized. Thus, his theorizing about history and its relation to personal freedom would leave humanity irrevocably and profoundly alienated. What I have attempted herein is to fathom the imperfection of Hegelian thought related to the subject of alienation, and to make a modest advance by constructing an alternative more adequate to a modern understanding of human freedom and rationality.

Beyond Myth and Metaphor

The grand religious metaphor of Hegelian alienation is the biblical expulsion from paradise succeeded by historically notable efforts of redemption taking various secular forms of reconciliation as described by Hegel's historical phenomenology. The odyssey of dealienation is a journey of the human spirit back to paradise, but one fully differentiated by history from its original amorphous and ambiguous significance. This odyssey is both personal and historical culminating in a return to the substance of culture taking the final form of acceptance of it and active promotion of its norms, practices and aims by the individual. As parts of the whole are separated from each other and as the individual is alienated from his culture, so is there a purpose of reconciliation guiding the process of dialectical progression. The purpose is to reconstitute the whole as made perfect through a phenomenological process representing a dialectic of Ideas of Geist worked through in history. Here Hegel reflects the Judeo-Christian belief that human history is the drama of a divine plan in the mind of God. The purpose guiding history represents a drive for re-unification of separated or lost parts, a Platonic Eros toward realizing truth, goodness and beauty in a perfect whole of being. Hegelian dealienation has this aesthetic dimension to its purpose. From Hegel's absolute idealist perspective, dealienation occurs with a communal self-objectification conforming to the Ideas of Geist.

Various forms of negation such as contradiction, opposition of ideas, denial, and human conflict drive a Hegelian dialectic: breaking the whole of reality into disparate opposed elements which are then reconciled and reconstituted into a whole expressing the perfection of being as such. The result of dealienation is an enriched return to a paradisiacal beginning where an alien *Other*, or object, is re-unified with the subject. The metaphor of this dialectic is of a reflected image in a mirror. When alienation in all its forms is finally overcome, and as the subject gazes at himself in the mirror, he sees a completely humanized world; a world which is his own objectification and thus no longer in any way alien to himself; a world he is completely familiar with and at home within. The reflected object in the mirror is recognized as an expression of the subject looking at it. And this familiar expression is synonymous with a particular culture that has been promoted and affirmed.

Being, finite or infinite, according to Hegel's conception, is an implicit whole, potentially complete and perfect. Alienation is a rent in spiritual substance with a consequent loss of wholeness, perfection and completeness in being. Differentiation of components of a whole is a process of disuniting and uniting it. Separated components are presented and experienced as Other or alien, with something missing or lacking; an incompleteness in being or in its complete development. Any part isolated from the whole is alienated, as is anything undeveloped and incomplete. For example, the self is alienated when isolated from fulfillment of its potential. It is also alienated when isolated from community, or from God.

Themes of alienation are loss and recovery, separation of part from whole, opposition and reconciliation. Dealienation is a dialectical process of negating what is separated in a development actualizing potentialities, re-establishing and completing a perfect whole enriched in meaning with components fully related. Metaphors expressing dealienation are the dissolving of something into a solution, the return of a reflected image in a mirror, and the circular return to a starting point. Alienation will persist until the actuality of the world conforms to its Hegelian Notions and Ideas instantiated by the intentional activity of the self. The world will reflect its image at the completion of its odyssey. In its end, it will recognize its beginning and everything intervening as its own development. In addition, it will be content with what it has become.

Since the beginning of recorded history, alienation and dealienation have been expressed artistically through myth and metaphor. Epic Homeric legends and the biblical expulsion from paradise still resonate after two millennia. Myth and metaphor carry deeply soul stirring cultural messages of accumulated ancestral wisdom. A modern recognition of this is expressed by Carl Jung's archetypal images of the collective unconscious. Alienation and dealienation have always been expressed with metaphors of circularity, departure and return, loss and recovery, emptying and filling and reflected mirror image. Odyssey mythology, although artistically conveying wisdom, is philosophically inadequate. For didactic poetical messages do not systematically analyze their subject matter and so hide as much as they reveal.

Alienation and dealienation, treated mythologically and metaphorically, reconcile self with cultural authoritative Others. Odyssey begins with an alienating departure, a dealienating adventurous maturation and a circular return home with the self changed; nevertheless expressing what was culturally authoritative to begin with. Yet, mythological metaphors leave too much out of account and so present a rather circumscribed conception of alienation. Dealienation is usually treated as a process of subordinating self to authority. This narrows the scope and understanding of alienation and dealienation, restricting its significance to reconciliation with authority. Alienation is set aside as a special human problem, thereby losing its general import for self-existence. And the problem of alienation is resolvable by a self-projection of cultural authority involving a sequence of historical events with a conclusive termination. Although this can be very dramatic and profoundly significant, the effect of such a narrow conception trivializes what is infinitely more important and significant, namely authentic self-realization. This requires transcending a mere accommodation to authority.

Preliminary Orientation

One sense of the verb to alienate is to give up or renounce something belonging to me, as in alienating property: where when I give something up, I cede ownership and renounce any claim to it. Such a dictionary definition is the narrowest signification of the term, providing the merest hint of its broader true significance. A better definition gives the term a much broader sense as a noun generally signifying an undesirable separation or loss, implying some intentional act of recovery with possible reconciliation. Absent a legalistic definition, alienation is commonly understood to be an undesirable separation from something previously possessed or enjoyed. The object from which one is separated can be anything that is prized or valued. It might be God, innocence, happiness, security, liberty, reason and so forth, which we struggle to achieve. Alienation might involve the loss of some ideal or real condition of life.

Implicit in the concept of alienation is human finitude in all of its dimensions of space, time, mortality and mutability. Typical of alienating finitude is confronting a limit; something needed, something frustrating the satisfaction of desire, an obstacle to be overcome. In this sense, the real and ideal are in opposition. As the opposition is overcome in a process of suffering and struggle, the ideal becomes a reality. The world is humanized as the self projects its wants and objectifies its potentiality. Being is revealed and affirmed in its myriad finite forms in a process of transcending limits encountered by self-existence. This overcoming of obstacles and transcending of limits, whether internal or external to the self is herein-designated *dealienation.*

Ontological negativity provides a theoretical foundation for and generic explanation of alienation. But the same theoretical basis was discovered to be generally applicable to describing dealienation, the nature of the self, freedom, rationality, the process socialization and culture. The locus of truth and value is found in a self, socialized beyond narcissism and egoism, possessing a highly developed capacity for rationality and freedom. Its values and norms are a derivative of its natural self-existence wherein obligation is implied by its needs and desires. Its behavior is guided by a conscience implicit in its own existential authenticity and autonomy. Its historically dealienating endeavor display an ethos expressed in the values and institutions of western civilization. From the equal claim of every self, sensed as obligation and integrated with an autonomous conscience, there follows a prescription for self-existence maximizing a human capacity for dealienation. Self-giving love becomes an expression of a *dealienating self.* This analysis implies an ethos underpinning personal liberty, human rights and democracy. An absurdly artificial modern abstracting of fact from value is rejected. Thus, this philosophy does what modern philosophy refuses to do, but what ancient philosophy did and claimed to be the perennial task of philosophy. It is to be synoptic in scope, to speculate where necessary, and to ethically prescribe.

Negativity forms the definition of alienation, whatever forms it takes. Yet, negativity is not simply a trivial attribute of formal logic. Consciousness itself is an act of negation in which an Other alien to the self is distinguished and encountered. As Hegel phrased it, "There is something in its object concealed from consciousness if the object is for consciousness an "other", or something alien, and if consciousness does not know the object as its self."[1] A deficiency in being or knowing something signifies alienation. Something is absent, lost, desired. And this something negates the very being of the self in some way. It opposes any being that contradicts the realization of its potentiality for being or knowing the truth about something. Absence of truth signifies something concealed that is implied by contradiction in thinking about it. This opposition becomes manifest where our idea of something does not correspond with an actual experience of it. To be alienated is sensed as something, which is not, but ought to be the case, an obligation providing an impetus for the self to think and act to negate the deficiency. Intentional thought and action respond, and in so doing, signify a being that is free. Every conceivable human form of alienation implies freedom. Moreover, the aim if not the outcome of exercising freedom is at once the satisfaction of need, desire, self-realization and self-objectification in a progressively humanized world.

Initially the self is an abstract undeveloped Other. It is neither this not that. This lack of substance has been interpreted to signify that the self is a being free to become something. This is undoubtedly true as witnessed by the process of self-development. Whereas the ancients and Hegel recognized the self to be free, they also thought it to possess an essential nature prescribed by a divine authoritative Other. Existentialism also recognizes the self to be free, but without an essential nature defined by an authoritative Other. However, although the self is free, is it nothing in the sense of a pure potentiality for being anything? Consider a mediating viewpoint. The being of any self is a potentiality for being actualized by the fact of its own needs, desires, rationality and freedom. Herein, a radical personal freedom is acknowledged while retaining an essential nature. Constituted by negation of the Other establishes the self as free to become something. It secures its identity through its development. By negating the alien Other that negates it, the self discovers who and what it is. And, through a historical process of exhausting every Other which negates it, the self discovers its world. If all possible alien Others were encountered and negated by the self, being would be completely revealed.

The odyssey of alienation and dealienation is a continuous encounter with and appropriation of an Other. This Other can be any object of consciousness. But no matter what or who it is, it is always alien to the self, even if it were the self. As consciously encountered the Other is a negation of self. And, as dealt with by the self, the alien Other is negated in some way. Being formed by negation, the Other is made alien by the specific way it is opposed to the self. Making the alien Other one's own is to remove its opposition to the self and to integrate it into an expression of the self. Appropriation of the Other requires the capacity of the self to think and to act for itself. After apprehending the Other as alien object or non-self, appropriation begins with thinking about it. It is translated into the thought and language of the self. Hegel thought this occurred dialectically as the Other is rationally comprehended or translated into Notions which are universal, thus relating it to a larger whole structure of meaning.

Appropriation is not merely an abstract exercise of rationality. Rather, appropriation involves the freedom and will of the self acting upon the Other. It is in some way possessed, controlled, and made to serve the purposes of the self. What the alien Other is in itself - its true meaning - is revealed by what the self makes of it. Made a vehicle for expressing the being of the self, the Other loses its alien quality of opposition. It is placed in a whole structure of meaning that is continuously enlarged and progressively comprehended. Therefore, an alien Other is necessary to initiate a process of dealienation that is both self-realization and a discovery of the meaning of being. When the alien Other is made known as to what or who it is, a part of the whole meaning of being is revealed.

Alienation is being in its incomplete aspect. The first negation in being presents the appearance of an alien Other. Thus is alienation an originating opposition in being. Every finite being has something lacking, missing, and encountered as Other. This Other is uncomprehended, strange, unfamiliar, not our own possession, or may even be lost and to be recovered. With finite beings, alienation is generally manifested as the need for something. To a self-conscious being, this need is experienced as a desire for something. A separation or estrangement in being is undesirable, often intolerable. The opposition in being, or contradiction in knowing requires resolution. Dealienation is a work of reconciliation performed by a self-conscious subject upon the opposition in being, whatever form it might take. Freedom to think and act purposively is required for the work of dealienation. As this work proceeds, the opposition in being is resolved by incorporation into an expanded structure of meaning and being. Yet, this is not just a logical exercise of thought. Rather, it is an ontological exercise expressing a continuity of thought, being and action, intentional or otherwise. The result of this ontological dialectic is to eliminate the isolation and incomprehensibility of the alien Other while realizing being in general and the being of a self-conscious subject in particular. A self, freely thinking and acting objectifies itself in a progressively humanized world.

Alienation can be defined within the context of the life of a developing organism. The life cycle generally consists of birth, development to maturity and then decay ending in death. Development of an organism moves in identifiable stages toward an aim of reaching maturity, the zenith of its development. Hegel characterized this in Aristotelian terms as realizing the potential or perfection of one's being. In terms of a process of development, alienation signifies not realizing or actualizing one's potential, not reaching ones aims or goal, a frustrated or arrested development, stunted growth. What is alienated is unfulfilled, unsatisfied, incomplete in being and meaning. Aristotle and Hegel thought of natural processes of development as driven by pre-ordained telos. Thus, anything with unfulfilled purpose is alienated. However, alienation in its generic sense, need not involve any pre-ordained telos. Rather, alienation may only signify arrested development of an organism that does not follow an empirically described pattern, or realize its potentiality for being, whatever that might be and however determined. To say that something is implicit or potential rather than explicit or actual is not to say it has a certain kind of essential nature or that its being implies a pre-ordained telos.

Phenomena of Alienation

Alienation is the central fact of the human condition. Humanity has suffered it throughout history and the likelihood of it ever being overcome appears remote. Its basic forms are disease and mortality with war and human privation following closely behind. In fact, alienation itself appears to have an infinite variety of forms. No sooner has one been overcome than another replaces it. Our destiny appears to lie in suffering one form of it or another. It even besets us when we are unaware of it or are ignorant of what it means for us. Something so pervasive and so pernicious calls for philosophical understanding.

Alienation is the triumph of negativity without affirmation. The phenomena demonstrating this are legion. Emotionally, for example, there is melancholy, boredom, anguish, and despair. Sartre believed physiological conditions such as vertigo and nausea indicate an absurd alienated existence. Freud viewed women patients reporting hysterical symptoms indicative of instinctual alienation. Strange or eccentric behavior manifests frustrated repressed desires. Ego defense mechanisms present striking examples of alienating negativity. Neuroses and psychoses present an array of ways in which the psyche is alienated. Social scientists present alienated persons as sensing a loss of meaning, power, hope and isolation from the polity. Specific responses to alienation can take any form and are infinite in principle. The self is disposed to respond to the alienating Other in various ways. Among the many general responses possible are asceticism, a religious turning to God for salvation, a secular ideological commitment to social change, submersion in work, suicide, hedonism and nurturing love. Successful dealienation displays human rationality and freedom as the most essential coping powers of the self.

To be human is to be finite and in this alienation is presented as limit, as the present non-being of the Other. But dealienation, as an overcoming of limits and an incorporation of the alien Other into the being in question, is also a fact of life. Potentiality is constantly being actualized. The liberation of humanity from undesirable imprisoning limitations is what life is all about. Thus is alienation relegated to an initial moment of negation, that recognition of a limit or opposing alien Other. Successive moments of negation realize the *ought* as Hegel called it, and in this the human spirit ascends into the infinite in spite of a burdensome alienating finitude. This implies that alienation is never absolute, but merely the beginning of a process of dealienation. Alienating finitude becomes necessary to the realization and expression of the infinite. This was Hegel's enduring ontological insight. Skepticism cynicism and despair are not conclusions drawn from this process of dealienation. Rather, they are important initial negative moments: the premises of dealienation calling forth a response of thought and action that liberates the spirit from its bondage to finitude. Without alienation, inspiration would be impossible and the human spirit could not soar in the realization of infinite possibilities.

Intellectual rationalizations of alienation may be found in philosophical schools of sophism, stoicism, hedonism, positivism, postmodernism, socialism and relativism. Alienating attitudes are perennially found in skepticism and cynicism. The alienated psyche is sunk in negativity. Appearances are deceptive and misleading. In fact, things are the reverse of what they appear to be. The language of negativity reflects this condition with understatement, hyperbole, irony and wit expressing a cynicism evading censorship. A linguistic style understood to express the opposite of what it affirms unmasks the truth hidden by convention. Hegel observed that alienated souls are perverse, counter-culture and vain. They scorn and laugh at a culture with which they cannot identify and of which they are completely skeptical.[2]

Philosophy itself often expresses what could be called *intellectual alienation* where no answer is provided to skeptical conundrums. Classic historic examples were provided by the epistemology of David Hume's despairing skepticism concerning knowledge and Immanuel Kant's unknowable nuomenal reality. This epistemological skepticism is continued by positivist emotive theory applied to aesthetics and ethics. Other recent examples include existentialism presuming personal freedom to be irrational, thereby finding no basis for ethical life. Intellectual alienation bifurcates human nature in some way leaving on one side of a dualism something denied or distorted by a faulty interpretation. Examples are thought versus being, fact versus value, cognitive versus emotive meaning, self versus culture and human nature versus God. Analysis invariably separates components of meaning with a loss only regained by a synoptic perspective. Philosophical synthesis must be speculative with implications to be experienced and realized at some future time.

Where there is a paucity of knowledge or fact, there is room for arbitrary or doubtful interpretation. Many beliefs can be made to appear relative in truth demonstrating that the capacity to reason is amoral and can even be put to immoral use. This misuse of rationality has profound moral and social implications in its destructive attack upon tradition and authority. Plato and Hegel believed that our capacity to misconstrue and misinterpret does not effect the true being of what is discussed. It just leaves us philosophically in error, intellectually alienated. Palliation for intellectual alienation lies, at least in part, in knowing the motive for constructing an interpretation. Whatever interpretation can achieve, what remains unquestionable is experienced fact. No interpretation can be admissible which does not accept the phenomena to be explained as actual or true to begin with. From an ideological viewpoint, this would undoubtedly be considered naive. Yet, any interpretation dismissing the actuality and validity of the phenomena to be explained presents a conclusion inappropriate to its subject matter, partially true at best, if at all. Such interpretations merely serve disguised motives and result in alienating gullible believers.

A Hegelian defined *Spirit* is both rational and free. Even if a Hegelian Spirit is no longer credible, the insight remains that rationality and freedom is essential to being human. This presumption runs through the history and culture of western civilization. The alienating finitude of self-existence draws out the infinite implications of conceiving rationality and freedom essential to human nature. Hegel speculated that the infinite whole is revealed by freedom driven by rationality with a divine source. Leaving aside its source, rationality and freedom remain as the secular nature of the self, to be explored in manifold human dimensions.

Humanity, although obviously finite, is also rational and free. The integration of these, herein designated *rational freedom*, signifies a capacity for being which is infinite. This infinite capacity contributes an infinite horizon to being in general and the being of the self in particular. Synoptic or speculative philosophy focuses upon the infinite capacity of the human spirit. Self-realization has speculative implications by the very fact of incompleteness in being and unforeseeable future consequences. Thus, any philosophical analysis limiting the human potentiality for being and knowing falsifies the essence of human nature. This is the root cause of intellectual alienation.

Hegel claimed that the empiricism, intuitionism and subjective idealism of his time provided distorted incomplete interpretations of man, culture and social institutions by misapplying concepts appropriate for understanding finite objects to infinite objects such as God. Rationality and freedom are not attributes of finite objects, but rather attributes with infinite implication, attributes constituting the spirit of humanity. Possessing the capacity for rational freedom, the self is more than just another object among finite objects of the world. Lacking an appreciation of what rational freedom implies combined with the loss of a synoptic speculative orientation characterizes analytic schools of philosophy intensely interested in justifying scientific knowledge without reference to the being who creates it. The inevitable result is a despairing skepticism and intellectual alienation. As a spiritual being, rational and free, humanity is the way the cosmos knows and reveals itself as a whole - a powerful speculative idea to say the least.

The self forms an identity and recognizes this in the product of its rationality and freedom. It also recognizes its identity in the public acknowledgment of its fellows. Universal norms and social roles provide a vehicle by which an identity is established. They are sensed as obligatory for self-realization to occur. Being universal, they are also publicly recognizable. Without them community cannot be formed and culture is not sustainable. With them, self-identification, self-projection and self-objectification construct both community and culture. Individuals participate, contribute and relate to culture and community as part to whole through a process of socialization aimed at dealienation. And, in this whole process of dealienation the self realizes the full potential of its freedom and rationality as well as the larger social and cosmic wholes to which it belongs. Alienation in its psychological and sociological forms results from a failure in the socialization process enabling dealienation. An alienated self, then, cannot create and sustain community. Its potential remains an alien Other, uncomprehended, unappropriated, unexpressed and unrealized. Oppositions remain unresolved within itself, between itself and other selves, between itself and cosmos or its God.

The crucial question about self-objectification and the resulting humanized world is what kind of self is objectified and what kind of world results. A different self-objectification produces a differently humanized world. It is precisely these different outcomes which need to be understood, compared and evaluated to establish their true normative value. Nothing can be established as superior in advance of being tried and it would appear that humanity would make trial of all available norms and roles. In humanizing the world, humanity sees its own reflection. However, a self who creates its own world is not necessarily a dealienated self. For that self can be sunk in narcissism and egoism operating without a social self and so disconnected from culture and community. Moreover, in a humanized world there may be found a poisoned environment, a victimized welfare state underclass, and all manner of undesirable unintended consequences for life.

Freedom

Forms of alienation are theoretically infinite, but can be classified as biological, psychological, and sociological including the political. Although particular forms of it can be overcome, the basic condition underlying all of them cannot be eradicated. This fact provides human beings with the perpetual task of overcoming any of its existentially encountered forms at any given time and place in history. Overcoming alienation is a perpetual task for individuals and societies. In other words, dealienation is a continuous and interminable process. Where there is no alienating condition, freedom has no meaning and signifies nothing for our lives. Human freedom only has meaning and significance as a generalized response to alienation. Since freedom depends upon the capacity to be rational, dealienation necessarily includes the integration of freedom with rationality to produce intelligent behavior. Rational freedom is the best hope of humanity for overcoming any particular form of alienation. This view is reflected in language by aphorisms such as, *the truth shall set you free.*

Western civilization is characterized by a faith in and historical development of freedom and rationality. While freedom is a precious gift requiring eternal vigilance and nurture, its exercise risks alienation. Major western thinkers have mistrusted freedom, associating it with anarchy and evil. Unguided by rationality, or uncontrolled by repressive authority, freedom can be alienating. Rationality and socialization have much to do with whether or not exercising personal freedom effectuates alienation or dealienation. Irrationally guided, personal freedom is self-alienating, as even those existentialists who glorified it understood. A defectively socialized self is unprepared to exercise personal freedom in a socially responsible manner. History, particularly that of the twentieth century, bears sad witnesses to the misuse of freedom. Therefore, what has to be understood about freedom is how it can serve to dealienate rather than to alienate the self. This is an imperative for a contemporary western culture continuously testing and extending the limits of personal freedom.

The nature of human freedom has been discussed by western philosophers in various ways for the past two millennia. Caveats have been often enough offered about the risk of its application and its dangerous consequences. Licentiousness, mob rule, anarchy and finally tyranny have often resulted when trial has been made of equality and democracy. So, philosophical wisdom acknowledges freedom, but distrusts its application and development. This philosophy of alienation and dealienation attempts to move beyond a distrust of freedom. Its basis in rationality, naturalistically defined, warrants trust in its continued expansive development and application to every aspect of human existence, personal and social. Contrary to its caveats, a developed capacity for rational freedom permits a dealienating self-existence. A self, whose existence is directed by rational freedom, discovers itself and its own capacity to be the locus of truth and value. Thus, within an existential context of dealienation, the normative is discovered and created. A sense of obligation arises from human needs and desires, tempered by rationality. In addition, conscience, expressing personal freedom can also be a guide for its exercise. A self, having developed its capacity for rational freedom is autonomous while existing authentically.

Freedom is best understood by analyzing it in multiple dimensions. How socialization develops or stunts freedom requires consideration. Its relationship to rationality needs careful examination. And, its potentiality for dealienation is developed in this work by relating it to nurturing love and conscience. Although major western thinkers have mistrusted freedom, when properly understood, it can be creative and normative for self-existence and social conduct. Some excellent critiques of freedom, fathoming its negative self-alienating dark side, are instructive and suggestive of a dealienating positive side. In spite of the many attempts to escape its burden, a universal demand for personal freedom persists. Absent defective socialization, but given a cultural milieu respecting personal freedom, a cultural ethos of freedom enables dealienation and self-realization of human potentiality. This work then, is a paean to freedom. Rational freedom is its refrain and mantra.

Hegel ontologically explained how alienation is necessary, since it is signified by finitude. He then correctly conceived of *Spirit* as freedom and rationality essential to the psychic and spiritual life of human beings. Nevertheless, his view of rationality is too narrow and locating it in the dicta of authoritative Others, be they social institutions, state or God, is questionable. However, locating rationality and freedom within humanity provides a better solution to the existential problem of alienation. Rational freedom can be described multidimensionally as aim, drive and process in human history. Rejecting a supernatural God and locating it within humanity itself as did Feuerbach, permits a superior understanding of religion and its vital social functions. The divine conceived as a human projection need be neither trivial nor dismissive of religion.

Hegel's view of human history as a spiritual process with an aim of realizing rational freedom correctly expressed the great idea and ethos of western civilization. This idea is defensible as an interpretation of history when rational freedom is redefined. It inspires and gives history a transcendent noble purpose. Thus, it is plausible to believe that the terrible human suffering of twentieth century wars was a working through of rational freedom. Its triumph lies in the worldwide defeat and rejection of Nazi and Communist totalitarianism. At a crucial twentieth century moment of history, rational freedom predominated in the refusal of nuclear war and world hegemony. Personal freedom and democracy are ascendant in a world led by American civilization, a relatively recent experiment. The twenty-first century promises a worldwide extension of liberty to all of humanity. Spectacular advances and an exponential growth in scientific knowledge and technology betoken a complete triumph of rational freedom.

Rational freedom is first and foremost a generic response to the alienating finitude of self-existence. Of all the responses tried throughout history, rational freedom is the most successful. Success aside, it is the correct response as witnessed by the fact that it does not allow humanity to be imprisoned by any particular form of alienation. Human life is then not a meaningless or hopeless repetition of any single form of existentially encountered alienation. This makes every form of alienation a challenge to overcome through an integrated exercise of rationality and freedom. Dealienation is then a continuous interminable process, a triumph of spirit that can be continuously enjoyed. Human history is then an odyssey of Spirit as Hegel saw it, an exciting adventure filled with hope and faith in human capabilities.

The central quest of this philosophizing lies in the question of freedom. That it is necessary to dealienation, both personal and collective, is not in doubt. However, if it is mistrusted, then authoritarianism must replace it. Yet, an authoritarian orientation has alienation built into it. Given the fact and drive for personal and social freedom, can it serve to promote successful dealienation? The answer offered herein is provided in multiple analyses of human processes and capacities related to freedom. First, socialization is considered along with how freedom can be suppressed or distorted in this formative process of self-development. Then freedom is related to an ontological redefinition of rationality. An integration of freedom with rationality defines intelligence, and developing it maximizes the human capacity for successful dealienation.

A self not alienated from its own needs and desires is liberated to live authentically. But can an authentic self be a moral being who can survive by sustaining the community upon which it depends? To live authentically calls for some kind of moral guidance for freedom. Who and what shall be an authoritative Other for each authentic self? The answer appears to lie not in traditional authority, but rather in an appropriate use of rationality or in human intelligence itself. While authenticity and autonomy working together are necessary for successful dealienation, they do not suggest an ethos for community. Moral guidance for an authentic and autonomous self is still required to complete the social answer. Investigations of the nature of freedom suggest something within it can provide moral guidance. This is conscience, understood in its positive creative dimension beyond its authoritarian root in a censoring internalized authoritative Other.

Freedom guided by conscience responding to the alienating finitude of self-existence constructs virtuous character indicative of a culture and even historical epochs. Still, the question remains how someone who is autonomous and authentic can live well. The answer is closely linked to biological survival. Nurture is deeply satisfying of biological and social need. A self-giving love expresses not only the power of personal freedom, but also its very development. A self who provides love realizes its own potentiality for being through acts of nurture. Simultaneously, that self receives the reward of affirmation, public esteem and reciprocity from those who are nurtured. In this, freedom finds its greatest flowering, power, and enjoyment of life.

Notes

1. Hegel, G. W. F. (1967) *The Phenomenology of Mind* (J. B. Baillie, Trans.). New York, NY: Harper and Row, 759.
2. Ibid., 547.

Chapter One

Negativity: Foundation of Alienation

Ontological Principle of Negativity

Negativity is central to any question about being. Historically, philosophical discourse about being has been expressed with a language and concept of negativity. Philosophy began with initial speculations about the nature of Being and Non-being. Parmenides and Heraclitus speculated about them, disagreeing about which would have priority in explaining their world. Socrates, Plato, Parmenides and Hegel employed negativity as a dialectical method designed to elicit wisdom and truth.

Theoretical speculation in the sciences depends upon negativity either implicitly or explicitly. It is employed as a method of critical evaluation where counterfactual examples are presented and their implications speculatively exhibited. Negativity appears central to the enigmas of philosophy. With an admirable exhibition of self-criticism the great Plato asked how the Many is to be differentiated from the One, thereby initiating centuries of theoretical speculation about the ontological status of universals.

With Hegel we see the full flowering of ontology based upon negativity in multiple dimensions. Moving negativity beyond a method of inquiry, Hegel expanded it to an ontological principle driving both thought and being. From the abstract thought of Being as a whole, Hegel discovered a logical equivalence, Non-being. Then negativity was used as a postulate for defining determinate beings and the process of their development, be it natural or spiritual. Being in process is described, if not explained by negativity. Herein lies its theoretical power for all of the sciences. Moreover, the Hegelian enhancement of negativity suggests a deeper understanding of alienation and dealienation as a process fundamental to self-existence which can answer the perennial question, "What or who is the Other?" or Heidegger's question about the meaning of being.

What is the mysterious One of which Parmenides speaks? Its meaning is derived from the method he employs in speaking about it. And it is spoken of by means of negativity. The One is neither this nor that. Since there is nothing to distinguish it from anything else, it is undifferentiated, indeterminate, and infinite in connotation. The One could be equally described by contradictory assertions without anything existential determining the truth of either. To be meaningful the One requires a difference to distinguish it from the Many. Without a distinct difference validated by some existential trial providing a specific result, a true meaning of the One remains elusive. For by implying every possibility of being it asserts none, which is to say that the One signifies nothing that can be said to exist. It is a signifier without anything signified. Therefore, the One is about the being of thought rather than the thought of being. The One remains that paradoxical abstraction constructed by the negativity of thought itself. Nevertheless, this is not a trivial observation.

Hegel told us that anything said to exist, has meaning only as it relates to something else, an Other. Therefore, to define anything existing is to specify what is identical and what is different about it relative to the Other(s). When thought is not so existentially determined, it signifies nothing but its own abstract processes, which are paradoxical and vacuous with respect to being. Plato's *Parmenides*, in effect, demonstrated this. Nothing of experience is signified by abstract signifiers such as the Parmenidean One, since it is not something experienced as existing with some but not other attributes. When the One is treated dialectically and so given every possible attribute, it is contradictory, signifying nothing in particular but anything generally, which Hegel referred to as the *infinite*.

Hegel believed philosophy began with Parmenides' assertion that Being alone is and Nothing is not. Parmenides made thought itself an object for investigation. Hegel considered every succeeding philosophy to continue differentiating parts of a whole structure of thought. From the Parmenidean standpoint, Hegel began his logic with the thought of Being signifying everything. This thought of Being is a grand ontological abstraction, devoid of differentiation, with maximum logical extension and minimum logical intension. Thus, Being connotes Nothing. For to signify everything is also to signify nothing in particular. Being, or Nothing, is then an undifferentiated intention to signify a whole structure of thought, anything one can call real. But this indeterminate intention posits negativity as the basis for thought to progress with successive differentiation of parts of its whole structure.

Hegel's linguistically oriented analysis of the ultimate abstraction says several things about the nature of thought. In effect, the distinction of Being from Nothing, considered indeterminate abstractions, is thought signifying its own activity. Thought is also a signifying activity with ontological import; whether what is signified is the whole of being or a component something said to exist. The negativity of a signifier is its implication, formal or material. Beyond this, negativity serves as a conatus for the progression of the thought and being to completion.

Hegel began his ontology presuming an equivalency of thought and being, and so suggesting a logic of thought traversing a totality of being. Being and Nothing were considered abstractions of pure thought, both equivalent in meaning, and yet distinct. Being, a thought of the whole of everything that is, the first philosophical abstraction, is the thought of indeterminate immediacy. "... it has no diversity within itself nor any with reference outwards." And, "... There is *nothing* to be intuited in it ... Being, the indeterminate immediate, is in fact *nothing*, and neither more nor less than *nothing*."[1] Being is empty thinking, or thought without specific content and so is Non-Being or *nothing*. Both Being and Nothing are real as thought, as empty intuitions. Moreover, of course, the reality of thinking *nothing* is confirmable by the fact that it is distinguished from thinking of being. This way of linguistically establishing an equivalence in meaning of Being and Non-being has ontological import, since language is an expression of thought which Hegel believed to found being.

The negativity of thought is the founding principle of Hegelian ontology. Identifying the being of thought with being in general makes of negativity a vehicle for a logical progression from indeterminate being of the whole to component determinate beings. At the level of determinate being - beings which exist finitely and are specifically defined - the principle of negativity appears as something and its Other, or something else which completes its being and meaning. Just as Nothing (Non-being) is the obverse of Being, so in the sphere of determinate being the Other is the obverse of something finite. The identity and difference of Being or of determinate beings constitutes their meaning; suggesting that meaning is a product of negativity. Without it, there would be no meaning at all, and certainly no meaning of being to be revealed by any interaction of thought and being.

As the most universal abstraction of thought, Being or Nothing is a distinction without a difference. Within ordinary discourse about finite things, a distinction without a difference is a mistake. However, when characterizing the basis of reality as thought, Being and Nothing - the distinction without a difference - is a meaningful beginning providing negativity with a significance well beyond what it ordinarily has logically or linguistically. The Hegelian beginning recognizes negativity to be an ontological principle. As identity and difference, as distinction, as contradiction, as opposition of some kind, negativity is the basis of thought and being, thereby providing an impetus for the processes of both.

When Hegel speaks of Being and Nothing, he is in effect speaking about negativity. And, as distinction within thought, negativity is the basis of meaning. That meaning is established by negativity is demonstrated by the fact that both Being and Nothing are meaningful even though the ultimate in abstraction. For Hegel, the identity and distinctness of Being and Nothing, or negativity, constitutes a principle of movement in thought and becoming in being. Non-Being is the not yet, the undeveloped or potential in being. Socratic negativity is found within a dialectic of discourse searching for true definitions by means of presenting negative examples. Hegel extends the negativity implicit in the ancient dialectic, giving it a greater significance by raising it to an ontological principle. Negativity became a ubiquitous attribute of thought and being.

Beyond providing the basis for meaning and thought processes, negativity describes any form of opposition in being, particularly within or between finite beings. Negativity provides an impetus for any kind of alteration. Every natural process of alteration is an instance of negativity whereby what is implicit becomes explicit: what is potential becomes actual. This applies to any process, be it a description of an internal or external change of state among finite beings. Hegelian ontological negativity breathes new life into an ancient dialectic, enormously expanding its scope and applicability.

Everything has an identity in virtue of its negating difference from an Other. The difference of something from its Other is a separation which bestows meaning and a unique identity or individuality. Separating with a difference unites the many Others within an environmental totality. Any act of recognition or definition acknowledges attributes common to the Others, but with a distinguishing difference. The meaning of anything presumes a whole and negativity of some kind to distinguish and relate its parts. The significance of the Other is its negating difference, and to fathom all differences is to traverse the being of any environmental whole. The thought of a whole is the meaning of a universal to which Hegel attached great importance. Universals with higher degrees of logical intension are made possible by negativity progressively incorporating the Other(s). Moreover, this is as true of thought as it is of being.

Synthetic propositions define an object of thought or perception by attributes with some implied specific difference. It is the difference, which allows the unification of object with attribute. Thought requires negativity as an ability to distinguish a difference. Contradiction is not the termination of thought, but rather expresses its basis in negativity, implicitly or explicitly acknowledged. Hegel clearly understood this when he said, "On this point, formal thinking lays down for its principle that contradiction is unthinkable; but as a matter of fact the thinking of contradiction is the essential moment of the Notion."[2]

A ubiquitous negativity describes thought, being and every process in the universe. The interaction of thought and being is driven by negativity. It is signified by any encounter with an Other in being, thought, consciousness and self-consciousness. Time conceived either abstractly or concretely is a negating sequence. Finitude is defined by a negating Other, by what something is not or by what stands in opposition to it. Within nature negativity is expressed as temporal change of state, as process, which when regular, repetitive and predictable is deemed causal. Implication, formal or material, requires negativity. It distinguishes truth from falsity, a principle that founds knowledge. Negativity is displayed as contradiction in the process of thought. Rather than terminating thought, negativity describes the essence of meaning, and contradiction provides a stimulus for thought and human activity effecting being. The very act of thinking requires simultaneously holding in mind something and its negating Other. Implicit contradiction is a necessity of thought. To think that S is both P and not P is the beginning of thought and human action which resolves contradiction and the alien character of the Other, leading both thought and being to completion. Driven by negativity, thought establishes a consistent homeostatic structure of meaning. Without contradiction and its existential counterpart in various kinds of opposition, nothing can be thought and the meaning of being cannot be revealed.

What or Who is the Other?

The meaning of being is posed by the question, "What or who is the Other?" The Other is a mystery, something hidden and to be revealed. Negativity, taking the form of opposition, contradiction, denial and refusal in an encounter with the Other, answers the question. It is continuously asked and answered in a progressive dialectic of finitude. This is suggested by Hegel's abstract words. "The other simply by itself is the other in its own self, hence the other of itself and so the other of the other - it is, therefore that which is absolutely dissimilar within itself, that which negates itself, *alters* itself."[3] Less abstractly stated, "Otherness thus appears as a determination alien to the determinate being thus characterized, or as the other *outside* the one determinate being; ... there is no determinate being which is determined only as such, which is not outside a determinate being and therefore is not itself an other."[4] Here Hegel points out that the Other is only Other as a negation of the being of something. Moreover, the Other becomes meaningful from a process of comparison, which discovers a distinguishing difference. This distinguishing difference unifies what is initially separate, thereby providing additional meaning. To the casual eye, negativity separates beings and meanings, but at a deeper level Hegel understood negativity as a unifying principle of meaning and being as well.

The quintessential Other for Hegel is nature: wherein everything is external and separated by the determinations of space, time and matter. Therefore, to discover the identity of the Other requires specifying differences from itself in time or from something else relating to it. The thought of something is not possible without the thought of its Other. Correlatively, the being of something is not possible without the being of its Other. Something in some relation to its Other makes up a finite world and their significance is as logical parts of a whole structure of meaning. The Other is being signified negatively, by implication. Everything finite is an Other in process of becoming determinate, moving from what it is not toward what it is, achieving identity and definition. The Hegelian *Notion* includes something and its Other in an achieved totality of thought and being driven by negating process. Notions are a product of inference and alteration in being that discovers the meaning of anything through its Other.

What does the Other signify? It poses a limit or deficiency in being to be transcended. It is a potential for becoming something else, a Hegelian telos for finite beings. To recognize the Other, is to be negated by it, whether the Other is an externally opposing something, or an internal potentiality for becoming something else. To become Other is the aim describing the development of any finite being. Expressing negativity, the Other is necessary for any finite being to develop and reveal its actuality, as Hegel would state it. The Other can be signified by human desire and purpose. A limiting Other elicits rationality and freedom as typical human responses. Purposive thought and action respond to frustrated desire. Thought and its active extension in the world reveal what or who is signified by the Other.

Nothing immediate can be true, for it is undeveloped, untested, untempered in the crucible of experience. To misconceive anything immediate and finite as true is to base the being of that something on an abstraction that fails to comprehend it in the richness of all its dimensions. Therefore, for Hegel, the immediate is never true. Only as mediated can the truth of anything be revealed. "The unintelligence of sense, to take everything limited and finite for Being, passes into the obstinacy of understanding, which views the finite as self-identical, not inherently self-contradictory."[5]

Meaning is to distinguish one thing from another. The essence of meaning is negativity in all its multiplicity of forms. Even an immediate presence of something is not simply something positive. What is present is Other in being, in time and within a structure of meaning. Language reflects this in that something immediately present as *this*, *that*, *here*, *now* has no meaning without relationship with something else or an Other. Hegel did not consider anything immediate to consciousness to be positive in the sense of possessing a being of its own unrelated to anything else. Rather, any affirmation of its being is derived from the negation of its initial presentation as an Other of consciousness or an Other of the Ego thinking or sensing it. This alien Other presents a possibility for its being and the meaning thereof. So the affirmation of anything finite is a product of a process of double negation in which what something is not implies what it is, both logically and in fact.

If being is pre-established by divine thought as Hegel believed, becoming Other completes and perfects its being, or realizes its telos. Although nature is no longer adequately explained by telos, it is evident in observable processes of natural development. These are describable as a negating sequence of events with an aim. A telos preestablished by the thought of a creator may well be an archaic and obsolete explanation of the world. Yet, telos is still a discoverable feature of any process. There is obviously a telos of human rationality and freedom, even if we are unable to precisely specify it in advance or predict its result.

Every something has an Other and is itself an Other of something else. Thus, to say A is the other of B is equally to say B is the other of A. But this kind of Hegelian analysis, although simply linguistic in appearance, has ontological import. Finite beings in fact develop through a series of negations, and universal Notions were intended by Hegel to describe such development. The answer to the question of the meaning of being - the question, "What or who is the Other?" - calls for a progressive development of being and meaning in a structure of universal Notions forming a systematic whole. Taken as a universal abstraction, the Other is the referent of an initial negation. After the Other is encountered, the process of negation continues by relating it to something of immediate interest. The meaning of finite beings is posited by the process of alien Others which negate and are negated. Consequently the Other loses its alien character as isolated, indifferent, hidden or unknown, and is related and incorporated into a larger meaningfully structured whole.

Heraclitus who said that Being is no more than Non-Being made an advance beyond Parmenides' acknowledgment of negativity. This thought places negativity in nature and so extends the scope of dialectic beyond dialogue. Everything in the world flows or changes ceaselessly and so Becoming is recognized as the fundamental feature of finite existence. Negativity takes the form of a relationship between things. Becoming makes the abstract identity and difference of Being and Non-Being explicit. Hegel believed Heraclitus' Becoming established a dialectical basis of attaining the truth about anything. "As the first concrete thought-term, Becoming is the first adequate vehicle of truth."[6] Becoming is here considered a resolution of the Parmenidean abstract opposition of Being and Nothing. Everything determinate, or every something, is a Becoming, a unity of Being and Nothing, a resolution of contradiction and real negating oppositions inhering in finite existence. Becoming manifests negativity in finite beings, which founds dialectic presenting the truth about them.

Negation by the Other(s) is the ontological basis of every finite being, creating movement, indicative of process, and reflected in thought. Dialectic describes finitude for Hegel.

> Everything that surrounds us may be viewed as an instance of Dialectic. We are aware that everything finite, instead of being stable and ultimate, is rather changeable and transient; and this is exactly what we mean by that Dialectic of the finite, by which the finite, as implicitly other than what it is, is forced beyond its own immediate or natural being to turn suddenly into its opposite.[7]

Dialectic is a process with a result in being, in thought and in truth. "For the negative which emerges as the result of dialectic is, because a result, at the same time the positive: it contains what it results from, absorbed into itself, and made part of its own nature."[8] Hegel cites Parmenides' deduction of the Many from the One, and Kant's *antinomies* as examples of a philosophical dialectic of finitude. Dialectic reflects the negativity of finite beings. "... its purpose is to study things in their own being and movement and thus to demonstrate the finitude of the partial categories of understanding."[9] Yet, since dialectic is based upon negativity, it points beyond the finite toward the infinite. Consistent with his Christian religious commitment, Hegel's dialectical logic ascends from understanding the partially true - the finite - toward comprehending the true and real basis of the finite, namely God, the infinite creator of the finite.

Being and Nothing are united in the Becoming of finite things which is to say that whatever is finite is mutable and subject to all kinds of change, physical, chemical psychological, etc. Anything finite *comes-to-be* and *ceases-to-be* in the Hegelian vernacular of process. Extinction is the destiny of finitude. Mortality and extinction are the essential marks of finitude. In fact mortality can be considered an archetype of finitude, or at least its most striking example. Mortality presents the most radical example of the negativity of a finite being. The appearance and disappearance of finite things and their characteristics means that anything finite is always described and defined by something *other* than itself. Stated otherwise, finite beings are dependent in being and meaning upon an Other. They are not self-sufficient. Being defined by an Other implies being part of a transcendent larger structured whole. As the Other is dialectically encountered, the meaning of being is revealed in part and in the whole.

Hegel explained the finitude of nature as a rational process wherein the being of something is logically driven by the telos of its Notion; or, in the case of rational and free spiritual beings, by the telos of an Idea. The being of nature lies in the action of negation, just as thought does. This follows the ancient way of explaining becoming or movement of determinate beings as driven by the same dialectic of negation applicable to thought. In effect, negativity forms a seamless whole whether it limits, differentiates, contradicts, denies, refuses, opposes, struggles, suffers, comes into being or ceases to be. Hegel believed a negating Other differentiates a divinely pre-established whole of being, thereby progressively revealing its meaning and structure. In short, negativity forms the ontological basis of every finite being, and change of its condition. By means of negativity, the potential becomes actual, the implicit becomes explicit, and the abstract becomes concrete.

To be finite is to be negated and to negate. Whether the being in question is non-human or human, finitude is marked by limitation and alterability. With finite beings, negativity appears as a limit to something. Anything with a limit generally defines finitude. The Other is what or who presents a limit to the being of something. A thing or non-human being is limited by an Other which it is not, but without which it cannot be understood as being anything. Hegel contended that negativity provides the principle of movement of all forms of being. A negating limit posed by the Other must in turn be negated thereby reaching a higher and more developed level of being. Negativity is the principle of every process, be it thought, natural necessity or the actions of a free will. For non-spiritual beings lacking rationality and freedom, negating a limit is understood as natural necessity, causal alteration. Limits that beset spiritual human beings are dealt with by rationality and freedom to produce desired outcomes. Human finitude suffers negativity manifested by existentially encountering the Other as a limit or a deficiency in being to be made good. Something is recognized which is not actual but ought to be the case. Limits encountered by human beings are negated by actions of thought and will altering the world and free agent's relationship to it.

To pose a limit to or deficiency in being is to encounter the Other. This Other is a negation of being and a negation in being. Finitude is this contradiction in being by the presentation of a limit or deficiency of some kind. A can be both B and not B in being, but at different times. Negativity without arithmetical abstraction is a time sequence of being. Without a distinguishable difference of being, time has no meaning. The present separates past from future first in being which can then be abstractly conceived as arithmetical sequence. The present, or actuality, is where past and present meet in a difference of being. This is what a potentiality for being means. It is a negating possibility of being something Other. So, the present is indeterminate, a genuine process of becoming Other.

The present resolves contradictions in being by disallowing the persistence of negating possibilities of being. Future negates the past in the present. Past appears necessary while future is a possibility for being Other. Thus, the actuality of something is not anything immediately positive. Rather, actuality is always constructed by a negating process in which a limiting Other or deficiency in being implies an *ought-to-be* as Hegel put it. That which limits and what it immediately implies Hegel considered logical components of meaning correlative with what he called *moments* of being in an ontological process of sublation. The present is then conceived as a transcending process of temporal existence driven by negativity and expressed in thought by dialectic of universal Notions, or Ideas of a free agent. In general, Being signifies a temporal totality; both potential and actual, with a meaning formed by the negativity of process and time sequence.

An analytic tradition in philosophy gained ascendancy with nineteenth and twentieth century empiricist and positivist schools of philosophy. They attempted to replace ontology and metaphysics with logical analysis based upon knowledge provided by the sciences. The paradigm of philosophical analysis was to avoid the bias of hidden presuppositions by being purely descriptive and value neutral. This comports with a paradigm of scientific method which deliberately attempts to eliminate bias in investigative procedure and observation. Scientific truth must be impartially verifiable by properly conducted experimental procedure that can be replicated by anyone at any time. Knowledge thus acquired is confirmed as practically certain, although never absolutely so. The building of a structure of scientific knowledge is then deemed a process of approximation to the truth. Skepticism is the standard attitude of a good scientist. It prompts scientific curiosity, investigation, and holds proffered theories to high standards of logical and experimental proof. However, at the highest level of theorizing, science and philosophy merge where coherence rather than any strict empirical correspondence are attainable.

While zeal in eliminating biased presuppositions, upholding rigorous logic and experimental verification are noble paradigms of scientific procedure; they do not directly present the truth of anything. Rather, they define a process of acquiring truth scientifically. It should not be forgotten that most of what is believed true and known true in fact, is secured without the use of rigorous scientific procedure. If, as positivists maintain, true knowledge can only be attained by the methods of science, then most of what is known is rendered mere belief or unknowable in principle. Hence, the classic ongoing historical confrontation of science versus religion, the bifurcation of fact and value, the inability to relate what is true to what is valuable. This modern problem stands in stark contrast to Plato's identification of truth with beauty and goodness.

Even more problematical is the effect of the modern scientific attitude toward understanding the psyche and spiritual life of humanity. For example, emotive theories applied to moral and aesthetic life, deny it the status of rationality, thus making knowledge of these bifurcated realms of human life impossible. Emotive and cognitive meaning are irrevocably alienated from each other. This curiously leaves humanity with a restricted knowledge of the world, but without the possibility of knowledge about itself. Such intellectually alienating theorizing aside, humanity proceeds to rapidly accumulate knowledge of itself and its culture in non-scientific disciplines variously called the arts, humanities, philosophy, religion, history and so forth.

An antidote to positivist intellectual alienation is to answer the fundamental question of how fact and value are related. Was the ancient philosophical attitude correct in not separating truth from value? The answer appears to be that the ancients were correct, although the answer offered herein is somewhat different from theirs. First, consider the implications of ontological negativity. Encountering an alien Other is to encounter a limit from within or without; a limit that implies a negation of whatever is limiting. Finitude is the presentation of a deficiency in being or a limit to being something. Deficiency and limitation is experienced as something which is not present but ought to be in the future. An expression of this general ontology is an experience of finitude, of something needed or desired. Value is this sensing of need and desire: something that ought to be the case, thereby providing impetus for intentional goal seeking activity. Human beings respond to this sensing of needs and desires with their peculiar intelligent capacity for dealienation, namely rational freedom.

Suffering the alienating finitude of self-existence establishes the value of anything. Thus, in effect the fact of need or desire is already value-laden. That self-activity is motivated by need and desire provides indubitable proof of this. The satisfaction of need or desire is a consummation both in the fact of something achieved and in the enjoyment of its value, emotionally and otherwise, as pragmatists John Dewey and C. I. Lewis claimed. Dealienating endeavor further enhances value-laden facts. Negative value resides in what alienates and positive value resides in the result of successful dealienation. Value is determined in degree by the extent of dealienating endeavor. The greater the degrees of suffering, sacrifice and work required, the greater the value of something. The converse is also true. A scarcity of what is needed and desired also determines its value. Thus, value is an attribute of dealienating endeavor. Value is measured by what is involved in satisfying the motivating need or desire to acquire something. The measure of value is usually stated by the price paid to get it, whether the price is expressed as money, an expenditure of labor, or in terms of some other aspect of dealienating endeavor.

Negativity describes any finite being in several ways. First, it appears as distinct from an Other. In fact its difference from the Other initially defines what or who it is. A distinguishing difference immediately sensed or perceived as the quality of an object provides its initial identity; but again, negatively and only in relation to an Other. Qualities cannot be comprehended or communicated except by noticeable differences from others. Qualities appearing and disappearing signify alteration in being, negativity in action. Causal relationships are successive negations existentially manifested by qualitative differences of something over time. Alteration of the quality of something over time implies alteration in a state of being. Its being is something definite and distinct from the Other(s), and becomes Other in time. So, negativity describes not only what something is now, but also what it was and will be. The ancient meaning of *Becoming* is described as a process of negativity as well as the more modern scientific concept of causality. In either case, negativity both describes states of being and changes in states of being, generally. Negativity equally well describes the actualization of potentialities for being, whether the operative agency is human or non-human. Neither does it matter whether or not the being in question is thought of as degraded, progressive, perfected, completed or merely continuously in process.

Negativity, considered an ontological principle, provides a foundation for explaining concepts of potentiality versus actuality and telos found in classical Greek and Christian philosophy. Hegel interpreted potentiality as the Other of a finite something while the resulting actuality of the process he interpreted as a final unification of something with its Other, providing the meaning of its being. Negation, then, is a way of explaining how the actual can issue from the potential, how the Greco-Christian telos of nature and spiritual life is revealed. However, beyond Hegelian philosophy, and in its most general sense, negativity is a ubiquitous driver of any kind of process occurring in the cosmos at any level of being. The power of this principle is evident in its universal applicability. It takes on various forms depending on the context of being under consideration. In logic it appears as implication, formal or material, a principle necessary to thought and knowledge. In nature it appears as causality applying to physical and chemical processes. In astrophysics it appears as anti-matter, cosmological black holes, other worlds. In theology, it appears as God creating the world from nothing. In psychology it appears as ego defenses and pathology. In sociology it appears as cultural conflict. It is equally applicable to an expression of human desires and ideal human aspiration in the realm of moral behavior. Its universal applicability ranges over the human, non-human, the finite and infinite alike.

As Hegel stated it, Being and Nothing imply the Becoming of determinate beings. The present condition of something is a continuous process of becoming something else, which is to say the Other mediates its being. Mediation is logical in the meanings generated by the process; but, more importantly, mediation is ontological, or reflected in the beings resulting from the process. What *ceases-to-be* is preserved and enhanced in that product of mediation Hegel called *sublation*. The resulting being signifies more in meaning and being than its original components due to the particular negating process creating it. This implies that actuality is a process of mediation in being, alteration of finite beings in a sublating process driven by negativity. Something and its Other Hegel considered *moments* of sublation characteristic of finitude. Sublation is an ontological process correlative to inclusion of particulars in the universal. Sublation is also equivalent to logical inference wherein a difference mediates between logical components unifying them to a conclusion. This outcome signifies more in meaning than the mediated components. Something with a new significance is revealed.

Negativity is essential to consciousness, thought and intentional behavior. Consciousness always either presents an Other alien to it or intends it as an object of thought with the Ego implicit in the background. The Ego is no more than a sensing and thinking of the Other, negating freedom, a conatus to become Other. Hegel characterizes the Other as an initial condition of being not what it ought to be, a deficient being, a mere potentiality for being which is realized by becoming Other than it is. An Other, considered as deficiency in or limit to being, has been referred to as a first negation by philosophers such a Paul Ricoeur. A second negation is said to amount to an affirmation of being. Alteration in being occurs through a negating process in which the Other is appropriated and assimilated into a fully developed self which has transcended the deficiency or limit initially negating it in some way. Successive negations transform being in general and the self in particular. The self remains finite, even though infinite in its power to transform itself and its world.

Initially, the Ego is abstract negativity, a presentation of the Other, recognition of limit and deficiency, and a demand for immediate gratification of need and desire. Primitive narcissism is the initial posture of the Ego and impetus for self-development. Ego is driven by negativity to comprehend and master the Other. In other words, its conatus is rationality and freedom. Alternatively, it could be said as did Hegel, and with equal plausibility, that rationality and freedom are its aim or telos. Dialectic of Ego and its Other constructs a self with an identity, which is recognized. Negating thought and action is a simultaneous discovery of self and world. As the Other is so assimilated, its hidden character is progressively revealed. This transformation of the Other is a humanization of the world and revelation of potentialities for being. Moreover, a negating Other provides an impetus for a process of realization in which being and meanings are created. What or who the Other is then becomes answered in the outcome of self-development. The process driven by negativity is continuous, eternal in fact. Being is open ended and always open to question. This more modern viewpoint is very different from Hegel's. He conceived of the Other as necessary to realize the potentiality of nature and human nature, of Spirit as rational freedom, of a pre-established divine intention and will. With or without Hegel's Christian beliefs and absolute idealism, a negating Other is certainly a necessary means for progressively developing the world, a self, and for any revelation of being and its meaning.

The Being of Thought

Thought and being are united by sharing the same characteristics. Both are driven by negativity. Both are active. Both constitute a process. Both progress sequentially with time. Both develop historically and become more complete. When being and being thought are consistent, the meaning of being is revealed and truth is secured. The task of ontology is to discover the meaning of being i.e. to think being as a logically coherent structure of meaning. In doing so, the meaning and relationship of both being and thought is comprehended.

Certainly, thought is the being of the thinker to begin with. Thus to the thinker, thought is indubitable when free of contradiction. Consistency establishes validity. Logic and mathematics are the generally recognized paradigms of this fact. Here, being and being thought is equivalent, since thought signifies only itself by definition or tautologically. The equivalency of being with being thought is also the case; but more subtly in psychic, spiritual and social life when something is to be made true by decision and volition. In such cases, being is created or made true as fact by thought and action. Dreams are said to come true by freedom of will and action. Obvious examples of this are faith: religious, in oneself, or in other persons. Other examples are found in a moral life driven by duty or in the self-conscious ethical behavior of individuals.

The test of validity is consistency within a structure of meaning. And, when inconsistency is detected, the being of thought is changed by a process of thinking and acting. Where the difference between being and thought lies in the coherence of thought itself, being and thought cannot be separated. For to be is to be thought. Whenever contradiction is detected, thought is compelled to work through it to form a new consistent structure of meaning. The degree of consistency and completeness of thought measure truth and falsity. Falsity is then a lesser degree of truth. Thus not only can being be thought, but it must be thought and thought through to a satisfactory coherent completion, to a conclusion if you will. The mark of truth for Hegel was consistency between thought and being resulting from a negating process of thought and human action creating a completed whole structure of meaning. At the end of this interactive process the truth is made known. With completed meaning, being thought is free of error. That being could have another structure of meaning is an abstract possibility. However, a nuomenal being has no content, cannot be known in principle and so is a meaningless abstract possibility.

Hegel's absolute idealism equated being with thought.

> We often hear it maintained that thought is opposed to being. Now in the face of such a statement, our first question ought to be, what is meant by being. If we understand being as it is defined by reflection, all that we can say of it is that it is what is wholly identical and affirmative. And if we then look at thought, it cannot escape us that thought

> also is at least what is absolutely identical with itself. Both therefore, being as well as thought, have the same attribute.[10]

Herein, Being is not something thought about, but is thought in progressive process. Being is misconceived when thought of as a mere abstraction, as simple and without related parts, as an attribute of existence, or as just one reality among others. No doubt Being is an immediate abstract certainty for the thinking Ego, but Being signifies a whole of implicit meaning and can be thought through. Therefore, being and thought are unitary and continuous with each other and with transformative action. Being encompasses both the subjective and objective, and as thought by the Notion, subject and object are no longer distinct but unitary. By conceiving of thought and being as continuous and unitary, Hegel sought to resolve the insurmountable dualism plaguing empiricism, intuitionism and subjective idealism of his time. Where this is not done, the result is a bifurcation of mind and body, subjectivity and objectivity, form and content, fact and value and so forth. These are subordinate to an originating bifurcation of thought and being. They all present an irreconcilable problem of how thought can correspond with being.

Since Aristotle, many philosophers believed thought could be described by a discrete number of *categories*. Hegel thought so, but insisted that the categories not be confined to finite beings. Categories of thought are not to be philosophically constructed from intuition, by induction from experience or deduction from knowledge in order to understand a being alien to thought. Rather, categories are implicit within the being of thought, and are made explicit through the dialectical progression of thought. This progression moves by differentiating a first category or Notion, examining its negation by an other implied by it, synthesizing the negation into a third signifying itself and the first, and implying another beyond its meaning. The process moves from an immediate abstraction through differentiation by an Other, returning to an object enlarged in meaning and significance to be taken once again as an immediate abstraction, and so forth.

Hegel's absolute idealism considered being as an instantiation and completion of thought. Plato held that thought pre-exists being which is a mere imperfect imitation of thought. This viewpoint, although problematical, is appealing due to its consistency with faith in a God creating everything that exists by thinking it. Within this context, the truths for humanity are God's intentions, particularly expressed in moral principles. These are held to establish a foundation for civilization and a structure of law. Although Hegel subscribed to a Platonic view of truth, he modified it. His addition was to view truth resulting from a historical process of human experience in which alienation from divine intention is suffered and worked through. Herein Hegelian thinking inadvertently suggests that truth is not pre-established thought prior to existence, but emerges from human experience and suffering. Truth is hereby revealed in the very human process of dealienation. Although truth is a temporal product of historical dealienation, truth transcends the moment. It need not be mutable, nor merely relative to place, culture or anything else extraneous to the process that establishes it. Truth, once discovered, endures and can be depended upon for future experience. Truth and wisdom are preserved with the human capacity to generalize and think with universals.

Thinking the Universal

When philosophy begins, it does so with abstraction, with thought removed from originating context, with universals. In effect, universals are abstract intentions signifying the identity of something composed of unspecified differences, which are implicit and can be explicitly developed. Hegel's recognition of negativity implied by thinking the universal, and more generally, a negativity driving both thought and being may well have suggested the possibility of traversing being by a dialectical logic as well as by a historical phenomenology.

Hegel gave universals existential import. "All things are a genus (i.e. have a meaning and purpose) in an *individual* actuality of a *particular* constitution. And they are finite, because the particular in them may and also may not conform to the universal."[11] Universal Notions ontologically support any abstract logic of concepts and deductive inference. For universal Notions carry implicit meanings with existential import. Thus, universal Notions constitute the basis of all thought forms and inference as mediated by dialectic of negation. Since universals have existential import, Hegelian Notions are considered objective to begin with, and so avoid the Kantian problem of how subjective mental forms applied to sensuous intuitions represent an unknowable being: how the *phenomena* correspond to the *nuomena*. Unlike Kant, Hegel begins with Being as given and implicit, whereas Kant begins with human subjectivity and tries to construct Being from an analysis of the implications of subjectivity.

Universals can be considered in their logically formal aspect a common or shared attribute of individuals. Hegel regarded this concept of universality to be deficient. For him the universal is what creates the individual. Without the universal, the individual would not in fact exist. I am first a human being before I am anything else. That is to say, the universal establishes the being of something, not the other way around.

> The individual man is what he is in particular, only in so far as he is before all things a man as man and in general. And that generality is not something external to, or something in addition to, other abstract qualities, or to mere features discovered by reflection. It is what permeates and includes in it everything particular.[12]

To give primacy to the universal rather than the particular is to defy common sense realism and assert the absolute idealist perspective toward the world. The individual is considered a universalized particular. In so far as he is particular, his being is isolated and lacking in meaning. As particular, he is merely a negation, merely Other. As universal, he is a human being with a fullness of meaning implicit in such a Notion. As universal, he is complete and fully incorporated into a whole of all Others, of the cosmos itself.

Hegel narrowly identified rationality with the ability to think with universals This ability to symbolize the Many as the One defines the universal. The identity of the One, the universal, disregards the differences of the Many which it signifies. Since the universal is an abstract signifier including implicit differences among the many signified, it implies complex relationships among them. Deductive logic is based upon the implications of the universal concept. A universal, the One signifying the Many and replete with implied differences, Hegel viewed not simply as a logical class, but more importantly as something with ontological import. Thus, it is possible to think of a universal signifying every possible Other, or the whole. A universal intended to signify every finite possibility, to include all possible Others, defines an infinite object of thought. The infinite can be thought as a universal unifying or sublating every difference among every finite Other. Hegel conceived it as the thought beyond which there is nothing more intended. He called it the absolute Idea, a culmination of a spiritual development of rationality and freedom. Everything finite or Other is therefore sublated in this temporal spiritual development in which the object of thought has nothing alien to itself to encounter. With this absolute Idea, alienating finitude is overcome. It is the Hegelian philosophical God, Spirit thinking itself, an unmoved mover, the Christian creator God become incarnate within history.

A universal is a signifier. Nevertheless, what is signified? Philosophy has provided a wide range of answers; a separate realm of ideas, essences embedded in substance, ideas constructed by some faculty of mind, mere words signifying nothing in particular or what the thinker chooses them to signify. The universal either signifies being or thought. Whether considered as real something or a product of thought, a universal makes an implicit distinction of differences in whatever is signified. Negativity is required to think about being and to describe being as a process. The meaning of anything requires negativity, a being that is Other. Abstractly considered, the universal implies something else with a difference, namely a particular. Their negating difference unifies them and provides a structure of meaning. That negativity creates meaning is illustrated by thinking the universal to which Hegel attached great importance, since he believed being derived from thought. Hegel's logic began with an abstract whole of Being, progressively differentiating it with a dialectic of universals in which all Others are enumerated as particular instantiations of the universal ending with Being thought through to completion in the absolute Idea. Thus it was that Hegel believed the infinite to be reachable in thought by finite increments through the universal Notion and Idea.

Thought is language, a complex system of meanings implying all possible significations. The abstract universal is the ancient One that implies and incorporates the Many. Both the abstract and the concrete are themselves negations. Negativity allows us to recognize the reciprocal reference of universal to particular. The universal, signifying many or everything excludes the particular. To think is to specify the identity of something and its differences, which may be implicit as when thinking an abstract universal, or explicit when enumerating or specifying differences. The identity of something thought about is kept in the foreground while implicit differences are kept in the background. Universals permit discourse to proceed without an impossibly laborious enumeration of particulars.

As differentiating activity, to think is to negate, to present an alien Other of consciousness. Hegel's point was that to differentiate is also to unify. Negativity makes it so. The alien Other must be comprehended and dealt with and doing so reveals a whole structure of meaning and being. Negativity drives being and the thought of it to signify every component of a whole, whether or not it is initially complete as a Hegelian abstract thought of Being, or complete as thought by God, or just a continuously expanding historical process. The negating capacity of thought to unify by differentiating is demonstrated by an analysis of predication. Universals unite what is disparate to form an identity with implicit differences. Whether thinking of implicit or explicit differences, a whole is presupposed consisting of parts reciprocally related to each other by some form of negativity. Science develops knowledge through a series of negations in either thought or being incorporating more parts with greater degrees of differentiation into an expanding significant whole.

The Thought of Being

Implication is derived from a negativity, which both separates and unifies. Negativity permits thought to proceed in either direction, and peculiarly enough, in both directions simultaneously. This forms the basis for the dialectical movement of thought. However, being is moved by the negativity of time in a single direction from past to future. Hegel considered dialectic as a process of thought and being driven by negativity. Equating being with thought suggests the possibility of revealing the meaning of being as a seamless whole traversed dialectically with a progressive series of universals with increasing degrees of signification expressed in Notions signifying nature, and Ideas signifying free agency.

A signifier, the universal implies finite differences without enumerating them. Focusing only upon a common abstracted element, the universal allows discourse to proceed without explicitly specifying what is signified. So, a universal functions in discourse as a shorthand signifier of what is signified by implication but left unstated. The universal, or One, is then a symbol for the Many. Logic of class and deductive inference is made possible by the unenumerated differences implied by the universal. It is a reflection of the negativity of thought residing in unenumerated differences. Meaning resides in difference or distinguishing something from its Other. Universals are important by functioning discursively as abstract signifiers of finite beings. However, this function is considered of secondary importance when attention is focused upon the common attribute or One, rather than upon the Many it implies.

Without abstract universals, discourse is impossible. However, discourse proceeds with universals signifying something finite with existential implications. Thus, discourse can discover hidden meaning among signifiers with existential import embedded in the structure of language itself. This is what philosophy does, since language has existential signification. The thought of being and being of thought reside within the structure of language. In addition, the meaning of being is revealed through discourse based upon self-existence and human experience in general. Universals function in the same way as a shorthand code or a high-level computer language creating a necessary economy in discourse. But, universals signifying existence do more than the logical syntax of any language. For then they offer further possibilities of being with a different meaning. The implication is material, not just formal. Possible existence and experience are suggested by their use. Herein is clearly seen negativity underlying the universal: a negativity of distinction creating meaning; a negativity presenting an alien Other(s) as the signified; a negativity implying complex meanings, suggesting possibilities of meaning, being, experience and action to be explored.

A universal is an abstract signifier with implication. It functions in discourse as indirect signifier with either formal or material implication. Without signifying anything finite, the meaning of a universal is formal but perfectly understood. For the negativity of thought constitutes meaning. And this negativity resides even in a completely abstract universal understood as a logical class with unspecified members. Here negativity forms the thought of a universal as an abstract signifier with formal rather than material implication. Thus, a universal can function abstractly as mere thought unrelated to being. The being of thought is thinking the universal and formal implication. However, the being of thought is not the thought of being. A universal signifying an abstract class with members is not equivalent in meaning to a universal signifying something finite with unspecified Other(s) encountered within conscious self-existence. Existential import of a universal requires enumerating differences among the finite many indirectly signified by it.

Universals with existential import can be thought about and acted upon to generate a specific result. Here negativity is ontological as distinct from logical, existential or material as distinct from formal. The Many signified by the One are the Others of experience, the meaning of which is revealed by a interactive activity responding to thought. The Other(s) signified and implied by the universal can be actively explored in the world with a further discovery of their meaning. The alien Other(s) implied by the universal then become a revealed meaning unavailable through the mere application of thought, by itself. When thought is about being, the process of discovering meaning is also a process of negating the alien aspect of the Other(s) signified and implied by a universal. Knowing something reflects this negating process wherein the world is discovered through intelligent behavior directed by a self seeking satisfaction of its desires and aims.

Rather than defining the universal as signifying an abstract attribute common to a class of objects, focus attention upon the differences implicit in the class thought about or objects signified. The differences exhibit the power of negativity both in the being of thought and in the thought of being. Regarding the former, meaning is formed with a distinguishable difference. Regarding the latter, a finite being is signified by its difference from its Other. Then the being in question is judged real. Whether the being of thought or the thought of being, negativity is comprehended as difference. Without difference, there is no meaning and nothing is signified. For example, if white were the only color, color could not be sensed, would have no meaning, could not be thought as a universal or attributed to perceived objects.

Meaning is the being of thought indubitable to the thinker, even when it consists of a false belief. What we think about something may be in error. Alternatively, that we think something, which has meaning, exists, does not make it so. What makes it so is our active experience. In science we dispassionately discover, observe, examine and verify what we hypothesize to exist. As we do so, a consistent structure of meaning is created which assures us that we know the meaning of the being in question. Truth then consists of a completed coherent structure of meaning. Since the sciences deal with finite beings altering with time, a completed coherent structure of meaning is not possible at any given moment. Thus scientific truth is held to be incomplete and probable, not absolute. But in fact at any given moment, the meaning of something free of contradiction is complete. So for practical purposes, the absence of contradiction or coherence is the test of truth generally and particularly for scientific knowledge.

Whether or not scientific, what we claim to know as the truth is established by a correspondence between signifier and signified. This is obtained existentially from immediate experience and public consensus concerning it. One directly observes, experiments and verifies what is claimed to be true. On the other hand, one indirectly infers what is claimed to be true. This is particularly the case at higher theoretical levels of abstract generalization where thought proceeds primarily with universals. Here, there is an increasing reliance upon implication and coherence to establish truth. Nevertheless, both direct correspondences with experience and indirect coherence establish truth in complementary ways.

With regard only to thought, the Parmenidean One is and is not. The abstract One consists of contradictory possibilities lacking any principle of determinacy. However, being requires determinacy. This is provided by the distinctions of existence. The contradictory indeterminacy of the One demonstrates that thought alone is insufficient to comprehend the meaning of being. The One is simply an abstract negativity characterizing thought itself.

With regard to consciousness, the One is always the negating Other. And with regard to the self, the One is its own indeterminacy, or freedom. Here, negativity moves beyond an abstraction of thought toward its true ontological significance. It becomes an ontological principle structuring thought, consciousness, finitude and self-existence. An alien Other initially encountered within self-existence is the being that provides an impetus for thought. The meaning of this being is developed by thought and its extension, namely self-activity. The result is a coherent structure of meaning signifying a totality of being. Negativity is the means whereby the structure is built. A self who thinks and acts is the locus of negativity whereby true knowledge is attained. The negating process of interaction between thought and being mediated by self-activity ceases when the Other is assimilated by the self so that it is without frustrating opposition and free of contradictory meaning. At this point the being of thought corresponds with the thought of being. The truth is established and there is no further impetus for thought to existentially interact with being.

The being of thought is not identical to the thought of being, since the referent of the former is itself thought while the referent of the latter is not thought. A being, which is not thought, is an alien Other to thought comprehended in a process of negative interaction with the self. Meaning is created and expands as being is progressively translated into a representation of thought. Being can be thought, can be changed by thought; can even be created by thought. There is no radical separation, no absolute alienation of being from thought. For both are unified and given impetus by negativity. Its operation provides their respective difference of meaning. Within the being of thought, negativity is evident in thinking the universal, in implication, and in contradictory meanings expressive of false belief. Negativity is also most evident as time, finitude and natural causality. With negativity, being and thought are coextensive as a process continuously creating meaning and discovering being. The process of interaction is interminable, disallowing any final knowledge of a totality of being. The negativity of time makes Hegel's absolute Idea no more than a vacuous abstraction, a wishful dream. Absolute knowledge would require the cessation of time, and with it there could not be any impetus for thought to further differentiate being, no revelation of the meaning of an alien Other, nothing to maintain a structure of meaning. Being would revert to an originating undifferentiated Nothing as Hegel put it.

Hegel conflated the being of thought with the thought of being. This is the fallacy of absolute idealism. It falsely presumes the universal to possess material implication or to imply the existence of something. Nevertheless, being is not merely a thought and something cannot be said to exist by the mere thought of it. Without the alien Other(s) distinct from and negating the self, there is no existential basis for the being of any kind. Without originating as a response to the alienating finitude of self-existence, thought is a vacuous abstraction. Linguistic symbols such as the universals, abstracted from the existential context in which they originate cannot signify being. So it is that Hegel began and ended his philosophical odyssey with speculative abstractions - Being and the absolute Idea. These undoubtedly display the being of thought itself with its power to abstract, but not the thought of being. Yet, even with such error, Hegel deserved great credit for recognizing that negativity drives both thought and being.

A Hegelian viewpoint claims that to think the universal is to symbolically represent the sublation of finite differences among many existent beings into a single meaningful signifier. Logic teaches that a greater degree of extension corresponds to a lesser degree of intension. Thus, a universal with infinite logical extension loses intension completely, connoting nothing in particular. There is left only abstract signifier without any finite object signified. Meaning everything or anything signifies nothing in particular. Now, meaning is derived from negation, by a specifiable difference of something from something else. Without this, meaning ceases as the signifier loses its function of representing reality. Thus to speak of Being, or God as infinite or absolute is to present an abstract universal signifier without anything finite signified. For what or who is signified must be a negating Other from which meaning can be developed by interaction with the self.

Note how God cannot be understood without being personalized. Yet, Being, God, the infinite or absolute are meaningful abstract universals intended to signify something, even if it's not a finite object capable of being perceived and interacted with. What such abstract universals signify is something about the nature of thought itself or about the nature of the thinker. So, even if the infinite cannot mean or be a finite object, it still remains meaningful when attributed to a self whose powers of rationality and freedom allow it to know anything or realize its potentiality for being. Then again, the infinite is meaningful when signifying a totality of being at the present moment. What originates meaning must be something finite existing as an Other with distinct differences. Minimally, thinking with universals abstractly intends the different Other(s) and this expresses a negativity of thought. Being requires differences determined by existential interaction of self with Other(s). In other words, being requires more than intended meaning and this more are differences existentially implied and verified in some way.

The claim that the self can transcend finitude by thinking the universal bears careful scrutiny. Certainly, the universal, absolute Idea, infinite and God all signify the power of thought. Yet, thought could only originate with and signify the Other(s), alien to the thinker. It must think about the Other and act upon it. If thinking the universal is to have existential import, and thus to deal with being, it is necessarily confined to finitude and self-existence. Thought requires a thinker, negativity and an alien Other. With these its movement occurs as a finite process Hegel conceived as sublation. In terms of process, all the infinite can be is an incremental movement of the finite, an expanding horizon. Since thought must be of the finite to be about being, its work is continuous and interminable. Hegel's analysis of the Ego as a negating encounter with an Other of itself, as freedom and rationality, suggests that its being is an infinite potentiality for being, but not that it can ever comprehend being with finality merely by thinking the universal. What rationality and freedom - that infinite essence of the self - allow is a continuous and interminable process of sublation wherein finitude is continuously transcended incrementally, if never with finality. Within this process the self develops and realizes its finite potentiality for being.

Conforming to an ancient mind-set, Hegel arranged universals in an ontological hierarchy. Presuming universals to have existential import, the higher the universal, the greater its value. However, if universals do not have existential import, it is difficult to ascribe any degree of truth or value to them. Glorifying the universal in a hierarchical structure of thought may be to celebrate the power of thought. But, to claim the universal signifies truth or goodness is to load it with freight it is unable to carry. Of itself, universality signifies thought. Only when universality is a thought product of existence can its meaning reveal the truth of being or anything of value. Only then can it obligate the self to respect and treasure its meaning. For then it is a result of what the self has suffered through and learned from.

Restricting the scope of rationality to thinking with universals arranged in an ontological hierarchy implies, for example, that the state is superior to the individual. However, to say something about a group of individuals is no more or less rational, valuable, or true than to say something about a particular individual member. The fact that a universal social norm or role is intended to apply to many individuals does not make it superior to what the individual might choose for himself. For universality by itself does not establish rationality in an evaluative sense of being worthy, or having reasons which obligate one to a course of action or judgment. Thus, it would be fallacious to presume the mere fact of universality to imply superior rationality. When the scope of rationality is not artificially restricted to universality, rationality can be seen for what it is: an ability to think logically with facts, evaluate and make intelligent choices for deliberate action designed to satisfy human needs, desires and aims.

Behavioral norms can be described as universal or at least intended to be universal in application. But the intention or fact of universality cannot make any conduct normative. It becomes normative when qualified in two ways. First, it must pass the test of experience requiring it to be rationally justified within a process of self-existence. Secondly, it must past the test of being freely chosen and acted upon by a self without coercion by any Other(s). Then, the norm in question is authentically expressed with personal conviction by an autonomous human being. That the norm ought to be the case, or is felt to be personally obligatory is an outcome generated by self-existence. Even if not having passed through the experience generating it, those expressing allegiance to it can understand how it came about and why it commands their allegiance.

Universal norms are not abstractions pre-established by thought, but originate existentially and are sustained by rationality and freedom operative in self-existence. Any departure from this rationale would make any norm or law an alien Other to the self. Unfortunately, this is generally how universal norms and laws are understood. They are simply commands of Others such as culture, community institutions, God and so forth. The manner in which universality is achieved is coercively by non-rational identifications or even irrationally by threat, punishment, violence or accidental historical circumstance. To be universally valid, a law must not deny what is essential to human existence, but rather express it. That is to say that laws must be existentially created while being spontaneous expressions of rationality and freedom. Where this is the case, laws would never be coercive and might even become unnecessary. Such a utopia of human existence is possible, but not probable, since human desires and aims conflict. Nevertheless, as human freedom and rationality historically develop and expand, laws could become less coercive.

The Truth of Being

Are there absolute truths, eternal verities, propositions about being which can never be refuted no matter what happens? Religious conviction might assert the ten commandments or the golden rule to be eternally true. Or, a philosopher might want to assert as an absolute truth that rational freedom is the essence of human nature. Deeply held convictions are often asserted to be absolute truths. The self wants to believe this, particularly after having identified with them, made them part of a self-concept that drives self-projective and self-objectifying behavior. A truth claimed absolute without reference to past, present or future human experience has lost existential significance while, at best, retaining egocentric significance. Asserting an absolute truth bespeaks an egotistical attitude; an inexcusable intellectual arrogance or hubris as the ancients would put it.

Truth is a quest to answer the question of the meaning of being posed by the alienating finitude of self-existence. Every self must answer the question of whom or what is the Other, and who or what it will become. The truth of this answer is temporal, approximate and ideal. In other words, the truth is an existential work in progress. Striving to learn the truth of being in general, or one's own being in particular, commands more respect than any claim to know it with absolute certainty. Such a claim provides a false sense of security by ending the continuously posed existential question of truth. For, whatever it is, or however claimed to be known at any given time, the quest for truth is eternal; ennobling of the human spirit.

Truth is not simply some abstract eternal verity, some proposition without reference to past or future human experience. Rather, truth is a product of an existential process of alienation and dealienation. Truth is not some proposition pre-established by an authoritative Other for self-existence. Neither is truth just there waiting to be discovered or merely confirmed by self-existence. No! A dealienating process of self-existence creates the truth, whatever it may be. And the same dealienating process confirms and sustains, or refutes and destroys whatever is believed true. Belief in the truth must be warranted by human experience. It is just that simple. Any claim to know the absolute truth disregards the existential conditions prompting the discovery of truth. Also disregarded is the process of dealienation necessary for the discovery and maintenance of the truth. Any significant meaning, or truthful proposition, is an outcome of an existential process of dealienation, which is approximate with respect to future experience testing of it. To remove a proposition from the conditions of its derivation is to eliminate its ontological significance thereby limiting its significance to describing the decision of the thinker about how thought is to progress.

Truths, other than tautological, have material implication, or existential import. Thought and intentional behavior respond to frustrated needs, desires and a virtually infinite diversity of human suffering. No truth signifying anything about human nature is conceivably possible without relevance to temporal existential circumstances. Truth can be revealed by reflecting upon past experience or discovered within present experience. However created, or whatever its authoritative source, it is subject to continuous testing by future experience that can confirm, refute or modify it. The deepest of human convictions are contingent upon the conditions of self-existence. Therefore, truth, as science recognizes it, may be virtually certain, but never absolutely certain. Rather, it approximates an ideal of absolute certainty that cannot be secured, in so far as a truthful proposition is a universal generalization about future experience that may refute or modify it in some way. Thus it is that science can never believe what it discovers to be true in any absolute sense.

If truth were not about human experience, it could not signify anything one could call real. Arising from, and sustained by experience, no truth can remove the possibility of contradiction. Absolute certainty has been said to reside in the *a priori*, in a tautology, a fiat, or a decision to choose a particular logic to achieve a pre-established aim. Although such a truth signifies something about thought or the thinker, it does not signify anything about the content of thought. The negativity experienced by existential finitude is the basis for any concept of truth and falsity. Ontological negativity is the origin of both correlative concepts of truth and falsity along with their content. Moreover, ontological negativity can only be existentially expressed through a temporal encounter of self-existence with alienating finitude accompanied by dealienating intentional interaction utilizing a distinct human capacity for rationality and freedom.

So, here are the attributes of truth. Propositions making the most significant truth claims usually take the form of universal generalizations, whether derived deductively or inductively. The truth is about an alien Other, be it the self or being of a different kind. Truths about thought should not be confused with those about being in general or the being of the self. Truth is formed by ontological negativity, posed by an Other, which limits or opposes in being. Ontological negativity is expressed by the alienating finitude of self-existence. The search for truth begins with unsatisfied human needs, frustrated desires and human suffering. A dialectical process of alienation and dealienation generates the truth as its outcome.

Truth addresses a perennial question of what is the Other and who shall the self become. Truth is necessary for self-projection, self-objectification and self-realization of human potential. The truth is derived from self-existence and what is learned from human experience rather than pre-established or prescribed by authoritative Others for self-existence. It depends upon the conditions encountered by self-existence. Thus, it can be confirmed, refuted or modified by future experience. The continuous possibility of contradiction makes the truth approximate; an ideal to be attained by the knowledge derived from self-realization. Over time then certain truths become virtually certain, but never absolutely so. Socrates, that most noble seeker of wisdom, intuitively understood this spirit of truth.

Alienation

"What or who is the Other?" is a question about the meaning of being. The question arises as an Other alien to the self is existentially encountered. However, the self is not a privileged being; encountering itself likewise as an alien Other. Initially, the self is uncomprehended, strange, hidden, lacking coherence, unstructured by most human needs, desires and aims. Through a negating existential interaction of self with alien Other, the question of being acquires an answer. The being of the self, initially an alien Other, is a potentiality for being which is realized by a process of negativity with respect to the alien Other. As self-realization progresses, alien Others are dealt with interactively. Being, thought about and acted upon, progressively acquires a coherent structure of meaning. As the self develops, every potentiality for being is realized and the meaning of being is revealed. The process is continuous and interminable. Answering what the Other is simultaneously answers who the self is. So the question of being is always being asked and answered by a potentially infinite number of human experiences in a world driven by negativity, characterized by finitude and temporal sequences of alteration in being.

The development of negativity and dialectic within the history of philosophy from Parmenides through Hegel into existentialism and beyond suggests a basis for understanding alienation and dealienation in terms of negating processes. Building upon Hegelian philosophy and existentialism, Paul Ricoeur thought of negativity as an existential process of alienation and dealienation. A first negation of being is alienating whereas, its second negation dealienates resulting in an affirmation of being. Ricoeur's first negation is an encounter with being in the form of an alien Other. It connotes a separation in being, a deficiency, something lacking or lost requiring a developmental recovery to make whole or complete. Negations succeeding the initial one are both logical in meaning and ontological in the fact of a process of temporal transformation of being. As the alien Other is negated, it is assimilated as something new is created. Hegel called the process *sublation*. However, negativity does more than merely demonstrate pre-established thought dialectically demonstrated by existential examples, as Hegel believed. Rather, negativity is an ontological principle of process governing both thought and being. Moreover, negativity is evident in every phenomenological transformation of being throughout history.

Hegelian sublation suggests a general explanation of alienation and dealienation. Encountering the Other as a limit to or deficiency in being is an initial negating moment of alienation. The Other signifies that the being in question is finite and alienated from what it can be. Its being is a possibility for it, a potentiality for being something, which it has never been and is not at the present moment. This alienating finitude fundamentally characterizes a world of finite beings. It is the impetus for alteration, transformation, and development in being. Everything finite is altered with time, comes to be, develops, is transformed, and ceases to be. Hegelian sublation is an absolute idealist explanation of this observation of natural finite processes.

A process of sublation driven by negativity was Hegel's ontological explanation of finitude. Sublating the limiting Other suggests dealienation as a process driven by negativity, a process revealing being and its meaning. Hegel thought of the process as an identification of differences in thought and being and an inclusion of them in a progressive logical structure of meaning with universal Notions or Ideas revealing what is divinely pre-established. Even if the Hegelian analysis of being and thought as divinely pre-established is now untenable, dealienation as a process of negating finitude remains a compelling general explanation of what it means to be anything, especially to be human. Sublation can be emended to a concept of dealienation driven by negativity. Alienation and dealienation would then generally describe being, not pre-established and created by God thinking it into existence, but rather emerging from a creative expanding process of existence structured by a negativity of finitude.

Negativity is the basis for thought, being, the self, and freedom. Being is not merely being thought. The thought of being is not equivalent to the being of thought. Universals do not have material implication and so cannot signify being without existential discovery. This is provided by the alienating finitude of self-existence. A self negated by the alien Other(s), alienated with frustrated needs, desires and aims provides the impetus necessary for thought to signify anything. The Other of thought is being; that which is encountered as an existing something, alien to the self. Being is something thought about and acted upon. But being can only be thought about as a finite something signified; something distinct or different from self and the many Others encountered by the self. Indirectly, universals signify being. However, universals presume the Other(s) initially encountered existentially through a consciousness of what is not self. Alien Others appear with undisclosed differences, hidden implications to be revealed in a further process of self-existence. Driven by the negativity of the alien Other(s) and its own desires, the self responds with intentional activity describing a process of dealienation in which self and world are revealed in being and meaning.

Alteration; a coming-to-be and ceasing-to-be; actualization of potential; birth, development and death: all are descriptions of finitude. Understood generally, finitude is the negativity of any temporal process whether it is a temporal alteration of being, a limit posed by the Other, or a deficiency of being. The essential attribute of existence is finitude; a central fact of being human, of existing in a world and with one's fellows where everything is at least initially encountered as an alien Other, including the self. Being, consciousness and thought cannot escape finitude, since they are all driven by negativity. An abstract Ego is no exception, since it always distintinguishes itself from the Other and determines what and who it is by means of the Other(s). Human finitude is exhibited by self-existence wherein desire implies a limit actively dealt with and so resulting in actualizing a potentiality for being something, be it human or otherwise.

The self exists as finite possibility of being an Other. Thus, its essential nature is a being, which it is not, but must become. Stated otherwise, self-existence connotes a being whose being is perpetually in question. Its future exists as the Other of what it was in the past or is in the present. As a potentiality for being Other, the self is alienated and so must develop and construct its being intentionally. Only through a self-realizing temporal process can the question of its being be answered. Self-existence points toward a being with a future, a being in continuous temporal transition, developing and revealing its identity and constructing its meaning.

The self is defined in terms of negativity by its alienating finitude and by its potentiality for being. To be nothing or always an Other is to be indeterminate. This indeterminacy of self-existence is the meaning of human freedom. Alienating finitude presents freedom in its initial negative aspect. The self is not the Other it is conscious of, or intends. Its non-being and potentiality bespeak its freedom. Being nothing poses the question of its being. Being nothing is its freedom to be. Therefore, the being of the self is an open question, an alienated potentiality for becoming something and for achieving its own particular identity.

Human finitude is an existential encounter with limits, barriers, restrictions and constraints. The alienating finitude of self-existence implies that human desires and aims are in principle infinite. A negation of desires and aims is a blocking of self-satisfaction and self-expression. In this, the self initially encounters its being negatively through alienating finitude. Alienation presents the task of self-existence, to actively negate that, which limits it. Doing so defines dealienation as a process of successive negations in which the self realizes an identity. As driven by negativity, alienation and dealienation is a continuous historical process with an infinite time horizon. Infinite in time, human needs, desires and aims are met by equally infinite powers of rationality and freedom that permit dealienation. Since the self is the agent of dealienation, its behavior is a choice of means. Some work, some don't work, and some work better than others do. None can be guaranteed to result in successful dealienation. But without the exercise of freedom and rationality, none can work. This contention requires proof. It lies in the lessons taught by what human beings have tried in their delineating endeavors. Historical self-existence, making trial of different means and behaviors teaches humanity what dealienates and what does not.

Negativity in being, in time, in consciousness and in thought makes alienating finitude a necessary and permanent condition of self-existence. But the negativity of being in general and self in particular also implies a freedom to think, will and act in the world. This amounts to negating the Other whether it is a deficiency from within or a limit from without. With the power of rationality and freedom, the self becomes Other than it was in the past or presently is in fact. The alien Other then serves as a foil for self-development, for realizing whom it is and what everything else is within its total environment. Positive freedom consists of thought taking the form of intentional self-activity responding to alienation. Rationality and freedom constitute a process of dealienation answering the question of what the Other is and who the self is. The question of being human then becomes how dealienation is effected, and the role played by rationality and freedom in the process.

Self-existence discovers its own deficiency of being by experiencing something needed, frustrated desires and what it aspires toward becoming. An initial experience of negativity is an alienating moment of being in which undesirable separation, a loss, or something lacking is recognized. Thought and activity respond to the alienating finitude of self-existence. Hegel thought of this as a temporal appropriation of the Other, a realization of a pre-established potentiality for being something universal. The self literally becomes Other. Human subjectivity appropriates its object, what it ought to become; the universal kind God intended it to be. This requires successive temporal negations in which being is altered from its initially alienated condition and returns to God as an example of what he intended for it in the first place. Hegel placed sublation, a transformation and enrichment of being, within Christian theology. In fact sublation can be considered his philosophical interpretation of the biblical story of creation. Yet, sublation does not require Hegel's absolute idealist and theological baggage. For Hegel described any natural process in terms of a sublating dialectic. And the essential meaning here is ontological negativity. Considering the interpretive power of negativity for understanding alienation and dealienation, it would seem relatively unimportant how it was derived; whether as a starting principle for Hegelian ontology, a metaphysical principle or simply a linguistic exercise.

Negativity, stated in terms of a process of alienation and dealienation, describes the natural world, and more importantly, human nature. Successive negations affirm or posit a being complete in fact and meaning. Sublation is then an ontological process of overcoming alienation, a dealienation. And, as the alien Other is assimilated to every finite being, being generally gains meaning and gets incorporated within a total structure of thought. Since the process is temporally continuous and interminable for finite beings, alienation and dealienation eternally recurs and describes being as such. Alienation and dealienation is that expression of negativity built into the structure of being. This continuous transcending of finitude posits or affirms the infinite to be an expanding totality of being and meaning. The infinite then is actuality, a reality of the present moment of time, which exists as a product of an ontological process of negativity in being and thought. As Hegel would have stated it, the infinite is posited through the sublation of the finite.

Dealienation begins when something is thought about, abstracted, analyzed and synthesized in various ways. As thought about, the being in question moves from the unknown to the known, acquiring a structure of meaning. By being comprehended its alien character recedes. When fully comprehended, it may be changed in being and controlled in accordance with the desires and aims of the self. If a product of the rational activity of a self, its being is a specific realization of the potentiality of the self whose general essence is rational freedom. A dealienated world is one in which being is comprehended and even created by a freely active rational self. When something we want is created by us, it is what we are. It is an expression of who we are; our identity, if you will.

Being is initially encountered existentially as an alien Other without any meaning other than the question of what or who it is. The meaning of its being is indeterminate. Only after the alien Other is incorporated into a structure of meaning can it become determinate, true and known. Any inconsistency in its meaning re-introduces its alien character, again with an indeterminate meaning. The thought of its being is false, not known. Thought is frustrated by incoherence. This provides an impetus for thought and being to again interact. The process of dealienation might include thinking, re-thinking, questioning, examining, observing, experimenting, discovering, changing or creating something. When the alien Other(s) in question is incorporated into a coherent structure of meaning, thought rests.

Alienation implies an incomplete development of being and meaning. Incomplete development is coextensive with a false conception of being. Hegel believed that complete development displays a perfection of being revealing its true conception. Thus, truth is the result of a process of dealienation. Since negativity and finitude are the necessary conditions of self-existence, the outcome of any process of dealienation is necessarily finite and so itself subject to being negated by time, space, material deterioration and what other human beings make of it. Yet, the outcome of dealienation is a self-objectification and progressive humanization of the world. Self and world are constructed and transformed simultaneously as alien Others are existentially encountered and dealt with. When fully developed, the self recognizes who it is and what the alien Other was that negated it and that it in turn negated. Being in general and self in particular become progressively less alien, less strange, completely familiar and known. Therefore, in a Hegelian sense, subject becomes object. Being is revealed when the alien Other is interactively judged and controlled by the self. Only then can any domination by the alien Other be overcome. The self dealienates by symbolically representing, enumerating and assimilating the alien Others in a coherent structure of meaning. Understood in this way, alienation and dealienation are built into the very structure of being. Furthermore, alienation and dealienation describe an existential process whereby being is revealed in a continuously expanding coherent structure of meaning.

Notes

1. Hegel, G. W. F. (1969) *Hegel's Science of Logic* (A. V. Miller, Trans.). London, England: Humanities Press, George Allen and Unwin Ltd., 82.
2. Ibid., 835.
3. Ibid., 118.
4. Ibid.
5. Hegel, G. W. F. (1830) *Hegel's Logic*: Being Part One of the Encyclopedia of the Philosophical Sciences (3rd ed., 1975) (William Wallace, Trans.). London, England: Oxford University Press, 165.
6. Ibid., 132.
7. Ibid., 118.
8. Ibid., 119.
9. Ibid., 117.
10. Ibid., 132.
11. Ibid., 243.
12I. bid., 240.

Chapter Two

Alienation: Impetus for Self-Development

Nature of the Self

Consider two kinds of abstract objects, *thing* and *self.* Both are described with certain attributes. Both can be said to exist. Both are finite, altering with time. Their unrealized potentiality is an aspect of their being alien to their present condition. However, their potentiality for being may be realized under a particular set of circumstances. Certain processes describe their historical development. So far, *thing* and *self* are indistinguishable objects. Yet, both are radically different. A self is conscious of itself and world as Other while a thing is not. A thing can neither think nor act for itself while a self can. A thing alters unintentionally by causes external to itself while a self can alter intentionally by its own powers. A thing is utilized by a self with certain intentions, but not vice versa. Processes describing the being of a thing and that of a self are different. This is reflected by the language used to describe each one. The behavior of a self is described as goal seeking. In addition, its development is intentional and social. A self is marked by intelligence, whereas a thing is not.

Thought and action are correlative and continuous, flowing from one to the other in either direction. Volition is the operation of thought and self-activity in the world. When the world is problematical as when the needs and desires of the self are frustrated, thought responds. A world is created in large part from intelligent volitional self-activity. Hegel thought of volition as a form of thought. Actualization of ideas occur by means of acts of will which is "... a special way of thinking, thinking translating itself into existence, thinking as the urge to give itself existence."[1] And,

> A man, however, can just as little be theoretical or think without a will, because in thinking he is of necessity being active. The content of something thought has the form of being; but this being is something mediated, something established through our activity.[2]

The being of thought is provided existential content and completed through volitional acts instantiating ideas, making something subjective objective in individual works or social institutions.

The self or unique personality of a particular individual is a spiritual entity, i.e. a free rational being with cognitive and conative capabilities active in the world. Personality originates from biological need and desire reflecting various kinds of alienation. Philosophically expressed by idealists such as Hegel, selfhood originates from an undeveloped abstract Ego with an indeterminate potentiality for becoming something temporally finite, thereby acquiring a unique history. Negativity constructs the self in multiple ways. First, what is presented to it is always Other than itself, i.e., consciousness is *objectively intentional.* Secondly, such a consciousness implies that the self is a nullity or an indeterminate potentiality for being something or other.

The alien Other(s), what the self is not, or that from which the self distinguishes itself, expresses its primitive freedom in a negative aspect herein-designated *negative freedom.* Contraposed to this is *positive freedom*, a far more complex process involving rationality and volitional self-activity in the world. Positive freedom begins with a desire of the self for something other than what it is. This negativity of consciousness and the null being of the self is the basis of its freedom - its freedom from the Other and its freedom to be something by creating its own being. Its desires active in its world bespeak the positive freedom of a self-objectifying being progressively developing itself in incremental finite determinations.

Desire is conative, a drive to be something by becoming something finite. A primitive self discovers itself to be a bundle of inchoate desires, needs, inclinations and impulses undisciplined by reason or experience of the world and its fellows. As the self develops, desires are structured by socialization, experience and reason. The finitude of nature, time, and place are confronted through the presentation of desire and endeavors to satisfy it. For a spiritual being, rationality, or cognition, is the means for satisfying desire. But to be something requires an active transformation of world and self. Stated another way, to be something requires freedom, both in its negative and positive signification. That is, the self is not something it desires and must become what it desires, or transform the world to satisfy its desires. In this process the self is at once rational and free, a spiritual being.

Every self is a creature of desire. The object of desire is something needed or wanted. When thought about, desire becomes an idea with an aim of attaining some particular goal. Actualization of an idea requires intelligence and practical action coexisting and cooperating. Deliberate action is the mark of intelligence, of a will free to think and act for itself. Motivated by desire and operating with its thought and volition, an Ego discovers and constructs the world. Hegel thought of the world as a mediated objectification of the self. The desires of the self express a nullity of being equivalent to an infinite range of possibilities including those that are contradictory. Although desires are always for something finite, the desiring self is an infinite potentiality for being. A desiring self, free and rational knows no limit and so possesses infinite creative capability, a power usually ascribed to one's God.

As opposed to an abstract reflection upon a Cartesian Cogito, the self is revealed existentially through its response to an Other, which alienates it in some way. The alienating finitude of self-existence finds its basic expression in the multiplicity of desires. The self begins to experience itself and know the world by sensing and responding to desires and their frustration. With need and a desire to satisfy it, a deficiency in the self is acknowledged. The self needs something. Its being is an alien Other with something lacking or something, which ought to be, but is not presently the case for itself. Something is wanted, or something poses a limit to what is wanted. This is sensed as unsatisfied desire. The presence of desire signifies an alienation in which self and world are alien Others. Desire is satisfied when the self becomes Other than what it is; when that which opposes its needs and desires is comprehended, possessed, consumed, controlled or used in some definite way that satisfies desire. To think about and act upon desire is to be rational and free. These twin powers make dealienation possible. Their use constitutes a process of dealienation in which need and desire is satisfied. The result is a world and self no longer alien, but related and understood in terms of each other. More generally, the result is a revelation of being and meaning in all its finite dimensions.

Self-existence rests upon a physical and biological foundation defined as conatus for life variously expressed as instinct, drive, need, or desire. Yet, the self is a spiritual entity with a potentiality for rationality and freedom. Through its dealienating endeavor, this potentiality is realized as the self is constructed. Its response to the particular conditions of alienating finitude, existentially encountered, answers the question of what and who it is. Sensing desires and negating the alien Other(s) defines a process of dealienation. Initially, the alien Other is encountered by the desires associated with what life requires to sustain itself. Thereafter, the alien Other is encountered socially through the opposition of other selves to a primitive narcissistic self.

Alienation and dealienation describe an existential process of self-development. With its dual powers of rationality and freedom, the self is a potentiality for discovering being, intentionally creating it and revealing its meaning. These powers are necessary for, and exercised to some degree, in a dealienating process of self-existence that defines self-development. An intentionally conscious self is a creature of need, desire, and purpose. By its own activity, an intelligent self creates its own being and its world to an extent far greater than it is aware of at any given moment. Every self constructs its identity continuously over time from when its existence begins to when it ends. Initially, its powers of rationality and freedom are an abstract potentiality for being. Upon its death, its potentiality has been realized to some degree through its own creative self-activity and self-development. Its being, to begin with is at least in part a potentiality, an alien Other, to be realized and made known. On the other hand, its being as tragically unrealized potentiality, may remain an alien Other. Such is the choice confronted by the life of every self.

A Hegelian orientation suggests that the self is best understood as a being that creates itself through a natural process of self-existence characterized by the negativity of alienation and dealienation. Understood as abstract Ego, the self is an agent negating the world whose finite being is an alien Other. Undeveloped, the being of the self is initially abstract potentiality, or implicit. Only through a process of existential dealienation can its potentiality for being become explicit, actualized as a concrete fact of the world. Clinging to traditional religious authority, Hegel continued to conceive the self as defined by the Other, namely God. Thus, the essential nature of the self is pre-established without regard to its existence. Self-existence has no creative significance, remaining confined to a confirmation of a divinely pre-established essence presumed true as thought by its creator.

Still, even with this ancient perspective, Hegel's conception of self-objectification suggests a self-existence that is genuinely creative of its own being and meaning. In other words, the self can be its own creator, given an existence characterized by alienating finitude and its active dealienating power of rational freedom. Then, the product of its own dealienation would be the meaning of itself and its world, something it both discovers and creates. The universal would not then be a pre-established model of meaning, but rather signify the being discovered in the process of dealienation. To think the universal would not be to think being, but rather to signify the existential implications of dealienation in which being is encountered and has thereby acquired its meaning.

Negativity is the origin of meaning, self, freedom and world. Existence and time are expressions of negativity. Finitude is to encounter an Other as a limit or a deficiency of being within time. A temporal encounter with the alien Other(s) signifies self-existence. Its essence is alienating finitude. Responses to alienating finitude define dealienation as a continuous existential process. Since alienating finitude is necessary to self-existence, alienation is a permanent condition of human existence, which although overcome incrementally, can never be overcome with finality.

The alien Other encountered by the self can be anything. It is the world we live in, become aware of and interact with. It is the basis of objectivity. Most importantly, it is ourselves. It provides an impetus for the self to develop and realize what and who it is as well as what the world is. There is nothing that is not initially encountered as alien Other. The Ego, or primitive self, appears to itself as alien Other just as the world does. Herein lies its freedom. Recognizing the negativity of thought and being, some philosophers conceive of the self as nothing, pure freedom, a mere spiritual entity. Yet, the self is a finite being existing in time whose spirituality is supported by its physical being.

Self-development proceeds from primitive needs through a process of alienation and dealienation. While negativity generally describes this process, it does not reduce the self to nothing, or absolute freedom. Rather, negativity serves as a vehicle for revealing the being and meaning of self and world. From primitive need and a consciousness of the alien Other(s), thought and self-activity respond providing freedom an impetus to develop. Within a negative process of alienation and dealienation the self discovers itself to be a complex of needs, desires and intentions related to Others of itself composing the world. As alien, the Other stands in opposition to be appropriated by the self in some definite way such as being owned, being used, being consumed and being controlled for some purpose. With such forms of appropriation, the Other is comprehended by becoming an expression and extension of the self. Negativity is the way of dealienation with an outcome that enlarges the being and meaning of the self by incorporating the Other(s) to signify its own being.

Alienation and dealienation is expressed in an individual and historical phenomenology of developing self-concepts. The self is alienated every time it encounters an alien Other in some way opposing it. Its historical responses constitute a developmental process of dealienation, an odyssey in which the opposing alien Other is comprehended and possessed by incorporation into the self. This self realizes what and who it really is through dealing with the alien Other in different guises. With dealienation the self is transformed and enlarged in being and in the comprehension of being.

A possession, control and comprehension of the Other signifies the occurrence of self-development, self-discovery and self-realization through an exercise of rationality and freedom integrating self with community and world. The result of dealienation is an autonomous and authentic self living in a world that is an expression and extension of this fact. The world loses its alien character when it is humanized or transformed into an objectification of the self. In addition, the self loses its alien character when the world reflects its own needs, desires and purposes.

Hegel's *Phenomenology of Spirit* described self-development occurring dialectically through a series of figures of consciousness. Each presents a self-conception more completely defined than its predecessor. Self-consciousness, or self-concept, develops from narcissism toward the social all the while confronting the desires and demands of other selves as alien Others dealt with dialectically. Adjusting to these alien Others involves their incorporation and modification into an enlarged social self-concept. This process defines social dealienation as a process of socialization. Hegel described historic figures of self-consciousness evolving from the slave to stoic, skeptical, unhappy Christian and beyond. In each of these, the alien Other changes its form as it is negated, incorporated and transcended into a new successor figure. Through each emerges Spirit expressing a self whose essence is rational freedom.

As the alien Other is assimilated and comprehended, the self realizes who and what it is. This evolution is a process of dealienation, of confronting the alien Other and overcoming its opposition by controlling, possessing and comprehending its meaning as it relates to the self. The alienating encounter with the Other progresses from perceiving and understanding the natural world to freedom indicative of the self to intentional rationality forming social life. The Hegelian significance of human experience, "... consists in its being the process of manifesting or evolving consciousness of self, in the subject's becoming gradually aware of or finding itself in its object, and so coming to be "at home" in its world."[3] Otherness and estrangement are overcome through the labor of the negative in which finitude is encountered and the self becomes substantial.

Narcissism and Self-development

In a primitive condition of undifferentiated innocence and symbiotic dependency, there might presumably be no alienation. Primary narcissism would signify a primitive absence of differentiation of self from Other. Although such a condition can be imagined, it never exists. For even infants experience an internal alien Other, if only in terms of urgent biological needs. Narcissism cannot be maintained since negativity drives self-development. Alien Others always provide an opposition to a narcissistic self, thereby necessitating its development. Narcissism, broadly conceived, is self-enjoyment, which would include any kind of pleasure. Consummation of intentional self-activity would involve narcissistic enjoyment. It can be pleasurable not as an aim in itself, but as a concomitant of achievement. Self-objectification would then be a narcissistic exercise. For example, recognition of the self in a work product is a narcissistic enjoyment. This is re-experienced with the repeated perception and contemplation of it.

Normal self-development is an expansive process. It begins with an unconscious maternal symbiosis and narcissistic isolation. A narcissistic self is related only to its own needs and desires. Frustration of these provides an impetus that compels a recognition and acknowledgment of the alien Other(s). Responding to the demands of alienating Others requires the self to develop beyond its narcissistic origin. Alienation from satisfying certain desires constructs a self related in definite ways to the alien Other(s) it encounters. The transformation of its desires is a construction of its self-concept and alteration of it. Self-seeking desires become bound up with the social needs and desires found in family, religious life, culture, community, commerce and government. Successive obligations taken by a self developing its powers of rationality and freedom are progressively more inclusive of the context of its expanding environment. Within this process, an initially narcissistic self expands its horizon, is transformed through socialization and its life experience.

Narcissism is implied by the core concepts of Hegelian philosophy. He speaks metaphorically of dealienation as a *circular* process wherein the self *returns* completed; including its original being and opposing others encountered in the path of its experience. He speaks of world as a *reflection* of self, and vice versa. What is it but narcissism to say that the self recognizes itself through the Other; that it recognizes itself as the other and the other as itself; that it recognizes itself in the product of its work. The Hegelian emphasis upon self-recognition is narcissistic in intention. The self wants to know what and who it is, to contemplate itself and take pleasure in so doing. In this consummation, the self recognizes the Other, not as alien, but as a completed expression of self; as dissolved back into the self, metaphorically speaking. This recognition of alien Other(s) as self is thus a return to and affirmation of narcissism, even if it were changed from its original undifferentiated form. In fact, the whole process of

Hegelian dealienation can be recast in terms of narcissism. The aim of Hegelian dealienation would then be to re-establish an alienated primary narcissism with a secondary narcissism within the context of an Other(s) comprehended as world and one's fellows.

Hegel's absolute Ego is a blind conatus of need and desire. Alienation is then a confrontation with reality, a frustration of true need and desire of the self. An absence of differentiation can mean either an initial primary narcissism of an undeveloped self, or the result of a process of development in which being is revealed and its meaning completely comprehended. The latter condition would signify an arrival at the truth of being, a self-objectification so complete that the world would have become completely humanized. This secondary narcissism would be equivalent to a Hegelian self recognizing its own being in a world comprehended and created by its rationality and free will. The truth would be witnessed by an absence of alienation and any opposition in being or contradiction in meaning. A final result of the dealienating process would be to re-establish narcissism with a comprehension of the absolute Idea. This philosophical culmination, expressing what might be called a secondary narcissism, is characterized by a self enjoying the recognition and contemplation of itself, except as incorporating the once alien Other(s). Secondary narcissism would be an enjoyment superior to the original; an enjoyment of the creations of the self, namely, culture and civilization.

Narcissistic Selfhood

The narcissistic self is defined relative only to its own desires. It refuses to recognize itself in the objective form provided by other selves. Hegel analyzed this primitive undeveloped self.

> The presentation of itself, however, as pure abstraction of self-consciousness consists in showing itself as a pure negation of its objective form, or in showing that it is fettered to no determinate existence, that it is not bound at all by the particularity everywhere characteristic of existence as such, and is *not* tied up with life.[4]

As blind egoistic conatus, a narcissistic self is alienated from its actual social dimension created by the fact of social dependency necessary to its survival. As infinite desire, the narcissistic self denies its social finitude. But not only is this impossible in a social setting, it is antisocial in so far as other selves are treated as obstacles to unlimited desire or competitors to the unlimited satisfaction of desire. The inevitable outcome of a confrontation of narcissistic selves is conflict and domination of one by the other. Hegel considered the demands of the narcissistic self so absolute that the conflict between such selves could easily issue in violence. The strength of narcissism is demonstrated by the willingness of narcissistic selves or groups of them to risk everything, even death, to secure dominance. History is replete with wars driven by narcissism.

The initial opposition in a Master and Slave allegory was dramatized by Hegel as a struggle to the death, or war. Each self desires to affirm itself as being only for itself by getting the other self to recognize it as such. But this is the recognition of servitude, of a Slave who in laboring to satisfy the desires of his Master is compelled to recognize him as independent and free of constraint in acquiring the necessities of life. The self appropriated by the victorious Master in battle is really not a fully developed social self at all, but rather a re-affirmation of a narcissistic self by means of violence and the coercive threat of death. So the Master is not of much interest compared to the Slave who develops a social self-concept through the dialectical dynamic of his servitude. While his choice of slavery rather than death forces him to be universally recognized as a Slave, his self-objectification takes place through the products of his labor. He is what his servitude creates and this is universally recognized by his Master and in turn by himself. Such self-objectification is not available to the Master who has no such social self, remaining a narcissistic egoist. This is reflected in the attitude of a master class denying itself the opportunity of such self-objectification by shunning any kind of labor. While the Master alienates and dehumanizes the Slave, his fear of death and toil dealienate and humanize the world; something Hegel considered immeasurably more significant for humanity.

The Master of the narcissistic conflict achieves the gratification of his desires through domination and servitude. The Slave is reduced to an instrument for the satisfaction of the Master's desires. Thus is the Master independent, free of the necessity to labor for the satisfaction of some essential desires. Although the Master is a *being-for-itself* and the Slave a *being-for-another*, both remain alienated from the dimension of their being possessed by the other. The Slave is not conscious of his inherent independence or freedom, while the Master is not conscious of his social dependency. Their social self, defined by another self, is an alien Other yet to be developed. Even within the context of society organized around slavery, the dialectical opposition continues. For the alien Other of the Master's and Slave's self-consciousness is an emerging social self constructed by the desires and demands of other selves in a social structure. This alien Other self is initially one of which each self is unaware and has not chosen for himself. Nevertheless, it can be appropriated without coercion by voluntary acceptance of a social role.

The narcissism of the Master is expressed by valuing the Slave only as a means, by considering him a sub-human or lesser being unworthy of respect by virtue of the weakness of his choice of servitude instead of death: unworthy by his immersion in doing and making things for others: unworthy by lacking that narcissistic freedom which makes one an equal commanding respect. Yet, by a curious dialectical inversion, servitude allows the Slave to realize his freedom in dealing with nature. Within the Slave's sphere of activity is discovered an independent self-consciousness producing things to satisfy desire, albeit that of the Master. Intelligence, nature and work - components of human freedom - are brought together in the process of servitude. Even in servitude is discovered a measure of stoic freedom and independence of the toiling self. Just as the Master's freedom is asserted through the labor of the Slave, so in turn, the Slave's freedom is discovered relative to nature serving as a means of self-objectification. Who can be essentially unfree and bound to nature when he can intentionally transform it to satisfy human desire? Moreover, is dignity not recognizable in the creative products of human toil irrespective of the condition under which it occurs? Can a Slave who produces a work of art, who is erudite, who teaches the Master's children, be undeserving of respect and be without dignity?

There is also a curious dialectical inversion of dependency established between Master and Slave. The Slave is certainly dependent upon the Master who lets him live in exchange for his toil. But, as time goes on, the Master becomes dependent in fact upon the Slave who provides what is needed, what is desired, what is enjoyed. Whereas the Master enjoys what the Slave provides, the Slave is able to enjoy the human power and capacity that goes into the process of providing—something entirely denied the Master. He is related remotely and only indirectly to nature and work, things vital to the realization of one's humanity, both individual and social. Dependency upon another self in any social setting, including slavery, cannot be avoided, even by a Master with absolute power over his Slave. History proceeds from the development of the Slave's self-consciousness. His self-concept is crafted by obedient toil and self-abnegation in which desire is negated, controlled and redirected in service to others; something required of all civilized human beings. He is socialized to accept the desires of others as definitive of his own, to recognize himself as an instrument for the satisfaction of the desires of others with one momentous difference: that he and his desires are not equal to theirs. Post-slavery historical development aimed to establish social structures that recognize the equality of human desires and those persons to which they belong.

Within a social context the self finds itself bifurcated into a being existing for itself to satisfy its own desires, and a being existing for another to satisfy the desires of its fellows. The Master is a pure exemplar of the former and the Slave of the latter. Each self negates the other thereby forming the opposing components of every self. The former is primitive, narcissistic, socially unmediated, egoistic. Since all that counts is its desires and itself, it is alienated from community. Other selves are treated as objects, unessential, except for their usefulness. They exist to be exploited. Their needs, desires and freedom are not acknowledged or accorded any respect. They make no claim and no obligation is felt toward them.

Reciprocity is acknowledged only in terms of the relationship of dominance and submission. Yet, dialectic between such selves reveals a mutually recognized dependency. Each recognizes himself defined by the expectations of the other, which is a fact not subject to choice. The ensuing dialectic enlarges their respective self-concepts revealing a social dimension each is forced to acknowledge. Each recognizes that he is an object of desire and use by his fellows with a claim equal to his own. Self-consciousness moves from recognizing itself to be merely a being-for-itself to recognizing itself to be a being-for-another. This is a psychic watershed event wherein a social self is irrevocably established. The dialectic moves the self from the alienating isolation of narcissism and egoism to a more universal, complex and higher plane of social life involving rights, obligations, roles, ethical conduct and respect for law. A social self has acquired a psychic apparatus allowing it to more effectively control and satisfy its desires within a community.

Hegel's genius, expressed in this allegorical dialectic of Master and Slave, is to present a self whose development proceeds from narcissistic desire. Unconstrained self-seeking desire cannot construct a social self that can be sustained in an interpersonal dialectic. War and slavery result from narcissistic self-assertion. This is worked through in a historical development of individuals and social systems. A superficial reading of Hegel's Master and Slave allegory might conclude that it is a rationalization of slavery. However, such an interpretation would miss Hegel's essential point about human development: that it occurs only in toil and suffering and within this historical process is discovered the meaning of freedom and self-realization. Without slavery, how could humanity discover the true meaning or value of freedom? In a historical working through of its opposite, freedom is revealed in its most complete social dimension. "It was not so much *from* slavery as *through* slavery that humanity was emancipated."[5] Considered by itself this statement seems bizarre, morally objectionable, a rationalization of evil. Obviously, slavery has catastrophic and evil significance from the perspective of the enslaved individual. Nevertheless, there is a broader philosophical interpretation of the historical fact of slavery that Hegel was interested in explaining.

Man in a state of nature driven by his own untamed desires is barbarous, lustful, unjust; in short, evil according to Christian theology. Serfdom denies the individual his own body, property and expression of his own desires. A dual lesson is taught humanity through suffering serfdom. First, untamed evil desire is suppressed. Second, serfdom imposes an external discipline upon the individual that becomes internalized and transformed to self-discipline necessary for the expression and development of Hegelian Spirit. Obedience to the untamed desires of the undisciplined individual is replaced by obedience to authority of a Lord of the manor. Then as Spirit is developed, obedience is transformed to a rationally based respect for the authority of an organized State and the laws it upholds on behalf of the rights of individuals. While the individual suffers bondage imposed by the terror of secular power, the Church terrorizes him with the threat of damnation. It takes serfdom and the Church working together upon the evil of untamed individual desire and will to elicit a self-disciplined rationality capable of expressing Spirit and developing it further in history.

Egoistic Selfhood

Narcissism is amoral self-seeking when operating outside a social context. An egoistic self, incompletely developed beyond narcissism, remains fixated in satisfying its own desires without acknowledging the claims of other selves. This egoism is socially alienating. For one's fellows are valued only instrumentally for the satisfaction of narcissistic desire. They exist to be manipulated, exploited and discarded like any common object when found no longer useful. Herein, the egoistic self enters the realm of the immoral. There, the desires of other selves go unacknowledged. If their desires do not count, then they may be considered radically different from the narcissistic egoist: possibly subhuman, although human. Thus, they cannot make equal claim to the satisfaction of desire. Any such claim limits narcissistic egoism. This makes them into alien Others to be subdued and made useful. Social conflict becomes inevitable. The resulting dominance merely confirms that the loser is undeserving of respect. Treated as a mere useful object, the alien Other self lacks the dignity of a person established by consensually acknowledging equality of desires, opportunity and rights.

Immorality and evil has its source in narcissistic egoism, in an absence of acknowledging the natural equality of the desires and claims of other selves. Acknowledging the universality of every individual with respect to the satisfaction of desires forms the basis of morality and civilized society. Hegel recognized that the equality of individual desires requires a transcending of narcissism, a relinquishing of an absolute imperious egoistic self and its replacement with a social self. This self can then function to further the survival of the individual and the social unit. Both are maintained in a mutually sustaining reciprocal relationship allowing for maximum satisfaction of individuals' desires. Some egoistic desires that annihilate or threaten the fulfillment of other individuals' desires would be considered antisocial and prohibited as unacceptable and disruptive to the social structure.

If a social structure with all its obvious benefits for the individual is to survive, unrestrained or uncontrolled individual desire cannot be tolerated. The degree and type of social control exercised on behalf of preserving the social structure is always a crucial question. When the control is vested in a dictatorial master with absolute power, the temptation to function as a narcissist is overwhelming. Kings, emperors and dictators who are absolute egoists mistake their individual desires for those of their people. They then represent the unrestrained, uncontrolled individual without any sense of social self. Their self-seeking behavior is outside the law. They are immoral narcissistic egoists with permission of the community, and tolerated for a time supposedly for the sake of avoiding anarchy.

The legitimacy of the demands of other selves resides in acknowledging the universality of human needs and desires. In this respect, all members of humanity are alike and equal to each other. Hegel was right, to center morality in the intellectual capacity to comprehend and act upon the universal, even if he mislocated the source of morality in authority. The moral sense residing in acknowledging the universality of needs and desires can even extend to the non-human, to nature generally. When it does, the treatment of the Other, whatever it might be, can no longer be exploitative. Domination and servitude are replaced with an acknowledged interdependence. Other selves need not be made alien, but can be treated with respect accorded to persons equal in dignity. Equal rights of individuals, opportunity in life, and justice then become supported by rationally based and mutually acknowledged obligations.

Hegel had a justifiable suspicion of narcissism that he referred to as an egoistic self with absolute imperious desires and the freedom to pursue them. The accidental and capricious nature of unrestrained egoistic desire is the source of immorality and the disintegration of social structures. Therefor, the guidance of the universal, be it located in the customs, norms, and laws of community or those of God appeared necessary to Hegel as a means preventing narcissistic and egoistic self-seeking from destroying civilization. An optimized social organization maximizes the collective satisfaction of human needs and desires. This is possible only when the individual acknowledges the demands of interdependency within a larger social structure. His self-seeking must be exercised legitimately by being acceptable to his fellows or with their consent. At the very least, individual self-seeking cannot be permitted to thwart the freedom of other selves to pursue their own desires.

No individual can survive alienated from the community necessary for the satisfaction of his or her needs and desires. The self must develop beyond the psychic realm of the narcissist. Absolute egoism and freedom must be sacrificed, if only for the sake of survival itself. A socialized self painfully learns to acknowledge and satisfy the desires of his fellows in exchange for their satisfying some of his own. Customs, norms, roles, practices and laws regulate the reciprocal satisfaction of human needs and desires. Since these are universal to human nature, they make an equal claim among individuals. To acknowledge this provides a foundation for morality, social justice, law and institutions supporting them. In fact, to make and acknowledge equal claim with other individuals to the satisfaction of desire is the social cornerstone of western civilization. From this flows recognition of the dignity of each individual: his personal liberty, his rights and obligations as a citizen, his equality under the law, and equality of opportunity.

Social Selfhood

The Hegelian insight is that the self is not merely abstract Ego, but is developed in time through a process in which antisocial desires are tempered by social demands. Negating oppositions to unbridled desire construct a social self. Its appropriation may take many forms other than the dominance and submission Hegel brilliantly portrayed. Submersion in the group, serving a cause, status seeking, accumulating wealth and conspicuous consumption name only a few.

Selfhood develops from an existential dialectic of human needs and desires. A frustration of narcissistic desires initiates the construction of self. An egoistic self originates with narcissistic desires. Development proceeds by encountering various alien Others posing limits to human needs, desires and aspirations. Who I am is that alien Other I want and act upon to get. Desire presents an ego striving intentionally. An immediately certain consciousness of what is desired is an existential presentation of an egoistic self. It is primary and primitive. While an abstract Cartesian Cogito is demonstrated with indubitable certainty by the logical nature of thought, it does not signify self-existence. Encountering other selves with desires of their own dialectically transforms a narcissistic and egoistic self into a social self. This social self is initially an alien Other presented by culture, parents, and various educational and religious institutions. The egoistic self is taught and often coerced to accept a social self, defined by standard norms, customs, practices and roles.

The problem of alienation is expressed in the perennial question, "Who or what is the Other?" The self is an alien Other in two senses. First, its own desires signify a being which is not yet present, but may become so in the future by exercising its powers of rationality and freedom. The subjective dimension of its being is a project for it to accomplish. Secondly, the self has an objective social dimension of its being of which it may be unaware, not of its own choice, but determined by the desires of its fellows. This follows from the fact that the self is social to begin with and survives only by living within an interdependent community. Community life demands a socialized self who participates and contributes to sustaining it. This requires a civilized individual who acknowledges and acts upon obligations, is honest, trustworthy, reliable, observing customary practices, respecting tradition, obeying the law and performing prescribed social roles. The transition from an egoistic to social self is learned by a sometimes-painful dialectic between self and its fellows. However, there is always the danger of arrested self-development with a fixation of behavior in narcissism, egoism, or both.

Replacing an egoistic with a social self occurs through an interpersonal dialectic. Both selves appear opposed, requiring a compromising reconciliation in which the substitute satisfies some of the desires of what it replaces while satisfying social requirements. Dealienation requires the self to want and in fact become what the community demands. The fact that this is most frequently the case with children striving to meet parental expectations and assimilate a self they prescribe escaped Hegel's notice. He focused exclusively upon the residual narcissistic and egoistic components of the self in conflict with a socially defined self. Of crucial importance then is that who I want to be is not who they want me to be. The dialectical construction of a social self begins from this initial alienating opposition. Hegel stated it this way:

> Self-consciousness has before it another self-consciousness; it has come outside itself. This has a double significance. First it has lost its own self, since it finds itself as an *other* being; secondly, it has thereby

> sublated that other, for it does not regard the other as essentially real, but sees its own self in the other. It must cancel this its other.[6]

This abstract discussion is somewhat misleading and was certainly so for Sartrean existentialism, which falsely elevated it to an ontological principle describing human nature as irrational conatus and blind self-assertion. Of course, this approach makes ethical life and community impossible. A more truthful conception of the self can be gained from the dynamics of socialization upon which Freud focused. Whoever the self is or becomes, it is in fact existentially constructed through a social dialectic. It is more fruitful to begin an analysis of the self-development with the social self it is initially given by its nurturer. Against this backdrop, an existential social dialectic is worked through to satisfy human needs and desires within a context of self-development achieving and expanding human autonomy and authenticity.

Socialization requires alienating narcissistic and egoistic components of the self. There is as well a confrontation with an alien Other social self, demanding that it be appropriated as a substitute replacement. When socialization is achieved, a narcissistic and egoistic self is renounced and transformed into a socially sustaining contributor with a predefined social role. Narcissistic and egoistic desire has been channeled and controlled in service to the social unit of which the self is a member and from which it gets social rewards and personal satisfaction. When the self wants to be, and has in fact become, what the community wants it to be, socialization is nearly complete. Until then, the self is presumed alienated. However, the question remains as to whether or not dealienation, understood exclusively as socialization, is successful. Hegel presumed it to be the case when any distinction between a subjective and objective identity is eliminated; when self-concept corresponds with objective fact. This is confirmed when self-recognition corresponds with public recognition from one's peers. The private has become the public self. In other words, the self has subjectively created itself conforming to the demands of authoritative Others, namely community and God. The truth of its being, prescribed by authoritative Others, is objectively manifested by its subjective conduct. It instantiates and demonstrates standardized universal norms and social roles. Hegel thought such a self true in the sense of illustrating a pre-established, idealized perfect standard.

Authenticity is presumably secured by the fact of having dialectically worked through possibilities of being for itself which are false to the standards of community and God. Thus, it is presumed, there is no alien component or internal conflict remaining in itself. However, upon scrutiny, this view is naive and false. Freudian psychoanalysis examined a highly socialized self of the Victorian era and found it to be filled with unresolved conflicts between unsatisfied desires. That self was found to be repressed, neurotic in its behavior, fixated, and therefore incompletely developed. Existentialism claimed that such a self dominated by an authoritative Other cannot realize its true potentiality for being. It lacks the autonomy and authenticity necessary for doing so. Thus, socialization is itself discovered to be an alienation of the self. A dialectically coerced Hegelian conformity of self to community and God still leaves autonomy and authenticity in question and self-alienation unresolved.

Psychoanalysis and existentialism describe an over-socialized self. Alienated from the satisfaction of its own desires, the self becomes neurotic and inauthentic. It is not free to express its desires. Outlets for self-expression are blocked by its bondage to a social self, which is an alien Other. Being so defined and controlled, the alienated self is not free to realize its own potentiality for being. Its social bondage is maintained coercively by means that are non-rational or irrational. This prevents it from rationally assessing or freely acting to change its condition. An over-socialized self is alienated from its powers of rationality and freedom and from any authentic potentiality for realizing its being. Yet, the same is true of an under-socialized self that so concerned Hegel.

Unlimited satisfaction of desire is antisocial and so destroys the very community necessary for the self to exercise its own powers and realize its potentiality. Contemporary society bears witness to this with its subcultures of drug addiction and violence. Attitudes such as, *anything goes* and *if it feels good, its OK* predominates. An under-socialized self follows from a disintegration of the traditional family and the supportive influence of religion. Behavioral norms and social roles must then be taken from the peer group or popular culture with its images of violence, sexual and drug induced euphoria. The resulting under-socialized self can be a defective human being lacking conscience and prone to violence. Such individuals are socially dysfunctional and often tragically spend their lives in prison rather than productively in civil society.

A willful egoistic self, certain of who it is as defined by its own desires can be dangerously antisocial and very hard to civilize. For its desires are infinite in scope, imperious in their demands, and capricious, without regard for the interests of its fellows or the law for that matter. A self defined by unbridled self-seeking desire must be tamed in order to exist within a society conferring collective benefits and requiring commonality of purpose. There must be reciprocity between the egoistic self driven by desires and social self driven by roles and behavioral expectations. Since the self is a creature of infinite desires, a coincidence of its individuality and socially contributive nature is difficult to achieve. The question of socialization then is how the objective social self - an alienated Other self - becomes the self desired by the individual. Hegel's Master and Slave allegory suggests how this might occur through a social dialectic of dominance and submission. The self can be conceived to be like an empty vessel to be filled or a *tabularasa* to be written upon by the experience of life. Initially, then, the being of the self would be nothing or indeterminate. Lacking being, the self needs to be something, whatever that something might be.

Although the self develops and must become something or other, its being is never completely indeterminate. For if this were so, then the self would be indifferently open to any possible identity. It would not matter which one were accepted. However, it does matter whether the self is cast into a socially dominant or submissive role. Dominance is overwhelmingly preferred. The construction of a social self and redirection of desire is generally achieved coercively. Whether cast by fate or chance circumstance into a dominant or submissive social role, the self cannot avoid accepting an identity at least initially alien to it. Yet, a non-coercive acceptance of universal social norms and roles remains possible. Also, it is possible for non-conforming individuals to create norms and roles accepted within a free society.

That egoistic desires should be subordinated to or replaced by the socially useful seems obvious and is arguable, but not to a mind untutored by reason. Thus, natural coercive rewards and punishments are employed, particularly in weaning the young away from narcissism and egoism. The trick of socialization is to channel egoistic desires to socially constructive rather than destructive purposes. A child is coaxed by rewards to adopt the ideals and behavior of a social self. In short, the egoistic self is taught to desire the social self. This process, beginning with an egoistic self confronting an opposing alien social self, ends with the latter replacing the former. The replacement is not simply one self overpowering another. Narcissistic and egoistic demands are provided socially acceptable substitutes, which channel desires into constructive communal life. Sexual desires are channeled by monogamous marriage and the institution of the family. Egoistic acquisitiveness is channeled by the institution of civil society and even by philanthropy and charity taught by the institution of religion. Aggression is channeled by state-sanctioned wars and so forth.

The result of socialization is an individual free to pursue his or her own desires within the boundaries of social norms, roles, laws and practices prescribed by the basic institutions of society that Hegel identified as the family, civil society, religion and the state. For social human beings, these institutions provide the basic structure for the individual to live within. His life activity sustains and transmits his culture and ultimately, his civilization. Hegel insisted that the higher and more universal - namely the social - control and structure the egoistic desires and impulses of the individual. A century later, Freud demonstrated how such an arrangement can make the individual psychologically ill, or neurotic, spreading to epidemic proportions in a Victorian culture.

The Alienated Self

The alienating finitude of self-existence is inescapable, since it is driven by the negativity of being, thought, action and time. Self-existence is defined by a perpetual encounter with an alien Other. It is manifest in the initial biological and physical basis from which a self originates. The invariable cycle of birth, development and death demonstrates a being that is always an alien Other over time. The circumstances of its existence are contingent. What and who it encounters, its existential *facticity*, is not determined by itself. Moreover, its being is reified by how its fellows perceive it and use it for their purposes. Since its potentiality for being something Other is perpetually in question, its destiny is essentially unknown to it in advance of its history.

Through existence in time the self becomes Other than it was or is at the present moment. Its dealienating endeavor answers the question of whom and what it is. Rationality and freedom are essential powers allowing the self to cope with alienating finitude. Thus, realizing its identity is to some degree a product of exercising these powers. When they are suppressed, a specifiable profile of an alienated self emerges. Its being remains deficient with unrealized potentiality. Its being also remains limited, by the world, its fellows and itself. What or who is alien to itself solely determines its destiny. In fact, such a self is not a *who*, but a *what* or an *it*. Its being is reified, as Sartre understood it, a Heideggerian *they-self*, a Freudian repressed self. It remains unconscious of what or who it is except as its authentic nature calls to it in eccentric behavior, wishful dreams, neurosis, and even in the illusions, delusions and the hallucinations of psychosis.

The desires of an alienated self conform to the demands of a controlling alien Other, whatever or whomever it may be. Since such an alienated self neither thinks nor acts for itself, it can be easily deceived, cynically manipulated and emotionally controlled. It is victimized and dependent upon an alien Other to satisfy its needs and desires. Its being is constructed for it by the Other as, for example, by public opinion, polling, focus groups, or media image spin. Reified into an object of social utility, apathy and isolation from community involvement are common outcomes. With respect to intellect, alienation is a world not making sense, standing as Other in opposition to the self. Hegel said it this way:

> The variegated canvas of the world is before me; I stand over against it; by my theoretical attitude to it I overcome its opposition to me and make its content my own. I am at home in the world when I know it, still more so when I have understood it.[7]

As strictly determined by the Other, an alienated self is not authentic. Without the power to think and act for itself, the alienated self is not autonomous. No doubt the self is an alien Other in so far as it is undeveloped in being and meaning. No doubt, the self requires the Other for it to develop and realize an identity. However, the self can never discover who it is, if it mistakes itself to be nothing but the Other.

While an alien Other is necessary for the self to develop, it is not entirely defined by the Other(s). For the self develops itself through its own needs, desires, rationality and freedom. The latter two are intrinsic powers of every self. Yet, they are also a potentiality that can develop or atrophy depending upon whether they are exercised. When exercised, the self becomes to a greater degree something of its own making, a being existing autonomously and authentically. Then, alien Other(s) do not dominate the self, but rather serve as a foil for self-development. The self does not simply obey the dicta of powerful authoritative Others and so become merely what they require. Rather, the self can respond to overcome the limit they impose. The means adopted can be in principle infinitely variable depending upon the circumstances encountered. Clearly, intelligence is indispensable for success. Therefore, the crucial question is whether the self has within its powers of rationality and freedom a guide sufficient for the task of dealienation. While this is not obviously true, if it were, then autonomy and authenticity would be marks of character necessary for dealienation.

Natural Self-seeking

Natural self-seeking behavior is dealienating activity expressive of a self defined by its needs, desires rationality and freedom. Hegel considered natural self-seeking within a civil society a positive good. "When men are thus dependent on one another and reciprocally related to one another in their work and the satisfaction of their needs, subjective self-seeking turns into a contribution to the satisfaction of the needs of everyone else."[8] Without a social context, self-seeking remains an unlimited activity. The self gets or does not get what it wants. It can be mistaken about what it wants or the means employed to get what it wants. Such mistakes are not condemned. Usually, natural self-seeking has social consequences, and so acquires moral significance. Self-seeking causing unnecessary human suffering is deemed evil. Proscriptive norms of conduct are then developed from the experience of human suffering to provide a warranted degree of social control.

Hegel would have considered evil to be an original form of alienation. Evil only is a product of natural self-seeking when it is chosen above duty toward community or God. Human rationality and freedom are prerequisite for successful self-seeking. Hegel recognized this as the foundation of civil society and its myriad universal benefits. He recognized the validity of Adam Smith's *invisible hand* where the general welfare of the community is secured by the natural self-seeking of individuals. Self-seeking needs not be antisocial. So to condemn as evil human subjectivity or the propensity for natural self-seeking is obviously false and inconsistent with Hegel's view of the goodness of civil society and how free individuals structure it.

Evil resides in subjectivity or the free will of individuals. Yet it is this very subjectivity that creates the social which Hegel claimed superior to the individual in being and goodness. It would appear illogical that the free will of evil self-seekers could establish a civil society superior in goodness to themselves. Of equal logical difficulty is how evil self-seekers can unconsciously realize a divine historical plan. Or, how they could be free rational beings while really being the unconscious instruments of Geist. Locating evil in the subjective will of individuals opposed to the objective will of community is inconsistent with other views Hegel held dear. Inconsistencies in Hegelian thought arise when subjectivity is condemned without qualification as the source of evil.

Where individual self-seeking is free, there will always be the possibility of antisocial outcomes. Such is the cost of freedom. Law often curbs it. Hegel identified individual freedom too closely with the irrational, capricious and antisocial. Certainly, it can have these characteristics, but it does not necessarily have them. In fact, it may quite as easily have the opposite characteristics. For Hegel, evil must reside in subjectivity, but never in the more universal culture, community and social institutions where it is often found. That something is rational or universal does not provide it with positive worth or merit. This is a false abstraction. The simple fact of something being rational or universal does not guarantee it against being corrupt or even evil. The identification of goodness with rationality misunderstood as universality is a typical Hegelian ontological error, a bias contradicted by fact, and most probably inherited from Plato's influence.

Placing limits upon self-seeking can alienate the self from the demands of its nature. Yet, those very same limits provide a secure structure of behavior and civility necessary for the reciprocal satisfaction of other needs and desires. Thus, morality and a structure of law, although limiting in some ways, can also liberate in others and so maximize human satisfaction. Understanding the reasons for limiting self-seeking creates an obligation felt to be universal and just. A law obligates universally when those to which it applies understand its reasons. When a law limiting some kind of self-seeking is deemed just, it has the force of a reasoned obligation, the effect of which is to secure maximum opportunity for the expression of human desire, rationality and freedom. A just law denies something harmful in order to affirm the nature and power of the self to proceed with its dealienating life activity. Unless every self is empowered by limiting natural self-seeking, that very limitation is alienating and may be declared unjust or evil in the sense of causing unnecessary suffering.

It has been philosophically proclaimed that natural inclination can enslave the self. Narcissistic or egoistic desires often do this. Yet, neither natural inclination nor desires are, of themselves, alienating. Rather, they are an initial response to alienating finitude. The complete and successful response that satisfies desire requires the self develops and applies rationality and freedom. These powers define its spirituality, which is only expressed partially and negatively by the suppression of natural inclination and desire. Rational freedom is more completely and positively expressed when serving as a means for dealienation. This requires meeting the demands posed by natural inclination and desire. Rational freedom allows such demands to be best satisfied by a recognition and consideration of the world and one's fellows. One's behavior must factor in the Other(s). This requires the prohibition of unlimited self-seeking, postponement of gratification, and substituted objects of desire. The needs and desires defining self-existence cannot be suppressed. If severely inhibited or psychologically repressed by non-rational or irrational means, they reappear in disguise as neurosis or psychosis, behaviors dysfunctional to self and community.

Roots of Evil

Many philosophers consider evil inherent to human nature. Following his Christian faith, Hegel conceived evil to be rooted in natural self-seeking and human freedom. The potential for evil which freedom confers makes a controlling authority necessary to restrain it in human affairs. Thus, at worst, freedom can create evil, and so construed, becomes problematical. At best, freedom is a gift of God or a power of human nature. Nevertheless, as a potentiality for evil, freedom remains ambiguous. Every self is guilty by reason of its freedom to sin against the dicta of authoritative Others - God and community - if not by the inevitable fact of doing evil in satisfying some natural impulses and needs.

Even where the authoritative Others are disregarded, existentialists still discover guilt in the freedom to realize or reject the self's authentic potentiality for being. However, for Hegel, since each self was created by God and is sustained by its community, they are authoritative for self-existence. Their dicta are required to restrain and dampen the evil done from self-seeking motive and willful freedom disregarding law, human or divine. Evil then, is defined by disobedience to the laws of established authority. This definition is too narrow, since it disregards whether or not the authoritative Other(s) or their prescribed dicta are legitimate. When judged illegitimate, authority ought to be disobeyed. In such instances, disobedience is not evil. Martyrs, civil disobedients and conscientious objectors are often among the most admirable persons. Opposition to error and immoral conduct may well be right and courageously noble conduct justified with perfectly valid reasons. The feeling and strength of obligation follows from good reasons in a mature self whose freedom and conduct is rationally guided.

A disregard for the dicta of established authority, or even a replacement of it by self-seeking interest, may or may not be evil doing. It all depends upon a judgment of legitimacy the self makes of the dicta and the authority prescribing it. Even in cases where disobeying established authority is evil doing, this definition of evil is abstract and dangerously narrow. For it may mislead one to make facile judgments about evil and false condemnations of conduct. This is acknowledged by any appeal to conscience whenever confronting a perplexing moral dilemma. A more complete comprehension of evil is rendered when freedom and its control by authority are not made the focus of analysis.

Set aside the view of evil as the freedom of a self to disobey authority. Instead, cast it within the context of self-existence from which it arises. To suffer evil is to be alienated by someone in some way from what the self truly needs and wants. Moreover, to do evil is to cause an unnecessary suffering which alienates something or someone in some very specific way. While there can be no doubt about the fact of evil or that it is a potentiality for any free and rational human being, it is not obvious that evil is an inescapable destiny necessitated by freedom. Existentially and naturalistically considered, evil is better understood in terms of incomplete or malformed social self-development. Evil, then, becomes a consequence of self-existence which remains alienated by a failure to develop beyond narcissism or egoism. From this developmental perspective, freedom can be viewed positively as a means of dealienation rather than negatively as the alienating possibility for evil doing. The dicta of authority are not presumed legitimate without being put to the tests of self-existence and rational evaluation. Furthermore, the sense of obligation can then become authentic to the self rather than merely the result of conditioning by the authoritative Other to obey and act upon one's duty.

Evil doing is most often attributed to a self who is morally, psychologically or sociologically, undeveloped or defectively socialized to some degree. In order to understand the basis of evil, it is necessary to adopt a gestalt perspective of the self. It is a philosophical mistake to view the self in only single dimensions of its being as social scientists are prone to do. Storywriters, novelists and dramatists, avoiding this mistake, often provide a richer insight into how religious, moral, psychological and sociological aspects of the whole personality are interrelated. Classical literature from ancient Greek to medieval European, English and modern offer excellent descriptions of a many faceted evil. Sophocles and Shakespeare had an intuitive understanding of evil in its multiple dimensions without benefit of modern psychoanalytic thinkers such as Freud who unintentionally described it in discussing narcissism and perversions such as sadism and masochism. Repression and guilt are now commonly recognized as sources of evil in many instances of human conduct.

Narcissism is the root of evil for several reasons. Unable to acknowledge the needs and desires of his fellows, the narcissist is so self-absorbed as to be oblivious to anything they need, want or suffer. Without any real consciousness of one's fellows, there is also no conscience regarding anything or anyone that may cause their suffering. When their suffering does not matter, the potentiality for evil doing becomes enormous and the actuality of it inevitable. The narcissist does evil without even caring about it. Where there is no social reciprocity of needs and desires among selves, community becomes impossible. The narcissistic self, if it can be said to be one, exists in social isolation, parasitically through symbiosis, or by the altruistic compassion of its fellows. For without acknowledged social dependency and reciprocity there can be no mutual satisfaction of most needs and desires of any self that would ensure its survival. Thus, narcissism is self-limiting and self-alienating.

Although it is a normal advance beyond narcissism to a higher level of social self-development, egoism has a potential for causing evil. Egoist conduct is a product of socialization, including a partial development of rationality and freedom. The social consequences of conduct are calculated prior to its execution in words and deeds. Social reciprocity is understood and practiced as well as the art of psychological manipulation by the skilled egoist. Yet, although the needs and desires of one's fellows are acknowledged, they are always subordinated to self-seeking interest. When self-seeking causes evil, it is usually deliberate. The egoist is developed enough to be aware of behavioral consequences and to have a socially defined conscience. Evil doing is blameworthy, precisely because the egoistic self knows that it is responsible for the suffering it causes.

The narcissist, where lacking consciousness of his fellows and a conscience from his own sense of agency is blameless for causing suffering. Not so for the egoist who is developed enough to know better. Whereas the narcissist has no friends, the egoist only calls a friend anyone useful to satisfying his interests. With limited social reciprocity, the egoist is less self-alienated than the narcissist. Although advanced beyond narcissism, egoistic socialization remains incomplete. For when the suffering caused by self-interest does not matter to him, the egoist will invariably suffer social sanctions. Refusing to acknowledge the equal claim of the needs, desires and suffering of one's fellows reaps the same in some measure from them. Socialization arrested in narcissism or egoism explains the psycho-sociological basis of evil.

Egoistic self-interest, when recognized for what it is, socially isolates the self from community. Egoism is limited with many kinds of social opposition ranging from punishments such as ostracism to imprisonment or even death. Lacking certain kinds of social reciprocity, egoism is discovered to be self-alienating. Many of the egoist's needs and desires remain unsatisfied and frustrated by its socially dysfunctional behavior. An egoistic self cannot realize its full potential since its psychological orientation blocks complete social development. Social reciprocity follows from a self who acknowledges an equal claim of the needs and desires of others in some way similar to itself. Without social reciprocity the self remains alienated and stunted in its development.

Clearly then, evil is an alienation of the desires and needs of those who suffer it as well as the narcissistic or egoistic self causing it. The roots of evil are found in incomplete socialization, which obviously include the underdevelopment of rationality and freedom. The demands of either the narcissistic or egoistic self, when frustrated become obsessive, even psychologically compulsive, or unfree. Satisfaction cannot be secured and normal enjoyment takes perverse substitutes. Unguided by rationality, freedom and an adequately socialized self, successful mature self-seeking, or dealienating behavior, becomes impossible.

Some philosophers claim that to do evil is to pursue one's desires in violation of a universal norm or some established authority such as community or God. The dicta of the authoritative Other(s) govern the self. Yet, there could be justifying reasons making such violations obligatory. Of themselves, neither the fact of universality nor authority provides sufficient warrant for the goodness or rightness of human conduct. However, natural self-seeking conduct is warranted by the alienating finitude of self-existence. Need and desire are immediately felt as self-justifying reasons, self-obligatory and serving as an impetus for dealienating self-activity. Here the norm is established by the demands of self-existence and the authority is the self. However, when the self and its demands cause unnecessary suffering, then there are countervailing reasons which may obligate its conduct in a different direction.

Is evil done when the self chooses and acts upon a particular natural desire violating the universal norms prescribed by established authority or commonly acknowledged by the community to be good for everyone? The answer depends upon the specific nature of the desire and the universal norm. Often, the norm violating desire is also found to be itself universal. Therefore, contrary to Hegel's presumption, universality does not necessarily signify anything good, or bad for that matter. Neither does universality signify rationality. For rationality is not reducible to uncritically endorsing a norm merely by the fact that it is mandated by authority or acknowledged by one's fellows.

Rationality requires the test of self-existence and the real work of critical evaluation. This authentic rationality, as opposed to an abstraction of it, makes the norm obligatory for any or every self. Beyond what authority prescribes or what generally prevails in the community, self-existence presents reasons why something is good and ought to be or evil and ought not to be. From such reasons, follows conduct felt to be obligatory. Certainly, obligations can be felt toward authority, which are non-rationally or irrationally based. Nevertheless, a non-rational or irrational appeal to authority of the Other(s) is not authenticated by the existence, rationality and freedom of the self and so cannot be genuinely obligatory upon it. Lacking the test of self-existence, the presumed rationality and universality of the dicta of authority remains an abstract unsubstantiated claim, unvalidated and non-obligatory.

If God, community, or an abstract universal norm cannot obligate the self to act, then what can? Hegel knew the answer by observing that what ought-to-be is discovered by what humans desire. Recasting this insight less abstractly, a felt sense of obligation originates within the alienating finitude of self-existence. Narcissistic needs are the most primitive expression of obligation. A more highly developed self finds its obligations expressed by its egoistic desires. In either case a sense of obligation, or what is not the case yet *ought-to-be*, is an impulse to dealienate by self-activity intended to satisfy a specific need or desire. Obligation follows from the fact of alienation, rather then from the fact of freedom. For, the fact that the self can do something does not obligate it to act. There must be natural existential grounds for acting or not acting in a certain way. A highly developed self who is both free and rational will invariably provide reasons why it is obligated to act as it does. Thus, maturity is marked by rationality determining obligations, but not an abstract rationality unconnected to self-existence, need and desire. Without these governing factors, obligation can be discovered in promise keeping. Again, it is necessary to ask why keep promises, just at it was necessary to ask why a free soul should choose or not choose to act in a certain way.

It is facile to identify the dicta of established authority with rationality by virtue of its merely intended universality. For then, exceptions pervert the norm and must be explained by viewing free will as somehow itself perverse. Freedom itself then threatens what authority prescribes, rather than validating it or having any role in creating it. Viewing freedom in this light, Hegel justified the dicta of established authority by ascribing rationality and universality to it. This attitude subordinates the self as a derivative of God and community, and is presumed to be of greater value by virtue of a greater degree of universality and rationality ascribed to either one. It then follows that evil is to falsely affirm the lesser as the greater: the self which is a part as superior to God or the larger social whole. Such abstract logic serves to support established authority without existential justification and masks the true nature of evil.

Defining evil as the self choosing its natural desires in opposition to authority merely asserts the authority of the Other(s) to govern self-existence. Unrelated to self-existence, authority is alien to the self. When dominated by the alien Other(s), the self is neither free nor rational. Its existence is inauthentic and alienated from its own essential powers. While it is true to say that evil is a potentiality of human freedom; it is not a necessary consequence of it. For evil can have non-human sources or can result from human behavior that is not free at all. When freedom is considered the source of evil, the essential nature of the self is unnecessarily condemned. Those who are convinced of the innate sinfulness of man might feel an unwarranted sense of guilt and so would be ripe for the social control of established authority.

A negative view of freedom places the self squarely in the hands of an authoritative Other(s) for its salvation. Consequently, freedom, a power essential for dealienation, is diminished if not denied when viewed as sinful or threatening to social order. Such a view might even make dealienation impossible, and so fundamentally alienate the self from realizing its potentiality for doing any good at all. A rational freedom serving the needs and desires of natural self-seeking is not, of itself, evil. For if this were so, then the free pursuit of happiness would be evil, and this is absurd. Just as pursuing happiness is not of itself evil, neither is a conflict with authority which cannot be presumed right or wrong without rational inquiry. Self-seeking and opposing authority, as well as the needs and desires of the self, must bear close critical examination to judge their potentiality for good or evil. A judgment of self-existence is clearly called for to decide what is evil. It is precisely here that an adequate conception of evil is crucial. Therefore, it is preferable to define evil as an aspect of self-existence wherein unnecessary suffering is caused as opposed to defining it as defiance of established authority.

The preferred definition of evil is an operational one that tests any experience. Beyond this, evil is herein viewed as a special case of alienated self-existence. Evil is more comprehensively understood in terms of socialization dynamics. Fixated or perverted self-development explains how evil is humanly created. Socialization arrested in narcissistic or egoistic self-seeking behavior causes evil. So do the common perversions of sadism and masochism. Both inflict unnecessary suffering and so can be considered species of evil. Both separately or together, involve the suffering of guilt and punishment, psychologically and sociologically inflicted. The dominance and submission required by either, or both together, leave opposing demands of self and community unresolved. Suffering continues with obsessive or compulsive sado-masochistic behavior without satisfactory consummation.

Neuroses and psychoses scientifically describe evil and a profoundly alienated self-existence. The emotions and behavior of the self do not express its authentic needs and desires. Rather, the desires of a presumed authoritative Other(s) alien to its own desires dominate self-existence. An alien Other(s) maintains social control by teaching the self to feel guilty. Notwithstanding the theological doctrine of original sin, an innocent secular self is persuaded of its culpability toward those presumed victimized by its society or history. Convinced of its guilt, of not measuring up to an alien standard imposed upon it, and filled with low self-esteem, the self is made ready to be socially controlled.

The penance or restitution prescribed by the alien authoritative Other(s) presumably assuages guilt. Instead, the self is made to suffer punishment and inflict it. Such unnecessary suffering is evil. The ensuing sado-masochistic behavior then becomes a demonstration of social control usually exercised by a governing elite. Guilt is maintained, not assuaged. Those repressed needs and desires definitive of authentic self-existence are ignored and this is what truly alienates the self. Thus, the behavior of such a socially alienated self is dysfunctional to itself and its community. Satisfactory self-seeking is perverted into evil doing not only by earlier narcissistic and egoistic phases of self-development, but also by a later more socialized sado-masochism. All these represent a dysfunctional, fixated, perverted and incomplete socialization process. Without rationality and freedom brought to bear, the opposing demands of self and community cannot be resolved. Alienation and evil inevitably result.

Evil originates in a primitive non-rational narcissistic response to alienating finitude. As blind conatus unguided by rationality, egoistic freedom can result in alienation from self and community. When the self acts in disregard of the equal claim made by the needs and desires of its fellows, their resulting suffering is evil. It is a loss, a negation of something desired, an alienation from something enjoyed. Such self-seeking is also self-limiting. Mutuality, reciprocity and the benefits of social interdependence are sacrificed at great cost. The narcissistic, egoistic or sado-machochistic self isolates itself from community. Yet, of necessity, self-seeking must be expressed in a social dimension. When the social rules for its expression are violated, the self, by its own behavior, bifurcates itself in opposition to the social. Cut off from genuine social interaction, it cannot realize its complete identity. Its desires and aims cannot serve itself while also serving its fellows, and vice versa. Such an incompletely socialized self can realize its own social potential in a severely limited way, if at all. Thus, its being is fragmentary, incompletely developed, lesser in being and value than it could be. It remains fundamentally alienated from its fellows and itself.

Evil doing teaches us to discern what is good and what is normative for human conduct and development. Wisdom is acquired in learning from the historical experience of a suffering humanity. Such wisdom must be culturally transmitted so that we recognize it when we see it. Narcissism, egoism and sado-masochism psychologically and sociologically describe the roots of evil. A self, so disposed, disregards rationality and so cannot be free to realize its true potentiality. Its behavior is counterproductive. Dealienation and self-realization cannot proceed with a self opposed to itself and its fellows. Invariably, social opposition blocks any self-objectification that is narcissistic, egoistic or sado-masochistic. In turn, social opposition blocks the formation of a complete relationship of self with any larger social whole, be it community or humanity, not to mention its own God.

Notes

1. Hegel, G. W. F. (1977) *Hegel's Philosophy of Right* (T. M. Knox, Trans.). New York, NY: Oxford University Press, 226.
2. Ibid., 227.
3. Hegel, G. W. F. (1967) *The Phenomenology of Mind* (J. B. Baillie, Trans.). New York, NY: Harper and Row, 49.
4. Ibid., 232.
5. Hegel, G. W. F. (1956) *The Philosophy of History* (J. Sibree, Trans.). New York, NY: Dover, 407.
6. Hegel, *The Phenomenology of Mind*, 229.
7. *Hegel's Philosophy of Right*, 226.
8. Ibid., 129.

Chapter Three

Alienating Work

Self-objectifying Work

Dealienation is a negating process responding to the alienating finitude of self-existence. Hegelian concepts of sublation and self-objectification, in effect, explain dealienation. Sublation was later elaborated with different terminology by Freud's concepts of repression and sublimation - both describing psychic phenomena driven by negativity. Similarly, self-objectification was also later elaborated by Freud's concepts of identification and introjection. Freudian concepts explain dealienation naturalistically as a non-rational process of socialization. From a psychoanalytic perspective, one result of self-objectification is pleasure and a narcissistic gratification in which self is reunited with an alienating Other(s). Yet, the work of self-objectification does not always achieve dealienation, which Hegel recognized. Where Hegel envisioned a self dealienated by obedience to the authoritative Others of community and God, Freud concluded that they repress the true antisocial desires of a primitive self into neurosis. With its true nature reformed by a distorting sublimation, the self pays a heavy price in instinctual gratification for the obvious benefits of civilization.

Self-objectification is work with a dealienating aim. As the work is accomplished, the self acquires an identity, the world is transformed with a humanized significance and the meaning of being is revealed. Whenever the process of self-objectification is successful, some specific form of alienation is overcome. The converse is also true. Moreover, the finite product of self-objectification can also be alienating as Hegel acknowledged. Self-objectification writ large is the basis for his speculative idealistic metaphysical theory of a *World Spirit* or Geist, molding history. Hegel thought of self-objectification as a spiritual phenomenon.

Only beings that are rational and free can objectify themselves in the world with their fellows. In essence, self-objectification is the intentional activity of a free agent who, being volitional, rational and purposive, causes a transformation of its world and itself. However, a Hegelian spiritual self-objectification driven by freedom and rationality is still too narrow in connotation. Conceived as a non-rational process driven by natural inclination, passion and social need, self-objectification acquires an even more general significance. For then it can be conceived as the most general response to alienating finitude in which the self appropriates the opposing Other(s) by making it an instrument of its needs and desires. A world so constructed and humanized is one in which the self is at home with the Other; in which the Other is recognized, not as alien, but as self. Its world has become its identity even where alienation persists.

Self-objectification is a product of work, however accomplished. As his own doing, any work product stands for the originator as an actual expression of his identity. He recognizes who he is by his work and so do his fellows. His work must have some universal social implication beyond mere self-satisfaction for it to be publicly acknowledged. If the work instantiates in some way pre-established universal social norms, then public acknowledgment is forthcoming. Dignity and self-respect is secured by a public acceptance of the work one does, particularly when its accomplishment is consonant with pre-established social norms and roles sanctioned by traditional authoritative Others.

From the perspective of its originator, it would seem then that the work of self-objectification is intended to achieve the aim of dealienation. However, from a more universal perspective, the result of self-objectifying work enters a complex social dialectic with the needs, interests and purposes of other persons. Hence, the work of one person may become the condition of alienation for another person, and when that work loses its original significance, it may even become alien to its originator. Hegel recognized that the process and result of work within the private context of self-fulfillment of individuals is dealienating in aim if not in fact. He also recognized that the result of work in a more complex social context could be a condition of alienation for and among individuals, a cause of social strife. But he did not fully recognize how the process of work itself can be alienating. This was left to later thinkers such as Marx reacting to the effects of the industrial revolution and to social psychologists reacting to contemporary consumerism of a post industrial so-called information age.

When work is understood solely from an objective perspective, the necessary connection of idea and actuality is lost, since the subjectivity creating that connection is not taken into account. It is then that work appears contingent, transitory, and fortuitous. The means to realize the sought after end also appear arbitrary when not chosen by the doer according to his purpose and what is available at hand under the circumstances. The mere fact of a work product, absent any comprehension of its human intent or purpose makes it a publicly indifferent object, an alien Other, possibly standing in opposition to the desires and purposes of other individuals. To anyone uninvolved with the work product, it is reduced to a mere impersonal fact. Consequently, the work product loses the human significance that it only has when it reflects its originating human purpose. For, it is human purpose and action expressed in the work product that creates the necessary connection between its idea and actuality. Without any involvement of human purpose and self-activity, the relation between idea and actuality of a work product is extrinsic or even accidental. Since different purposes or chosen means can effect the same end, the natural intrinsic unity between idea and actuality of any work product is severed. Idea and result secured through self-objectifying work thereby suffer a loss of significance.

Reflecting upon work accomplished compels an awareness of the opposition of between idea and actuality, willing and executed result, human ends and chosen means. The individual performing work demonstrates the unity of these moments. His thought and free intentional activity provides their necessary connection. As Hegel might have stated it; with purposive human activity, the Idea is concretely realized, reality humanized and truth revealed as a correspondence of Notion and reality. Thus, self-objectifying work has a profound ontological significance. Working and work product reveal the meaning of being, if not occasionally creating it. The dealienating work endeavor also reveals the being of the self. What and who it is, is what it does with the alien Other(s). It or they do not define the self. Rather, the self discovers who and what it is by the work it does with the alien Other(s). They are the vehicles for self-discovery. Working and work product present reality in both its subjective and objective aspects as Hegel might have put it. Just as work is a fundamental response to alienation, a dealienating process with subjective aim, so work when completely objectified in a public social context, may again present alienation. The dialectic of working is a continuous process of alienation and dealienation.

Minimally conceived, *necessity* is implication where something signifies something else. Necessity is a special kind of implication that is invariable. What is implied cannot be otherwise. Obvious examples are a tautology, a mathematical demonstration or when the contradiction of something is false. Such considerations suggest that necessity originates from the implication of thought without existential import. Meanings are intended to be used only in certain ways expressed by rules of formal logic and linguistic syntax. Thus, invariable implication applies to thought driven by negativity. Observation of natural events in temporal sequence does not provide any reason explaining why the sequence could not be otherwise as David Hume pointed out by his analysis of causality. Where necessity is conceived as invariable implication characteristic of thought, it cannot be derived inductively from experiencing predictable temporal sequences in nature. Yet, intentional self-activity provides a reason why something cannot be otherwise.

A self, free to think and act, is aware of its own needs, and aims to satisfy them. Something must be accomplished to alter an alienating situation limiting the satisfaction of human needs and desires. The limiting situation is investigated and evaluated by thought relative to the satisfaction of an aim. Strategies are devised utilizing knowledge and complex means-ends relationships in order to achieve successful outcomes. The self then acts intentionally and often in a complex manner to achieve its aim. A successful result utilizes the negating power of thought and action to bring about a different situation. While the formal implication of thinking is a symbolic representation of existential possibilities, the material implication of free intentional self-activity is a changed existential situation: a sequence of temporal consequences experienced by the self bringing about the satisfaction of its aim. It is in the result of this complex work that necessity is ontological, not merely a formal attribute of thought. Necessity is then discovered residing in freedom of thought and action existentially applied. What the self creates for itself in the world demonstrates necessity in an ontological, as opposed to a logical dimension. Necessity is experienced in what results from thought and the intentional activity of self-existence in a process of dealienation.

The debate over what constitutes *necessary connection* can be resolved by analyzing what is involved in self-objectification. Necessary connection is embedded in the relationship between working and the work product. Self-objectifying work establishes the necessary connection of idea with fact. Statistical correlation and probability used to establish causal relationship cannot define necessary connection. Nevertheless, self-objectifying work leaves no doubt about the who, what, when, where, why and how of its accomplishment. The connection is made, not abstractly, not logically, not subjectively, but objectively through self-objectifying work and its public work product. As Hegel would have put it, work makes the Idea actual, establishing its truth.

The work product demonstrates a necessity that is ontological, rather than merely logical or subjective. Necessary connection is not an a priori logical notion superimposed by the mind to structure experience. Neither is necessary connection provided by an Ego intent upon acquiring knowledge. Rather, necessary connection is discovered in the life processes of an individual acting intentionally in the performance of his own work. Necessary connection is discovered as a feature of self-objectification and in the very process of dealienation. That necessary connection originates with self-objectification is implicit in judging any result accomplished by a free agent. Moral judgment presumes that responsibility and accountability is determined by examining the self-objectifying result. Self-objectifying motives are sought to affix guilt or determine an appropriate penalty. Curiously enough, necessary connection can be discovered in the freedom of the self to think and act for itself in its self-objectifying work.

Social Dominance and Submission

The world becomes humanized through the work of self-objectification. This process is anything but straightforward, since it is driven by negativity in aim, execution and result. Work is inherently dialectical as demonstrated by the dynamics of interaction in Hegel's famous Master and Slave allegory. The original significance of work for the Master is to shun it and compel his Slave to do it for him in order to subsist, enjoy luxury and leisure for the cultivation of a preferred higher spiritual life. His identity is to be independent of the natural necessity to work, to be spiritually cultivated, and to be socially dominant over his Slave. This identity is recognized and acknowledged by the fact that his Slave is dependent for subsistence, if not life itself, upon the absolute power and magnanimity of his Master.

However, the relationship between Master and Slave is fraught with dialectical reversals. For the Master, with all that he has, is dependent upon the Slave to satisfy physical needs and provide an identity resulting from acknowledged subservience. The Slave discovers an identity created by work and the self-objectifying opportunity it offers. His dependence is counterbalanced by the outlet work provides for his stifled freedom. Curiously, through his coerced work he discovers independence resulting from his own productive use of the physical world. His freedom is exercised and displayed in the creation of his work product. This is ennobling; requiring public acknowledgment and respect for his demonstrated knowledge, skills and abilities. Even in his servitude, a measure of dignity is secured and freedom is not altogether suppressed. In fact it is required and develops through the work of servitude, although barred from its complete expression within a social context of persons with equal rights and opportunity.

Both Master and Slave in the original conflict risked death to avoid servitude and assert their freedom. Nevertheless, after the conquest, the Slave chose servitude to suicide. This coerced choice is self-demeaning, confirming his inferiority and justifying his enslavement. Social superiority and dominance is here determined by which party is physically stronger or better at violent coercion. Hegel did not notice that choosing servitude is perfectly rational under the circumstances. Merely by staying alive, there is hope of regaining the freedom necessary to live the good life. In addition, it must not be forgotten that although the Master does no physical work, his self-objectifying work must consist of the arduous endeavor to maintain social dominance, ultimately by coercive, violent means.

The Slave is forced to express his potentiality for freedom of thought and action through coerced work. Self-objectification is severely limited to doing what the Master, an alien Other, dictates. Yet, even in the servitude of physical work, self-objectification occurs in the result of work. Depending upon the nature of the work, there may be some limited opportunity for the exercise of freedom to create something expressive of the Slave's personality and talent. Hegel overemphasized these opportunities thereby creating a false impression of servitude as itself creating opportunities for self-development. The Slave would be forced to develop whereas the Master would not. Nevertheless, the menial work of the Slave is no more self-developing than the indolent luxury of his Master. He has the advantage of not working to subsist, and putting leisure and luxury to good use, but whether he cultivates himself spiritually is his choice and therefore uncertain. Spiritual self-development is not guaranteed, but remains for the Master no more than a possibility provided by the personal freedom, luxury and leisure. Since self-development requires work, and he shuns work, then self-development could not be expected to occur. Thus, his self-objectifying work would consist of nothing more than coercively maintaining social dominance.

The absence of the necessity to work is a freedom that provides no more than the possibility for self-development. Since Hegel discussed the Slave's self-development through coerced work, but not that of the Master freed from work, it would appear as if self-development would not occur without coercion. Of itself, the freedom provided by luxury and leisure would be insufficiently motivating for self-development to occur. Furthermore, the endeavor to coercively maintain an identity of social dominance thwarts self-development. Hegel undoubtedly understood this. Although an absolute chasm of inequality is maintained between Master and Slave, curiously enough the latter has more motivation and opportunity to develop through the necessity to work. This might explain the historical decline of slavery without considering the sociological, economic and moral factors of industrialization.

Alienation expressed by human need and desire requires dealienating work. Self-objectifying work is not only necessary for survival, but also creates one's identity. This whole process must occur within a structure of social interdependence. The self is the interdependent social function it performs; its publicly acknowledged social role. From this is derived one's self-concept. Hegel intuitively described a theoretical interpersonal dialectic and resulting self-concept emerging from one kind of social structure based upon the dominance of a Master and submission of a Slave. With respect to an identity resulting from the social feedback of public recognition and acknowledgment, both the Master and Slave are necessarily equals dependent upon one another. Both are also independent, but with a crucially distinguishable difference; the necessity to work or lack thereof. As the dialectic proceeds, the independence of the Master is counterbalanced by a dependence upon his Slave; and, the dependence of the Slave is counterbalanced by independence gained through the necessity to work. Both are dependent upon each other, and both are independent in different ways.

Freedom is still common to Master and Slave, even if radically different in degree, or expressed in radically different life-styles and work. Self-objectifying work requires some degree of freedom that is reflected by one's self-concept. Even in slavery, freedom may find its outlet in certain kinds of coerced work and the self-objectification it provides. Historically, self-objectification through work has replaced the coercive social dominance of slavery. The forces of technology, economics and moral activism have progressively made slavery obsolete. Machines have replaced the need for arduous human labor. Work, so necessary for subsistence, is inherently satisfying and preferable to inactivity. Working infinitely enriches life with its consequences. Without work of some kind, any realization of rationality and freedom - the Hegelian human essence - becomes impossible. The Master remains primitive and undeveloped relative to the Slave compelled to strive for self-objectification and liberation through work. In the end, work proved more ennobling of the human spirit than coercive social dominance by threat or violence.

Survival and dealienation compels everyone to work, self-objectify and develop a self-concept reflecting their social role. Beyond survival and on a more subtle level of self-existence, work can be a social contribution, which is enjoyed rather than simply coerced. Under certain exceptional circumstances of servitude, or of equality among free individuals, work can express an authentic self-realization, not alien in performance, result, or coerced by an alien authority. For example, an artistic or educative work product, even that of the Roman slave philosopher Epictetus, can be universally admired and acknowledged to be an authentic self-expression partially dealienating in its consequences. There is dignity in some if not most kinds of work. However, the value and significance of work change with the social dialectic surrounding it. Work is inherently social in that its result is an object for someone else's interest and purpose. When taken out of a simple social context of Master and Slave and placed in a more complex social context of free and equal individuals, the social dynamics of work changes the dialectical interaction of the parties involved. In this context, work was still discovered to be alienating under the circumstances of industrialization and bureaucracy.

Alienating Self-objectification

Dealienation is the aim of self-objectification accomplished through work. Self-objectifying work can by its motive, intention or consequence be good or evil, right or wrong, responsible or irresponsible, social or antisocial, and so forth. Understood as abstracted from self-existence, self-objectification is reduced to amoral process and may be considered value neutral by a social scientist. Nevertheless, in practice, self-objectifying work always has a value implicit in its motive and intention. Otherwise, what would give it impetus? Certainly, the consequences of self-objectification reveal something of positive or negative value, depending upon whether it achieves its dealienating aim or further alienates the self.

Straightforward and unproblematical self-objectification results in dealienation. Beyond defining it, there is not much that might generate philosophical interest. On the other hand, existentialists such as Sartre, believed that the result of self-objectification is a *reification* of the self, a contradiction of its freedom, invariably alienating. Although this viewpoint is interesting, not much can be said about it, since it does not theoretically permit the possibility of successful dealienation. Such an extreme view of self-objectification is invalidated by the fact of successful dealienation. Frustrated self-objectification or cases of alienating outcomes capture immediate interest and stimulate careful analysis. A process of working and a work product are aspects of self-objectification, both of which can be alienating. Hegel described how any kind of work product could become alienating to its creator, given certain social dynamics surrounding it. Marx further elaborated upon this by describing the social dynamics of exploited industrial labor, and emphasizing the alienating aspects of both working and the physical work product for the industrial worker. In a post-industrial information age, bureaucracy has become the focus for the analysis of alienating aspects of working and work products that are social services rather than tangible goods.

Self-objectification is accomplished through work. Although dealienation is the aim of work, it still can have alienating consequences, according to Hegel. "The work is, thus, in general something transitory, which is extinguished by the counter-action of other powers and interests, and displays the reality of individuality in a transitory form rather than as fulfilled and accomplished."[1] Physical work transforms and humanizes the world by destroying or reforming something from its natural condition. Yet, work products are temporal and transitory having a life cycle from birth to death. Decay over time and accidental circumstance enters the formation and duration of a work product. So do the interpretations and uses others give it in a social context.

Work is an expression of human finitude. Yet, work can transcend finitude. Great cultural works expressing the truth of being do not vanish into historical oblivion. Rather, they persist and are cherished by posterity. Everyone recognizes their true meaning or timeless wisdom. Such works have no alien quality. They are a perfect expression of the original intention of their creator, which remains undiminished in time by nature or circumstance. Posterity recognizes in such works something universally true transcending their creator. As Plato might have said, everyone couldn't help but acknowledge the universal truth, goodness and beauty perfectly expressed and embodied in an artistic work.

The most perfect moment of existence for any work product is upon its successful completion when it reflects the original intention of the agent(s) who performed it. The self-objectifying purpose of work is lost with the changes wrought by time and circumstance. A work product becomes imperfect when not reflecting the creator's original intention or by contradicting it. Work products embody degrees of perfection, depending upon the creator's purpose, the means chosen, circumstances of its production, chance environmental conditions, the skill or competence of the doer, blunders, erroneous judgment, errors of omission as well as commission. When a work is completed, then the vicissitudes of nature, culture and time take their inevitable toll. As workers come into being and vanish, so does their work.

Finitude is not escaped by self-objectification and alienating finitude may be its outcome in virtue of how the world is constituted or what one's fellows intend. But this may not be the case where the intended consequences and the intentions of others are identical to my own with respect to the action one has taken and its outcome. So, there is nothing inherently alienating or self-defeating in self-objectification. Not everything we do is problematical for others and ourselves. The Hegelian way of ensuring this is to act simply for the same aims and in the same way as one's fellows. In other words, embrace the universal; conform to accepted mores and prescriptions of traditional authority and express dealienating work only within standardized social roles. This is good advice most of the time. But not always, as when restrictive social norms and roles prevent one from realizing some aim of his or her own which does no harm to others. Then the embrace of the universal and conformity to it may in fact alienate the self from its true potential and unique expression, which may also be a loss to one's fellows.

Self-existence never escapes alienating finitude, even in the outcomes of dealienation. Outcomes are often beset with uncertainty. Unintended consequences abound. Other persons may construe an outcome differently from its originator. Natural forces, time and contingent circumstance have their inevitable effect contradicting original intentions. The self may lack knowledge of the conditions or consequences of its actions. Yet, the doer is always responsible for what he or she intends. However, the doer cannot be held accountable for unforeseeable outcomes. The ideal case of dealienating work occurs when there is perfect knowledge of intention underlying human action, the circumstances surrounding it, and a perfect correspondence of outcome with intention. All the impediments to dealienation point toward the condition of its success, a will free to act upon its intentions and subordinated to rationality. However, given the finitude of self and its world, the ideal rarely occurs and only in the simplest circumstances. Most often, the alien Other(s) intrudes in unexpected ways that make a self-objectifying work product itself an alien Other.

A self-objectifying work product, although a fact signifying my own intention, may not possess the same significance for my fellows. They provide what is created with significance commensurate with their own intentions. When these are different from mine, what I did gets a different meaning and value from them. This makes what I did an alien Other to me of which I may or may not be aware. When it is something I did not intend, it is an indifferent Other. Moreover, if it is something I do not want or something I disapprove of, it takes on an alienating aspect. Unintended consequences often contradict the intentions of the doer. In such cases, self-objectification is dysfunctional in its result: alienating to the will that brought it into being. This being so often the case, the moral worth of a deed is determined by its original intention rather than its unintended consequences or different significance overlaid upon it by the intentions of others.

Self-objectification also has the dimension of reification akin to a static snapshot pose at a given place and time. In the work product, something of the self is abstracted and reduced to something external. With the reification, comes a loss of control over what the work product signifies. Its meaning invariably changes with time, place, unintended consequences, chance, accidental circumstances, misinterpretation, reinterpretation, and various uses other persons attach to it.

Self-objectification through work can be problematical and even alienating. Marx viewed it this way by pointing out how alienating the work product can become when it is neither owned nor enjoyed by the worker whose labor produced it. Once my work is public, it is no longer strictly mine, no longer bears only the significance I gave it when produced. In fact, its significance can even change for me personally as I change my views and circumstances relating to it. Therefore, self-objectifying work is partially definitive of myself, but never completely so. It is who I was or am now, but not who I may become tomorrow. Work is an exercise in finitude through which we become aware of our own limitations and those set for us by nature, culture and historical circumstance. The work we are compelled to do represents a potentially infinite variety of human responses to a potentially infinite variety of alienating circumstances confronted by life itself. Being an outcome of an interminable process of dealienation, no work product escapes alienating finitude. Work defines human destiny.

Self-objectifying work has a subjective and objective dimension. The former has the intense personal significance of one's own doing while the latter involves the social significance of its result. A personal work product is also an impersonal social object. To those who are uninvolved in its creation, it may be entirely impersonal, with or without interest or value depending upon its usefulness. Any absence of human significance makes the work product something alien. The intentional significance of its originator is invariably lost as it becomes a mere indifferent fact of the world, or is given contrary social interpretations and uses, or has unintended consequences.

Furthermore, moments or conditions that gave work its originating significance are necessarily not experienced by persons indirectly involved with its performance. For them, a work product cannot be a coherent totality resulting from the dialectical moments of its creation. They did not emotionally react to the alienating deficiency prompting the work and so cannot experience its original purposive significance. Therefore, the original moments of work undergo *diremption* as Hegel called it; a separation in meaning and being when the work product is complete. For uninvolved persons there is no necessary connection between the idea and fact of a work product. Where it rectifies some deficiency, its original intention tends to disappear. Particularly where the work product is a social structure, we reap the benefits of the suffering struggle of our forbears while foregoing a true comprehension of the original intention animating their legacy. This often requires painfully relearning old lessons.

When an individual is dissociated from his work or its product, both cease to be regarded as his own, reflective of his thought, feeling and behavior. Working or work product neither express nor satisfies the full range of needs and desires motivating every self. Then, working and work product are regarded as a necessary means for subsistence - something merely incidental in life, if not accidental depending upon good or bad fortune; something determined by a fate alien to the self. The work one does could just as easily have been accomplished by someone else, by some other means, or from some other purpose. The world of work and its product is impersonal, something the self is indifferent toward. Unrelated to its needs and desires, working or work product is alien, even incomprehensible to a great extent. Under such circumstances, the connection between self and world is substantially severed. In a word, the world is dehumanized in significance. Self-objectifying work or work product are reduced to their barest significance. Subsistence and security are its only purposes. Working and work product have no personal significance at all beyond their fungible value as money. Working is just a way to put bread on the table for oneself and family, but nothing more. Working is not enjoyed as a creative expression of ones own knowledge, talent and skill. There is no pride of personal achievement associated with work or its product. One gives one's labor and time in exchange for money. Whenever possible, work is to be avoided or minimized in time and effort expended upon it. Social reciprocity is also minimized where the work product is undervalued or not valued at all. Without reciprocity of working and work product, the self is isolated along with a concurrent loss of community.

Socially, any work product becomes an object of interpretation and can be used by others for purposes quite different from that of the originator. In the normal course of events, any self can encounter an alienation of his self-objectifying work within a social context of conflicting interests and purposes. As Hegel expressed it, the individual cannot recognize himself in what others have made of what he has done. When the social feedback from self-objectifying work negates its purpose, the significance of the work is distorted into something unexpected, unintended and possibly unwanted. If the social feedback is lacking or disinterested, the identity-establishing aim of self-objectification is thwarted. Without its originating significance, work simply exists as mere impersonal fact, as mere object for somebody else, as not one's own, and so incomplete in meaning and being.

An individual free to think and act posits through working the necessary connection between idea and actuality. This connection, established ontologically, is derived from and demonstrated by the process of thought and action in working and in the result of work accomplished by individuals. The significance of work resides first in alienation, then in a process of dealienation, and finally in the resulting work product which Hegel understood to be an actual self-objectification. What this self-objectification signifies to the worker and to his fellows provides the deep meaning of work as a response to alienation, as a humanization of the world, and as a source of further social alienation. In the biblical myth of the fall, work is God's curse necessitated by alienation and alienating in result. The necessity to work demonstrates that alienation is unavoidable and dealienation is an interminable work.

Alienating Collective Work

Collective work, or working for a social cause is often discovered to be alienating. How many times are the immediate social or historical consequences of collective *work for the cause* unintended by the participating individuals? How many times does one hear that the extraneous interests of its participants perverted a good cause, or that the good intentions of the founders were never realized? That elusive original intent is all too often altered in its collective execution. It is as if the intended consequences of collective work results in a puzzling realization of some other unanticipated consequences having some other purpose set by something or someone alien to the doer. There is the sense that what the individual wanted was not really what the collective endeavor was all about to begin with. Thus, the collective product of common cause can stand against the very individuals who have worked so hard to bring it about. Scrutiny reveals hidden purposes and effects seemingly not amenable to deliberative choice by the individuals involved. Obviously, *the cause* has different signification depending upon concealed motives and intentions that vary widely among participants. Lacking perspective on the social whole and unaware of the true dynamics of collective work, the individual is not empowered to fathom or control its complexity. The implication is that personal autonomy is a delusion within a context of collective work.

Often a social cause is perverted into something the individual does not recognize as his own and which does not comport with his values or intentions. In the interaction between diverse participants and in the result, the consciously avowed aim is subverted and perverted to such a degree that it becomes alien to the individual whose sacrificial work it was. The sense of disappointment and disillusionment is profound; so profound perhaps, that it may be an awakening to alienation typical of social phenomena. Within any group working for a common cause is found disagreement among individuals and attempts to influence others in the group by praise or condemnation. The attempts by individuals to influence the common work among themselves produces a transpersonal outcome effected by strong self-assertiveness and interpersonal compromise.

Collective work, always a socially dynamic interaction of individuals, is a gestalt: greater than the sum of constituent interests, motives and intentions, but created by them. In effect, what is signified by the individual as the common cause is not what is signified by its realization. A collective social work product expresses something substantially different from that of an involved individual or collection of them. The social resultant is something unexpected, unintended, unpredictable, novel in character, previously unknown, mysterious and strange. The impression is that in common work, we are flying blind, so to speak; unaware of what is really driving us to do what we do. It is as if the outcome is pre-ordained by some force or power other than our own and outside us. So, at a social level, the interactive dialectic reveals an alienation of its own, an alienation even more profound than that experienced by any single individual.

Self-objectifying work, be it individual or collective, is infected by negativity of one kind or another. In a contemporary world of bureaucratic institutions, the law of unintended consequences often prevails in executing social policy and government programs. The original intent of a law or regulation is frequently circumvented by what special interest groups or individuals make out of it to satisfy their own purposes. Good intentions seem to generate contradictory results. As is often said, "The road to hell is paved with good intentions." A confluence of diverse social interests by groups as well as individuals creates a degree of complex social interaction with consequences impossible to predict or even understand in advance of policy implementation.

It is plausible to suppose that self-existence could be dominated by alien Others such as destiny or a Hegelian Geist. Neither can be comprehended primarily by reason of the finitude of self-existence. The fact of freedom introduces indeterminacy into the time sequence of historical events. What may alienate the self at a future time is as indeterminate as what the dealienating response will be. A radically free individual has the capacity to transform and even create the conditions he confronts. Radical freedom dictates the indeterminacy of social outcomes. If who we are is what we will become, then we can never know ourselves in any final sense. We are literally a self-realizing process with unknown outcome, contrary to the Hegelian predestination of Reason, Ideas and Geist.

If the existentialists are right about a radically free individual lacking an essential nature, then the social outcomes of the activity of such beings is indeterminate. All we can know of history is then retrospective, not prospective. Even if the existentialists are wrong and there is an essential human nature, which is free and rational, the future would still remain indeterminate. For our nature is revealed to us through a process of a radically free human response to the prevailing conditions of alienation, whatever they might be at any given historical moment. Even a scientific determinist would have to admit that uncertainty and unpredictability reside with a perpetually incomplete knowledge of a complex interactive social dynamic causing specific outcomes. The alienating outcome of collective work can be explained by the indeterminacy of self-existence, the fact of human freedom and incomplete knowledge of the social dialectic. This is certainly a simpler explanation and less problematical than supposing individuals personally engaged in collective work are merely dupes of a Hegelian Geist.

There is much truth in Hegel's analysis of social action. The collective is complex, a real objective entity larger than and beyond the complete comprehension and control of the individual. Living in a bureaucratic institution gives one this humbling sense - that the individual counts for very little, if anything. In a cosmic sense, we are as nothing. However, am I as an individual deceived concerning the intent and effect of my behavior? Are we all so deceived? And is Geist the deceiver? How can this be the case if I am aware of being so deceived (to echo a Cartesian rejoinder)?

Even more interesting is why Hegel cast history in a disguise and made Geist a dissembler. Why must we be duped to do Geist's work? Might it be because we would not choose it as our own and so would be unwilling workers who would have to be coerced. Must Geist dupe us, since our rationality and freedom cannot be trusted with free reign? Is individual rationality and freedom so threatening, so dangerous, that it requires a limitation placed upon it by Geist who deceives and dupes us into doing what is right against our wild antisocial will - a will which would not do Geist's work otherwise? So Geist must deceive and coerce such an individual: must alienate him from that which makes him a most noble creature; that which is his essential nature, and which bestows dignity and worth upon him - namely his own capacity to think and act on his own for himself. It would seem as if Hegel had to have Geist alienate the individual in order to save him from himself. However, such a solution to the perplexity of social action and history denies rationality and freedom, that human essence universal to individuals.

If we are alienated and duped by the Other(s), be they the collective or God, how is dealienation possible? One despairs of an answer, yet hopes, maybe through Christian faith in salvation by God's grace. Alternatively, dealienation might be possible only by some miracle. But, dealienation, if it is to be possible, requires an absolute assertion of rationality and freedom, not located in some alien Other, be it the collective or God, but in the individual with all the risk of abuse, misuse and immorality that this entails. We must know what motivates us and why, both as individuals and collectively. The truth of this cannot be hidden from us by any form of deception, be it personal, collective or Godlike. For without honestly confronting the truth about ourselves, our fears and anxieties, dealienation is impossible.

It would appear as if human nature is continuously being revealed in a self-defining process of alienation and dealienation whereby the most successful response seems to require freedom and rationality working together. Both then constitute a human essence supporting a continuously self-defining and self-realizing being. Western civilization has so defined human nature through the classical Greek emphasis upon rationality and the Christian emphasis upon freedom. These two fundamental characteristics do not, of themselves, make history predictable, since the conditions generating their response are not known in advance. Human historical indeterminacy is mandated then by the complexity of alienating circumstances coupled with a choice of alternative dealienating responses, which may not always be rationally based.

Hegel seemed correct in asserting that rationality and freedom are the human essence, and that social outcomes cannot be determined in advance. These conclusions are unaffected by whether one believes history to be driven by the Hegelian Geist with its hidden purposes and Ideas, or by the rational freedom of individuals. With regard to the trend of human history, and given rational freedom as the human essence, one could speculate that it would be continuously reinforced by historical outcomes. In addition, the conditions of alienation will more and more be created in a humanly created environment. Recent history would seem to warrant this much with its exponential explosion of knowledge and technology, given their attendant problems.

Hegel's view of collective behavior is unacceptable for several reasons. First, it irrevocably alienates the individual. Second, it denies his essence as a rational and free being. We are nothing, if not free to think and act to bring about what we intend. By positing the collective as different and superior to the individual, and placing Geist at the ontological apex, Hegel makes autonomy of the individual mere self-delusion, if not completely illusory. As secretly directed by an Other, individual authenticity is sacrificed. Without autonomy and authenticity, alienation cannot be overcome. History is just a tragic series of events not amenable to human intelligence and will. If Geist rules absolutely and we obey as pre-programmed automatons, dealienation is impossible. Nevertheless, as soon as we realize this, we rebel against it. We refuse to believe it. It is not considered an acceptable or even an accurate interpretation of unpredictable and tragically undesirable historical events. We sense that it does not comport with an intuitive apprehension of our own rationality and freedom, individually or collectively.

Hegel viewed collective work as utterly unlike individual work. The transpersonal dimension of collective work unites the individual with the social and God. The bond is secured by a Geist that alienates the self from its own power to think and act for itself. This makes Hegel's interpretation of history and the place of the individual in it problematical. A manipulative Geist makes a self free to think and act for itself mere self-delusion. That self is treated as a puppet, duped by Geist to do what it wants. Such a self, manipulated and enthralled by Geist, cannot exist authentically or autonomously. The work of self-objectification is contradicted by collective work. Yet, this alienation of collective work, when the individual is conscious of it would not be accepted. For it is a denial of freedom, rationality, and human dignity. If alienation of individuals is to be the price of their connection with their fellows and the divine, then the price is too high and the sacrifice is too great. For to be driven by the Other is to be alienated, something to be overcome. This, in the Hegelian vernacular, *ought not to be*. It generates refusal and the imperative of dealienation.

Self-objectification requires Socialization

Every self is an alien Other whose potentiality for being someone is realized in time. The perennial question of self-existence is "Who am I?" The *who* gets answered by dealienating self-existence. Establishing an identity is a self-objectifying work. Its product presents the being of the self, its particular acquired identity. The work product also provides an opportunity for narcissistic enjoyment of the world as an extension of self. The same enjoyment is also secured from being recognized by one's fellows. They provide a public identity for the self secured by being named and given a social role to play. For a variety of reasons, a private and public identity often differ, since any self-objectifying work product may have unintended consequences or acquire a different public signification, possibly one that might not be publicly esteemed. When this is the case, there is negative feedback to its creator and narcissistic enjoyment is denied. An identity lacking public confirmation is painful, particularly where the purpose of the work was to achieve some specific social goal. In such a common circumstance, the self stands isolated from community and alienated from complete satisfaction expected from its work.

The true significance of self-objectification transcends the individual and includes that of the larger social whole. This is a significance of which we are mainly unaware and cannot completely know from our finite perspective of place and time in history. However, that there is such a larger significance cannot be doubted. For it is expressed in the universal norms and social roles of culture. If self-objectifying work is driven by an acceptance of the norms and social roles of one's culture, then an alienating isolation from community is avoided. Social feedback is positive. There is a genuine reciprocity between self and community with each sustaining the other. The self feels secure in the enjoyment of public approbation for its work.

The aim of self-objectification is dealienation. However, that aim can be contravened in a variety of ways. Too often self-objectifying work becomes alienating. Hegel offered a paradigm for successful dealienation. He believed the self had to introject authoritative Others, namely community and God. Their dicta provide pre-established universal norms and social roles. Through a process of identification with these, a self-concept is developed. With it, the work of self-objectification can proceed in channels that ensure successful dealienation. The result is the historical creation of self-identity in a progressively humanized world. This paradigm, although plausible and appealing, remains problematical. For, even where it is fully operative, alienation remains. Why the Other is authoritative for the self rather than merely alien to it always remains to be answered. It is not clear how the Hegelian paradigm provides self-existence with sufficient autonomy and authenticity necessary for successful dealienation.

Placed in a straight jacket of authority, pre-established norms and social roles often thwart self-realization. No doubt dealienation always requires self-objectifying work. What kind, for whom and for what purpose cannot be prescribed by the Other(s) in advance of self-existence and the specific form of alienating finitude encountered therein. Self-objectification can occur without the Hegelian paradigm. Nevertheless, the Hegelian implication is that successful dealienation is impossible without adopting it. Historically, all efforts of self-objectification without the dicta of God and community Hegel interpreted to end in failure with the Roman Empire and French Revolution providing classic examples. However, historical examples can also be adduced which indicate that the self can upon occasion be a creator of norms and roles. Hegel acknowledged this much with his concept of heroic world historical individuals. Operating according to their conscience and against prevailing traditional norms and authority, they transform culture and make progress for humanity, even though unconsciously directed by Geist. However, such elaborate interpretations are unnecessary. For, self-objectifying work makes its appeal by the successful dealienation it provides in resolving the problems encountered by self-existence. When satisfying the needs and desires shared by other selves, a particular self-objectifying work sets an immediately appealing example.

Certainly, Hegel's analysis of self-objectification through work explains the mechanism of alienation seen in social institutions, particularly centralized bureaucratic governments. His insight into the consequences of self-objectification through work demonstrates an inescapable alienation of the individual. Also implied are subtler forms of alienation within the social fabric itself, which would include institutions. However, Hegel's concern with defending the status quo of existing social institutions and traditional authority prevented him from expanding his insight about self-objectification and work into a critique of social forms of alienation. This was left to later thinkers such as Marx.

Dealienation is the aim of self-objectification. Any kind of dealienation requires self-objectifying work. Since human beings are socially interdependent for survival, almost all their needs and desires arise in a social context, and are satisfied or frustrated therein. Self-objectification requires a process of socialization culminating in the development of a self-concept. It is projected upon the world and one's fellows in any kind of self-objectifying work. The development of an enabling self-concept is a very complex process involving a cooperative effort of parents, peers, and community with familial, religious, educative, economic, civic and governmental social institutions.

Hegel described the development of a self-concept with his famous Master and Slave dialectical allegory. He emphasized that a viable self-concept requires renunciation of self-seeking desire with substitutes defined by community and God. These authoritative Others assisted by social institutions of family, civil society, state and religion provide limiting channels for the use of personal freedom. Freud further elaborated upon the psychological dynamics of socialization. A self-concept is constructed by processes of identification with cultural norms and social roles transmitted by parents. They are the authoritative Others for the child who, by a process of introjection, acquires a self-concept or personality with particular attitudes, dispositions and values. What Hegel described as a necessary renunciation of unlimited self-seeking, Freud described as a psychological process of repression of particular antisocial desires.

Socialization, although mainly a non-rational natural process, becomes subject to some degree of control once it is understood as Hegel and Freud described it. The question arises as to what kind of self-concept one would prefer, if given the choice. Today, peer group and popular culture transmitted by the mass media have a greater influence upon the development of a self-concept than ever before. Different self-concepts emerge depending upon the relative predominance of parents, religion, government and competing ideologies. The perennial question is what kind of self-concept shall prevail in the self-objectifying work of individuals whose lives transmit culture. Competition in socialization raises important philosophical questions. Which cultural norms and social roles are worthy of self-identification? Can this process be rational as opposed to irrational or non-rational? What kind of self-concept and self-projection result from introjecting a non-authoritarian as opposed to an authoritarian Other? Since the aim of self-objectification is dealienation, a self-concept maximizing it is preferable. So is one maximizing self-realization of human potentiality. Freed from the domination of the alien Other(s), self-existence can become authentic and alienating finitude can be dealt with by the fully developed power of an autonomous self.

Socialization is a work of developing a self-concept enabling dealienating self-objectification. Socially driven negating processes progressively develop a self-concept from narcissism to a completely socialized self. Antisocial desires and behavior is prohibited by saying *no* and coercively by a variety of punishments. The process continues until renunciation of certain self-seeking desires is internalized. Overt social prohibition is then no longer necessary as the self punishes itself with guilt for a violation of its *ego ideal.* Both Hegel and Freud understood the process of socialization to be dialectical. Both understood that no desire could be completely renounced. A substitute is always found for desires that are socially prohibited and self-renounced. The substitutes define a social self-concept. This poses some interesting questions about the nature of the process and nature of the substitute. Expressed with Freudian language, is a sublimated desire merely the original in disguise, or has it been transformed into something completely different? Within the process of socialization, is a *choice* of substitute possible?

Socialization transforms primitive desires by creating substitutes. The desires of a socialized self are expanded in number and complexity. Such a self is often called sophisticated in tastes and lifestyle. A socialized self has identified with cultural norms and social roles provided by various social institutions. Both Hegel and Freud understood that identification is a natural process requiring training of the young through coercive rewards and punishments. In effect, Hegelian philosophy provides a rational justification for identification. Cultural norms and social roles ought to be chosen because of their universal applicability and ontologically superior source, namely, community and God.

Integration of self with community and God aside, what is important here is the suggestion that identification can be a rational choice. At first glance, this view might seem naive; a simple reflection of an uncritical ancient attitude toward established cultural authority. Yet, where identification is formed by rational choice, neither the source nor the content of what the self identifies with is alien to the powers of its essential nature, namely rationality and freedom. Self-realization not imposed by alien authoritative Others can express an authentic potentiality for being. A rational identification has explicitly expressible reasons why it is worthy that are derived from personal experience of alternatives. These have been worked through and thought over. When one identification is seen as better than another for good reasons, the mechanism for sustaining it is free of unconscious unresolved oppositions. Then the social product of identification is not unstable and liable to disintegration. Rationally based identification is not a fiction, but a fact for both youths and adults alike.

Freudian Repression versus Hegelian Sublation

Alienation is signified by the presence of desire or the frustrated satisfaction of it. Desire is painful and its satisfaction pleasurable. The development of a self-concept enabling dealienating self-objectification begins with an alienation of certain antisocial desires. Powerful authoritative Others frustrate their satisfaction. A narcissistic self is forced to develop when the parent says *no.* An egoistic self is likewise forced to develop in particular channels by moral or legal prohibition of particular socially harmful self-seeking behavior. Alienated satisfaction of certain antisocial desires force the self to develop in ways that sustain survival of the individual and group. Freudian repression is a species of alienation, since it denies some desired object that would satisfy an instinct, urge, impulse, need, or drive, however named.

Both Hegel and Freud believed the alienation of certain desires necessary to construct a self capable of dealienating self-objectification in a social setting. While Hegel described socialization as sublation, Freud described it as repression. These processes are very differently conceived and have very different results with respect to alienation. However, both end with a substitute for alienated antisocial desires and a socialized self-concept that sustains civilization. Whether created by spiritual sublation or instinctual repression, the great works of civilization originate from how antisocial desires are treated; whether suppressed, repressed, sublimated or entirely transformed with substitutes.

Freud applied a mechanistic model to socialization. It consists of forces and mechanisms which resolve forces to act in specific directions with specific strengths, analogous to the vectored forces of physics. Psychic forces operate unconsciously and in a non-rational fashion like the physical forces of nature. They coerce behavior. That part of the psyche that is conscious, self-conscious, rational and free is essentially inconsequential. Negating psychic forces maintaining repression may or may not be successful. When not successful, neurosis results and self-development is arrested with the psyche fixated upon unresolved conflicting desires. Psychic conflicts may be controlled by repression, but are never reconciled.

With repression, instinctual denial is traumatic. The desired object is forgotten, placed into the unconscious realm of the mind where it is operated upon by natural non-rational mechanisms of association and displacement. The psyche contains ideas *cathected* with energy acting as forces. However, the substitute for the prohibited desire that repression puts in place is never completely successful. The illicit displaced desires reappear disguised in various ways as eccentric or neurotic behavior.

Although individuals are civilized and socialized by repression, its process remains unstable, a result of unresolved conflict. Civilization then acquires only a paper-thin veneer in danger of disintegration with neurotic individuals alienated from their natural desires. In effect the self is submerged in a culture alienating an expression of its true nature. The conflict between instinctual desire and social prohibition is continuous, taking a great deal of psychic energy to maintain. Unconscious repression of prohibited desire is maintained by coercion, by natural forces in or out of balance which act upon the self as if it were a physical object without consciousness, rationality and freedom. Since there is no final resolution to the conflict, neurotic symptoms may result. Individuals are always in danger of becoming sick, eccentric, or behaviorally dysfunctional in some way. Civilization with its great works of *sublimation* is at best tenuously maintained at great cost in psychic energy and with the prospect of disintegration with outbreaks of mass neurosis.

Repression maintains alienation with unchangeable forces and desires that can never be transformed, but merely overlaid with partially successful substitutes. However, with a spiritual model of the psyche as rational, free and self-conscious, any desire can be transformed and completely satisfied. For example, although primitive sexual desire is physiological, the quality of pleasure and satisfaction are very different within a marital relationship in which there exists self-giving love and personal commitment to family. These social relationships give sexual desire an enhanced significance, quality and value. When present, there can be the most complete satisfaction of sexual desire without maintaining any alienating opposition of primitive desire with social demands. For these are not overlaid as substitutes for satisfying primitive desire. So, there is no basis for an unstable compromise substitution. Primitive desire is completely satisfied; enhanced and expanded socially in a way that transforms it into something different. The original form of primitive desire is not retained. Thus, when socialization is conceived as sublation rather than repression, primitive desires are transformed rather than retained with inadequate substitutes.

Hegel uses the term *sublation* to refer to the process of reconciling or overcoming alienation. The concept of sublation presupposes alienation and expresses dealienation as a process involving negativity and dialectical progression. A primitive unity of self and Other is followed by separation or loss, which is a dialectical stage of alienation. A process of recovery of loss ensues by means of a negating conflict, struggle and opposition. The contradiction of the self and separated alien Other is resolved by incorporating the Other as part of the self, which Hegel considered a rational synthesis re-establishing the lost unity. With reconciliation effected, contradiction is eliminated, truth secured, the self enlarged in meaning and being with a higher level Notion. This process goes on existentially and according to a logic of thought. The new Notion and unity of self and Other is a return to the originally implicit primitive unity, resulting from an existential and logical working through of the alienating opposition. Opposing differences are reconciled in a higher level universal Notion.

Sublation reflects the wisdom of recognizing the validity of conflicting demands with a logical compromise incorporating both, while being different from either in some significant way. The logical advance resides in the difference. Therefore, sublation describes a process we are intimately familiar with in everyday life. Nevertheless, sublation is more in its implication. It means that a whole is implicit within any part and reachable by a dialectical process driven by ontological negativity. The part is something finite, expressing the finitude of life. A particular part, signifying the universal, is an instance pointing toward a larger whole. Thus, the process of dealienation or movement of sublation, has a Hegelian telos, namely, to reveal and express a larger infinite whole.

Contrary to Freud, Hegel treated the psyche as a spiritual being whose primary attributes are consciousness, rationality and freedom. As with repression, negativity drives psychic processes, but in accordance with a rational dialectic. Sublation is a different process of dealienation with a different outcome. The behavioral substitute of repressed desire is a partially satisfactory compromise without complete resolution of opposing instinctual and societal demands. Alienation remains in force with a self bifurcated between conscious and unconscious, but with occasional subconscious communication. However, sublation reconciles desire with social prohibition through a process of development consciously driven by rationality and freedom. The outcome of sublation is the complete satisfaction of the original desire expanded in significance to include the social as well. The self is required to transform and expand its desires to include the social. This is what the original opposition truly signified. Within a social context, desire is expanded and transformed. So, for example, sexual desire is channeled by marriage into sustaining a social unit, the family.

By becoming more inclusive, desire comes to serve the social, which transcends the self. Being a parent allows the self to satisfy its sexual desire and many other desires resulting from the creation of a family. Community is also sustained in the process. So, sexual desire, rather than being displaced by repression into the unconscious and remaining an antisocial force, can be transformed to include other social desires. In this way desire can be completely satisfied and any conflict with social demands successfully resolved. Social institutions, particularly religious, assist the self to transform primitive sexual desire by providing moral norms and family social roles for self-identification. Sacraments such as marriage are provided to those aspiring to be a parent and create a family.

Desire is a constant in the process of dealienation. It never changes its alienating impetus or dealienating aim, but its object can change. Desire can be transformed in two ways. It can remain the same with a substitution of its object. Freud thought of repression in this way. Instinctual drives always remain the same, but are sublimated with substitute objects. However, it may be possible for desire to change with a substitute object. Certainly, the significance of a particular desire changes with a substitute object. Moreover, with this the quality of desire cannot remain the same. It is experienced as something transcending its original meaning. This is what Hegelian sublation implies. When sublated, the being and meaning of something is transformed. It incorporates the original with an additional difference. It is more differentiated, richer in meaning, significance, value and quality of experience. Might it not be possible for desire with a substitute object to be a transformed desire, which possesses only traces of its original meaning? When primitive desire is sublated, it is literally transformed with a socially constructive aim. Primitive desire then gets its universal and transcendent significance different from what it was originally. Socialization of desire does more than overlay it with a social aim providing its original primitive expression with a thin social veneer.

The mechanisms of repression are non-rational, irrational, and coercive. A conflict of opposing psychic forces deflects the aim of sexual desire to produce a secondary byproduct, namely civilization. Primitive desire is displaced and sublimated. That first negation of primitive desire is never sublated and so dealienation is impossible. A repressed self cannot develop in a way that satisfies its whole nature as both a sexually aggressive and social being. How could successful dealienation be expected without the application of rationality and freedom to the alienating situation? Freud acknowledged psychoanalysis interminable, not curative.

Hegelian sublation provides the possibility of successful dealienation. A sublating compromise integrates the opposing demands of primitive desire and social prohibition into a new desire with different significance and value, which can be fully satisfied through self-objectifying work. In addition, this process accomplishes dealienation by means of exercising the essential powers of the self, rationality and freedom. Self-identification with that which satisfies opposing desires is a prerequisite for dealienating self-objectification. Moreover, that self-identification must be rational, or self-consciously chosen for good reasons. Hegel thought of the more inclusive goals reconciling self and community as pre-established by God, traditional authority, culture and social institutions such as religion, family, civil society and the state. They offer the norms and social roles with which the individual can rationally identify. A commitment of personal freedom in service to them purportedly allows complete self-realization and complete connection to a larger social and cosmic whole to which each individual belongs as an actively sustaining integral part.

Alienation and Identification

The psychic product of self-identification with a cultural norm or social role has been variously called identity, self-concept, ego ideal, and social self. Whatever called, it is formed by the alienation of desire by an authoritative Other(s). Its demands and prohibitions are alien to the self who is forced to accommodate with a substitute satisfying its desire. Even though the self gets its identity from the interpersonal dynamics of a dialectical opposition between its own desires and those of the alien authoritative Other(s), its identity is not reducible to what the Other says it is or acknowledges it to be. For the self is a work in progress meeting its own needs and desires in a social context. Thus, self-identity continuously changes with the particular conditions of alienating finitude and self-existence.

Socialization is a continuous process of self-identification. What or who the self identifies with determines its self-concept which when self-projected by self-objectifying work has alienating or dealienating consequences. What the self identifies with are cultural norms. Who the self identifies with are social roles. Both cultural norms and social roles provide the self with an identity. This is obviously true. But, the question Hegelian philosophy raises, is whether identity can only be secured by identifying with norms and social roles established by authoritative Others such as parents, peer group, popular culture, community, educative, religious, economic, civic and governmental social institutions. Yet, cultural norms and social roles do not appear to be pre-established by authoritative Others as Hegel believed. For both continuously change as witnessed by an older generation unable to understand the lifestyle of its youth. If cultural norms and social roles were pre-established, then there could be no new lifestyles. However, the evidence is overwhelmingly to the contrary.

The source of changing norms and roles is to be found in needs and desires not predictable in advance of self-existence. This implies that the very process of dealienating self-existence generates novel cultural norms and social roles. From an existential perspective, the self has a far greater degree of autonomy and authenticity than Hegel or Freud suspected. Its being encompasses far more than any pre-established definition of it by an Other, no matter what or who the Other might be. And, since the self must existentially create its own identity, its being is far more than any particular social definition imposed upon it. Thus, it is not necessary to have authoritative Others alien to the self completely define and determine what or who it shall be. Doing so often has alienating consequences.

What or who the self identifies with will determine how it is alienated and set the task of dealienation. Hegel thought of self-concept in terms of historical figures of self-consciousness progressively developed in an interpersonal dialectic in which some desire is alienated. A self-identification with some norm or social role then presents a substitute desire that can be satisfied. The transformed self-concept is projected and objectified in a new interpersonal relationship. Again, some other desire is alienated and the process is repeated with a progressively more socialized self. The dialectical progression is from narcissistic to egoistic to social self as different self-identified norms are chosen such as power, wealth, honor and virtue. They become guides for the dealienating work of self-objectification and so are, in effect, ideal masters of freedom.

Using Hegel's allegorical Master and Slave dialectic as the archetype of social analysis, it is recapitulated between seventeenth century Nobleman and absolute Monarch. Both are socially defined and sustained in being by each other. The Nobleman renounces his freedom to do whatever he personally desires, ceding it to an absolute Monarch he flatters, addresses as *your highness* and pledges fealty. In return he acquires honor and titles bestowed by the Monarch to whose will he is bound and at whose pleasure he serves. Replacing wealth, honor has become the substitute object of desire with which the Nobleman self-identifies. Nevertheless, an identity provided by an Other is always found alienating in unforeseen ways. The Nobleman's identity is contingent upon the inclination, gratuity, will, or even whim of the Monarch. Being so, the Nobleman's identity is reified, inauthentic and outside his control. His alienated freedom is discovered to have alienating consequences. For the absolute Monarch has self-identified with narcissism and egoism which is an expression of absolute freedom without social limits.

When misused in self-seeking for the unlimited satisfaction of personal desire, the Monarch's freedom is misdirected into perversions of sadism and masochism with evil consequences for his subordinates. Of course, such consequences are self-destructive for the Monarch. There are several messages forthcoming from this interpersonal Hegelian dialectic. Any self-concept constructed solely by an authoritative Other will reify the self who cannot recognize itself as its own doing. Disabled from exercising its freedom for itself alienates it from realizing its authentic potentiality for being. Self-identifying with any social role which either alienates freedom or possesses unlimited freedom has alienating consequences. Social structures organized upon alienating freedom to a single individual are prone to disintegration. Self- identifying with norms such as wealth, power, honor, virtue and so forth can have alienating consequences. Self-identification is less alienating, less self-isolating and more successful when it is more inclusive of the needs and desires of one's fellows.

The reification of the self by alien Other(s) is also a loss of autonomy. When the Nobleman senses this about himself, he is conscious of his alienation as a feeling of humiliation and powerlessness. The noble self-consciousness

> ... finds that, as regards its own ego, its own proper and peculiar actuality, it is outside itself and belongs to an other, finds its personality as such dependent on the chance personality of another, on the accident of a moment, of an arbitrary caprice, or some other utterly irrelevant circumstance.[2]

The natural response to this impotence of the self is to revolt against the absolute Monarch who keeps the Nobleman in thrall. A *base consciousness*, as Hegel calls it, becomes ascendant. Obviously, the Nobleman has discovered that alienating his freedom to an absolute Monarch was a mistake. There is the sense that a reified self lacking autonomy does not correspond with the true identity of self as a free human being with dignity. The drive to express this authentic identity cannot be suppressed.

As the dialectic of self-existence between Monarch and Nobleman continues, the self-sacrifice of the latter is discovered to include a larger social whole transcending the self. From a deposed absolute Monarch, the allegiance of Noblemen finds a substitute in the state sustained by their collective will and energy. The state then becomes a substitute object for self-identification by those who seek honor through self-sacrificial service to it. This in turn paved the way for ever more inclusive self-identifications with culture, law and God. Hegel thought of this ideal Platonic ascent as rationally driven and dealienating.

Socrates self-identified with reason and moderation, virtues of classical Greek culture and norms for self-conduct believed essential for happiness. Acquiring a virtuous self-concept is an arduous work of self-discipline recognized by one's fellows as admirable, since it expresses common cultural values and ideals difficult to achieve. Virtue is therefore a distinction of noble character. The practice of virtue by outstanding individuals can mitigate an alienation of self from community. For virtues are already publicly acknowledged as having universal merit transcending that of an isolated private self. A practice of virtue places personal freedom in service to something that can build community. However, Hegel thought identification with and practice of virtue insufficient to establish social cohesion, since its effectiveness is set voluntarily only by the example of exceptional individuals. Most cannot be relied upon to have the strength of character, courage and discipline required to universalize virtue. Its practice is therefor not obligatory and compelling for everyone. If rationality cannot make virtue obligatory, then non-rational coercion in the form of custom and law is necessary to sustain community.

It may be believed that total identification and participation in social life signifies an absence of alienation. This belief is plausible, but false. Complete unconscious submersion in the group, or Hegelian *Sittlichkeit*, can be alienating as witnessed by totalitarian societies. Hegel understood that self-consciousness is compelled to dialectically develop beyond *Sittlichkeit*. When culture or community poses alienating conditions, an unconscious identification and participation is tantamount to being manipulated and coerced by an Other alien to oneself. The suppression of anything beyond the norms and social roles prescribed for the self by traditional authoritative Others often denies certain needs and desires vital to self-realization. Such repression may end in neurosis with unnecessary and unacceptable loss to the self and community.

Conversely, it is also commonly thought that a lack of identification and participation indicates alienation. This belief is also plausible, but false. For nobody would voluntarily either identify with or participate in anything that thwarts his own needs and desires. Making social participation a virtue and inculcating it as a duty does not avoid alienation. For individuals must be personally convinced that their participation can make a difference for themselves or others. If not, their response will be apathetic. The self will opt out of what it considers irrelevant to its perceived needs and desires. Alienated from certain norms and social roles, individuals in a free society will proceed with their lives unhindered, and if they are numerous enough, will by so doing transform society by example and with an authentic expression of different values. Of course, if sufficiently hindered, they will rebel and try to change alienating social conditions.

Alienation can be described as an initial negation whereby something desired is denied to or renounced by the self. A first step in the process of dealienation is then to identify with a substitute that compensates for what has been alienated. When identification is made, the self-expression of desire is channeled to a substitute object replacing the prohibited original. Ensuing behavior tests whether the identification promotes successful dealienation. If it does, then the original opposition is resolved and desire is satisfied. If not, alienation persists with the substitute, or even with a series of different ones. Hegel described a historical series of failed self-identifications. With each failure, what is identified with remains alien in some way.

For example, the self doesn't know what to do with its own freedom. Its culture or the state turns out to be unworthy of its allegiance. Divine perfection is beyond its human grasp. In every case, the object of identification does not allow a complete expression of the human essence, its freedom and rationality. Self-objectification cannot be completed. One's identity is not confirmed through a public acknowledgment of who he is corresponding to a self-recognition of what he did.

Culture is created and sustained by the lives of individuals. In order to receive the benefits of culture, the individual must sacrifice unlimited satisfaction of personal desires and unlimited self-seeking. The renunciation or alienation of these aspects of individuality is a necessary first negation in a process of forming culture. The process of finding an adequate substitute is a work of identification by the individual. This work can be non-rational, coerced by rewards and punishments provided within the family or through other social institutions such as religion or the state. Educative institutions also provide indoctrination and training necessary for a self-identification with culture. Of course, there are always customs, traditions, and laws. Identification can also be non-coercive as when one is convinced of the value of one's culture upon rational grounds. In this case, reasons can be provided to support cultural beliefs and practices. This is a sophisticated way of making a cultural identification. Whether the identification is made non-rationally or rationally, once made, the individual has found the necessary substitute social self replacing a narcissism and egoism, which do not sustain culture.

With a cultural identification, the individual proceeds to create and sustain culture as his own work and with his own freedom. This work aims at dealienation. It is a negation of already alienated primitive self-seeking desire: a second negation that affirms culture through the life work of the individual. The satisfaction of primitive unsocialized desire, first renounced, is recovered by the substitute replacing it. If the substitute is inadequate, alienation remains as unresolved repression or neurosis described by Freud. However, if the substitute brings adequate satisfaction of renounced desire, then there is a genuine resolution of the opposition of primitive desire with culture. There occurs a sublation in which primitive desire finds satisfaction within a social context as when sexual gratification is achieved by parental identification, marriage and the creation of a family.

Dealienation is successfully completed when the individual's identification is followed by successful behavior both satisfying personal desire while realizing a social aim. The norms and social roles with which the individual has successfully identified set limits to individuality. However, their substitution also allows and even requires a free exercise of individuality. One can perform ones role well or poorly. And in performing it, culture is sustained by a participant contributing to it, connecting its past with its future and self with humanity, past and future. This connection is buried deeply within human genes. It is given to everyone as his or her natural potential, and yet is formed deliberately by the life work of individuals who are rational and free.

Authenticity is derived generally from the dealienating endeavor of self-existence. Simply stated, authenticity is a self-expression of rationality and freedom. Just as authenticity is necessary for dealienation, so it is also a reinforced outcome of successful dealienation. A self is authentic when its being is its doing, not the direct or indirect doing of an alien Other. Liberated from domination by anything alien to its own nature, the self can be authentic. The essential meaning of authenticity is to make something an expression of oneself.

One way of being authentic is to identify with a social norm or role, projecting it with self-objectifying work. Hegel thought God's laws and pre-established social roles require self-identification and are the necessary bases of self-objectification giving freedom its legitimate purpose. From such a view, it might be thought that any successful identification is sufficient to establish authenticity. However, this is false when the Other with which the self identifies remains alien to its essential nature, or produces alienating consequences when self-projected and objectified. Whether the Other alienates in these ways is determined by the very process of self-identification. When it proceeds irrationally, or is non-rationally coerced by natural rewards and punishments, what or whom the self has identified with remains an alien Other opposed to some aspect of its nature, be it rationality, freedom, need or desire. Without satisfying all of these, the self is dominated in some way by an alien Other. Authentic self-expression and self-realization are then not possible.

Authenticity requires self-identification, uncoerced by an Other; a free self-conscious choice with reasons and evaluated consequences. The alienating Other cannot remain hidden. It must be identified, understood and dealt with in a fully conscious manner thus providing the possibility of resolving the opposition of self with alien Other within self or external to it. It is certain that dealienation cannot occur without meeting the conditions for authenticity. Of course, there is no guarantee that the consequences of self-objectification, even by an authentic self, will not be alienating. Nevertheless, it is clearly more likely that dealienation will be successful when self-identification is rational and free rather than coerced by an Other alien to the self.

Irrational or non-rational self-identification always runs the risk of generating alienating oppositions within the self or between it and its fellows. An example of irrational identification would be the fanatic whose mission is to kill enemies by a deliberate sacrifice of his own life. Identification is certainly complete in this case. But to alienate oneself from life itself is an irrational self-objectification that does not resolve the opposition of the fanatic to his alien Other, the enemy. For identification to work as a step in a process of successful dealienation, the identification must not be irrational. It must be capable of successful execution. Non-rational identification fares no better. For it runs the same risk of not resolving opposition with the alien Other. The most common example is a child identifying non-rationally with a dysfunctional parent thereby becoming dysfunctional in a similar way.

Dealienation is unsuccessful under various circumstances. It may be that the culture does not offer anything believed worthy of identification by the individual. Cultural norms and social roles then appear as Other to the self who feels estranged and isolated from the culture. It offers nothing to truly satisfy needs, or what it does offer is irrelevant to them. No self-seeking desire can be renounced in favor of what is deemed unworthy. If identification with a substitute is coerced, then it cannot have the authenticity conferred by a deliberate self-conscious rational choice. For, since some Other imposes the identification, the substitute is alien to the self. This would be the case where indoctrination occurs by propaganda or punishment such as terror. Obviously, identification by non-rational or irrational methods can fail when attempted, or fail by its unintended consequences. If a substitute for primitive desire cannot be found or does not work when it is found, alienation persists in another form. For the substitute must be equally as personally satisfying as the original to be rationally chosen. If the substitute is non-rationally imposed or irrationally chosen, it must be at least partially as satisfying as what is renounced.

A process of negation between self and Other generally describes appropriation. The self temporally alters its being, becoming Other than what it once was. An appropriation of the alien Other is a good Hegelian beginning for understanding dealienation. However, this definition is incomplete. For, it could mean that the self merely appropriates something alien to itself. Consequently, its being would consist of unreconciled oppositions or a bifurcated self, acknowledged by Hegel and Freud, even if differently described. Therefore, it must be the nature of the appropriation that would determine whether alienation remains or dealienation is successful.

Appropriating the Other, when understood as a process of identification has several aspects: identification with *what* or *whom*, the manner in which it is carried out and its consequences. If the *what* or *who* remains alien to the self, then self-identification does not permit successful dealienation. A self that renounces its own desires by identifying with a substitute provided by an authoritative Other may remain alienated from what it renounced and alienated by the consequences for self-existence of the dicta of the authoritative Other. Identifications are always tested by their consequences, which are found to be alienating or dealienating for self-existence. In addition, if the identification serving as a substitute for an antisocial desire fails, then alienation may well be compounded. For neither the substitute nor the prohibited desire can be satisfied. Moreover, the consequences of repressing desire with an alienating substitute are devastating to the self. It becomes disabled, neurotic, as described by Freudian repression.

The Hegelian dialectic has the self continuously becoming Other. Yet at each stage, self-consciousness again finds itself alienated in a new way. This implies that merely becoming Other does not signify dealienation. The authoritative Other, Hegelian community or God for example, must meet certain conditions for successful dealienation. Such conditions are embedded in the very nature of the self. First, it is a creature of universal needs associated with survival and well-being. Second, each self has particular desires; many of which are different from other selves. And, of course, the self has its essential powers of rationality and freedom allowing it to cope with the alienating conditions of its existence. A self whose being is both authentic and autonomous then marks successful dealienation. When self-identification is uncoerced and meets the test of self-existence, it is authentic and autonomous. Autonomy and authenticity cannot be separated, just as freedom and rationality cannot be separated. For both bespeak a self who can think and act for itself. An autonomous self is rational in an existential, creative and problem solving sense. The self then is not rational in a rule-bound sense; not compelled to obey some Hegelian logic of Ideas, pre-established for self-existence by the dicta of authoritative Others alien to self, be they social institutions, the state or God.

The Other, whatever or whoever it is, defines an alienated self. Dealienation is a process in which the self appropriates the Other by becoming Other than it was in the past or is in the present. However, this Other, whatever or whoever it is, can remain alien Other or make the self into an alien Other. Where appropriating the Other involves self-identification with cultural norms and social roles, certain conditions are required for successful dealienation. Self-identification coerced by non-rational or irrational means makes the appropriated

Other alien. For it is imposed contrary to rationality and freedom, powers of selfhood demanded by it for dealienation. An alien Other is then superimposed upon its true needs and desires.

Where self-identification is rational, it is non-coercive, freely decided and relevant to satisfying the needs and desires of self-existence. An Other appropriated by rational self-identification cannot be alien to the self, since it is a product of its own essential nature and dealienating capacity. The result of rational self-identification is then necessarily an authentic self-realization of potentialities for being residing in the very nature of the self, not in the nature of an alien Other. A rational self-identification with the Other promotes both successful dealienation and authentic self-realization.

True, the Other often initiates a process of dealienation by a sometimes-painful socialization process. Still, the Other need not serve as a pre-established and fixed norm or role model, simply to be uncritically or slavishly imitated. Rather, the Other is suggested to the self with the purpose of assisting it to maximize its needs and desires within a structured social context. What or whom it suggests the self become enables it to realize its authentic hidden potentiality for being. So, when the self accepts the suggestion from the Other, it is not suppressing or repressing its essential nature. Neither is it simply obeying a law or the dictum of an unquestioned authoritative Other. For it is free to change the norm or role it has identified with to comport with the conditions of self-existence. This happens continuously as dealienation proceeds with a projected self-concept and self-objectifying work. The Other, then, does not dictate, but enables self-development and self-realization. The result is sometimes quite novel and not entirely predictable. It reflects the nature of the self as need, desire, rationality and freedom.

No doubt, the Other signifies alienation in a very general sense. No doubt, the Other when it is a social norm or role is necessary for dealienation. But that a socially based Other dealienates largely depends upon how it is appropriated. Any self-identification with the Other which is coerced by non-rational or irrational means will alienate the self from its essential dealienating powers, rationality and freedom. Self-existence will be neither autonomous nor authentic. True needs and desires will be disregarded. The self will not be able to realize its authentic potentiality for being.

On the other hand, rational self-identification expresses the essential nature of a self utilizing its powers in a way that satisfies all the requirements for successful dealienation. With rational identification, the self does not simply conform to what an alien Other dictates. The self is enabled by the Other to develop and realize its authentic potentiality for being. An immigrant American provides a good example of rational identification. He or she is alienated from satisfying certain needs or desires deemed essential to self-existence. America is that Other holding the promise of a better life for them and their progeny. Arriving past the Statue of Liberty at Ellis Island, New York, the immigrant has non-coercively and rationally identified with and acted to achieve the American dream of liberty and prosperity. When accepted for immigration and in taking the oath of allegiance, a process of linguistic and cultural assimilation begins that sloughs off the identity of the old country, replacing it with an American identity having attendant life-style consequences

Appropriation of the Other may take many forms such as possession, consumption, domination, and comprehension. When the Other is social, appropriating it takes the form of self-identification, be it non-rational, rational, irrational; and whether coercive or non-coercive. Hegel suggested that when an alien Other is appropriated by the self, it affirms its identity through what it negates. Furthermore, this occurs by acts of self-abnegation wherein the self relinquishes within it what opposes an authoritative Other alien to itself. Hegel and Freud thought this process essential to socializing the individual to form community and sustain civilization. Becoming Other by self-abnegation certainly signifies an endeavor of dealienation with respect to social demands. However, the endeavor cannot result in successful dealienation. For, by negating its own needs and desires the self becomes an Other alien to itself. Suppressed or repressed needs and desires do not permit any reconciliation with social demands. Instead, authentic self-expression and self-realization is crippled by operating with an alien self-concept which when projected and objectified neither satisfies authentic needs or desires nor the demand for rational freedom requisite for dealienation.

Social Roles and Alienation

Hegel once asserted of the individual,

> Unless he is a member of an authorized Corporation (and it is only by being authorized that an association becomes a Corporation), an individual is without rank or dignity, his isolation reduces his business to mere self-seeking, and his livelihood and satisfaction become insecure.[3]

Without a social role and certified membership in a social class, Hegel believed the self to be a nullity without any basis for self-objectification. Robbed of what is necessary for contributing to community, the implication is a profoundly alienated self. Dignity, or being a *somebody*, is conferred by self-objectifying work with a self-concept conforming to a universal social role pre-established by various authoritative Others. Membership or certification is accepted as public evidence of some standard of individual competence. This does not guarantee competence, since incompetent individuals are often certified by the mere fact of membership. Dignity, reputation, respect and esteem are still dependent upon notable accomplishment, upon what the self makes of the social roles offered to it.

Certified membership in a social class is not, of itself, enough to establish human dignity. The self might eschew certified membership in a social class with its standardized social roles, or even create a new social role, which contributes to community in unpredictable ways. This happens continuously with unorthodox methods of dealienation. Social roles do not have eternal life, but change continuously depending upon prevailing social conditions and needs. Role stereotypes can become obsolete and are often abandoned in time. When oppressive, social roles may be deliberately abandoned. Yet, this does not portend social dissolution. In fact, it may just as well be a harbinger of social renewal. Rather than being exclusively provided by an authoritative social Other, human dignity resides in the power of the self - its freedom and rationality to delineate - even under oppressive social circumstances.

Reducing the self to its universal social class or role ignores its creative social role. Now this does not deny the obvious merits of class membership, social certification or social contribution by identification with standardized social roles. While necessary to sustaining community, they also may offer a measure of satisfying self-realization. Performing the role of parent well can provide enormous satisfaction. But, to claim that membership in a social class or performing standardized social roles are the only options for satisfying self-realization is a distorting exaggeration with socially alienating consequences for exceptional individuals.

Human beings are more than bees with specialized functions for the hive. The self is more than its abstract social function. A Hegelian universality of social institutions and roles does not capture the multidimensional being of the whole personality. The merit of social roles and institutions depends upon what they in fact do, and must be judged on that basis. Otherwise, for example, bureaucracy or bureaucrat could be falsely glorified. That they are socially dysfunctional would be overlooked by not examining their built-in incentive to waste human and non-human resources, their rule-bound inflexibility and the unintended consequences they produce. Such facts are masked by unnecessarily glorifying the universal and asserting its ontological superiority to the individual. This Hegelian abstraction has alienating consequences. For alienating finitude is necessarily experienced by the particular circumstances of a particular self-existence. Conceiving of universal social institutions and universal prescribed social roles as superior to the self alienates its capacity for dealienation and denies the possibility of harm, or even evil, emanating from the fabric of social institutions, roles and behavioral norms.

Civil society places individuals into a class and offers a wide range of social roles, particularly those that are occupational. Each role, publicly defined, is universal since it can apply to anyone. Identifying oneself with a social role and objectifying oneself with it has beneficial consequences. First, the individual secures an identity as exemplar of the role. He is a *somebody*, a person of substance publicly recognized and respected. Secondly, the individual contributes to a system of satisfying human needs. Authoritative Other(s) pre-establish and prescribe social roles for self-identification. Playing or projecting a social role is a work of self-objectification whereby the self recognizes itself to be what it is publicly recognized as being. Its sense of worth comes from the respect or even honor accorded by the authoritative Other(s) to its successful role-playing. One is a good father, businessman and so forth. Moreover, the converse is true. Poor role-playing can bring opprobrium.

Nevertheless, playing a social role can be self-alienating when coerced into doing so; when driven merely by what *they* want the self to be; when the self has no aptitude for the role; or when other choices of what the self could be are excluded. Playing the role of a good bureaucrat can alienate by frustrating the needs of those intended to be served. A rule-bound bureaucrat lives in a completely rationalized predictable environment and is obligated by the role played to ignore factors that would otherwise make a critical difference in outcome. Behaving otherwise, the bureaucrat is stigmatized as a misfit penalized with exclusion and social isolation. Knowing this possibility, the buck is passed up the line. Personal responsibility and accountability disappear. The innate power of rationality and freedom possessed by the self is restricted, if not denied by such stereotyped role-playing. A self who projects a bureaucratic self-concept is not whole, but fragmented with its autonomy and authenticity set aside.

How role-playing effects the authenticity or autonomy of the self determines the extent of its dealienating capability. If the self behaves only as *they* prescribe and not from its own choice and conviction, its character loses both autonomy and authenticity. It may not itself be free, but live merely a shadow life dictated by the Other(s). Such considerations indicate that role-playing can cut both ways. By contributing to the larger social whole, role-playing dealienates. But, if not expressing the autonomy and authenticity of the self, role playing can just as well alienate the self from realizing its own desires and unique potentiality. Contemporary examples abound of how oppressive and restrictive social role stereotypes can be. For example, every woman is destined to be nurturing wife and mother and not much else, like it or not, and every man cannot nurture, but is destined to be the breadwinner, like it or not.

Notes

1. Hegel, G. W. F. (1967) The Phenomenology of Mind (J. B. Baillie, Trans.). New York, NY: Harper and Row, 427.

2. Ibid., 537.

3. Hegel, G. W. F. (1977) Hegel's Philosophy of Right (T. M. Knox, Trans.). New York, NY: Oxford University Press, 153.

Chapter Four

Freedom

Freedom and Rationality

Part of the trouble with freedom lies with misunderstanding what it signifies. In discourse, its use is often vague or ambiguous. Hegel noted,

> But that this term "Freedom," without further qualification, is an indefinite, and incalculable ambiguous term; and that while that which it represents is the *ne plus ultra* of attainment, it is liable to an infinity of misunderstandings, confusions and errors, and to become the occasion for all imaginable excesses - has never been more clearly known and felt than in modern times.[1]

A self who can think, choose and act in the world and with other selves is free. Primitive freedom is a natural capacity or power of the self with many significations. There is *freedom from* something limiting choice and action, which connotes personal liberty or liberation. Then there is *freedom to do* something, which connotes self-empowerment and self-realization. Freedom can also be a condition of self-existence wherein thought and self-activity are uncoerced by an Other alien to the self, whatever or whomever the Other might be. Any form of coercion generates a response of the self that defines its primitive freedom and develops it. Limits or restrictions placed upon the self define its alienating finitude, experienced as need and desire for something. Thus, freedom cannot signify an absence of an existentially encountered limit or restriction. No! Freedom is a self-response to alienating finitude. A coercive Other that restricts or limits is necessary for freedom to exist and develop as a power of the self. Moreover, when it does, it is a self-realizing power.

Ontological negativity is necessary to think, to be and to become. Taking the form of intentional self-activity, ontological negativity signifies freedom. It is a capacity to intentionally become or change something. To be conscious of the world or self, and to think, is to intend an Other distinct from self. Thought is an activity that intends the Other, representing it with symbols possessing implication. Just as thought is a negating activity of symbolic signification, so also is freedom a negating activity with conative intention directing self-existence in the world. From the perspective of ontological negativity, thought and being are continuous. Freedom creates this continuity, extending it in either direction. Thought, even at the highest level of logical abstraction is translatable to being by existentially directed intentional self-activity. Human freedom is commonly manifested by self-activity following thought. The reverse also occurs. Just as thinking makes one free, so freedom makes one think.

That freedom resides in rationality has been asserted through the ages from ancient philosophy to contemporary psychology. Without thought, freedom is not possible. Freedom is encountered in the very activity of thinking that represents reality of the Other(s) through a public language and with abstract symbolic codes. Imaginary models of reality can be constructed by thinking which contemplate logical possibilities, anticipate future events and behavioral consequences. Strategies relating chosen means to resulting ends can be formulated to secure human purposes. The ability to think secures freedom in both its negative and positive aspects. Reasoning allows the self to obtain or avoid consequences, satisfy desires, achieve aims, and successfully deal with the Other(s). Thinking can liberate the self from the alienating Other thus allowing it to transform its world and even itself to correspond with its desires and satisfy its needs. Moreover, reasoning provides the freedom to behave in ways not pre-determined by natural inclination or emotional impulse. Gratification can be postponed, given a different priority, or even suppressed to secure certain advantages.

Since it occurs as a natural private activity without immediate behavioral manifestation, to think for oneself can never be eradicated or socially suppressed. This fact implies that thought is inherently free. To think is to be free and this cannot be eliminated or controlled. Even in its most primitive form, self-activity in the world and with others is an extension of thought. Self-existence demonstrates a continuity of thought and behavior. The sense of being *free from* something signifies an avoidance of alienation as restriction to thought or self-activity. Yet, by negation, being *free from* implies being *free to*, which signifies freedom as an exercise of self-activity. Freedom has many nuances of meaning. Its narrowest sense is mere abstract negativity: something not desired, denial, refusal, rebellion, or just saying *no*. However, its broadest sense implies rationality and knowledge. Between both senses lies a development of freedom from primitive non-rational and irrational narcissism to a highly rational socialization. This fact is demonstrated by distinguishing between the fact of desire and what is desirable. For the former lacks reasons while the latter is a conclusion with reasons formed from an evaluative process of self-existence.

Rational freedom is the most important dealienating process defining self-existence. This very process has an infinite potential for revealing being and its true meaning, if not creating being by human self-activity. The breadth of dealienating responses is vast and can be generally classified as non-rational, irrational and rational. Successful dealienation is more assured when self-activity responds rationally. For rationality broadens the field within which self-activity operates. A greater number of factors influencing an intended outcome are considered. Contingencies and consequences are evaluated. Deliberation prior to choice of alternatives for self-activity represents the ideal case maximizing chances of success in a finite world. Non-rational responses driven by natural inclination and desire succeed often, but not always. Irrational responses driven by capricious impulse rarely succeed and almost never in the long run. A narcissistic self stands little chance of achieving successful dealienation, since its self-activity tends to be non-rational or irrational.

The primitive aim of human freedom is the satisfaction of natural desire. As such, freedom is a means for all the basics related to survival. It serves natural instincts, drives and needs. It is the most primary response to alienation, and a basis for successful dealienation. Initially, freedom is exercised in goal seeking behavior. It is most dramatically demonstrated in self-seeking activity driven by a desire for something and the thought of how to secure it to satisfy a need of the organism. Any successful exercise of freedom requires a fairly high degree of rationality. In fact without rationality, freedom is liable to failure. Considered as mere means without rational direction, freedom is ambiguous. It can be used to secure anything and so is a potentiality for either good or evil. Therefore, the critical question about freedom always concerns the purpose of its use. In fact, the value of freedom is determined by the purposes it serves and the consequences of its application. These can in large part be determined by character or personality. A narcissistic or egoistic self will use freedom in counter-productive ways stunting self-development, preventing self-realization and resulting in social isolation or worse. The same is true when freedom is misdirected by psychic compulsion, obsession, or when driven by sado-masochistic perversion. In such cases, the self is enslaved to non-rational or irrational forces that fixate development in dysfunctional patterns of behavior.

A completely dependent narcissistic self cannot be free. Neither can an independent egoistic self, pursuing its desires without regard to social consequences. In fact freedom is maximized and guaranteed by certain restrictions placed upon self-seeking that would cause unnecessary suffering and social disintegration. A self completely unconstrained has no freedom. Nobody ever had it or could possibly have it. For the existentially alienating conditions generative of freedom would be absent. Thus, *absolute freedom* is a theoretical fiction. Conceived as non-rational or irrational conatus, freedom becomes self-contradictory, resulting in bondage. If the self could get everything it wanted, freedom would have no meaning and would not signify anything about self-existence.

Absolute freedom can be understood to mean a self, unconditioned and unrestricted in satisfying its needs and desires. However, no such self can exist. Alienating finitude always has some specific content. Some limitation is to be overcome grounded in history, culture, environment, and the makeup of the self. Without encountering some real limit, there is no impetus to activate freedom and no aim for an exercise of its power. Without impetus and aim, freedom is meaningless. If freedom were absolute, there would be no need for it to exist or develop. Since absolute freedom contradicts finitude by implying an impossible absence of limit and necessity, any demand for absolute freedom is irrational. For existentialists such as Sartre, this was the case. He did not fully comprehend the Hegelian wisdom about freedom dialectically sublating necessity.

Human finitude signifies a discontinuity of thought and being. The self is beset by finitude. An alien Other is encountered and the self encounters itself as an alien Other. What and who the self is do not correspond with what and who it thinks it is. It must discover this through interacting with the alien Other, namely the world and other selves. The task of every self is to become Other, to respond to need and desire, and in so doing to realize a potentiality for being human. Therefore, human freedom consists of human activity to effect a change in being in accordance with rational intention. Freedom requires intentional self-activity driven by thought. Correctly conceived, freedom requires an integration and continuity of thought and action. Hegel thought of action as a special case of thought with both together effecting any distinctly human transformation of being. Pragmatism also recognized the intimate relationship between thought and action, emphasizing the latter contrary to the Hegelian idealistic emphasis upon the former.

Freedom and rationality are the twin pillars of western civilization. Both express the spiritual essence of being human. Together they define intelligent behavior and constitute the human power necessary for dealienation. The negativity of being in general and alienating finitude of self-existence in particular provides the impetus for their development within the individual and throughout history. Even if we do not know their precise relationship, we intuitively sense their connection. Taken singly, either can alienate the self. Without rationality, freedom is impossible. Without freedom, rationality is severely restricted, if not entirely sacrificed to irrational impulse or non-rational social forces. Of great concern, then, is to precisely understand how freedom and rationality are related - their common signification. Understood as a whole, a concept of rational freedom enables the self and has far-reaching dealienating potency. The importance of rational freedom cannot be overemphasized. Authentic self-realization becomes possible with it. Without it, alienation persists and the self becomes sick and atrophies. Any loss of freedom is not often tolerated, and its complete loss is intolerable. An essential power, it is both something needed and deeply desired, not very different from basic physiological needs. It could even be said that freedom is a human drive with dealienating aim. Beyond this primitive characterization, freedom and rationality require cultivation much like any human discipline.

Confronted with an alien Other dominating or frustrating us, thinking is a natural response maximizing the prospect of successfully resolving any problem. However, thought is often not the typical response elicited from a human being confronted with an alienating situation. Thought is rarely the first response or even an automatic response to a problem. Undisciplined minds respond with emotion, irrational passion or according to the dicta of authoritative Others. When thought is not the response, alienation is not usually overcome. Thinking is learned and must be made into self-discipline to be effective for the individual. Only the civilized and learned can think, and do so successfully to solve their problems.

The ontological principle of negativity explains alienation and dealienation generally. Beyond this, it explains consciousness, be it of the world, of the self, of the social. A consciousness of anything always presents an Other alien to the self. Freedom originates from this fact. Self and Other are always juxtaposed. Negativity is again expressed by human need and desire. The Other is something needed or desired. The Other also can oppose or frustrate the self in some way. Self-existence is alienating finitude. The Other is also what or who the self must become to satisfy its needs and desires. Negativity constructs the self in its response to the alienating Other.

Freedom is manifested in the response of the self to the alienating conditions of its existence. Through thought and intentional self-activity in the world and with one's fellows, freedom is discovered and developed. This can be abstractly characterized as a double negation. Nevertheless, double negation is not merely a trivial logical abstraction. For it is a shorthand description of an ontological process. The initial negation is an experience of alienation while the second is a dealienating response affirming being, as Hegel, and his modern exponent Paul Ricoeur, suggested. With the second negation, freedom becomes creative since its exercise involves rationality. Whereas negative freedom is merely the denial or refusal of something to the self, positive freedom is a response which negates what or who alienates the self from its needs and desires. This response is usually complex, depending upon the exercise of rationality, broadly defined as intentional thought and self-activity in the world and with one's fellows. Positive freedom, unlike negative freedom, is not merely a given, but rather a hard won result of socialization, education and maturation.

Whereas negative freedom is a primitive response, as in just saying *no*, positive freedom requiring rationality must be developed by degrees as a power of the self to cope with alienating finitude. Rationality, conceived as a developed ability to consider and evaluate all possibilities, both expresses freedom and enables it. The philosophical habit of thinking about something in multiple perspectives or *outside the box* is to be free. Restricted conceptions of rationality make of it some kind of logic or some set of propositions presumed authoritative or lawful. Rationality is better conceived as a power of the self establishing freedom and maximizing its exercise.

Failure to comprehend the intimate relationship between rationality and freedom can only lead to alienating misunderstandings. Hegel sensed this intimate relationship, but subordinated freedom to rationality, narrowly conceived as the dicta of the authoritative Other, be it culture, social institutions or God. Placed higher than the self in his ontological hierarchy, the authoritative Others cannot be questioned or evaluated. Their alienating dimension cannot be properly dealt with. Existentialism, glorifying freedom to the exclusion of rationality, alienates the self from the very power it requires to be free. An irrational exercise of freedom usually brings something unwanted or unintended. The mistake is to concentrate upon the object desired without evaluating its desirability. Outcomes lacking rationality usually frustrate what we want and so do not permit the enjoyment expected from an exercise of freedom. Without rationality, the self loses its dealienating capacity and sinks into an alienating abyss of domination by irrational antisocial impulse, by non-rational forces of social conformity or destiny. Even Freud, conceiving the psyche to be irrational antisocial impulse dominated by non-rational social forces, presumed freedom and rationality capable of successfully dealing with repressed ideas psychoanalytically made conscious.

Not many would disagree with placing freedom in service to rationality. For, were this not so, freedom could not develop or accomplish its dealienating aim. The question here is the locus of rationality. Is it found in authoritative Others such as social institutions and God, or is it a capacity inherent to the self? If the former, then the self can never be autonomous and its existence can never be authentic, but merely an example of some universal kind. Moreover, self-existence would be nothing more than a particular instance of a universal norm or standardized social role prescribed by authoritative Others alien to the self. If, however, rationality is a power located within the self complementing freedom, then it cannot be a source of alienation. A human nature so constituted cannot be a Sartrean irrational useless passion

Rationality provides the possibility of liberation from alienating conditions and when rationality is translated into intentional activity, dealienation is underway. Freedom driven by rationality tends to dealienate whereas, freedom driven by the irrational or non-rational tends to alienate. An initial experience of freedom is as a self-consciousness negatively expressed by denial, refusal and rebellion. This negative freedom rejecting the limiting Other, while necessary to dealienation, is only its first step. Just saying *no* acknowledges some kind of alienation, but is insufficient to dealienate. A self cannot develop without in some way transcending *no.* Further negation is required by thought and its extension with intentional self-activity. This is rationality in its most general signification wherein alternatives to the limiting Other are revealed, possibilities of being then actualized as the self realizes what and who it is.

Hegel drew attention to a self who does not transcend the first negating response signifying alienation, and therefor remains trapped in it. Without rationality, primitive freedom becomes an absolute, a capricious negativity with destructive outcome never affirming anything of the self or world. Emotionally, the self is left with anxiety, melancholy and despair reflected in attitudes of skepticism, cynicism and nihilism. Hegel's analysis of negative freedom and its alienating consequences are valuable and instructive, notwithstanding his limited conception of rationality as universality and confusion of rationality with the dicta of traditional authority.

There can be little doubt about the dealienating power of rationality. However, rationality can alienate as well when lacking freedom, when misconceived as obedience to authority, when in service to evil. Modern examples abound. Genocide was once carried out with a high degree of rationality. The policy was deliberately formulated, clearly communicated with the means worked out with engineers. Meticulous records of Nazi atrocities were maintained. A less horrendous example was the industrial revolution in which individuals lost their autonomy and creativity in the rationalized machinery of monotonously repetitive production processes. A subtler example is a modern bureaucracy structuring thought and human behavior to a rigid conformity with rationally pre-established outcomes. The mindset of the bureaucrat is so rule-bound that no thinking or behavior outside standard organizational prescriptions can be tolerated. Clearly, rationality, of itself, is not enough to ensure dealienation. Narrowly conceived as instrumentality with no evaluation of its purpose, rationality is not free, and so becomes ambiguous with respect to alienation. Without the freedom to evaluate possibilities and consequences, rationality may even risk becoming an instrument of evil.

Industrial production organizes human labor into bureaucratic hierarchies. So does government with its specialized departments performing specific narrowly defined functions. Bureaucratic organization fragments the self by its compartmentalization of life. Successful behavior is rationally designed to promote pre-established replicated outcomes. Complexity increases with the degree of functional specialization. Rationality is expressed in a labyrinthine morass of rules and regulations designed to govern every aspect of life. Thought and self-activity is rule-bound. Freedom expressed by the human capacity for spontaneity and creativity tends to be suppressed. Thinking *outside the box* is prohibited. The transformative power of free thinking, when not operative, prevents reform of dysfunctional rules. Nothing new is possible. Unintended consequences and dysfunctional behavior tend to be maintained.

Bureaucracy perverts rationality by narrowing its meaning to the logic of a certain set of rules, not evaluated or tested with regard to their consequences. Without the freedom to put something to the test of self-existence, rationality becomes a mere facade contradicting its dealienating aim. Authentic rationality requires freedom. Successful dealienation requires rationality and freedom operating in a complementary manner so intimately as to be indistinguishable. The bureaucratic mentality misconceives rationality by defining it too narrowly and making freedom irrelevant to its exercise. Thus, rationality is not allowed to function as intended, which is to serve human needs and liberate self-existence from whatever alienates it. A rule-bound rationality makes bureaucratic social organization at best problematical, and at worst alienating. The excuse of the bureaucrat is to blame failure on the system. The sharing of responsibility and the obligation to be rule-bound robs the self of autonomy and authenticity. Nobody can be held accountable, since everyone is responsible. An abstract *system* made me or us do it.

Hegel, Marx, Freud, existentialist and bureaucratic viewpoints provide deficient responses to alienation. The deficiency is always that rational freedom is not maintained. Either freedom or rationality is sacrificed. Hegelian freedom is reduced to obedience to traditional authority with rationality falsely located in its abstract dicta pre-established for self-existence. Marx sacrificed freedom to the presumed rationality of an economic pseudo-science and ideology. Freudian psychoanalysis dismissed rationality, subordinating it to irrational impulse and non-rational social forces resulting in neurosis. The irrational ideas of the unconscious, where freedom is inoperative, replace rationality. Even bringing those repressed ideas to consciousness does not help, as analysis remains an interminable process without curative result. The existentialist glorification of irrational freedom makes it the source of alienation. Rationality is so completely overlooked that freedom cannot cope with an absurd existence, which the self must face with resignation. Bureaucracy completely replaces freedom with a rule-bound rationality prohibiting innovative thought and action. These considerations indicate that rationality and freedom are complementary and must be integrated to achieve successful dealienation. Singly, either tends toward alienation and is insufficient for dealienation. With both properly conceived and operative, self-existence is autonomous and authentic. Herein lies an adequate response to every possible kind of alienation.

Rationality and freedom are correlative concepts, coextensive in signification. Successful dealienation requires each complementing the other and both integrated in operation. Thus, separating them is a mistake. Equally mistaken is placing them in opposition. Subordinating one to the other destroys their combined effectiveness. One cannot be rational without being free and one cannot be free without being rational. Each implies the other as recognized by aphorisms such as *the truth shall set you free.* Certainly without freedom, the truth cannot be discovered. Without either, self-development and self-realization are blocked. Intentional self-activity, self-objectifying work, overcoming obstacles, satisfaction of human needs and desires display the relatedness of rationality and freedom, or *rational freedom*, more truly named. Without rationality, we cannot know what is true and without truth, our behavior cannot be either correct or successful. Without freedom, we cannot act experimentally to ascertain the truth or any proper course or action to take toward achieving a successful conclusion. Within the context of self-actualizing human development, the relatedness of rationality and freedom become manifest. Both appear as necessary and complementary aspects of the self-actualizing process of life. Both are the necessary means for the satisfaction of human desire and any goal-seeking behavior.

Rationality and freedom are fully integrated with common significance when thinking through alternatives or consequences of any prospective behavior. Confronted with needs, desires or their frustration, the self seeks satisfaction by means of symbolic thought. Existing circumstances and possible outcomes are evaluated relative to achieving certain aims with intentional behavior, which alters a condition alienating the self. Therefore, the conclusion is inescapable that rationality and freedom, if not at bottom the same in meaning, reinforces each other and is required by the self-actualizing, self-developing creature that we are.

Narrowly defined as license or unlimited self-seeking power, freedom presents the possibility of lawlessness and antisocial behavior with evil consequences. Of course, licentious freedom then becomes potentially dangerous and destructive of self and society. Hence, from Plato onward, many philosophers have distrusted freedom and proposed to socially control it with rationality located in an authoritative Other. However, such a proposal also results in too narrowly defining rationality. Separated and placed in opposition, freedom and rationality are misconstrued with unfortunate alienating consequences. The dicta of an Other, whatever or whomever it might be, cannot be presumed either rational or authoritative. For nothing can be authoritative or presumed so for self-existence that is not critically evaluated, tested by experience and freely accepted with personal conviction. The dicta of authoritative Others can only be validated by the power of a self free to think and act upon what that dicta signifies for self-existence.

A self both rational and free in the broadest sense listens to what the Other prescribes, evaluates it relative to existence, and tests the consequences of operating with it. A more broadly defined and integrated rational freedom relating to self-existence is required to establish the rationality and authoritativeness of anything prescribed for the self. Authoritative Others such as culture, custom, community, law or God may in fact alienate self-existence. If they do, they can be neither rational nor authoritative. How often have authoritative Others alienated the self by denying its needs, desires, and freedom to think and act for itself? That the dicta of an Other are neither rational nor authoritative is also proved when non-rational coercive means such as natural rewards and punishments are required for enforcement. Respect for authority compelled by assiduous indoctrination can create a disciplined self with repressed antisocial desires. They are liable to resurface out of control upon occasion.

Subordinating freedom defined as license to rationality defined by traditional authority destroys authenticity emanating from self-existence. For traditional authority casts personal existence into pre-established molds. The self exists for the Other as a universal Other alienated from rational freedom. Unable to determine its own existence, it is alienated in the most fundamental way conceivable. For it cannot determine itself, cannot cope with its own alienating finitude, cannot satisfy its needs or desires. It is entirely dependent upon the Other to tell it what and who it is and how it ought to exist. This, the world knows as authoritarianism or totalitarianism.

Hegel interpreted history as the actualization of human potentiality by means of its freedom. Freedom has degrees, which correspond to the degrees of alienation it overcomes. Thus, for oriental cultures, history exhibits freedom in its most primitive degree, that of the individual despot who has unlimited satisfaction of his accidental natural capricious desires. Greco-Roman culture raises freedom to a more universal if not imperfect degree with some individuals free while others remain slaves. Christian Germanic culture in turn raises freedom to an even higher degree by recognizing it to be the universal essence of human nature. Even if such Hegelian speculation reflects some degree of cultural bias and parochialism, it is highly suggestive. For hasn't the Spirit of freedom been developed through the history of western civilization, and doesn't this development constitute its greatness?

Freedom or liberty is the essence of man, but it is also hard won as chronicled by Hegel in his history of civilization.

> World history is the progress of the consciousness of freedom - a progress whose necessity we have to investigate. ... Freedom is itself its own object of attainment and the sole purpose of Spirit. It is the ultimate purpose toward which all world history has continually aimed.[2]

Hegel made the Idea of freedom God's will or divine plan that human history works out. Therefore, history is a theodicy. Spirit carries a final purpose and so a destiny. Nevertheless, how are men free by nature and in fact when they just work out a divine plan as actors on a world stage? In what sense are they free when what they express is unknown to them and prescribed for them by a God whose plan they do not understand or consent to in advance of their historical actions? If man is truly free, then he must be free to choose and to express in his own history the divine plan. Who or what is this Other, God, whose plan is alien to man? Obviously, there is a logical tension between the free expression of man and the predestination of a divine plan.

Alienation provides life with its perennial task. Rational freedom is first and foremost a generic response to alienating finitude. Of all the human responses tried throughout history, rational freedom holds out the greatest prospect for successfully dealing with every possible kind of alienation. Human existence then does not have to be alienated by either damnation or absurdity. Resignation and despair are not inevitable and destiny need not be entirely determined by an Other(s) alien to the self. Dealienation is then a continuous interminable process, a triumph of spirit conceived as rational freedom. This is the greatest idea and hope of western civilization. Although Hegel narrowly defined freedom and rationality placing the former in service to the latter and misconstruing it as the dicta of traditional authority, his vision of human history moving toward ever greater degrees of rationality and freedom was accurate. Modern history provides abundant evidence to support this belief.

Freedom and Necessity

Rational necessity is exhibited by the negativity of thought that distinguishes an Other with implications. Alienating finitude, or an Other negating the self in some way, presents necessity in an existential dimension. Alienation and dealienation exhibit necessity. It is ubiquitous: found in coercive forces of nature, in destiny, in natural inclination, need and desire. Necessity is also felt by the self as an obligation, as something that is not present but ought to exist and must be made to exist. The necessity to satisfy need and desire is the origin of obligation and provides the impetus for any exercise of freedom or any development of it. Rational self-activity or intentional behavior exhibits a necessity of thought and being. Self-objectifying work confirms a sense of necessity resulting from agency, from forethought of means and consequences. The self responds to internal and external necessity and utilizes it in the processes of dealienation. Necessity is incorporated into every dimension of human nature including any positive exercise of freedom utilizing rationality. Freedom is a necessity for dealienation and self-realization. This becomes dramatically manifest when freedom is lost. Its recovery is urgently felt. The most strenuous actions are taken to recover freedom. In such situations of loss, or even the threat of loss, humanity affirms the necessity of freedom for its own being.

It would then be a mistake to conceive of freedom as an indeterminacy of the self. For freedom, responding to some alienating necessity always has a determinate dealienating aim. The self needs to rid itself of something or change something. Without the burdensome necessity of finitude, the self cannot exercise its power of freedom either by negating what it does not want or affirming what it does want. Without necessity, freedom is not conceivable and would not exist. Hegel understood this.

> A freedom involving no necessity, and mere necessity without freedom, are abstract and in this way untrue formulae of thought. Freedom is no blank indeterminateness: essentially concrete, and unvaryingly self-determinate, it is so far at the same time necessary.[3]

Abstracted from the context within which they originate, freedom and necessity can be regarded as mutually exclusive. But Hegel considered this mistaken.

> ... freedom presupposes necessity and contains it as an unsubstantial element in itself. A good man is aware that the tenor of his conduct is essentially obligatory and necessary. But this consciousness is so far from making any abatement from his freedom, that without it real and reasonable freedom could not be distinguished from arbitrary choice - a freedom which has no reality and is merely potential."[4]

Hegel thought of freedom as signifying independence from coercion, either external or internal, a condition therefore of self-sufficiency of one's being. This sounds plausible, but it is incorrect. For complete independence from the Other, or self-sufficiency, is virtually impossible. If it were possible, alienating finitude would not exist as it obviously does. There would be nothing that could provide an impetus for the use or development of freedom, which obviously occurs. Freedom would have no aim, which it obviously does have in satisfying the natural necessity of human needs and desires. Complete independence from any determination by an Other is ambiguous regarding the self. For rather than being fully developed through dealienating interaction with the Other, such a self could also be radically narcissistic and undeveloped.

Complete independence implies indeterminacy in being and this is not freedom, but mere abstract possibility without any determining principle. For a finite self compelled to decide and act, indeterminacy is alienating. Hegel recognized this.

> Man, if he wishes to be actual, must be-there-and-then, and to this end he must set a limit to himself. People who are too fastidious towards the finite never reach actuality, but linger lost in abstraction, and their light dies away.[5]

Here we see self-alienation to consist of a complete capitulation to finitude by a refusal to actualize human potentialities. The self remains indeterminate, lost in contemplating the mere possibility of being something, never changing or growing as a person. One's potentiality for being something lies fallow in a refusal to think and act to overcome existing limits and impediments confronting self-existence. Existentialists such as Kierkegaard observed a self suspended in abstract possibilities and indecision, remaining alienated from realizing its potentiality for being by the normal exercise of freedom. Indecisive individuals, Kierkegaard himself or Shakespeare's Hamlet, make no active attempt to cope with alienating finitude and so are overcome by it. Their capacity for freedom is not exercised in some crucial circumstance of their life. They unnecessarily accept something they encounter as an insurmountable barrier, a personal limitation, and rationalize it to be an irrevocable fact of life determining their fate. Stuck in indecision and self-perpetuated alienating finitude, their being is determined by default, implying that alien Others dictate who and what they are.

Indeterminacy, signifying a refusal to become something while remaining lost in abstract possibilities, contradicts freedom. Personal freedom cannot be abstract independence. Neither is abstractly defined by complete self-sufficiency, as Hegel suggested. Self-sufficiency suggests existing in isolation rather than reciprocal relationship with Others alien to self. However, an isolating independent self-existence is not possible. The fact of alienating finitude never permits self-sufficiency in any absolute sense. Always dependent upon and interacting with alien Others; the self necessarily exists in reciprocal relationships. Rather than signifying an abstract self-sufficiency in being, freedom is a response to an insufficiency in being. In fact freedom can only be meaningful when it signifies a response to alienating finitude, reciprocity of self to alien Others and intelligent interaction constituting successful dealienation. An isolating self-sufficiency can be neither freedom nor some postulated dealienated condition of self-existence.

Many philosophers have understood self-consciousness to directly present freedom. The negativity of consciousness and self-consciousness always presents an Other distinct from a thinking Ego. This may be an indubitable intuition that even Descartes' devil cannot mask. But it says little beyond the fact that freedom is evident with the negativity of conscious thought. The impetus for freedom, its aim and development remain to be explored in the works of self-objectification. Whether freedom develops to produce a self fully capable of dealienation depends upon the content of self-identification, the projected self-concept and process of self-objectification. For it is possible to project and objectify that which alienates the self and limits its freedom in ways which prevent the satisfaction of needs, desires and self-realization.

There is no contradiction of rationality or necessity with freedom. For freedom, responds to necessity and requires the application of rationality. Without the necessity inherent to reason, freedom could not be developed. So, the positive use of freedom requires following the necessity of reason both in thought and action wherever it takes us. This is not without risk, uncertainty and insecurity. These aspects of exercising freedom are reasons for the abortive attempts to alienate it from oneself. Considered simply as abstractions, both freedom and necessity are misunderstood. Hegel correctly conceived their correlative relationship. Each requires the other and each is implied in the larger whole of being to be comprehended and realized.

The very negativity that creates the distinction between necessity and freedom synthesizes them. This is understood when necessity, natural and rational, along with freedom is placed within the context of a developmental process. Freedom then becomes a response to a necessity that alienates. Destiny is an expression of necessity. Stoic resignation has been the most common response to destiny. However, when it is burdensome enough, it may be refused. Alienating destiny is a limit to be overcome, a challenge for rational freedom. The ensuing dealienating process presents a logical progression from necessity to freedom in its liberating sense. Freedom in the sense of intentional self-active power negates the alienating finitude of destiny. A self fully empowered with rational freedom makes its own destiny.

Anything driven by necessity is not foreknown but merely suffered. The ancients knew necessity as destiny, accepting it as a matter of course. Destiny was rationalized to console the suffering it brought. What must be and cannot be otherwise is somehow as it ought to be, where no reason for it being so can be found. History is a Hegelian metaphorical slaughter bench upon which is sacrificed the happiness of people, the virtue of individuals, and the wisdom of states. The destruction of noble civilizations and defeat of private virtue in the history of the world filled Hegel with melancholy. He said the only consolation we can have at this devastation is a belief in fate -a belief that history had to be worked out the way it turned out. This belief consoles us. "We can endure it and strengthen ourselves against it only by thinking that this is the way it had to be - it is fate; nothing can be done."[6] Destiny was therefore unquestioned and normative for life.

Resignation was the ancient attitude and response to destiny. Without any alternative to it or the means to negate it there is no way to cope with destiny other than with resignation. Stoical resignation implies that destiny is alienating. For resignation is an act of giving up on trying to change the inevitable. Therefore, resignation is the triumph of destiny, an acknowledged inability to cope with alienation and a denial of any human capacity to negate it. Resignation implies the acceptance of alienation. Yet even in resignation there is at least the wish that it be otherwise expressed in the belief that God(s) are not subject to destiny. When knowledge and freedom are sufficiently developed to effect desirable transformations of the world, then destiny is no longer a necessity and resignation can be abandoned as a response to alienating finitude.

Even if the ancients were naive, innocent and unconscious of their capacity for freedom, this does not mean they were unaware of living in a world that controlled their destiny without their consent. The ancients were undoubtedly aware at a minimum subconscious level of being alienated by destiny. Otherwise their response of stoic resignation would not be necessary and would make no sense. Mythology may present a prehistory to alienation in which innocent and naive selves existed in paradise without human need, desire and work. However, this vision is an impossible fiction. For, even in a paradiasical garden of Eden, those mythical creatures of nature would have been alienated from realizing their divine gifts of rationality and freedom.

Whether it is the biblical myth of estrangement from a nurturing protective God or an awareness of helplessness confronting nature, a self-recognition of freedom need not be alienating. In fact, the opposite is the case where freedom signifies a dealienating power of self. Traditional authority, or the so-called establishment, may consider a free self threatening and a curse to orthodoxy. Hegel thought of freedom in this way and so located alienation in a self free to defy traditional authority. Appearing as *hubris* and a defiance of authority, secular and divine, alienation is a sinful consciousness, guilty conscience, and an estrangement from the authoritative Other(s). Hegel thought it to be dialectically worked through in the history of Christianity terminating with the Protestant reformation. This view is made untenable by the fact of historical alienation prior to Christianity and after the Reformation. Alienation is not a mere historical stage in human development. Neither does it suddenly appear with some cataclysmic historical event such as a mythological expulsion from paradise. Nor does it depend upon any particular kind of self-consciousness. Conceived as merely a passing historical phenomenon, alienation is not properly comprehended. Alienating finitude is an ontological condition without regard to history or state of self-conscious development.

Normative Freedom

Freedom, considered as a power of the self, has dealienation as its aim. Thus, freedom is itself of inestimable value. But, is freedom normative? Considered as a means to achieving any end, freedom is ambiguous and value-neutral. It cannot establish the end for which it is exercised. If then, freedom is mere means, then it is not normative. The question then becomes what or who determines the end for which the self exercises it? Hegel made freedom a vehicle for the purposes of Geist, social institutions and traditional authority held to be ontologically superior to the self. The problem with this perspective on the question is that an Other, presumed authoritative for the self, establishes the aim of its freedom. However, authoritarianism, totalitarianism and collectivism alienate freedom of thought and action essential for dealienation. If neither freedom nor an authoritative Other can be normative for self-existence, then the question is what can be? Recasting the question in terms of alienation may prove more fruitful.

What is true or right is normative for the self. Norms have to be universal in the sense of applying equally to everyone. If norms are not an outcome of dealienation, then their actual universality can be taken as evidence of their validity. This reduces what ought to exist to an empirical actuality, to what generally prevails, even with some exceptions. What ought to be the case is just what is and what the self should be or do is merely what everyone else is or does. Universality is here not absolute and the exceptions to the norm require explanation. Classical Greek and Christian explanations are that the exception results from an ignorance of what is truly good for us, or a perverse free will.

Considering norms to be validated by their actuality is problematical. For why should the self believe or do what everyone else believes or does? The mere fact of something actual does not make it normative. By such logic, anything can be justified. If what *they* do is immoral, so is what I do. Mere conformity is taken as establishing and validating the norm. Thought and choice are not required; just obedience to what everyone else thinks and does. Intellectual indolence and ignorance prevail. The hard process of experience testing and rational evaluation is avoided. Without this, normative significance vanishes. When not revealed existentially and by the power of rational freedom, the acceptance and promotion of a norm is inauthentic, abstract and alien to the self. Rather than a demand placed upon self-existence and determining it, what is true or right is an existential result of a dealienating process. Self-existence discovers and creates its norms.

A crucial question for every self is whether the norms which govern its existence are pre-established by an authoritative Other, or are a product of the process of dealienation itself. If the latter, those norms are the creation of the self and therefore authentic to it. If the former, those norms must be experienced at least initially as alien, if not always so. Their validation would consist of a dialectic of self-identification with them. The power of the self to think and act for itself need not be factors in this process. Natural processes of self-identification psychologically describe sudden conversions and faith. Dealienation has a much broader significance then a self-identification that accommodates to the alien demands of an authoritative Other. Resigning oneself to authority does not reconcile the self to either its own demands or those of external authority.

Let us assume for a moment that the outcome of dealienation is pre-ordained. How then can that which initially alienates the self come to express its true nature? The only answer possible is by some process of identification. Now anything imposed upon the self is alien to it. If the self is coerced to accept it by imposition of external power or by a natural process of identification, then it remains alien. An identity so established is not authentic, since it has not defined itself, but has been defined by the alien Other(s). A dealienated self is authentic by virtue of having worked through the alienation of its own existence. It is authentic when its being is a product of its own existence, of the processes and activity of its own life. The acceptance of externally imposed norms, although providing the self with an identity, does not allow authentic self-realization. Norms governing self-existence must come out of confronting alienating finitude with the power of rational freedom.

It is difficult to comprehend how dealienation can be successful if the self is inauthentic; if its being is not self-determined rather than determined by alien Others. How can alienation be overcome when the Other defines what and who we are? How can dealienation and self-realization proceed when the alien Other dominates us? How can rationality and freedom be the genuine essence of the self, if it is only determined by the alien Other(s)? How is wisdom and truth created or sustained, if not by and through the existence of the self who rejects and transforms the alien Other(s)? The history of humanity is a discovery of what it means to be human through suffering alienation and responding with dealienating activity. In this process, the self discovers who it is and what is normative for itself. The history of western civilization has been a progressive discovery that every human being is rational and free. Human suffering and dealienation has been a working through in specific detail of the implications of rationality and freedom. These are the twin pillars of western civilization generally describing our being in both dimensions of potentiality and actuality. The truth of what and who we are is demonstrated in the process of human existence, alienation, suffering and dealienation. That truth endures, as does wisdom acquired from the process of dealienation.

Self-existence governed by rational freedom provides human destiny with a direction but leaves it otherwise indeterminate in outcome. If what were normative for the self originates from within it, the very process of existing would authenticate those norms. They would truly express the nature of the self as inner not other directed. Rational freedom makes coercive obedience to established norms unnecessary. The actuality of norms would be a product of the existence of an authentic self, not a self coerced by authority and power alien to itself. The self would not simply be Other, or what *they* want it to be. Dealienation would then be much more than resolving a conflict between the self and external traditional authority. In addition, dealienation would be more than an unstable compromise between self and Other, or an acquiescence of self to the power of an alien Other. The dialectical process of dealienation would amount to more than just self-accommodation to the pre-established and pre-ordained; more than resignation to destiny. Dealienation would reveal meaning and a potentiality for being not known in advance of existence.

Self-existence is to be conscious of something, an Other which limits and requires the realization of some potentiality for being. As previously argued, a negative response of the self, signifying alienation, is also an initial response of freedom and a requirement for its development. Something stands in opposition to the self. Something needed or desired provides an impetus for self-activity. Something obligates the self to think and act. The self ought to possess or be something that is not presently the case. What it does not want implies what it does want. Saying *no* to something implies saying *yes* to something else. The reason for refusal affirms a deficiency in being signified by something sought after. Thus, it would appear as if human need and desire originate what turns out to be normative. Yet, what is desired may not be what is truly needed. In other words, desire can be mistaken. This possibility is minimized when desire is subjected to rational appraisal. Rationality, broadly conceived as a trial of means and evaluation of consequences, can make something desirable and obligatory for intentional self-activity. Need, expressed as a desire for something put to the test of experience, and rationally evaluated, determines what can be normative for self-existence.

Whatever is normative for self-existence is discovered in the whole process or alienation and dealienation. First, the self discovers it is alienated from something it needs or desires. The discovery of this fact is a negation of self by the Other. Distinguishing self from an Other which opposes it or is a deficiency of its being is an initial primitive manifestation of negative freedom. In other words, negative freedom is a sensing of alienation. It provides an impetus from which a dealienating process commences. The self feels obligated to respond and it does so with its own powers of rationality and freedom. The object of desire satisfying need is identified by thinking about it. Then the object selected provides an aim for an exercise of positive freedom. The question is always how to achieve the aim. Existing circumstances and possibilities are rationally evaluated. Means are selected. Possible consequences are evaluated. Interaction with the world and one's fellows are undertaken. Outcomes are evaluated relative to the satisfaction of need, desire, and aim.

The whole process of dealienation defines intelligent behavior in which language, thought and complete existential interaction are integrated. Rational freedom sums up the process of dealienation. What is normative for the self is established by an alienation, which presents need, desire and an aim. When rationality is fully operative with self-activity and successful outcomes of dealienation are evaluated, norms are fully developed and existentially established. Rational freedom is normative. This almost states the obvious when rationality is broadly conceived within an existential context wherein dealienation proceeds by intentional self-activity.

Negative freedom is a first response to an alienating situation. Of itself, negative freedom cannot determine the direction of self-seeking activity. Negative freedom without aim cannot dealienate. Unguided by rationality, negative freedom is alienating. The self discovers itself driven by non-rational or irrational impulse. So directed, its existence is controlled by an Other alien to itself. Contingent circumstances of the moment determine behavior, and over time behavior is inconsistent, arbitrary and unreliable. A narcissistic or egoistic self, lacking the capacity to consider socially relevant possibilities and evaluate consequences of intentional behavior cannot successfully dealienate and so construct norms. Whatever satisfies need and desire signifies successful dealienation and so becomes normative. Positive freedom driven by rationality has an aim, obligates intentional self-activity and can successfully dealienate. In other words, successful dealienation requires rational freedom. Therefore, it establishes whatever is normative for human existence.

Negative freedom distinguishes the Other from the self and rejects the demands of the Other. Consequently, such a being is bereft of the direction required for constructive self-objectification. Negative freedom leaves the self alienated and unable to express anything other than rebelliousness. The attitude of negative freedom is skeptical, cynical and despairing. These attitudes of negative freedom persist throughout the ages from the ancient Sophists to contemporary life. Postmodernist counter-culture deconstructs a social order and values transmitted by traditional authority. Contemporary examples are gender feminist rejection of the male sex, the movement to deconstruct the family by allowing single sex marriages, the legitimizing of homosexuality in culture and law, and the elimination of merit from determining social rewards. Such instances of negative freedom pose questions without answers; certainly a cause for anxiety. How would a society without gender difference, without marriage, without family roles, reproduce itself or socialize its progeny? How would a society not respecting individual differences of merit sustain its liberty and secure its general prosperity?

Abstract possibilities, represents the negative aspect of human freedom. The choice among abstract possibilities would be entirely arbitrary from a theoretical viewpoint. Nothing would determine one's choice except the contingent circumstance of the moment. Whenever this is the case, the subject is not self-determining, since choice is not free but determined by an alien Other. Such a situation signifies a subject lacking free will, not autonomous, a subject in bondage to alien Others. Therefore, the negative freedom of abstract possibilities is not freedom at all, but its contradiction. For choice is never arbitrary. Abstract possibility determines nothing. The point of being free turns on what drives choice. In other words, one is truly free if choice originates not from an Other outside oneself, but from within oneself. The ideal of human freedom is autonomy where choice is determined by rational considerations. Freedom is rational self-determination, not the absence of any factors determining choice.

The self experiences its negative freedom by thinking of possibilities for itself, alternatives for choice and action. Abstract possibilities present a potential self-identity, but do not realize it. A self existing only with its possibilities and without any principle determining their choice and action is left alienated, abstract and undeveloped. Kierkegaard in *Either/Or* and Shakespeare in *Hamlet* described such a self. Its being is simply possible and so nothing finite. Its will is paralyzed in possibilities. It remains entrapped in indeterminacy, unable to get what it needs and desires. A self whose being is mere possibility consists of unresolved oppositions, mutually exclusive options. For to exist, or to be actual, the self must become finite as this possibility rather than that one. Choice, decision and action by the self resolve the contradiction of possibilities. Some possibilities cannot be actualized by a self limited in certain ways within itself or by its environment. Choice without an impetus or aim is arbitrary, leaving possibilities of being undetermined. Positive freedom consists of possibilities with some principle determining choice to a finite actual outcome. Rationality can be that principle of determination. A deliberately chosen possibility has reasons why it was chosen and acted upon.

Negative freedom presents alienating self-existence. Although negative freedom implies an aim for self-activity, it provides no assurance that it is the right aim or that it will dealienate and provide the satisfaction of what the self truly needs. Thus, negative freedom is limited to initiating a process of dealienation, which may or may not lead to successful dealienation. Negative freedom becomes highly problematical when understood as permissiveness or license. For unlimited self-seeking with probable antisocial consequences is never socially acceptable. In fact, it can threaten or destroy the social fabric. Suspicion of it then is well founded. How this suspicion is answered becomes crucially important. A most common answer is to distrust freedom and subordinate it to authoritative Other(s). Nevertheless, doing so is a mistake in principle and in result. For it alienates the exercise of positive freedom, a capacity of the self essential for dealienation in general. Freedom denied contradicts the very being of the self, establishes unreconcilable conflicts and diminishes its capacity for self-realization. Freedom is what the self needs to survive. Without the most complete exercise of freedom, the self atrophies. Self-existence becomes impoverished.

If rational freedom is normative for self-existence as has been argued, then the locus of what is necessary and universal - the law - resides within the self. Hegel, arguing against the Romantics and Kant, viewed law to reside in authoritative Others molding the self, namely in the institutions of community and God. Such authoritative Others and the presumed rationality of their dicta counterbalance the social abuses of negative freedom residing within the self. What the Romantic Self feels as necessary for itself often proves to be the exception rather than the universally normative rule.

Kant correctly located law within the rationality of a free self. The *categorical imperative*, excluding contradictory exceptions, is an expression of rationality, albeit narrowly based upon a principle of formal logic. Unlike Hegel, Kant did not misconceive rationality as instantiated in the dicta of authoritative Others. This was an advance toward a self who brings its power of rational freedom to bear upon the alienating finitude of its existence. Hegel was right to believe that universalizing a *law of the heart* as he called it is a wanton unjustified act of egoistic self-assertion when based solely upon subjective feeling.. Yet, law cannot be coercively imposed by some authority external to the self without alienating consequences. Neither can law be justified as universally normative merely by applying some formal logical test without reference to self-existence. Laws are necessary and universal, or normative, when they originate from and address self-existence in a rational manner. Moreover, this requires a completely free rational discourse among individuals to whom the law is meant to apply. From this process, laws in fact express commonly experienced problems, interests, inclinations and aspirations among individuals, which could be arguably true without exceptions.

With the Kantian categorical imperative, rationality is presumed to emanate from the self; whereas, Hegel constricts the existential import of rationality. Rather than reflecting a capacity of the self, rationality consists of knowing what the authoritative Other(s) command and require the self to be. Moreover, the function of human freedom is similarly restricted to obeying those norms external to the self. Nevertheless, training is not equivalent to rationality, and obedience is not equivalent to freedom. For, if this were true, rationality and freedom would be deprived of its relevance for self-existence. Rational freedom would not arise from within a process of self-existence. Neither could rational freedom develop or expand from the process of self-existence. For to allow this, was for Hegel, to unleash the potential for radical evil from a self unconstrained in self-seeking. To allow the self rationality and freedom sufficient to establish the truth for itself and authenticate its own conduct would have very dangerous antisocial consequences. To counter this anarchy of the self, laws or norms universally applicable to every self are required. Their source lies in an authoritative Other(s) with power to coerce obedience whenever necessary. Coercion would not be necessary to achieve civility if the self were trained to feel obligated toward the Other(s) or awestruck by its power, or convinced that the Other(s) are the legitimate source of truth and conduct for itself. Obligation here would be a natural non-rational or possibly irrational feeling; not a feeling resulting from a reasoned choice made by the self.

Reason without freedom is dead. Freedom without reason is blind. Rational freedom, that universal power exercised to some degree within every self-existence, creates an authentic obligation. Since the source of obligation lies in the needs, desires, rationality and freedom of the self, the mere dicta of the authoritative Other(s) cannot ultimately command it. Their dicta is neither rational nor obligatory by merely being intended to apply universally, or even by the fact that it is actually universal in practice. Such presumed universality is an abstraction justifying nothing. No! Whatever is universally obligatory is discovered consensually within the process of collective dealienation. Often, the dicta of the authoritative Other(s) are not discovered to be rational or universally obligatory. Such dicta are continuously subject to evaluation and validation by every self possessing the universal power of rationality and freedom. The self can only feel authentically obligated when it has evaluated and existentially established what is right for itself. When other selves do the same, a consensual basis for law exists and becomes universal by being established inductively. Beyond naturally sensing personal needs and desiring certain things for itself, conscience, rationality and freedom establish whatever is socially obligatory. Herein resides the legitimization of authority, a basis for liberty, justice, law and social duty.

A law is not alien when it originates from the conviction of the self, according to Hegel. This implies that a law must be an authentic expression of a free self. Then, notice how authenticity and freedom are limited in relation to law. It is presumed objectively pre-established and thereby universally obligatory. An authentic expression of the law by any self merely consists of internalizing or self-identifying with the law. However, this process, if naturally coerced by non-rational or irrational means, cannot make the law an authentic expression of the self. The only way the law can be such is if it originates within self-existence and from rational freedom, its dealienating capacity. Where a law is projected and objectified coercively, the self is neither autonomous nor authentic. Hegel implicitly acknowledged this in his analysis of oriental civilization where the law is reduced to the coercive will of a despot alien to the self. What the oriental subject internalizes is not a respect for the rationality of the law itself, but merely a natural fear of the sovereign. Obedience to law is not rationally obligatory, but coerced by an alien authoritative Other, the despot. The source of law is and remains an alien authoritative Other, regardless of historical period or culture. This could be otherwise if the source of law were re-conceived to reside in rational freedom, self-existence and collective dealienating endeavor.

Hegel believed the locus of truth and value cannot reside within the self, but must be found in external sources of community and God. Freedom is therefore constrained to seek guidance from such sources. There are several Hegelian reasons why the desires of the self cannot be universalized for all selves. First, the self is particular, singular, and individual rather than universal. Second, free selves can and will disagree about anything. Third, when a norm established by an individual becomes social, it becomes alien to its originator by virtue of what other selves make of it and its alienating consequences, unintended by the originator.

However, from such obviously true reasons, one still cannot conclude that the self cannot be the locus of truth and value: an originator of laws, necessary and universal for everyone. For does not the self, free to think and act, project and objectify itself into the world and with its fellows? Does not its self-created identity express what is true about it and something valued positively or negatively? Is it not possible that what is true and good for one self can apply equally to everyone else, particularly where it is established by rational discourse among selves who may disagree? Whereas freedom cannot obligate one self to agree with another, rationality can do so. Free selves guided by rationality can arrive at consensus, even universal consensus, at times when the reasons for a belief or course of action are overwhelming. Therefore, it would seem that a self who is both free and rational could be not only the locus of universal truth and value, but also its originator. The Sophists were right to say that man is the measure of all things, implying that humanity is the locus of truth and value. Culture, community, law and God are human creations and not the repositories of a rationality alien to the self.

Critique of Personal Freedom

The trend of western civilization is to subordinate culture to the self. The locus of truth and value is presumed to reside within the self rather than traditional authority and cultural authoritative Others. Self-realization is highly prized. Personal freedom is rapidly expanding in scope of application. Its limits are being extended as so-called *glass ceilings* are being broken. Toleration of deviancy has been replaced by permissiveness. This is expressed in certain attitudes such as *if it feels good, it must be OK.* It has recently become socially impermissible to be judgmental of other subcultures, deviant behavior or lifestyles; all of which are presumed to command equal respect. Condemnation of them is *discriminatory.* Deviancy is continuously expanding and being redefined as normality. This provokes anxiety from cultural conservatives opposed to counter-culture. Yet, the trend toward ever-greater degrees of personal freedom prevails, particularly in contemporary American culture. The implications of expanding personal freedom in contemporary democratic cultures are being worked out with unforeseeable consequences.

Beginning with the biblical myth of expulsion from paradise, freedom has been suspect. Used to disobey divine authority, the gift of freedom was abused. At best, freedom is ambiguous with respect to producing good or evil. At worst, it is self-alienating, a barrier to self-realization and a contradiction of the intentions of a divine authoritative Other. Possessing the potential to subvert traditional cultural authority and institutions, freedom is considered potentially threatening, if not actually dangerous. Where freedom is license, the specter of social disintegration and anarchy looms large. Permissive personal freedom lets loose the demons within us, normally constrained by traditional cultural authority and civilizing institutions. Hegel believed that without religious and cultural control of personal freedom, a community ethos maintaining social cohesion is not possible. Freud believed civilization would disintegrate without cultural repression of antisocial instinctual gratification. The predominant view of western thinkers as diverse as Hegel and Freud has been that unconstrained personal freedom is self-alienating and socially alienating.

Radical freedom isolates the self from culture and community. According to Hegel and even existentialists such as Sartre, a demand for absolute freedom is irrational and self-alienating. Unlimited freedom can only lead to a narcissism and egoism disregarding the dealienating claims of other selves. Placed in the hands of a single individual, unlimited freedom permits the creation of evil by perversions such as sado-masochism. Hegel believed that historical periods such as the late Roman Empire and French Revolution bore witness to the egoistic excesses of tyrants whose will became law. This also is confirmed by the dictators and totalitarianism of the first half of the twentieth century. Given the historically alienating abuses of freedom and its future potential for evil, a distrust of personal freedom would seem justified. Its threatening aspect and dangerous exercise warrants social control. Yet, contemporary western culture promotes a permissive personal freedom. Can this expansion of freedom be trusted to produce a dealienating result? Or, would increasing personal freedom only lead to social disintegration, as notable social thinkers have feared?

The current permissive attitude toward personal freedom bears a striking similarity to eighteenth century Romanticism. Therefore, the Hegelian critique of freedom made with arguments against Romanticism also becomes a critique of contemporary permissive personal freedom. Every self wants to be a lawgiver, at least for itself. It demands autonomy and authenticity, the means for dealienation. Laws mandated by authoritative Others contradict the demand for autonomy and authenticity. Laws, which are necessary and universal, serve as a basis for social life. Hegel argued that freedom couldn't make the self a lawgiver. For what one self discovers good and necessary for itself, may not be so for another. Moreover, a capricious or perverse will cannot be universalized. When socially imposed, a perverse will merely compounds alienation. Contrary to the Kantian autonomy expressed by the categorical imperative, Hegel believed that laws sustaining community must rest upon grounds other than the autonomy and authenticity of the individual. Neither consensus among individuals nor Rousseau's *general will* could be a basis for law. A law, necessary and universal, can only be established in fact when all selves can instantiate it without logical contradiction, or exception, or opposition among themselves. This requires that every self identify with a law posited by an authoritative Other of culture, or God.

Contemporary permissive freedom encourages the self to set its own lifestyle and trust its own feelings about itself. Hegel described a similar Romantic disposition calling it the *law of the heart.* What is felt to be necessary for a particular self can be universalized to be a law for everyone. Hegel believed this view falsely glorifies personal freedom making it a source of law. He also believed that the necessity and universality of law must be applied to self-existence and cannot be derived from it. An activist self will use its freedom to socially universalize what it discovers necessary for itself. However, Hegel believed that universality couldn't be created by self-existence or induced by social activism. Neither can it be created inductively by generalizing the desires of a majority or plurality.

The universality and necessity of law is found in authoritative cultural sources extrinsic to self-existence, namely social institutions and God. Acknowledging these extrinsic authoritative sources and their dicta obligates the self to doing its duty accordingly. The necessity and universality of law, rather than being created subjectively by self-existence, resides in the very Notion of law. It is *a priori,* categorical, and absolute: never empirically derived, nor admitting of degrees, or contingent upon the action of any particular self or circumstance. Yet, laws are in fact a historical result of collective dealienating endeavor. And this issues from the alienating finitude of self-existence encountering commonly shared needs and desires. Dealienating self-existence, rather than being condemned as a fallacious process, in effect establishes the efficacy of law by inductive generalization. No authoritative Other can be expected to validate what is in fact taught by reasoning about the conditions of self-existence.

Hegel's argument that personal freedom cannot be a basis of law rests upon emphasizing negative freedom. Since all selves are free, what anyone claims necessary for himself can be refused by others. Dissent is the posture of negative freedom. What is law for one will be alien to another. This is confirmed when a law is universalized by one self coercing another. Furthermore, when a law is socially operative, it often becomes alien, even to its originator. The inductive leap generalizing from the desires of a particular self is not only logically unjustified; it is an indulgence in self-conceit. Narcissistic or egoistic personalities would be prone to making their freedom the basis of law for everyone else. Nevertheless, negative freedom is merely an incomplete aspect of freedom. In its positive aspect, it is not simply self-assertive, but tempered by rational considerations of the desires and needs of others.

Often a self-objectifying outcome is alienated from the original intention of its creator. This is common where other selves are free to interpret, use or oppose what any given self publicly projects. Subject to the personal freedom of others, a self-objectified product takes on a life of its own. As socially interpreted and used by one's fellows, it can become alien to its originator. Also, it may present some undesirable limit to someone else, thereby generating a further dealienating dialectic. Such are the unintended consequences of self-objectification. Yet, social outcomes are not invariably alienating. Although common in bureaucratic social structures, the so-called law of unintended consequences is the exception rather than the rule. Personal freedom is not so perverse as to always contradict the original intention of a social projection.

Freedom and Authority

Dealienation is the general aim of freedom. Whether dealienation is successful depends upon who or what shall be authoritative for the self. Authoritative Others can be just about anything such as God, an elite social class, capitalists, priests, academics, a political party, a social institution, prevailing mores or traditions, an ideology, and so forth. Any of these and many others can determine self-existence. Every self confronts the problem of authority and answers it by making someone or something the master of its own freedom. Whether authority is located in an Other or in the self determines the scope of freedom and extent to which it is exercised. The historically prevalent view is to locate authority in an Other separate from self-existence. Plato postulated a separate realm of Ideas providing self-existence with a perfect model of meaning that imperfect self-existence could imitate. Hegel added to this view that Ideas originate with the intentions of a creator God. Then self-existence follows from a pre-established meaning of the self provided by an authoritative Other(s). They create whatever is meaningful and valuable for self-existence and so govern it.

The first question to resolve about any authoritative Other is whether its thought can precede self-existence. Existentialism and naturalism deny this possibility. The former claims that existence precedes essence. The latter, particularly pragmatism, view thought as originating in existential circumstances which is problematical and frustrating to the self. Both viewpoints are based upon fact, not abstract speculation. That thought could precede existence is false and contradicted by the fact of alienating finitude. For without the alienating finitude of self-existence, there is no impetus which could generate thought, no reason to think about anything.

Narrowly conceived, alienation is a discovery of the self with its negative freedom taking the form of refusal and rebellion against authority. Many philosophers, notably Hegel, claim that negative freedom cannot be normative for the self. It offers no constructive aim and so fails to replace the external authority rebelled against. Negative freedom is an alienation of self, a recognition that, of itself, the self is nothing. Its negative freedom must be harnessed by being provided a constructive aim from a source external to itself. An Other must be accepted as authoritative for the self. An authoritative Other defines its nature and provides self-existence with purpose. Dealienation then becomes a process of overcoming the vacuity of the self and the alienating consequences of its negative freedom. This is accomplished by the *introjection* of an authoritative Other and a self-identification with its dicta.

Negation of a self and its vacuous negative freedom can be considered a second negation, which affirms the being of the self as substantial rather than nothing. The refusal and rebellion of negative freedom is replaced by positive freedom, which works on behalf of introjected authority. Thus, dealienation is narrowly conceived in terms of working out the problem of authority confronting the self with a process of self-identification and introjection of various authoritative Others. Still, the question arises as to whether or not self-identification and introjection of authority can dealienate in principle or in fact. The self does not appear to be an entirely vacuous being. Its physiological needs primarily define what it is to begin with. What it desires are aims implied by what it needs. Its freedom although negative is also positive as demonstrated by its capacity to think and act for itself. Introjecting an authoritative Other may alienate the self with respect to its own needs, desires, rationality and freedom.

Narrowly conceived, alienation can be disobedience to authority, a loss of self-orientation. Dealienation is then a process of recovery of self-orientation by obedience to authority. Freedom describes alienation, first as an act of willful disobedience, then as a dealienating act of obedience. Dealienation is then an odyssey in which the self first disobeys traditional authority and then finds a way back to it. However, the way back does not require freedom. For obedience to authority is secured coercively by natural rewards and punishments meted out by powerful authoritative Others. Obedience is secured through a process of socialization involving self-identification and introjection of an Other who thereby becomes authoritative for the self. Such processes do not require any exercise of rationality or freedom. The process of alienation and dealienation moves from rebellion to a resignation to traditional authority. Freedom, although expressed negatively in rebellion, is not operative thereafter.

A self merely reflective of the Other is not free, is not necessarily rational, is not authentic and has a destiny not of its own making. If dealienation is reduced to an identification and introjection of authority, then rational freedom is not operative in providing the self with an identity. The resulting identity is neither rational nor free. It is an identity established by an Other, alien to the self and its essential powers. Therefore, identification and introjection, although describing a natural process of maturation, may not signify dealienation. Rather, identification and introjection signify a non-rational psychological process, an immature commitment of faith without reasons, a blind trust in a controlling authority. Self-identity is constructed coercively by natural rewards and punishments. A self confronted by coercive authority is alienated not only from its own natural inclination, but also from the exercise of its own powers. Authentic self-realization is not possible. Natural processes of self-identification and introjection of authority may very well alienate the self from its authentic potentiality for being. The least that can be said is that successful dealienation requires something more than what is offered by the natural processes of socialization and maturation. An autonomous self can challenge and reject any authority not consistent with its own needs.

Freedom, misconceived as merely negating power, is cloaked with a threatening or destructive aspect. Hegel could not recognize that identification and introjection of authority is not an exercise of personal freedom, but rather a validation of an authoritative Other by submission and emulation. To introject an authoritative Other requires neither rationality nor freedom, particularly when accomplished by coercive processes of socialization. Disobedience to the dicta of authority, rather than a misuse of freedom, may be a rational exercise of it. Freedom loses its more general significance for dealienation when restricted to self-objectification driven by a projection of authority. The same can be said for rationality. For obedience to authority does not require thoughtful evaluation or experimentation. When tried out, the dicta of authority may be found wanting. Self-existence may not confirm it. Then, what is to be done? The self must use its own powers to decide and thereby become authoritative for itself. The necessity for responding to any given alienating situation requires autonomy. When it is operative, self-realization is authentic, not an expression of anything alien to self. The alienating finitude of self-existence invariably requires a self who is autonomous and authentic.

Assume for the sake of inquiry that the exclusive aim of freedom is to uphold authority. The dicta of an authoritative Other would construct a self-concept. One must do or say what the Other(s) do or say. One must live as *it* or *they* want no matter who or what *it* or *they* is. Authority external to the self rules its existence providing the only identity deemed possible. Self-existence is merely illustrative of an authoritative Other, not creative of its own meaning or anything novel. Self-objectifying work, would then be a projection of authority, as well as its instantiation in social affairs and the world. Self-objectification may require the exercise of freedom, or it may not when authority dictates what the self shall think and do.

The outcome of self-objectification is to provide actual self-identity, moving the being of the self from nothing or vacuity to become something substantial, a *somebody* so to speak. But a self-created identity conforming to the dicta of an authoritative Other and lacking autonomy cannot enjoy freedom as the condition of its existence. The complete power of freedom to dealienate remains undeveloped. A self-objectified identity acquired from the authoritative Other is not an authentic expression of either the dealienating powers of the self or the potentiality for being that those powers imply. Clearly, a self whose being is dominated by an authoritative Other is a mere expression of it. Its being is an alien Other, not self-created by its dealienating power of rational freedom. Being what an authoritative Other wants, an uncompromising conformity to the universal kind, or to a behavioral norm or social role, invariably alienate the self from realizing its authentic potentiality for being.

Obedience to what authoritative Others proscribe and prescribe makes conformity the basic condition of life. Self-existence is here inauthentic as existentialism claimed. For the work of self-objectification, is not aimed at satisfying the needs and desires of self-existence, but rather those of an authoritative Other alien to the self. Whenever what it does and how it does it is mandated by an authoritative Other, self-objectification neither emanates from nor expresses any personal capacity for rational freedom. Now the self may obey authority and socially conform, even with strongly felt personal conviction. Nevertheless, this fact does not signify existential authenticity. For no process of socialization can make the self authentic in the sense of acting on behalf of its own nature, or from that nature. Becoming what the authoritative Other prescribes is realizing a potentiality for being Other and a destiny which is Other than that possible for self-existence whose potentiality for being is a realization of its own inherent power of rational freedom.

Freedom exclusively aimed at upholding authority is so narrowed in significance as to be misconceived. For then freedom becomes an exercise in obedience to authority. Depending upon the content of its dicta, obedience to authority may or may not be justifiable. When not rationally justified, the result may well be a denial of freedom understood in the sense of liberty, and in the broadest sense as the capacity to cope with alienating self-existence. Freedom validates authority, not by simple acts of obedience, but by evaluating its dicta and by experience testing. Thus, obedience to authority is not necessarily a demonstration of freedom. Neither is it necessarily a virtue. Authority can be wrong. A presumption of its superior wisdom may be false. Obedience to it may only serve to exercise social control, or serve covert interests and aims contrary to those of the self. Existence for the sake of authority robs the self of autonomy and authenticity. Since individuals compose any social group, authority exists for their sake. It is they, not it, which has the capacity to be rational and free. Only they can evaluate authority by what it does to them or for them. Just as the self can evaluate its own needs and desires, so it can evaluate the demands of authority. Without genuine reciprocity between self and authority, the latter cannot be sustained. Authority is validated only when subject to criticism and when meeting the needs of individuals.

If truth and norms are pre-established by authoritative Others to govern self-existence, then rational freedom, a power essential to dealienation, cannot be exercised or developed. The connotation of freedom is narrowed to obedience to authority, thereby distorting its general dealienating function. Rational freedom is not required for identification and introjection, which are non-rational natural processes of socialization. Dealienation, when reduced to the processes of socialization makes freedom irrelevant and unimportant. However, alienating finitude makes freedom critically important to self-existence and its capacity for dealienation. Introjected authority leaves the self alienated in several ways. First, it is formed by forces alien to its essential nature. Secondly, the existential outcome of introjected authority signifies a self dominated by an alien Other, not created by its own powers. Thirdly, any self-existence not originating from within the distinctive powers of the self cannot validate its being, cannot establish what is true and normative for it. Fourthly, self-realization is reduced to a repeated example of the universal, rather than a result of an authentic process of dealienation.

Assume for the sake of inquiry the following conception of alienation. It consists of a self, free to refuse the dicta of an authoritative Other. Dealienation then would consist of making the dicta of the Other authoritative for the self. This presumably requires a personal act of freedom such as can be found in sudden religious conversions. Kierkegaard described it as an absurd leap of faith, a demonstration of radical freedom responding to the absurdity of self-existence. Lacking the power within its own nature to cope with an absurd existence, a Kierkegaardian self decides to accept the dicta of an authoritative Other as definitive of its own being. Following such a radical decision, freedom serves the aims of authority understood to be one's own. This is a plausible interpretation of alienation and dealienation. Nevertheless, there are objections to it. Alienation is too narrowly conceived as rebellion against authority. Freedom is misconceived as obedience to authority. Freedom is not required for self-identification and introjection of authority. For these are effected by non-rational or possibly irrational coercive means of socialization involving various rewards and punishments. Dealienation may not result from doing and being what the Other dictates. In fact, more often than not, the result is an alienation of self from satisfying its own needs and desires. Bound by authority, the self fails to develop its own capacity for dealienation, namely rationality and freedom.

A process of socialization in which the self identifies with and introjects authority can have alienating consequences. For authority remains an alien Other to the self, if it cannot choose it with reasons for doing so. Socialization to authority depending upon some form of natural coercion is at best non-rational and at worst, irrational. In either case it does not originate in a self who chooses its norms based upon rational deliberation. Cast into the mold of traditional authority, a mold that is alien to and imposed upon the self, it is inauthentic and lacking in autonomy when the most important choices of its life are externally directed. Only the rational exercise of its freedom can make it autonomous and its existence authentic.

Human history presents many examples confirming whatever authoritative Others have prescribed and proscribed for self-existence. Still, their dicta require validation by self-existence, or invalidation, as might be the case. Limiting freedom to obedience to an authoritative Other narrows its general aim, which is to effect dealienation. Self-realization need not be limited to illustrating certain universalized identities and social roles prescribed by authoritative Others. Subjecting the dicta of an authoritative Other to the test of self-existence is a demonstration of the fact that the self can be autonomous and influence its own destiny. It's potentially for being then becomes an open question, not entirely determined by an Other alien to its own needs and desires.

Escaping Freedom

Since freedom originates, develops and is exercised within a context of finitude, it is necessarily disjunctive. From finite options, only one may be chosen and acted upon to the exclusion of others. Decision and action is imperative in many circumstances of life. Doing nothing might not even be possible, or might even be the worst alternative. Any particular course of action may entail undesirable but unavoidable consequences. In such situations, an exercise of freedom results in something necessarily alienating. Finitude may require choosing the lesser of two evils. Alternatively, one may tragically negate one good in order to assert another when both are in some way opposed. Sophocles' play *Antigone* depicted the paradigmatic case of this, according to Hegel, in the clash of human and divine laws and loyalties personified by Antigone and King Creon. Equally obligatory duties alienate both protagonist and antagonist. Both alternative laws are equally attractive and desirable. Choice of one is the rejection of the other making either party guilty of violating a law recognized as valid and obligatory. After violating King Creon's state edict by burying her brother according to religious law, Antigone acknowledges her obligation to the former by her admission of guilt and willingness to suffer the penalty of death for her violation.

Something becomes valuable only when we can be said to objectively need it, subjectively desire it, or both. Its value can be unconscious or conscious, objective or subjective, good or bad for us, something we can truly or falsely understand. But there is no doubt about the value of something when it is an object of intentional thought or action. Anything, be it nature, our environment, other persons or social organizations can deprive us of freedom. All human history bears witness to the struggle to gain, sustain and enhance freedom. We can suffer a loss of freedom in many ways. Someone can deprive us of liberty. Something beyond our control, such as disease, can deprive us of it. Frustrated freedom is the frustration of an essential human need; something immediately desired and actively sought. Its recovery is an imperative of our nature and of supreme value.

The demand for freedom is absolute. This is clearly demonstrated by any situation where life is risked for freedom. How many times in history has it been more honorable and preferable to die in battle or commit suicide rather than suffer the loss of one's freedom by acquiescing to enslavement. We are so in need of freedom that we cannot live without it, and this is made unmistakably clear when we suffer the threat of its loss or its actual loss. Its value is expressed by an urgent need to regain it in order to live. In fact, it can be said that the value of freedom varies inversely with the degree of its actual enjoyment. That is, the lesser the degree of freedom enjoyed, the greater its value becomes to us with the converse also being true. The extreme cases are represented by preferring death to a complete loss of freedom, or taking freedom so much for granted that we do not defend it against the threat of loss. With the latter case, freedom is so ubiquitous in our lives that we are entirely unconscious of its value. This seems true of aging well-established contemporary democracies.

Alienated freedom is self-alienation in its most radical form. For what is lost is a general capacity for dealienation. Without freedom, there is no possible response to alienating finitude. Therefore, alienated freedom has a peculiar and special ontological status as an archetypal form of alienation, its worst case. Every self is condemned to be free by the fact of its finitude, the necessity of choosing and the attendant consequences. The burden of freedom is to be responsible and accountable for personal behavior. A free self accepts the prospect of being wrong, making mistakes and being penalized. Punishments for failure or error can be severe, are always painful, and can be self-inflicted by remorse. As existentialists and various religious philosophers have claimed, being free brings with it a deep sense of guilt. For there are consequences regardless of whether the self chooses to act or not to act. Many tragic situations require choosing the lesser of two evils. Nobody enjoys being castigated, censured, criticized or ridiculed. Humiliation is never pleasant. The natural tendency is to avoid a public or private loss of respect, honor, status and esteem. Just as there is no escape from freedom, so there is no escape from its burden.

It is common for the self to attempt an escape from the burden of its freedom. The bureaucratic attempt is to either shift responsibility or socially share it. The latter is to be preferred, since any penalty for failure is applied to the group, not to any individual. Collective penalties are easily shared and less painful. On the other hand, a shared penalty is reduced to no penalty. Since everyone was responsible, nobody in particular is blameworthy. The *system* is conveniently blamed. Without the pain of blame, there is no motive for learning from mistakes, correcting them or changing a system that displaces personal risk, failure, blame and penalties. Bureaucratic incentives for avoiding the burden of freedom preserve the status quo, depresses original thinking, maintain dysfunctional social organization and make the self dysfunctional through disuse of it own rationality and freedom. The collective and a rule-bound system masks burdensome freedom. What everyone does is just OK, even if it does not make sense.

The way to escape the burden of freedom is to displace authority from the self to the Other, whatever or whomever it might be. When the stakes are high, the temptation can be overwhelming. Moreover, the self may not even be aware of displacing its own freedom onto an authoritative Other. Or, it may rationalize doing so by presuming the authoritative Other to have wisdom superior to its own. The mere fact of authority and its power does not warrant allegiance. When misconceived as mere obedience to authority, freedom is dismissed. Authoritarian control of freedom disconnects it from rationality. And when this occurs, freedom loses its dealienating power. Freedom placed exclusively in service to authority invariably results in a loss of freedom. For simply being and doing what authority prescribes, may not be an exercise of freedom. Refusal of authority may not in fact be the path of error and loss of freedom as is often claimed. Only a trial of self-existence can prove such a claim. In fact, refusal may be the better choice. For refusal may well be the initial response to alienation and therefor a first step in a dealienating process.

Freedom, an essential human capacity, is not alienable. Authoritarianism, totalitarianism, and collectivism are social forms of escaping freedom by ceding its exercise to an authoritative Other alien to the self. But, fleeing freedom only creates alienating consequences making its exercise more imperative. By the fact that the self is free and rational, it is authoritative for itself. It, not an authoritative Other, must in the end proscribe and prescribe for itself, determining which potentialities for being it objectifies as its own identity.

Modern philosophical discussions of alienation often treat it as a flight or escape from freedom. Sartre believed any attempt to alienate freedom merely confirms it. Fromm thought of attempts to alienate freedom as an irrational defense against its burdens. Escaping freedom is impossible, since human nature cannot be reified. Any attempt to do so must be maintained by repeatedly choosing to do so, as in Sartrean *bad faith*. The burdensome choice of what and whom the self must become cannot be avoided. Hegel discussed the abortive attempt to escape freedom with his description of the religious Alienated Soul. Its identity is exclusively determined by its authoritative Other, namely a priest. The result is not to unite with the unknowable

Other - God - but to reify one's own being, reducing it to an Other or external thing, equally unknowable. In ceding his freedom and capacity to reason to a priest of the medieval Roman Catholic church, the alienated believer denies the truth of his own essential nature, and so that which he seeks, namely union with God, becomes impossible to achieve.

Hegel sensed the implication of abstract possibility for immorality and alienation. "In practical life too it is no uncommon thing to see ill will and indolence slink behind the category of possibility, in order to escape definite obligations."[7] Furthermore, existentialists such as Kierkegaard and Sartre recognized an alienation of the self by its abstract possibilities where everything is an option. This provides an excuse for not choosing and taking decisive action on a matter of importance. Equal possibilities excuse accountability for ones actions, since one possibility is as good as another, or the self can be one possibility as well as another, even where both are contradictory as in Sartrean bad faith. Equal abstract possibilities, when used as an excuse to evade responsibility or accountability, undermines any sense of obligation, justifies immorality and so threatens social order.

The denial or contravention of free will is an attempt to alienate the self. This can be socially imposed or perversely self-imposed by a renunciation of freedom or by a deliberate choice of evil for self-projection in the world. In either case the actuality and potentiality of the self are separated so that the normal expression of free will that realizes any potential is cut off. Alienating freedom to an authoritative Other, whomever or whatever it might be, provides no solution to the problem of alienation, but only emphasizes and makes it worse. Hegel acknowledged this.

> Herein lies the possibility of the alienation of personality and its substantive being, whether this alienation occurs unconsciously or intentionally. Examples of alienation of personality are slavery, serfdom, disqualification from holding property, encumbrances on property, and so forth. Alienation of intelligence and rationality, of morality, ethical life, and religion, is exemplified in superstition, in ceding to someone else full power and authority to fix and prescribe what actions are to be done (as when an individual binds himself expressly to steal or to murder, &c., or to a course of action that may involve crime), or what duties are binding on one's conscience or what religious truth is, &c.[8]

However, the implications of ceding freedom to an authoritative Other could not be fully explored, since Hegel was so suspicious of the abuses of egoistic freedom and so bent upon upholding traditional authority.

Without behavior making it public, thought is private, inherently free and inviolate. Every self inhabits a world in which it is free to think anything it wishes. It is this freedom of its own thinking that is unique to itself, undeniable and inalienable. This freely thinking self cannot be other than the content of its own thought. To say otherwise is to say that what I am actually thinking is not what I am actually thinking - a contradiction terminating thought. Therefore, although the products of self-objectification are constantly alienable, their basis - the freedom to think for oneself - is not.

Hegel distinguished what is alienable from what is not. Property is alienable by renunciation, sale, and disinterest in ownership or the social obligation that accompanies it. Nevertheless, that which creates property and gives it value, a self-objectifying being, is not alienable. As opposed to property, spirituality is inalienable. That which follows from freedom, namely personality, human will, ethical life and religious belief are imprescriptible or inalienable. The alienation of our essential nature as a self-expressive rational free will cannot be accomplished either unconsciously or intentionally, since the truth of our human essence is the actual reality of our being and so cannot be denied or falsified.

Constructed by negativity, a primitive Hegelian Ego is conscious of itself by its power to abstract everything from itself. Not being the Other of which it is conscious, an abstract Ego is vacuous. It is simply nothing: an infinite potentiality for being and meaning objectifying the universal. It can become anything by its choice from among possible options presented, upon which it can act. The Other, a possibility alien to its being, can be made its own through self-identifying and self-projecting activity in the world. Volition or a free will is the means for a dealienating self-objectification. And freedom, understood to be an infinite self-realizing human capacity, cannot be alienated.

> It is the will whose potentialities have become fully explicit which is truly infinite, because its object is itself and so is not in its eyes an 'other' or a barrier; on the contrary, in its object this will has simply turned backward into itself. Further this will is not mere potentiality, capacity, potency (*potentia*), but the infinite actuality (*infinitum actu*), since the concept's existence or its objective externality is inwardness itself.[9]

Freedom expresses a self-objectifying process transcending alienating limits. Self-objectification provides the proof of a being, which is self-determined, self-sufficient, independent. Such a self is complete, whole, without contradiction or opposition within itself. It is true in being, having realized the actuality of the Hegelian Idea it has of itself.

Certainly, most self-objectifying work products are intended to be alienable. Their value resides in the reciprocal satisfaction of human needs. One's property, material or intellectual, is exchangeable when somebody else needs it. In certain ways, the self and its powers are alienable in the marketplace. Personality as public image is packaged, bought and sold every day. In this sense, it is considered alienable property from business and legal viewpoints. Products of self-objectification are considered property with ownership rights legally protected. Such property is alienable. One's labor, personality and talent are saleable. Such powers are highly valued in the marketplace. By selling these, is the self not selling its own essential capacity for rational freedom? It would seem so. Yet, rational freedom is not an alienable product when considered in an existential context broader than the marketplace. For, first it is a power necessary for dealienation. As such, its self-realizing potentiality is infinite. Self-objectified work products are alienable, but the creative power that generates them is not.

Social Implications of Rational Freedom

Freedom is ultimately based upon the negativity of being human. A self beset by alienating finitude must choose between alternatives, excluding one in favor of another. Choice is a necessity of life whether the basis of decision is deliberative, irrationally impulsive or driven by non-rational forces. That the self is free is intuitively obvious. More than that, an overwhelming evidence of human freedom surrounds self-existence. For example, the self is guilty of acting one way or another, or not acting at all, and this is factually determinable. Applications of law presume freedom where condemnation and punishment depend upon discovering whether one's deed was intended. Emotionally, remorse is evidence of personal freedom as well as any expression of regret.

Language, ordinary, moral and legal is filled with words and phrases to express the fact of personal freedom. Conscience, whether or not associated with guilt, also bespeaks human freedom. The process of socialization is intended to deal with freedom as license, its primitive form, driven by underdeveloped narcissistic and egoistic personalities. Any social structure presumes freedom by the fact of holding individuals responsible for their behavior and accountable for its consequences. The social consequences of freedom, in its primitive licentious form, makes morality and law necessary. Repression of primitive licentious freedom is socially necessary and justifiable. However, carried beyond this, such repression becomes counterproductive by interfering with the dealienating power of freedom. Since its aim is to satisfy basic human needs and desires arising from the alienating finitude of self-existence, freedom demands the maximum possible scope and minimum possible restriction. Exceptions are only justifiable and desirable when responding to specific human actions that cause unnecessary human suffering, have antisocial consequences and promote social disintegration. Licentiousness and anarchy are enemies of freedom in so far as they subvert a structure of law intended to guarantee personal security and protect personal freedom from abuse.

Freedom can be misconstrued as license, an absence of any limitation to self-seeking activity. In a brute state of nature where individual caprice and license prevail, there can be no liberty at all. Unlimited self-seeking abusing the liberty of others is socially destructive and counterproductive. So, it is justifiably limited by the state with the intention of universally securing liberty. A true exercise of freedom lies in rationally directed purposive behavior rather than self-seeking license. Freedom is hard won by a process of civilizing the individual, and the state ensures this through laws governing self-seeking behavior. Without supporting the state when it acts as the guarantor of rational freedom, there can be no freedom for anyone.

Alienating the freedom of citizens to a single individual is intended to prevent self-seeking individuals from warring upon each other thereby creating a horrendous condition of civil anarchy. When every individual cedes his natural right of unlimited freedom to a single master such as an Emperor, civil order is supposedly secured and guaranteed by the power invested in him. However, unlimited power naturally driven by self-seeking inclination abuses the governed, even to the point of making them slaves. Ceding personal freedom to an authoritative Other, whomever or whatever it may be, can only lead to tyranny and a loss of freedom. That *power corrupts and absolute power corrupts absolutely* is a wise observation. Tyranny is the temptation of absolute power, and the tyrant must be deposed to regain foolishly ceded personal freedom. Constraint of abusive power by authoritative Others such as God and law have been historically required to curb the abusive power of narcissistic and egoistic individuals. Authoritative Others with superior power provide moral direction channeling narcissism and egoism in order to secure the civil order so desired by the governed. However, personal liberty and its concrete expression acknowledged as human rights are best guaranteed by a deliberate commitment of every citizen to support them with constitutions, laws and institutions.

Human rights follow an acknowledgment of rational freedom being the essential nature of every self. Just as that nature cannot be falsified, so rights cannot be surrendered voluntarily or by coercion. For a right is an expression of freedom with a specific content. Freedom is protected by rights with universal equal applicability to every individual. Each is obligated to acknowledge its universality. Rights signify a public respect for the autonomy and dignity of every individual. Essential kinds of freedom are made inviolate by rights, implicit in law or explicitly stated in a constitution upon which law is based. Just as freedom is an inalienable fact of being human, so are the rights guaranteeing the expression of that freedom.

Rights take the form of prohibitions against infringing upon a rational free will in pursuit of natural interests and happiness. No matter whether the source of human rights is considered human nature itself or a divine gift, rights are inalienable. Hegel argued that what is internal to the self is inalienable, as opposed to what is external such as owned property.

> The right to what is in essence inalienable is imprescriptible, since the act whereby I take possession of my personality, of my substantive essence, and make myself a responsible being, capable of possessing rights and with a moral and religious life, takes away from these characteristics of mine just that externality which alone made them capable of passing into the possession of someone else. When I have thus annulled their externality, I cannot lose them through lapse of time or from any other reason drawn from my prior consent or willingness to alienate them.[10]

By this distinction of what is internal versus what is external to the self, Hegel wanted to establish the inalienability of personality. By implication then the persona of its ideas, beliefs, emotions, values, attitudes, character, moral principles and religious beliefs become inviolate.

Social structures facilitate dealienation by providing some degree of satisfaction to human needs and desires. The optimum society empowers its members by maximizing their freedom and rationality. Democracy tends to do this although its natural tendency is toward the lowest common denominator, mob rule, corruptive populism, anarchy, autocracy and tyranny. Every society has an organizing principle implicit in its laws or constitution. Can the rational freedom of every self be an organizing principle? An economic marketplace composed of individuals reciprocally satisfying their respective needs by voluntary association provides a natural principle of social cohesion. Adam Smith's *invisible hand* rules the free market. However, social cohesion is less easily secured by government and laws coercing individuals into involuntary association. Universal agreement is practically impossible to secure from individuals free to form their own opinions. What is meat for one is poison for another.

It would appear as if individual freedom couldn't be a basis for the universality of law. Every self, free to think and act as it desires can place itself into opposition with every other. Hegel pointed this out and demanded some other principle establishing universality of thought and action, or social cohesion.

> The universal here presented, therefore, is only a universal resistance and struggle of all against one another, in which each makes good his own individuality, but at the same time does not come off successfully, because each individuality meets with the same opposition, and each is reciprocally dissipated by the others. What appears as public ordinance is thus this state of war of each against all, in which every one for himself wrests what he can, executes even-handed justice upon the individual lives of others, and establishes his own individual existence, which in turn vanishes at the hands of others.[11]

An undesirable anarchic freedom can be limited by an authoritative Other, alien to the self, imposing laws and penalties.

Obedience to authority is one kind of solution to anarchic freedom. The authoritative Other may be God, a law giving person or the collective. Obedience often takes the form of conformity, a submergence of individuality in the mores of the collective. This appeals to relieving the burden of freedom, i.e. exercising one's power to think and act for oneself. Obedience to authority and submergence in the collective is based in non-rational or even irrational processes of socialization. The price of conformity and submergence can be very high with many individual needs, aspirations and enjoyments remaining unsatisfied. The mores of the collective can be just as alienating to the self as its own narcissistic and egoistic excesses. Contemporary alienation is rooted in popular culture and bureaucracy even more than in the oppressive will of the dictator. Alienation psychologically described as neurosis results from excessive authoritarian control. Dealienation will then take the form of liberation from unacceptable restrictions by the authoritative Other upon natural self-expression and self-seeking.

A just law applies universally and equally to individuals. Since anyone can disagree with what the law intends, perfect universality is an ideal almost never practically realized. Thus, enforcement of violations is practically necessary to maintain the universality of law. In addition to authoritarianism, law can be created by democratic consensus. This method presumes each participant has the capacity to think and act upon what is of common concern. All voices, although not equal in wisdom, make equal claim by virtue of a commonly alienating situation that the law is intended to address. Rational freedom allows each self to be a lawgiver for itself and participate in creating the law. What each self determines to be necessary for itself, its peers may recognize as necessary for themselves. Through common dialogue consensus is reachable. Of themselves, enforcement and consensus do not make a law just. The universality required of a just law can be assured by knowing the true needs and circumstances that the law is intended to address. Presumably, the truth is best revealed in the result of a free rational dialogue among those with differing points of view who are equally effected by the consequences of law. Even with incomplete experience and partial knowledge of the truth, democratic consensus establishes the universality of law inductively. Although imperfect, this is at least practical. A majority or plurality will do.

How consensus is achieved is critical to avoiding alienation originating from coercion by an authoritative Other. Democratic consensus utilizes the rationality and freedom of every participant who creates the law. Rational and free participation by selves with equal claim to the benefits of law assures its success. For then, law is consistent with the nature of every self, errors tend to be minimized, and consequences can be re-evaluated. Even though inefficient, democratic consensus is self-corrective. The dicta of authoritative Others alien to the self is not so easily amenable to rationally based correction.

Freedom for every self is maximized in a democratic organization of social life. A democratic culture is therefore worthy of acceptance and support by every self interested in liberty. The collective life of selves exercising their freedom creates a dynamic social fabric continuously responding to the circumstances of alienation encountered at any given historical moment. There is nothing sacrosanct about any social organization within which one lives. In fact non-democratic social structuring tends to diminish or even eliminate personal liberty, and this loss of freedom has been profoundly alienating to whole populations. For this reason, totalitarianism has been found wanting and unworthy of self-identification and self-objectification.

In a free society, the individual may or may not choose to identify with or project cultural mores which tend to alienate him in some way. He may respond by ignoring them or experimenting with substitutes. Alternatively, he may rebel and change them through public advocacy or political activism. If successful, alienating mores or laws can be abandoned, changed, or replaced along with those social institutions which promote them. Responding in this manner allows individuals to make a difference and transforms culture within a social structure permitting rational freedom to flourish. Social institutions sustain norms established by the freedom of individuals. Hegel recognized this fact but explained it away in deference to traditional authority. Great world historical individuals did not address the alienation of their time in an authentic way or with any degree of autonomy, but were considered unconscious puppets carrying out the pre-established Ideas of Geist. Freedom is here minimized and misconceived as obedience to an authoritative Other.

The self-projection and self-objectification of each individual member of any group concretely defines how it exists and what it is. Free selves behaving rationally can create community. Rational freedom, whether potential or actual, is of the highest value to every individual. From this, and the fact that it creates community, follows a whole democratic civilization that respects individual dignity, demands personal liberty, equal rights and equal opportunity for everyone. Narcissistic or egoistic selves cannot create stable communities. Only a fully socialized self who is autonomous and authentic can do so. Both anarchic self-seeking and absolute power of authoritative Others generate similar alienating consequences. The history of western civilization is plausibly a progressive realization of the dealienating power of rational freedom, a potentiality of every self. The terrible human suffering of twentieth century wars was a working through of rational freedom. There has been a worldwide rejection of totalitarianism. Freedom has been emphatically re-asserted by the triumph of democracy. Moreover, it has become a real worldwide possibility for the twenty-first century. The refusal of self-destructive nuclear war was a triumph of rationality currently undergoing near exponential growth with advances of scientific knowledge and technology.

Notes

1. Hegel, G. W. F. (1956) *The Philosophy of History* (J. Sibree, Trans.). New York, NY: Dover, 19.

2. Hegel, G. W. F. (1953) *Reason in History* (Robert S. Hartman, Trans.). New York, NY: Macmillan, 24-25.

3. Hegel, G. W. F. (1830) *Hegel's Logic*: Being Part One of the Encyclopedia of the Philosophical Sciences (3rd ed., 1975) (William Wallace, Trans.). London, England: Oxford University Press, 55.

4. Ibid., 220.

5. Ibid., 136.

6. Hegel, *Reason in History*, 26-27.

7. *Hegel's Logic*, 204.

8. Hegel, G. W. F. (1977) *Hegel's Philosophy of Right* (T. M. Knox, Trans.). New York, NY: Oxford University Press, 53.

9. Ibid., 30.

10. Ibid., 53.

11. Hegel, G. W. F. (1967) *The Phenomenology of Mind* (J. B. Baillie, Trans.). New York, NY: Harper and Row, 399.

Chapter Five

Religious Dealienation

Religious Alienation

Every religion is concerned with alienation, particularly with its manifestation in human suffering and mortality. These are religiously interpreted and ameliorated with general prescriptions for dealienation known as ways of salvation. Generally described, salvation is achieved by faith in, love of, and obedience to the dicta of an authoritative Other of the self, be it a prophet, God, or however defined. Salvation is promised or earned by a self-objectification of the faithful conforming to certain prescriptions involving love, prayerful contemplation and ritual observances.

Religious moral prescriptions socialize the self and create a community of the faithful with all its attendant spiritual and practical benefits. Religious socialization assists the family generally, by reinforcing the self-development of its youth, transmitting mores, and providing a sense of empathy with and compassion for the plight of others through charitable works. Historically, religion has provided a moral foundation for law and government effecting every social institution. Religious ritual celebrates significant life transitions with sacraments for birth, adulthood, marriage and death. Religion has actively confronted various alienating conditions of life and offered various palliative responses to human suffering which are more than resignation or mere opiates. Any adequate understanding of religion must consider its response to alienation from psychological and sociological perspectives. Without such an analysis, religion can be easily overlooked or dismissed as ignorance and superstition, an unfortunate conclusion indeed.

The alienating finitude of self-existence prompts a religious attitude and religious questions such as, "Who or what is God?" Or, in critically important and perplexing life situations lacking self-guidance, "What would God have me do?" Any chosen way of salvation answers such questions and provides self-identity. A religious orientation defines the self through its authoritative Other, its God. The self is alienated from its fellows and its God by a natural self-seeking disregarding the evil consequences of its behavior. An incompletely socialized self, be it narcissistic or egoistic, with unconstrained freedom, is by its very nature an evil doer. Freedom is problematical in its potentiality for evil doing and sin. An unconstrained freedom invariably results in sin, which disobeys one's own nature and God. Since the self is a blind conatus toward unlimited self-seeking desire, an authoritative Other is necessary to constrain the evil consequences of freedom. Fear of punishment and obedience to the commands of an authoritative Other socializes a primitive self whose freedom is otherwise undisciplined and dangerous. A religious self fears its God, humbles itself, self-identifies with an identity pre-established by its God, and projects itself in the world with others in conformity therewith.

Negativity structures self and world always as alien Other. The world alters continuously and the self must become what it is not in order to satisfy the needs and desires which eloquently bespeak the deficiency of its present being and its future potentiality for being. A God, conceived as perfect being lacking nothing, can provide the archetype for that Other which the self and world must become. Nevertheless, any prescription for dealienation is subject to the test of self-existence and religious salvation is no exception. The manner in which one's God is conceived and its prescription for salvation can alienate the self. This occurs whenever that prescription contradicts natural human needs, desires or the capacity for rational freedom. Under this circumstance, one's God cannot be self-projected or self-objectified. A self without autonomy cannot exist authentically and so dealienation is generally prohibited. Religious authoritarianism generates this tragic result.

The Judeo-Christian religious explanation of alienation is found in the biblical myth of the fall whereby an original sin of disobedience to the dicta of the authoritative Other, God, is committed. The sinners are punished by an expulsion from paradise and are condemned to labor for survival. Alienating finitude is a burden along with the necessary work of dealienation. The manifold messages of this myth are deeply significant and have effected western civilization for many centuries. The myth recognizes the alienating finitude of self-existence, provides an interpretation of its origin and consequences, interprets the significance of knowledge, human freedom, its relationship to evil, and offers a general religious prescription for dealienation.

In perfect mythological symbiosis with a nurturing creator - its God - all biological needs and related desires of the self are perfectly satisfied. Nothing threatens its survival. It is completely secure. There is no incentive for it to develop. Primitive narcissism is a paradisiacal existence without distinction of self from its nurturing Other. A narcissistic self exists in unself-conscious ignorance and innocence without fear, guilt, shame or freedom. Its life is that of amoral nature not requiring any morality or laws to constrain self-seeking behavior which might cause the suffering of others. However, this narcissistic paradise is ruptured by a cataclysmic event. A being created in God's image, free to think and act for itself, and curious, disobeys its nurturing authoritative Other.

Eating the forbidden fruit is the occasion of an original sin against the dicta of God. An act of disobedience ruptures paradisiacal narcissism. The self is alienated from its nurturing authoritative Other. Its loss is mythologically signified by the shame of nakedness. Narcissistic symbiosis with God is forever lost. The effort to recover it is to reunite self and God by means of the very power by which it was lost; namely, the ability to think and act for oneself. Yet, this capacity prevents any retrogressive restoration of lost narcissism. There is no choice but to continue with what is initiated by radical freedom. The only available path to restoring the lost primitive narcissistic harmony of man with his environment springs from the labor of the human spirit to create its culture and civilization. Thus begins an odyssey of the human spirit. Development proceeds from an amoral childlike innocence to acquiring the wisdom of an adult, who knows through suffering what is good from what is evil. The infinite human power of rational freedom, an image of the creator, is a divine gift bestowed upon every self. Just as it is misused in an alienating act of disobedience to the authoritative Other, so must it be reused to dealienate. And in its use, the self, its world and authoritative Other are recreated in a completely unexpected and different way.

The rupture with narcissism brings with it the alienating finitude of self-existence. The self is forever cursed by the requirement of its finitude to labor to satisfy its own needs and desires. It must work simply to survive. This is the divine penalty for having the power to disobey a nurturing authoritative Other. Dealienation of a finite being is the penance for disobedience to a nurturing authoritative Other. Yet dealienation does not effect a reunion, but rather transforms the relationship of authoritative Other to the self. It develops a new self-concept from exercising its own powers in egoistic self-seeking. Its identity progressively becomes its own doing, rather than one pre-established and governed by an authoritative Other. In fact the authoritative Other is progressively transformed into a self who is autonomous and whose existence is authentic rather than an alien given. The self discovers itself to be a historical product of its power and dealienating endeavor. As it becomes Other than it is by its exercise of rational freedom, the locus of authority shifts, progressively residing within its own being rather than in an external authoritative Other. Its God progressively becomes its own divine power, expressed in the outcome of dealienation, tempered by the mistakes it has made, the evil it has perpetrated, and wisdom it has obtained through its own suffering.

Alienation, however understood, begins with finitude, meaning a being existing and altering over time. When that being is human, its being is deficient. Its being is a potentiality for being, something to be realized over time. It has needs and desires. It senses an obligation to become something or someone other than it is at present. Alienation, then, is that separation of what it is from what it ought to be and can become; a potentiality for being to be actualized. Religion acknowledges self-existence burdened with alienating finitude. However, religion narrows the scope of alienation to a separation of self from a specific authoritative Other, namely God, however conceived. Judeo-Christian religion believes that separation is effected by a misuse of freedom in acts of disobedience to divine intention or law. Ethical prescriptions for escaping alienation from God are offered with the promise of achieving a different state of being, be it a heaven of an afterlife or nirvana. That specific forms of alienation can be overcome incrementally is generally acknowledged. That it can be overcome with finality within the finitude of self-existence is impossible. Human finitude in all its dimensions makes heavenly bliss or nirvana an impossible dream. Religion promises it as a reward for obedience to the dicta of God. Such inducements to the faithful undoubtedly contribute to the power of institutionalized religion and its socializing ethos.

Religious salvation has its counterpart in secular dealienation. Both are an exercise of spirituality, defined as rational freedom. The religious exercise is devoted to a life of faith and obedience to divine authority and law. The secular exercise is devoted to realizing human potentialities in a finite world. Hegel wanted the secular exercise of rational freedom to be coextensive with the religious. He wanted finite secular life to express infinite divine purpose. The secular work of dealienation Hegel intended to be the religious work of salvation. Obedience to divine authority and law has its secular counterpart in obedience to the authority and law of the Hegelian-conceived State, justified as reflecting the divine. Hegel believed the Reformation historically marked the end of ecclesiastical alienation. Lutheran Protestantism allowed the self to recover a lost personal relationship to the divine with an enhanced personal freedom objectifying divine purpose and law into secular life. A religiously guided secular life would then be a seamless whole. All social institutions, including the State would be actively sustained by selves performing social roles sanctioned by religion.

Spiritual life begins with freedom expressed through disobedience alienating self from its authoritative Other. This can be a parent confronting a rebellious pubescent teenager as well as the creator God of Adam and Eve. The biblical myth expresses what can be observed in the natural development of every self. Freedom and self-identity are initiated by rebellious disobedience to authority. Self-development requires freedom. With it, the self constructs its own identity by its own choices and self-objectifying work. Without an outlet for freedom the self remains in symbiosis with its original authoritative Other, whatever or whomever it might be. The historical odyssey of dealienation commences with the freedom exercised by each self. Just as the self constructs its life history, so humanity constructs its world history.

The result of dealienation ensuing from the narcissistic rupture is a symbiotic reunion with a nurturing authoritative Other not possible by any simple act of obedience. For the self has developed beyond an authoritarian solution to its alienation. That originally sinful act of disobedient estrangement from authority is also an occasion for the development of the divine gifts of reason and freedom. A self who thinks and acts for itself is condemned to do evil and discover what is good or bad for itself. Self-development must experience the hubris of egoistic freedom, an awakening from narcissistic innocence and ignorance through guilt, shame and punishment. Just as freedom inflicts the wound, so must it heal it. The enormous potential for evil flowing from egoistic freedom is only ameliorated by suffering its consequences and acquiring wisdom therefrom. To know the difference of good from evil is not simply to be taught the duty to obey the dicta of an authoritative Other. That precious knowledge is taught by the very process of existential dealienation.

Authoritarian Evil

The biblical myth of the fall casts evil as a result of a divine gift of freedom. Evil is not just something that happens accidentally. It is a self-inflicted wound motivated by natural self-seeking inclination placed in opposition to authority by freedom expressed as disobedience. The temptation to disobey lies in the non-rational or irrational impulses of nature. Thus is nature held to be opposed to the spiritual, which is presumably based upon rationality and freedom. Natural inclination and self-assertive freedom are the reasons for disobeying authority. Doing good, or what is right, consists of doing one's duty, which is obligatory by reason of its presumed authoritative source and rationality.

The religious doctrine of original sin ascribes evil to being in bondage to nature. Hegel expressed this religious conviction in these words.

> For the very notion of spirit is enough to show that man is evil by nature, and it is an error to imagine that he could ever be otherwise. To such extent as man is and acts like a creature of nature, his whole behaviour is what it ought not to be. For the spirit it is a duty to be free, and to realize itself by its own act. Nature is for man only the starting-point which he has to transform. ... In that finite sphere man pursues ends of his own and draws from himself the material of his conduct. While he pursues these aims to the uttermost, while his knowledge and his will seek himself, his own narrow self apart from the universal, he is evil; and his evil is to be subjective.[1]

The alienation of evil doing results in an isolation of self from realizing its true nature and community as pre-established by the intentions of its creator and authoritative Others. Hegel disagreed with the enlightenment notion that man in a state of nature is inherently good and, by following his natural impulses, does good. Such a doctrine is presumed naive, false and socially dangerous. Unlimited self-seeking without reference to the universal interests of community or laws, human and divine, is what makes human beings evil. Its source lies in an untamed lawless subjective will indicative of freedom in bondage to natural appetite and irrational passion; unguided by rationality expressed by categorical propositions and universal norms guiding human behavior.

Enslavement to nature denies freedom, implies a self driven by need, natural inclination, impulse, irrational passion, perverse desire, all of which are self-defeating and dangerous to collective survival. A narcissistic or egocentric self whose freedom is unconstrained by any authoritative Other is a recipe for evil doing and social disintegration. Selves with such an absolute degree of freedom become uncivilized in their disrespect of the needs and dignity of other persons, their rights and the law itself. Thus would civilization degenerate into hellish anarchy. An authoritative Other is then required to coerce lawless self-seekers to respect their fellows and obey the law.

The paradigmatic case of authoritarian defined evil is a self choosing to act upon its own natural desires in opposition to the dicta of authority. In doing so the lesser is mistakenly placed above the greater, the particular above the universal, which Hegel presumed absurd. The root of evil is then a personal exercise of freedom, which is irrational by virtue of defying the true nature of the self as pre-established by an authoritative Other(s). Rationality would here consist of using freedom to establish self-existence conforming to a universal definition of it.

Traditional authority establishes the truth of human nature from which follows whatever is normative for self-conduct. Thus, in order to avoid evil doing, every self must be carefully taught to know what traditional authority prescribes for its existence and, that its duty is to obey the customs, behavioral norms and laws established by authoritative Others. Since whatever traditional authority prescribes is presumed universally true of and for self-existence, any rational self is obligated to obey and instantiate it. Not only is disobedience to authority evil doing, but it is also a falsification of the true being of the self, self-contradiction, an alienation of self from itself as well as its authoritative Other. Self-identity is not possible without self-objectification proceeding from a conception of self mandated by authoritative Others. Freedom, conceived negatively, has no content except that provided by an authoritative Other. Thus, freedom is a mere means for self-objectification and is unable to establish self-identity. Self-realization is limited to instantiating the prescriptive ideas of authoritative Others. Life in every dimension, be it personal or social, is then structured in an authoritarian mode.

Religion presents an authoritarian conception of evil excellently depicted by the biblical myth of the fall. Evil doing is held to be disobedience of the self to its true definition as prescribed by the dicta of an authoritative Other. However, disobedience to authority is too narrow and problematical a conception of evil. What it presumes true of human nature is dubious at best. That it presumes self-existence can be pre-established by an authoritative Other is falsified by a being who is free, rational and self-realizing. The inadequacy of an authoritarian conception of evil is supported by many considerations.

Disobedience of authority does not comport with evil doing commonly understood as causing unnecessary suffering. That disobeying authority is evil requires validation. However, if the dicta of authority are pre-established to govern self-existence, there is no way for the self to validate it. For it does not originate with, and is not subject to being tested or developed through any process of self-existence. Existential authentication of the dicta of authority can only consist of confirming it through subservience and obedience. Such behavior is not validating, since it is not based upon the rationality of the self. An autonomous authentically existing self would be free to question, even to rebel, if not make trial of alternatives. Nevertheless, such a self would be condemned as a perpetrator of evil from an authoritarian perspective.

Evil, then, is held to be a misuse of freedom in a natural self-seeking opposed to the dicta of authority. Yet, as with everything else, the dicta of authority requires the application of rationality herein defined by the capacity of every self to critically evaluate it within an existential context. When meeting such a test, the dicta of authority is validated and authenticated by each self and so generally legitimized. Elaborate philosophical rationalization, non-rational appeals to faith, collectivism and social coercion are not necessary to support traditional authority, since it is in fact being continuously tested by self-existence. Authority is created and sustained within a process of dealienation driven by natural self-seeking desire tempered by rational freedom.

Without, or in defiance of direction from the Other(s), personal freedom is claimed to be a source of evil. A freedom which negates authority is suspect, not to be trusted, threatening and dangerous to the self and society. Yet, freedom is an essential capacity of the self necessary for dealienation. Such a dealienating power cannot be itself evil and alienating. Certainly, desire and self-seeking are universal and not claimed to be intrinsically evil. Without self-seeking desire, nothing of value, good or bad, could exist. In fact, self-seeking given impetus by natural desires defines an existential process of dealienation requiring both rationality and freedom indicative of an autonomous self, existing authentically. Moreover, natural desire and self-seeking establish whatever is normative for the community. Therefore, neither community nor authority is necessarily opposed to natural self-seeking. In fact both depend upon it and likewise support it. Institutions, laws and authority most often support the liberty of individuals to seek whatever they desire with minimal restrictions imposed only for good reasons.

An authoritarian conception of evil acknowledges the rationality and freedom of the self, but limits both by subordinating them to traditional authority. Rationality is narrowly defined as knowing what is universally good to be one's duty. The self is carefully taught to distinguish good from bad, right from wrong, and that its duty is to do what is right and good. Can what the prevailing authoritative Others prescribe to socialize the self be considered knowledge? If socialization were a kind of knowledge, it would be true of and for every self, at any time and under every circumstance. However, socialization to the dicta of traditional authority often does not meet this criterion for establishing knowledge. Thus, socialization of the self can be wrong or bad particularly when its demands unnecessarily limit the satisfaction of human needs, desires, freedom and rationality. Too often, authoritarian socialization has this effect.

If the dicta of authority were knowledge, it would be true of and for self-existence. However, knowledge is not reducible to socialization. Knowledge is not simply social conformity in belief, attitudes and behavior. Neither is knowledge a product of natural social coercion based upon feeling and emotion rather than thought. Obedience to authority is secured through a process of socialization, which cannot masquerade as knowledge. An authoritarian socialization is doing what the Other(s) commands rather than knowing what is true or right. Here there is no appeal to rationality, since socialization is achieved by coercive non-rational means with reward and punishment of conduct. Knowing and doing what an authoritative Other dictates does not require rationality defined as the capacity of the self to think for itself and critically evaluate what is commanded. Authoritarian socialization makes the self obedient, not autonomous or authentic in being. Virtues of authoritarian socialization are subservience and obedience.

The self is a product of its own historical development. Ultimately, its temporal existence and dealienating endeavors reveal what it true of it as well as for it. The outcome of this existential process of dealienation determines the truth or falsity of any prescription intended to describe or socially control it. What authoritative Others prescribe for its existence may or may not be true of what it is or what it ought to become. An indeterminacy of being is the truth of self-existence. This does not mean there is no truth to be learned from existence. Self-realization reveals the truth. Whatever is true of or for the self is continuously being tested, formed and reformed by the temporal process of dealienating existence. Given a self-existence characterized by alienating finitude, desires, needs, rationality and freedom; every self must realize what and who it is in time.

Atonement

Alienation and dealienation are the themes implicit in Hegelian philosophy. Alienation is loss of something and dealienation is a process of recovering the loss. The process would be simply circular, except that the process of recovery enhances the significance of what was originally lost. The metaphor of loss and recovery is expressed religiously for Hegel by the crucifixion and resurrection of Christ. Hegel's notion of sublation reflects a distinguishing and a dialectical reuniting resulting in an enriched meaning which is more than the opposed components, and so novel.

Hegelian-interpreted history proceeds in stages of alienation. First, the divine is lost. Then the self discovers its own capacity for freedom. Reveling in its own nature and freedom, the self attempts to make itself the basis of dealienation. This fails sending it into deep despair over itself. At this stage, the self is receptive to a religious conversion in which it identifies with divine dicta to achieve salvation. Conversions typically occur only when the self is brought to despair over its own capacity to cope with its alienation. Once the self renounces its own capacity for dealienation, it is receptive to a religiously prescribed salvation. A converted self prays to its God for salvation and avows its self-identification with the prescriptions founded in scripture and institutionalized religion. Participation in religious ritual continually renews and reinforces self-identification and commitment by the faithful.

Hegel viewed religion as providing a moral foundation for civil law and social institutions. His early critique of *positive religion* was that hypocritical formality and religious ritual weakened the personal bond of self with its God. Positive religion locates the moral law in an alien Other, namely God. The source of that law is alien to the self and contrary to its natural sinful inclinations. Therefore, the problem of positive religion always is how to internalize religiously presented moral law. In other words, how can the moral law become an authentic expression of the self? The Kantian solution, embraced by Hegel in his early theological writings but later repudiated, locates the source of the moral law in the autonomy of the self. If so, the moral law is authentically expressed. If not, the self must internalize a moral law alien to itself. Hegel's early Christian theological training and conviction emphasized love as *the* mechanism for religious self-identification. Later, Hegel dismissed this power of love, believing it unreliable, since it is voluntary and based upon natural inclination he presumed capricious and subject to contingent circumstance.

If human love is an unreliable means of religious self-identification, then a sinful self-concept might be more effective since it brings into play coercive psychological and sociological dynamics. A sinner's guilty conscience is an effective psychologically painful form of punishment. The emotional reaction to sin is remorse associatively followed by repentance and redemption. Sins are forgiven when the sinner is judged truly repentant and this is confirmed by an avowal of faith coupled with righteous living conforming to religious prescription and practice. Without intense personal involvement, redemption is inauthentic and hypocritical as claimed by the Lutheran reformation. If the sinner continues to view either the law or its divine source as alien to himself, then atonement and salvation become impossible.

Believing that his God is inaccessible or an alien authoritative Other, conjoined with the repeated temptation to sin and dreading God's wrath, the self lives with the angst of the sinner over his moral deficiency of character. In desperation, he can turn to the forlorn hope of divine grace. Alternatively, he can rely upon the intercession of a clergyman who persuades him, for his fealty, that he is still worthy in spite of his sinful thoughts or misdeeds. Nevertheless, such intercession is inauthentic to the self. Believing its identity to be defined by the intercessor for a price amounts to crass self-deception. The sinner cannot help but recognize the inauthenticity, deceitfulness and falsity of this self-image. Thus, any palliation of sin or guilty conscience by intercession proves ineffective. For it maintains the powerless condition of the sinner to religiously dealienate in an authentic manner. The chasm between human and divine remains along with a self whose being is inauthentic and conflicted about its own nature held in low esteem. Not only is the sinner nothing next to his God, but his value is next to nothing. There can be no solution to this religious alienation unless the divine is located within the human. The conditions necessary for expressing the divine necessarily involve self-identification, self-projection and self-objectification. Without this, God is not real or realized in the world, and religious culture is jeopardized.

If fear of damnation is insufficiently coercive of the sinner, then love may be an option for redemption and salvation. Certainly, self-identification with the divine is achieved through love. The Bible exhorts the faithful to seek salvation through love:

> And thou shalt love the Lord thy God with all thine heart, and with all thy soul, and with all thy might. And these words, which I command thee this day, shall be in thine heart: And thou shalt teach them diligently unto thy children.[2]

Extending love to human relationships, the Bible again exhorts, "... thou shalt love thy neighbour as thyself..."[3]

In effect, such exhortations proclaim the necessity of self-identification through a love which must be taught and learned. Love socializes the self and saves the alienated soul. A philosophically matured Hegel was skeptical that emotion alone, such as love, could overcome religious alienation. When love is understood as a mere fleeting emotion, then loving devotion, by itself, is insufficient for religious dealienation. The alienated worshipper cannot maintain the emotional force of love, or love strongly enough, to breach the chasm with an unreachable God. The endeavor to maintain the relationship to God must then become obsessive in practice, only resulting in a heightening consciousness of absolute separation from God. However, Hegel may well have been wrong to emphasize the emotional aspect of love while de-emphasizing the practical redemptive power of a love that drives self-objectification.

A sinful self-concept acknowledges a deficiency of character. Remorse and dread follow sinful behavior. The sinner lives with the emotional burden of guilt and a dread of divine retribution as the price to be paid for sin. Although guilt and dread are painful punishments, they need not be morbid or indicative of some pathology. Rather, both function positively to socialize the self. Guilt and dread are the internalized levers for social control by religious authority, or any authority for that matter. Religion offers redemption from sin through conversion, a profession of a creed and religiously prescribed righteous personal conduct.

Even if the historical fact of personal sin is ineradicable, atonement can proceed by acts of forgiveness and *agape* illustrated by religious figures such as Christ. Acts of forgiveness for sins committed assuage personally felt guilt and dread. Religious redemption requires forgiveness by an authoritative Other and oneself. The young theologically schooled Hegel argued that redemption is not achieved by means of punishment for violating a law. For punishment returns like for like thereby seeking to restore equality between the demand of the law and the lawbreaker.[4] Such justice diminishes the life of the sinner. Redemption recognizes the sinner is more in being than his sin. He has the possibility of choosing to redirect his life. If he does so, his sin becomes part of a dead past, no longer operative in his present or future life. Unreserved agape, giving impetus to his powers of freedom and reason, redeems the sinner casting his fate as his own doing rather than the result of sin. With a demonstration of agape, guilt can disappear, since the sinner's self-concept is no longer determined solely by his past sins. A self-concept redirected away from sin by a faith commitment and agape allows the sinner to eventually forgive himself.

The prophetic tradition of Judaism interpreted misfortune to signify divine retribution for sinfulness. A dealienating response of the faithful to their misfortune was to assume collective guilt, warranted or not. Penance is then a personal repudiation of sin. The penitent, renouncing sinful desires and aims, proves it with sacrificial behavior. This might consist of giving up some personal property, mortification, or adopting some kind of ascetic self-discipline. While the avowed aim is reconciliation with the divine, the penitent atones with practices prescribed by religious authority. The practical effect is to reinforce social control of the faithful and achieve social cohesion through common religious purpose.

Apocalyptic religious tradition has advocated pacifism as a possible response to alienation. Instead of opposing a prospective loss, the self renounces it, adopting an indifferent attitude. Hegel called a *Beautiful Soul*, the self who renounces the natural desires of life. This negative freedom was admired for its assertion of spirituality above natural desire, something very difficult to achieve. "Beauty of soul has as its negative attribute the highest freedom, i.e., the potentiality of renouncing everything in order to maintain one's self."[5] For the sins committed by his enemies, Christ responded with a pacific love, a presumably reconciling forgiveness and a renunciation of life itself. While it is true that pacifism does not subject one to the risk of a fate decided by violence and accidental circumstance, it is hard to see how the alienation of one's freedom is effectively dealt with by renouncing it, by undergoing enslavement, by accepting death or choosing suicide. Hegel thought of pacifism as fate, self-determined. Nevertheless, it is not, since the alienating Other(s) deny one's freedom and control one's fate.

Returning good for evil would appear to be acquiescing to it. Forgiveness and love of the evil doer enables his conduct rather than changing it. The sinner, if he is to be redeemed, must himself atone. No pacific example by those sinned against can do this for him. Neither can any practice of agape toward the sinner. Nor can forgiveness by an authoritative Other. Forgiveness must be warranted and merited by an authentic eschewal of sin and evil. Authentic repentance, a transformed self-concept and conduct warrants forgiveness. A pacifism which renounces what has been forcibly taken away and forgives sin without any warrant merely rationalizes misfortune. Believing it to be divine retribution for one's own sins does not rectify the situation. The passivity and impotence of pacifism contradicts its intended effect serving only to promote victimization and martyrdom. Pacifism asks too much of the oppressed and provides little comfort in apocalyptic belief and the promise of heaven for the righteous.

Escaping Finitude

Death is the quintessential signifier of human finitude, a final limit to human existence. Observed by the living, death is oblivion. In death, the physical no longer supports the psychical or spiritual, and the self ceases to exist. Death signifies that the self is not present in or to the world. Nothing is signified and there is no meaning. Negativity is no longer operative as a consciousness of the alien Other or of the self. Existence is no longer a negatively determined possibility of being something Other in the future. Death is a cessation of time, the nothing of eternity. Conceived as extinction, death is an escape from alienating finitude, but only in the narrow negative sense of its absence. There is no conscious presentation of a limiting Other or reactive self. There is nothing beyond. Yet, religion imagines the possibility of escaping finitude to a condition of being sometimes called nirvana or heaven. Since what is beyond human existence cannot be experienced, it can only be imagined in terms of existence. Such beliefs are acts of faith without rational grounding in self-existence. No evidence can be adduced for believing that disembodied souls leave the body at death and migrate to some realm beyond the natural world, be it heaven or hell.

Death is the ultimate signifier of finitude. The life of every individual ends in death. For the dead there is only nothingness or oblivion. The significance of death is for the living. It is first an absence of a loved one and a grieving over the loss. However, death signifies much more. For the dead are remembered for what they have contributed to culture and posterity. The lives of forbears, serving some surviving purpose for posterity to enjoy, is often celebrated with gratitude by the living. Their self-objectifying work survives them and lives on in the culture of future generations. Immortality consists of this for finite human beings. Every self-existence links past to future by what is achieved in the present. Any life that has counted for something and for others maintains a deep transcending continuity with humanity and being in general. Religion senses this significance of death. Thus, it refuses to acknowledge death to be merely oblivion and a return to nonbeing. Hence, the appeal of belief in an afterlife, even without evidence.

A religious attitude toward death demands that life have a meaning transcending death. Therefore personal extinction, without any purpose transcending finitude, is rejected. Nevertheless, the demand for self-affirmation and transcendent meaning would appear to be universal. Every self wants its existence to contribute or count for something. One's life has to make a difference. This demand is shared even by atheistic existentialists who consider life absurd and without purpose. For they have taken particular notice of how impending death gives life a certain urgency. It becomes important for a self contemplating its death to realize whatever potentiality for being it has. This gives freedom its importance, making it in fact a necessity for self-realization.

Hegel, a committed Christian, recognized finitude and death to be an inescapable human fate. "The being as such of finite things is to have the germ of decease as their being-within-self: the hour of their birth is the hour of their death."[6] This is a most melancholy thought for Hegel, an emotional realization of alienating finitude. Yet, he refused to become resigned to an absurd life without purpose. Finitude could not merely signify a perpetual encounter with an alien Other without any final reconciliation. The very process of finitude seeks closure and reconciliation with the totality of being. Contrary to existentialists, Hegel refused to despair over the alienating finitude of self-existence. Instead, he demanded and attempted a philosophical reconciliation of finitude with infinite being. Hegel's religious response was to embrace Christian beliefs in redemption, resurrection, salvation and union with an infinite God in an eternal afterlife.

Hegel considered finitude a self-contradictory notion when understood to consist of an interminable process of negation that also terminates in Non-being. It is a mistake to think of the infinite as absolutely beyond the finite and unreachable by it. If finitude were an infinite negating process, it would contribute nothing and affirm nothing. Finitude without telos becomes an abstract and absurd process of negation. Negativity drives the process of finitude, but is not its aim. The telos of finitude is not the nullity of everything. Hegel offered in opposition to this view a different conception of the infinite. It is considered a whole that is the outcome of a process of expanding finitude. The negating aspect of finitude signifies an affirmation of being in its infinite aspect. Extinction in the death of individual finite beings is not their true destiny signifying a mere return to Non-being. Death can signify a positive contribution to an expanding infinite whole being. The negativity of finitude then affirms being thereby leaving in its wake a positive outcome. Thus, the truer significance of negativity lies in the being that it affirms, rather than in the fact of negativity itself. Finitude is certainly a process of negation, but a process that transcends negativity in outcome by presenting the infinite.

Among many philosophers, Hegel believed it possible to escape finitude and offered an absolute idealist interpretation of how it might be done. The *infinite* is an escape from finitude, since it can not only be defined as such, but also demonstrated by a continuous sublating progression of the *finite* in the progress of history. This re-conceived *infinite* is revealed by the intentional temporal activity of a self writ large, namely Geist. Still, this model is based upon the alienating finitude of self-existence from which meaning is derived, and upon the intentional dealienating activity of a rational and free self. Just as finitude is the condition of alienation, so must finitude be reflected in the result of dealienation.

Death can be considered a final determination of finitude, its termination. In death, life as a process of changing determinations of finite beings, ceases. The ceasing-to-be process of finitude terminates, is negated, left an unresolved contradiction. Finite being remains unreconciled with its alien Other. There is no satisfactory closure. In death, a finite being becomes simply nothing lacking any structure of meaning. In effect, alienating finitude is considered absolute. This is unacceptable to Hegel in several ways. First, calling the outcome of a finite being Non-being is contradictory. Second, if finitude simply terminated as Non-being in death, then finitude and life itself would have no meaning. Hegel disagreed, arguing that finitude points beyond itself to an infinite whole of being which gives it meaning. Death is not finality, but rather a carrying forward of what was affirmed by life. The result of alienating finitude cannot be merely a return to a Non-being, which is simply the obverse of Being, an abstract beginning and a driver of the whole process. Rather than implying such an alienating absurdity, finitude implies the infinite. This is for Hegel the true significance of finitude. Finally, Hegel was committed to sustaining religious faith in a creator God, whose death in the person of Christ signified an escape from alienating finitude and the promise of union with God in an eternal afterlife.

Another approach to escaping finitude is to identify the *infinite* with the *universal,* which is thought to be a whole including all possible finite instances of a kind. Thinking the universal could then be considered an escape from finitude, from the temporal limits of human existence, from the opposition presented by its the limiting Other(s). Geist or a divine mind might be the thinker, but still without any existential basis. A divine thinker, thinking itself, does not think the Other of itself: thus, it is thinking nothing, or not thinking at all. There is here no thinker and no existential impetus for thought to occur.

Now Hegel correctly recognized that thought and its extension in intentional behavior constitutes a process by which a finite self creates its finite world. Considered as a continuous finite process, negating thought and intentional behavior transcend finitude. The infinite then is this spiritual process of self-transcendence; thinking and acting with the universal to concretely realize it. This spiritual process transcends the limits of time, space or place, and the determinacy of past history. Its movement is liberation from finitude within finitude by means of a self-objectifying process generating a history. Yet, the outcome, although a continuous transcending process, can only produce a finite result. While the *infinite* can be conceived as a continuous process of transcending of the finite, there can be no transcending of the continuous process itself. Thus, transcending finitude either in thinking of acting cannot move the thinker or actor to an infinite that is beyond finitude.

Religion depicts God(s) in various ways thought of as an *absolute universal* ideally unifying all differences among finite things of the world. Hegel's God was known philosophically as a being transcending the finite. Hegel speculated that his own infinite creator God is the object of every historical religion, although imperfectly comprehended and revealed to each one in varying degrees of truth. Understood as a component of the absolute Idea, Hegel believed he had philosophically made a final statement about his God. Dealienation was thought to be at least intellectually achievable by a contemplation of the divine by finite mortals. A religious contemplation of God,

> ... is the region of eternal truth and eternal virtue, the region where all the riddles of thought, all contradictions, and all the sorrows of the heart should show themselves to be resolved, and the region of the eternal peace through which the human being is truly human.[7]

Religious contemplation aims at transcending finitude.

> In the region in which spirit concerns itself with this aim it unburdens itself of all finitude and gains ultimate satisfaction and liberation; for here spirit no longer relates itself to something other and limited, but to the unlimited and the infinite instead. This is an infinite relationship, a relationship of freedom and no longer one of dependence.[8]

Unfortunately however, dealienation is not achievable by mere contemplation, philosophical or otherwise.

Thought originates only when a finite self existentially encounters the alien Other(s). Alienating finitude is the impetus for thought and its translation into dealienating behavior. Removed from its originating existential context, thought becomes mere abstraction, signifier without signified. It loses the Other that it is about. Beyond losing significance, it loses impetus and ceases in abstraction, which is merely about itself and nothing more. So, alien Others, existentially encountered and distinct from the thinking self cannot be removed for thought to occur, proceed and be significant. Stated otherwise, an existentially based alienating finitude is a necessity for thought. The infinite can never be comprehended as anything but an abstract negation of finitude. Any suggestion that contemplating the infinite is a final dealienation then becomes absurd. How could contemplating an abstraction dealienate? For dealienation is a process of dealing with alienating finitude by thought and behavior in finite ways and with finite results. Meaning and human satisfaction reside, not in contemplating an abstraction, *the infinite*, but rather in an existential context wherein alienating finitude is continuously encountered, thought about and freely acted upon in finite increments of human experience.

Spirit, understood to consist of rationality and human freedom is instantiated in the world through the self-objectifying lives of individuals. Matter is embodied spirit. So, spirit might be considered ontologically prior to matter. Yet, without living matter, there can be nothing spiritual. When certain parts of the brain cease to function as in brain death, psychic life and any manifestation of spirit is gone. There are physical parts of the brain controlling sensation, thought and action. Such facts do not reduce spirit to matter. However, they indicate that spirit is a derivative of highly organized living matter. And this supports several philosophical contentions: that the process of self-existence is prior to the creation of meaning; that what is signified is prior to any signifier; that spirit and thought cannot be prior to matter and existence, but must arise from them.

Hegel believed speculative thinking could justify a belief in God. The mere negativity of thought alone speculatively implies an elevating movement from the finite to the infinite. This is based upon the negativity of thought that intends an abstract Other with abstract implications. Thinking with the universal has the same abstract negative significance, since the universal abstractly implies some unspecified Others, we know not exactly what. The abstract implications of the universal are in principle indeterminate. They require existential determination to be meaningful and to signify being. The reason why Hegel cannot elevate us from the finite to the infinite is that the alienating finitude of self-existence cannot be escaped by contemplation. A contemplative escape could only be a philosopher's dream. The alienating finitude of self-existence provides the impetus for thought, which must remain about it and be based upon it. The negativity of thought alone, of the universal, of a consciousness intending an abstract Other with abstract implications, cannot signify any being except the being of thought itself. Thus, abstractly thinking an *infinite universal* neither moves the self beyond its own finitude nor logically demonstrates a being that is infinite.

Dealienation is a movement of self-existence transcending alienating finitude. Yet, even though a free self-activity aims at transcending finitude and in fact does so by overcoming specific instances of alienation, the finitude of self-existence can never be transcended. It abides along with alienation signified by desire and goal seeking behavior. If finitude could be transcended, self-existence would not describe the human condition. Moreover, if subject and object could become identical in meaning as Hegel claimed, being would collapse into nothing. The Other would be neither intended; nor would there be any consciousness of it. Objectivity would have no meaning without distinct differences in the Other or among Others. The self would not be negated by the Other(s): nor could they in turn be negated. The meaning of an unknown Other(s), or knowledge, would not be discoverable. All that could remain would be an amorphous secondary narcissism in which there is no self and no Other.

Without thought applied to existence, meaning constituted by distinction of self from Other(s), negating implication and self-activity would cease. Existence would terminate in an extinction of self and its world. Death would describe an indistinguishable uniting of subject and object. An infinite indeterminate being cannot exist. Therefore, if God were to be conceived as infinite and indeterminate, God could not exist. Some appeal for faith in the supernatural would be called for. However, this would be unnecessary, since it is based upon fallacious reasoning about the meaning and significance of finitude.

Alienating Religion

Just as religion has successfully responded to alienation, so it has also at times fostered alienation by certain beliefs and practices. History is replete with instances of religion tending to alienate the self rather than serving as a means for dealienation. In each case God(s) is conceived as an alien Other of the self. Too extreme a contrast between the self and its God(s) maintains or increases religious alienation. The self, acknowledged to be finite and imperfect in being, is by negation entirely isolated from its God, believed infinite and perfect in being.

A conception of God *via negativa* makes a supernatural transcendent being unapproachable to an absolutely different finite human self. Philosophically, such a God(s) is reduced in significance to an impersonal abstraction thus removing its socializing function. For a finite being cannot identify with Hegel's *infinite universal*. The deity must be personalized to avoid becoming meaningless and uninteresting. Personalization is supplied by artistic myth and imagery. Some of the greatest works of art are attempts to give God(s) concrete representation. God(s) may also remain alien to the self when what they prescribe for self-existence contradicts vital aspects of the nature of the self defined by its needs, desires, rationality and freedom. Any self attempting to meet the impossible demands of an authoritative Other invariably becomes neurotic or possibly worse. Impossible ego ideals make self-existence itself a burdensome trial creating a longing for nirvana or a heavenly afterlife.

Historical religions illustrate in varying degrees alienating doctrines and practices. Enormous suffering has been caused by holy wars, inquisitions and pogroms. The innocent has been hunted down, persecuted as heretics, convicted of witchcraft and burned at the stake. Galileo's forced recantation suppressed intellectual freedom. Books have placed upon the Index Expurgatorius or destroyed. That ignorance, superstition and prejudice have been promoted by religion at various times is well known. However, to disregard or deny religion or religious institutions a place in modern society risks overlooking their primary socializing and educative functions. Institutions such as the state, not formed for such purposes, have failed as substitutes for family and religion, which together, perform these vital social functions.

History presents conditions of alienation prompting a religious response. An incompletely socialized self, be it narcissistic or egoistic, is often the cause of unnecessary suffering in the world. Uncontrolled self-seeking easily degenerates into evil doing, thereby creating a high degree of social insecurity and instability. Assume for a moment that every self exists in a Hobbesian described state of nature.

> ... during the time men live without a common Power to keep them all in awe, they are in that condition which is called Warre; and such a warre, as is of every man, against every man. ... no Arts; no Letters; no Society; and which is worst of all, continuall feare, and danger of violent death; And the life of man, solitary, poore, nasty, brutish, and short.[9]

No doubt, unrestrained self-seeking would represent a hellish condition of anarchy. Religion responds with an authoritative Other. Its function is to socially control antisocial behavior resulting from the excesses of narcissism and egoism. This is accomplished by an authoritative Other prescribing a moral code of conduct which every self is obligated to obey. The majesty of the authoritative Other lies in its awe-inspiring omnipotence assuring swift punishment for disobedience. Social cohesion is maintained by punitive intimidation.

Anyone who fears the wrath of God will obey his commandments and can therefore be trusted by his fellows. The Old Testament proclaims, "The fear of the Lord *is* the beginning of wisdom."[10] Obedience to the authoritative Other contrary to the natural proclivity for self-aggrandizement does not go unrewarded. The return for obedience by the faithful is God's protective nurture and promise of eternal bliss in a spiritual life beyond death. Besides intimidating power, civil order is religiously maintained by psychological mechanisms. An authoritative Other presents an idealized role model with which every self can identify, introject and objectify. The dicta of this authoritative Other - religious law or moral prescriptions for self-existence socialize the self thereby sustaining a stable community. Each self is taught to love and obey the example set by its nurturing authoritative Other.

A Judaic God of Abraham was conceived as a lawgiving Other and nurturing protector. The relationship of self to this God is one of subservience and obedience similar to that of the Hegelian Master to Slave. Obedience is rewarded by nurture while disobedience is punished by collective suffering. This is reflected in the religious tradition of prophetic interpretation. In the land of Canaan Judaic religious culture flourished. There the Jews where unified with a God who chose them and gave them a homeland.

The Babylonian and Roman expulsion were cataclysmic historic events bringing prolonged collective suffering which was interpreted according to a relationship with the authoritative Other founding and sustaining a Jewish community. Why were they abandoned and left unprotected by their God thereby exposing them to tyranny and evil? Why had they suffered such punishment? The answer, dictated by an authoritarian orientation, was to presume that their unfortunate fate was punishment, a result of God's wrath for sinning against his dicta. The solution was to atone for their sins. The response to their external condition of helplessness and oppression was to turn inward to establish a relationship with their almighty authoritative Other who could save them. They yearned for a lost homeland and life as the chosen children of God's family. Their attention was necessarily focused upon propitiating their God through strict obedience and walking the righteous path of holiness. Such was the ancient religious prescription for dealienation intended to overcome the alienating conditions of human existence.

The hallmark of both Judaism and Christianity is a self-concept of the sinner. A self feeling guilty of sin is subject to social control by its nurturing authoritative Other. The sinner acknowledges his guilt by placing the blame for his alienated condition upon himself rather than projecting it upon the world or his fellows. This is an appealing alternative for a self fearful of public reprisal, overwhelmed and made helpless in a hostile oppressive world, as were the persecuted Christians of the Roman Empire. The subjective focus of a sinful self-concept attempts to overcome its alienating condition through changing itself, particularly when it cannot change the conditions of its existence. Changing oneself by atonement sets a proselytizing example, which may be hoped, or may in fact, change the world in time. Convincing someone of their guilt opens their behavior to social control, or even deceptive manipulation. Christianity, at least in part, subverted the Roman Empire by converting the psyches of the oppressors to a sin-consciousness needing to atone for guilt feelings. The oppressed ascended to power by using a psychology appropriate to socialization in an authoritarian culture.

An authoritative Other, human or divine, with absolute power may well avoid anarchy only to present alienation in another guise. Despotism is the usual result of an authoritative Other with absolute power. Examples abound throughout history. Such was the case with self-deified Roman Emperors whose narcissistic and egoistic abuses corrupted the moral fabric of the Empire. The failure of such authoritative Others to provide socializing models for self-identification capable of maintaining civil order invariably led to their replacement and the extinction of a civilization. Still, the social need for an authoritative Other was maintained by its psychological displacement from Emperor to medieval Christian God. Both are similar in absolute power. A Judeo-Christian sinful self-concept rationalized and retained an alienation of self from its authoritative Other. Salvation from this condition of alienation maintained social control and a social structure for the medieval era. Yet, any religion requiring the annihilation of natural self-seeking, excessive piety and guilt, risks alienating the self by placing it in senseless passivity and bondage to an authoritative Other. Any self-existence lacking autonomy and authenticity is deeply alienated from its own rational, free and self-realizing nature.

Hegel referred to the self-alienated medieval Christian as an *Unhappy Consciousness* or *Alienated Soul*. This self is bifurcated by the contradiction of its being. Imprisoned by finitude and sin, it is considered non-essential and mutable as opposed to its divine opposite, a being that is essential and immutable. The Alienated Soul is able to negate its finitude in thought by conceiving of the infinite. But it cannot make of its being what it can think of as its God. Thus, its authoritative Other remains alien to itself. Salvation consists of negating finitude and sin, thereby affirming its opposite. Hence, the otherworldly attitudes such as piety, humility, self-abasement and asceticism adopted in the vain hope of reaching union with the infinite. But to reject finitude and embrace the infinite does not resolve the contradiction of a bifurcated self, since denial and the means employed to effect it both acknowledge and re-affirm finitude. Prescribed mortifications merely affirm as its being what the self endeavors to negate.

Mandates upon the faithful for salvation emphasizing personal renunciation of property, wealth, sensuous pleasure and self-seeking are problematical. Asceticism risks alienating the self by denying the very fact of its finitude. Ascetic self-denial is arduous self-objectifying work. Although ascetic self-objectification certainly humbles the self before its God, that very same activity affirms the very opposite as the being of the self. Hegel thought of the ascetic as, "... a personality confined within its narrow self and its petty activity, a personality brooding over itself, as unfortunate as it is pitiably destitute."[11] The more the ascetic tries, the more he merely reaffirms about himself what he attempts to deny. Any flight from finitude is therefore futile. The ascetic, by attempting to deny his own alienating finitude, is unable to exercise its own dealienating powers necessary for self-realization. Boredom, melancholy and despair emotionally signify this alienated condition of self-existence.

Although the intention of religion is dealienation, it can alienate the believing self as well. Medieval ecclesiastical alienation, marked by cynicism, and hypocrisy, was well chronicled by Luther in the Protestant Reformation. Professing to despise wealth, the church devoted itself to accumulating wealth. It encouraged bequests, engaged in simony, dispensed indulgences, became a secular power by sanctioning secular authority, maintained secular power through coercive interdicts, excommunication, threats of damnation and grants of divorce for the powerful wealthy. Moral character and virtue were eroded by the ecclesiastical bestowal of titles and privilege without regard to personal merit. The faithful relied upon superstition and miracles rather than themselves to satisfy their desires. Conscience was weakened by the Confessor listening to the sins of the faithful and prescribing atonement such as hearing mass, performing penance, repeating prayers and undertaking pilgrimages. Supererogatory works of saints could be purchased from the church by the faithful.

Startling contradictions existed between piety and the expression of its opposite in barbarous beliefs and behavior. The life of the Church was rent with debauchery, corruption, hypocrisy and deception. Pious individuals showed utter disregard for truth telling and promise keeping. Self-seeking replaced personal integrity, honesty and trustworthiness. Worship became adolatrous focusing upon relics, places and saints. Possession of holy objects and territory became consuming passions. Crusaders slaughtered the conquered inhabitants of Jerusalem, collected sacred relics and sent shiploads of earth from the Holy Land back home to Europe. Pogroms were conducted against Jews.

Socially, God(s) remain alien to the self by ecclesiastical interposition of an authoritarian clergy and bureaucracy. This interposition exaggerates the alienation of self from its God(s). For the intercessor, possessing the proxy of the faithful robs them of the autonomy necessary for religious dealienation. Salvation for sale did not require self-objectification through an authentic commitment of faith. Rather, salvation was coerced by ecclesiastical threat, penalty, or considered ultimately a matter of grace completely independent of personal works or merit. Salvation by means of self-identification with a divine authoritative Other and the self-objectifying work of each believer is replaced by a process of intercession. The effect of this is to further remove the divine authoritative Other from the self and weaken the power of its dicta upon the lives of the faithful.

Medieval Christian religious culture was corrupted by making obedience to ecclesiastical authority the price of salvation, and excluding personal freedom from the process of achieving salvation. Intercession gave the clergy the proxy of the faithful who were kept illiterate and unable to understand or participate in a Latin liturgy. As the ecclesiastical bureaucracy redefined salvation in terms of its own interest, its example weakened the attractiveness of religious self-objectification thereby promoting secular directed living. In return for ecclesiastical intercession, the faithful sustain the ecclesiastical bureaucracy by their obedience and loyalty. Intercession replaces the agency of the self with that of the intercessor. This allows a convenient escape from the burden of freedom. Objectified not by itself but by an intercessor, the self is reified. It's being, worthiness of salvation and fate are determined by an Other alien to itself. Just as the self is bifurcated by its inability to relate to an unreachable God alien to its own finitude, so is it further bifurcated by the fact that its self-concept and self-existence become ever more incongruent over time. Religious belief is not related to practical secular behavior.

A self defined by the Other becomes an Other to itself, sacrificing authenticity. This loss is evident in hypocritical differences between professed belief and practical behavior. The degree of this difference defines a religiously imposed alienation as well as the degree to which religious prescriptions intended for self-identification and self-objectification are weakened. Each Sabbath day the believer gives thanks and praises a God he cannot personally understand. Personal autonomy is absent on the Sabbath, yet resumed in the practical affairs of life during the remainder of the week. The believer might be considered one-seventh religious, if at all. Faith is then reduced to a public facade without personal conviction; disguising idolatrous secular interests such as status and power. The relevance of one's God for self-existence recedes, remaining a mere abstraction and an alien Other. Modern philosophers such as Kierkegaard agonized over the loss of religious self-objectification in an increasingly secular world in which conviction is replaced by hypocritical public displays of inauthentic religiosity.

A social existence makes authority necessary for Hobbesian reasons. However, authority, whether human or divine, can be alienating to those governed by it depending upon the degree to which it limits freedom. The least limitation necessary to secure social control will produce the least alienating effect. Authority succeeds when it permits enough freedom for the self to grow and exercise its natural capacities. One way religious authority provides this is by leaving room for individual conscience to operate alongside eccestiastical authority. Also certain religious rituals and festivals function as safety valves against excessively repressive religious authority.

God as Other of Self

Any religious creed requires acknowledging its God as ultimate substance and ground of being including self. Any authentic affirmation of creed requires the work of self-identification and self-objectification. The self must strive to negate its pride, humble itself, surrender its natural self-seeking propensity and discipline its own freedom to objectify itself in conformity to the dicta of its religious authoritative Other, usually prescribed by traditional ecclesiastical authorities and institutions. Every religion requires some degree of self-renunciation in preparation for religious self-objectification. God must be loved before self. Religious devotion or worship reinforces self-identification with a divine Other that enables religious self-objectification. A self fully identified with its creator and objectifying itself accordingly acquires an identity pre-established for it by its authoritative Other.

Monotheism conceives God as a transcendent supernatural being. God is an absolute Other of the self. It is claimed that a supernatural God can be known via negativa. However, when this is attempted, divine being is reduced to a vacuous abstraction and the self cannot relate to an absolute Other that remains completely enigmatic. Divinity must be personalized to be understood. If God is to be meaningful to the faithful, God must be a projection of finite self-existence. All religions beginning with primitive animism are compelled to be anthropocentric and anthropomorphic to some degree. Furthermore, an impersonal God robs religion of its socializing purpose. For no human self can identify with a being completely unlike itself that it cannot understand. Therefore, monotheistic religions are compelled to personalize God in order to facilitate self-objectification with its dicta by the faithful. Personalization is reflected in conceiving of a triune deity or of a man-God such as Christ. Hegel, a defender of his own Christian faith, philosophically personalized his God. Although the way he did it was highly problematical, the effort suggested the possibility of a naturalistic interpretation of God as a human self writ large. This interpretation is suggested by the following critique of Hegelian absolute idealism as he applied it to thinking about religion and his own God.

Hegel chose to understand religion and God as historically established fact. A Hegelian God is personalized as a thinking self writ large which he called Geist, or Spirit. Our finite world is *posited* by Spirit thinking dialectically with universals. Personalizing God is extended by human selves who are vehicles of what Spirit thinks and intends. God's intentions define rationality for every created self. It uses a divinely bestowed gift of freedom in two ways. The first is to secure faith by identifying with its creator. The second is to express divine intentions in finite works of self-objectification. Self-existence is illustrative of the divine and so cannot create anything from a self, which is as nothing before its creator. The result is an odyssey of human history that also expresses a divine plan. Hegelian Spirit philosophically incorporates and justifies orthodox Christian doctrines.

Finite human beings exist within history and are products of it. Hegel accepted religion and God(s) as historical fact, interpreting their significance from a traditional Christian perspective rationalized and justified by his worldview. However, this methodology represents an uncritical attitude presuming historical fact to be a manifestation of rationality and spiritual agency, of pre-established meaning and divine intention. What is ought to be so, if divinely predestined. Also, since traditional authority and the ideology of existing culture are presumed to be self-justified by a preceding historical dialectic, they are not really subject to critical evaluation. For no trans-historical standpoint is possible. Yet, Hegel's selection of historical phenomena to support his Christian interpretation of history is not altogether unbiased.

This approach is uncritical. Its effect is to rationalize traditional authority and the ideology embedded in the culture of the time. The status quo is taken as it is and interpreted to be as it ought to be. This inherent conservatism palliates rather than reconciles. For it robs the rebellious critic of any legitimate grounds of grievance against existing traditional authority and culture. More importantly, the rationality and freedom of the rebel to question authority and change his condition is subject to condemnation as hubris, sin, heresy, deserving of punishment. The burden of alienating finitude must be born by an uncomplaining resignation to the actuality of human suffering. For there is no alternative; and, to suffer is the rightful fate of a sinful humanity within the larger scheme of world history driven by inscrutable divine intention. The suffering of humanity is thereby philosophically rationalized and dismissed. Small comfort!

Hegelian ontology is based upon Parmenidean negativity and Platonic dialectic expanded into an organismic idealism. Thought occurs by means of universal concepts - Hegelian Notions. Negativity drives a logic of universal Notions and Ideas reflected in alterations of finite beings. Formal implication is presumed material by identifying the being of thought with being. Thus, being conforms to pre-established universals of thought moving from the universal to particular to individual as modeled by a formal deductive process of inference with a major premise, minor premise and conclusion establishing the identity of the individual existent by the universal kind to which it belongs. This deductive mode of thinking structures nature, self and its social world. A structured hierarchy of deductive categories of thought describes being in a cosmic sense. Everything has its place in an ontological hierarchy that rationalizes authoritarian culture of ancient origin.

The self writ large, Hegelian Geist or Spirit, thinks being. A thinking Spirit is simultaneously both subject and object. Hegel speculated that Spirit thinking the universal is not only an immediately certain presentation of its own being, but also the creation of finite beings, the Others of itself, a knowing consciousness of the finite world. Spirit thinks being and the world is a divine thought. Hegel's Christian creator God thinking with universals wills everything finite into existence. From the infinite divine thought of the universal guiding the free negating activity of a self, there emerges a differentiated finite world. What is implicit in the infinite thought of the universal kind is thereby made explicit in a finite world. What is potential within the universal is thereby actualized. What is unconscious becomes consciousness of an Other(s) by thinking the universal. Instantiating it by self-objectifying work creates a self-consciousness that is not alien, but identified with the objects it creates.

Self-identity is secured by a free agent whose self-objectification is guided by those universal norms and social roles pre-established by divine intention and prescribed by authoritative Others such as parents, priests, kings and Gods. A self-objectification conforming to traditional cultural authority reveals being. This process of instantiating the universal finds its metaphor in an odyssey, with its departure and return. For, the universal by being thought and acted upon by an adventurous self, returns a pre-established meaning implicit within the originating thought of an authoritative Other(s). These, including a hierarchical social structure crowned by God, govern self-existence.

Hegelian absolute idealism has thought creating being with God as thinking self. Finite human selves introject God's thought of universals and project it to finite instantiation by their free self-objectifying activity. The result is history revealing divine intention through a human instantiation of the universal. God creates man in his image and man's self-activity realizes divine intention. Human destiny is to express what divine thought pre-establishes. The world is not alienated Spirit as some Hegelian scholars contend, but rather a realization of divine intention and human dealienation. Divine self-consciousness is of the works of man. Finite objects of every description are a reflection of the divine self who pre-established them by thinking the universal. Ideas are the universal realized in the finite objects of the world by means of an extension of thought in intentional activity of a self. The process of instantiating the Idea in finite objects is deductive, akin to casting an object from a mold. Thinking the universal is the mold. Making the casting is an activity of a free agent or self. The resulting material casting is a finite object recognized as instantiating some universal kind or essential nature. Finite individual objects are thus particular instances of thinking the perfect universal kind by a free self whose activity temporally produces it with some imperfect difference.

God is the absolute in thought and being, a *being which is in and for itself*, as Hegel stated it. There is no *Other* of a God who is self-sufficient, who in thinking itself, creates being. Hegel's God is unlimited or infinite. By mistakenly identifying being with being thought, the activity of Spirit thinking the universal creates being. Hegel believed the universal does not merely symbolically represent or signify being. Rather, the universal implies the Other(s). Being is immanent to the universal. It signifies what can and does exist. Stated otherwise, universals possess existential import. However, this material implication of the universal concept is a fundamental mistake of absolute idealism. Notwithstanding these two mistakes, Hegel believed the negativity of thought, or Spirit thinking the universal, dialectically creates a finite history of the world also expressive of a conceptual logic encompassing the totality of meaning and being. One universal sublates the meaning of another while also signifying being in a progression expressive of divine being - its actively creative intention. Hegel's God - a Spirit thinking the universal - is a philosophical rationalization of a Christian theology claiming God, a super-self, to have created the world from nothing, man in his own image with freedom, but subject to his pre-established laws and destiny.

Rationalists and idealists such as Hegel believe the to be is to be thought. But being is not simply thinking. Rather being is what thought signifies. *To be* is not *to be thought. To be* is *to exist.* Thinking is derived from and a response to self-existence. Thus, thought cannot be by itself. To say that something thought could be *on its own account* apart from self-existence is nonsensical. For without self-existence - meaning a finite self encountering the alien Other(s) - there is no impetus for thought.

Placing signifier prior to what it signifies is the reverse of how meaning is created. For it is derived from self-existence and historically develops through human experience. If signifiers are to have any real meaning and not represent abstractions that might signify anything we desire, choose or wish; they must be existentially created and developed. In other words, no signifier can be allowed arbitrary definition. Nevertheless, this is precisely what Hegelian absolute idealism permits. What is actual can be interpreted as justifying any kind of preconception, prejudice or false belief. Stated otherwise, since a belief is actual, it is presumed to be true. Since evidence rationalizes actual beliefs presumed true, no evidence can contradict it, but can only confirm it. This standpoint is entirely uncritical of culture and beliefs promulgated by traditional authority.

What is signified by asserting that God is an Other of the self? The Other of consciousness, or the Other intended by thought does not establish that the signifier *God* signifies any object other than the self. An abstract unformed self can be said to be mere conatus, an indeterminate potentiality for being, a being signifying thought rather than determinate being. Whether identity is pre-established by an authoritative Other or realized from its own powers, the self must be existentially constructed. Whatever identity the self acquires results from its desires, intentions, and conative activity in the world.

A Hegelian viewpoint claims that to think the universal is to symbolically represent the sublation of finite differences among many existent beings into a single meaningful signifier. Logic teaches that a greater degree of extension corresponds to a lesser degree of intension. Thus, a universal with infinite logical extension loses intension completely, connoting nothing in particular. There is left only abstract signifier without anything signified. Now, meaning is derived from negation, by a specifiable difference of something from something else. Without these, meaning ceases as the signifier loses its function of representing reality. Thus to speak of the *infinite* or *absolute* is not to refer to being but only to abstract thought itself. Meaning everything or anything signifies nothing. However, this is what Hegel's absolute Idea appears to mean. For it cannot summarize a historical dialectic which is not yet terminated. Universals such as *God* or *universe* cannot be meaningful without some specifiable difference from something else. If such universals mean the negation of every conceivable difference from anything finite, they would be reduced to meaningless abstractions, signifying nothing. The meaning of being is not revealed by such universal abstractions even with the Hegelian presumption that they signify being.

How can merely thinking the universal mediate and posit being? How being could spring forth from thought is a mystery. If it were possible, fantasy could become reality. Or, at the very least, one would not be distinguishable from another. And truth would not consist of any correspondence of being with being thought. But this is all absurd for mere mortals such as us. Yet, Hegel maintains that the universal is equivalent to being, and finite beings are posited as particular instantiations of the universal. What is necessary to posit finite beings is Spirit - modeled upon an existing self writ large - whose activity consists of thinking the universal. Now, a human self cannot *posit* the existence of anything merely by thinking it. In fact being and existence cannot be posited at all. Rather, it is natural self-existence with its alienating finitude and dealienating endeavor that permits a discovery of being and a revelation of its meaning. The universal is how we think, not what we think. The universal is an abstract structure of thought, a symbolic representation of being with abstract implications.

Being and self interact. From this negating process is derived meaning. Of itself, the universal has no concrete existential content. Its implication is formal, not material. Stated otherwise, the universal is abstract signifier with abstract implication, not what is signified. For what is signified can only be determined by a process of self-existence, in which the abstract Other becomes significant as a product of experience and an intentional self interacting with being so as to discover its true meaning. Even Hegel had to recognize that an abstract universal requires the activity of a self to realize meaning.

Meaning cannot be realized merely by thinking the universal. Meaning is existentially discovered within self-existence by self-activity intentionally responding to the alienating Other(s) in a process of dealienation. The universal cannot objectify itself, since, as abstract, it has nothing to objectify. Self-objectification is derived only from finite self-existence. The model of Spirit must remain human self-existence. A Hegelian Spirit thinking the universal is a soul without substance, an abstract disembodied self without existence. This model taken from finite self-existence just does not do the speculative job Hegel intended for it. God as the self writ large thinking things into existence can neither explain nor replace the significance of human existence. In fact, such a view distorts its true significance, relegating human freedom to mere subservience to authority.

Hegel thought of immediate being as abstract implication evident in thinking the universal. Finite being was considered a determination of thought, an implication of the universal concept. Thus, God, defined as infinite Spirit thinking the universal, creates a finite world.

This is a neat rationalization of Christian theology where God creates the world from nothing by merely thinking it into existence. It is difficult to understand how being could spring forth from thinking the universal, as if by magic. Moreover, the being of thought cannot be the thought of being. For, if so, being could not be a content for thought, an Other of the self, something discovered by existing. The objectivity of being, our sense of a world independent of us, would disappear. However, being has implications for self-existence. Self-activity discovers the consequences of being. Something limits the self, harms it, and needs to be changed to satisfy certain desires and aims. Being always makes a difference that is distinguishable and important to the self. Being is something the self can interact with, test, verify, validate, and alter in some specific way. Being has existential implications for the self who encounters it, interacts with it, and discovers what it is. Being negates and is negated by the self. The implications of being are specific, temporally continuous and possibly infinite in principle.

Being and thought are only identical with regard to negation, i.e., the self is conscious of the Other(s) as not itself, and intends what is not present to it at the moment. Thought symbolically represents an existentially encountered Other consciously experienced by the self. Both thought and being have implications. Those of thought are abstract while those of being are discovered by an existentially interactive self, negating what is Other symbolically, and in fact. The result is a discovery or even a creation of being as, for example, in artificially created materials or free self-development.

It is through a negative process of existential interaction that being and the meaning of being is revealed. Thus, to elevate the universal concept to the status of being is a mistake. For then the world and objectivity are sacrificed. Self-existence loses its vital ontological significance. The door is open to flights of speculative fantasy, which misinterpret the true significance of what is derived from self-existence. For example, if we say as Hegel did, that God is an infinite universal, a being which is *in and for itself*, God then becomes a philosophical abstraction without existential significance, without being; a mere intending of being by thought and nothing more. A universal concept not related to existence either directly or indirectly cannot be conceived. Believing that it can is a mistake perpetrated by the fact that thought abstractly intends the Other. Yet, for the abstractly intended Other to be real and meaningful, it must originate existentially or have existential consequences. Universals without existential import are the mere form of thought, not signifiers of being.

What does it mean to say as Hegel did that God is an *infinite universal?* A *universal* is meaningful due to the fact that it is an abstract signifier with formal implication. The *infinite* is also meaningful as signifying a whole including every possibility of finite being and meaning. Both components of this concept of God are meaningful because of their negative logical formulation; i.e., God is negatively defined as not anything finite. Such a God is completely Other, not capable of being experienced by mortals who are finite and who can only think about what is finite. Such a God is incomprehensible, an unreachable absolute alien Other. Moreover, if *infinite in being* connotes every possibility, then it would include contradictory finite possibilities. A God of infinite possibilities, including those that are contradictory, could not be thought. Hegel met this difficulty by speculating that the infinite can be comprehended as a sublated enumeration of all possibilities of actual finite beings. This required re-conceiving God as Spirit (Geist), a self engaged in a temporal process rationally reconciling finite oppositions and contradictions through free agents of human history.

Hegel asserted God to be an object of human consciousness, an inclusive universal signifying the totality of being. Such a universal implies everything *Other*, or finite, including ourselves. Yet, Hegel denies that God is conceivable as substance. This *One* including the *Many* is an activity of Spirit, which is concrete rather than abstract. Spirit, thinking the universal, *posits* concrete existence, the actuality of our finite world. Spirit, through the agency of freely existing selves, realizes existential implications of the universal, enumerating its particular instances. It takes the activity of a human spirit to express the material implication of the universal. The result is history created by self-projection and self-objectification. Thinking with the universal and acting according to it expresses in concrete form the intentional thinking of Spirit.

Hegelian Spirit reflects the traditional major proofs for the existence of God. There is the teleological proof wherein a finite world appears *as if* it were intelligently designed. Who could this designer possibly be if not Spirit, the anthropomorphic speculator himself, writ large. Then there is the logical or so-called ontological proof, wherein it would be contradictory to think of a perfect being, God, without including existence among its many attributes. Here is a clear example of the fallacy of both rationalism and idealism. Being is implied merely by *being thought*. Self-existence and material implication is hereby completely overlooked. What is signified is the signifier with any meaning we choose to give it. Nonsense! For what is signified must have existential implications. If a self behaves toward what is signified in a certain way, some specific consequences will occur.

What is signified always makes a difference that is determined by actively altering its relationship to the self encountering it. Such differences constitute the material implications of the signified. Self-existence establishes material implication and demonstrates by intentional interaction that what is signified is real, and in some way independent of any thinker. For if this were not so, there would be no certain predictability of what is signified relative to a self which acts with and upon it. Whatever does not make a difference to human existence is not significant. The abstract Other, which the self thinks and intends, is a signifier without anything signified, a potential for meaning derived solely from intentional existential interactions characterizing self-existence.

At the macro level of history, Hegel claimed human freedom only has the significance of a means for God's purposes. Freedom is merely a vehicle for Geist's expression. This brings up a question as to why Geist, in its total perfection of being, requires human freedom to express itself. Hegel answers, "... God is the absolutely perfect Being, and can, therefore, will nothing other than himself - his own Will."[12] Geist appears alienated from the actuality of its thought. However, God cannot be independently self-sufficient, infinite and perfect in being if requiring finite expression through human freedom. Rather, Geist must be as finite as the human self upon which it depends to actualize the Idea in a finite world. Stated another way, if God requires a human historical objectification of his intended purpose, then he suffers from the same alienating finitude as does man i.e., his thought or idea - by itself - is not actual or complete in being. Apparently, an infinite God lacks the active freedom he has given to finite man. However, this anomaly is not the orthodox Christian doctrine Hegel wanted to defend. His theory of history subordinates human freedom to divine reason in order to conform to biblical predestination.

Hegel establishes reciprocity between man and God by alienating the former from rationality and the latter from freedom. Yet both attributes remain dealienating powers the self. There are tensions and even contradictions in Hegelian views of the relationship of humanity to the divine and how human history is created. First, the emphasis is upon denying rationality to the self in order to assert it as the divine guide for history. Yet, created in God's image, man must also be rational. Hegelian ontology acknowledges both powers to be human. However, when explaining history, Hegel emphasized man's freedom while denying him the rationality necessary to determine his own destiny. Freedom is irrational conatus requiring governance by divine rationality. Humans must obey divine law. History becomes significant when understood as an authoritarian relationship between blind human freedom and divine rational intention.

Alienation is multifaceted depending upon the specific nature of the undesirable separation or loss. Man can be alienated by nature, by destiny, by other men. Authority, whatever its source, can be the cause of alienation. The source of authority be it an Emperor, God, State or community is no guarantee of its legitimacy. Hegel was right in recognizing reason as establishing the legitimacy of authority. But he was wrong in presuming those traditional sources of authority, or the law itself, to be inherently rational. Neither may be rational and so their legitimacy always remains subject to the test of rationality. Assent to authority or law can only be secured after rational examination of their intent, consequences and merit. Authority and law need questioning about their rationale, who is subject to them and whose interests are served by them. The universal validity of authority and law resides not in any Hegelian abstraction of their meaning or in their ontological status presumed superior to the individual. Legitimacy is a self-imposed obligation created by the rational judgment of everyone concerned.

The correct response to alienation is rational freedom. This much Hegel suggests. Locating freedom within the individual is obviously correct. However, Hegel's refusal to so locate rationality is a mistake. Humanity has been alienated by nature and by the arbitrary subjective will of individuals as Hegel correctly claims. The traditional authority of community, the state and religion has also equally alienated humanity. The correct response to these sources of alienation lies in the complete rational freedom of individuals to test and change them whenever necessary. The marks of dealienation are individual authenticity and autonomy. In this context, the obligation to authority and law is not alien to the individual. Knowledge and duty are not simply instruments of obedience to an alien higher authority. Rather, knowing one's duty is a product of the rationality inherent to every individual. The law is independently tested by the rationality of each individual and its obligation is naturally self-given. In such a circumstance, obligation is not felt as obedience, but as inner need, as natural desire.

Christianity believes that overcoming alienation awaits the day of judgment as human history ends. Hegel viewed alienation as overcome by the human work of history. However, to view alienation as a mere part of the dialectical progress of human perfectibility, as a mere historical stage, is too circumscribed. The deeper, tragic and more sobering ontological view of alienation as built into finitude is more adequate from several perspectives. First, it allows for an endless variety of forms of alienation enduring as long as human life and history. Secondly, it allows for alienation within social organization and institutions. Thirdly, it allows for a critique of social organization and institutions. Hegel was unaware of these advantages while being keenly aware of his commitments to classical Greek reason, human perfectibility and Christian salvation. The deeper view of alienation as a permanent feature of the human condition relinquishes the Hegelian philosophical demand for closure, and relinquishes the Christian promise of overcoming alienation with finality.

Since Hegelian absolute idealism, philosophy has generally repudiated the possibility of overcoming alienation with finality, either contemplatively or existentially. Religion and utopian ideology with its social engineering have not succeeded. Alienating finitude appears intractable as it changes historical form. Yet, the aspiration to dealienate is never quelled and dealienation of every conceivable description occurs. The process itself appears as a continuous and interminable feature of finite human existence. As history advances, so does the dealienating power of rational freedom. Recent developments in genetics present an incredible panoply of possibilities for life. This quantum jump in freedom provides humanity with God-like power, but also demands ever-higher degrees of rationality and socialization to successfully cope with it.

God as Self

On the micro level of the individual, Hegel does not rationalize what is as what ought to be. In fact, what is means an unacceptable limitation to be negated, changed and transformed by intentional human thought and action. That is the meaning of freedom and the generic response to an alienating finitude. On the macro level of world history, Hegel defends traditional religious beliefs in human predestination by a divine plan with a traditional belief in God as ruler of us mortals. However, God cannot be an inscrutable manipulative master of man without profoundly alienating man's nature as a rational and free being, a dealienating being transforming and humanizing the world. That God is the master of world history and man's destiny means that man is not autonomous, and this is reflected in the proposition that what is actual in world history is in accordance with God's will and so is as it ought to be. Only human reason itself can judge this so or not so.

The Geist of world history is an enigmatic alien Other, a master puppeteer depriving its puppet - a human self - of the autonomy and authenticity which Hegel claimed to characterize its secular existence. What Hegel needed to do, to keep his micro level analysis of the self from contradicting the obvious implications of his macro level theory of world history, was to locate God within the being of self, not external to it. Repeating the metaphor of Master and Slave describes neither the relationship of God to self nor the development of human history. For Hegel meant the relationship of Master and Slave to metaphorically describe only the origination of a historical dialectic of dealienation from which the self is spiritually developed and entirely transformed into a higher socialized being.

There is in Hegel's view of the relationship of human to divine an alienation conundrum. On the one hand historical man suffers a loss of autonomy and is alienated from reason by a God with inscrutable purposes. On the other hand, God himself is alienated from the actuality of his Idea and must depend upon manipulating historical man to actualize the divine will. A solution to this would be to locate the source of freedom and rationality within the human self. Then reconceive God as a potential within the self for the perfection of freedom and rationality. God would represent the best within humanity, the best that we could become. History would then be the realization of human potential against a backdrop of alienating finitude instead of predestination by a being alien to the self. We could then say of history that it is truly an authentic expression of human freedom in both its rational and irrational dimensions. History would also represent a spontaneous creativity of humanity confronting alienating finitude in its potentially infinite variety. If we believe rational freedom constitutes the essence of humanity, we can hope and accept as an article of faith that rational freedom will prevail in human history. The issue will always be in doubt as it must be if humanity is truly free.

Religious identification and self-objectification does permit some degree of self-realization along with the formation of community. Nevertheless, it must not be forgotten that religion can also alienate the self from realizing its potentiality for being resulting from its own powers of rationality and freedom. With religion, the question remains of how the individual directed by any authority external to himself, rational or otherwise, can be authentic and autonomous. Dealienation requires both. They are denied the self by any religion presenting an authoritarian Other for self-identification and self-objectification. A self-realization which expresses both would also express the divine, if human beings are courageous enough not to fear the means they have to effect dealienation, and if they are not coerced by an authoritative Other in their self-objectifying life work. Successful dealienation teaches the self what and who it is. A culturally transmitted self is a continuous product of historical dealienation. Such a self serves as an authoritative Other necessary for the self-development of future generations. A well-socialized self learns to respect the desires, freedom and rationality of its fellows. Such respect promises the possibility of developing culture beyond authoritarianism toward one respecting human dignity and law.

Hegel ontologically explained how alienation is necessary, since it is signified by finitude. He also correctly conceived of Spirit as freedom and rationality essential to the psychic life of human beings. However, locating rationality in sources external to the self such as community, state and God falsifies a human nature whose inherent essential powers are rationality and freedom. They permit dealienation and drive human history. Supernatural divine purpose is unnecessary to explain the direction of history. Locating the drivers of dealienation and history within the self takes the Feuerbachian philosophical turn. The divine is located within humanity and can be correctly said to be a projection of it. The projection is not trivial and does not dismiss the divine, but correctly relocates its source within each self.

The thought of God as absolute ground of being, perfect being, infinite being, or any other omni attribute negating finitude is a metaphor for self-existence. This consists of a self confronting the existential limitations of space and time and responding with its negating power to think and act freely in the world to get what it wants. Hegel's God is then a projection of the powers that are possessed by a finite self. The process of thought by a divine mind mirrors a process of free thought and activity responding to alienating finitude. The infinite Hegel referred to is really a continuous process of human dealienation without escape from finitude. Contemplation, or the power of thought alone cannot escape finitude even in the creation of finitude, and Hegel acknowledged this. The Hegelian God is Spirit, thought thinking itself, pure negativity, and a sublating movement of thought expressed in logically progressive instantiations of the finite constituting the history of the world. Since modeled upon a process of self-existence, this speculative veiwpoint is superfluous.

Hegel glorified thought identifying it with being. He conflated the being of thought - the universal as signifier - with the thought of being - what is signified. A Hegelian God creates being by thought. It is cognized by humans through thinking with universals and freely acting to finitely instantiate them. However, thought and freedom are essential human attributes. Therefore, God as creative thinker and doer finds its image in human nature. Which comes first is a question of one's philosophical orientation. It is simpler to presume that God, as creative thinker, is a projection of human powers rather than the reverse required by faith. Hegel's God would then seem to be the finite human self writ large, a self whose infinite power lies in its capacity to think and act freely and intentionally to create itself and its world from its own intelligence. Hegel considered God and universals to be Others, objective for the self. Being thought, both Others are perfect as standards for the conduct of human life; molds into which human existence ought to be cast. But this view sacrifices human autonomy and authenticity. For, autonomy is lost when rationality is located outside the self in divine intention and pre-established universals. And, freedom is not indicative of authenticity when restricted to submissive obedience to the dicta of God, an authoritative Other. The self cannot create its own identity, but must replicate the identity divinely intended for it.

History is replete with all kinds of religions and Gods. An answer to the question, "Who is your God?" also answers the question, "Who are you?" In other words, the identity of the self is an expression of whom or what it believes its God to be. God as alien master defines the self as obedient subordinate. Or, God as agape, defines the self as autonomous nurturer. To know oneself at the deepest level is to express the being of one's God. What does this historically based observation say about what God really is? Better posed, who is God? Feuerbach suggested that God is the self writ large, a projection of the self with its powers, and its foibles. This makes sense of the historical variety of religions.

Hegel's God is a philosophical self who by thinking and willing creates its own world. God's thinking transcends the finite while its instantiation by free agents, namely ourselves, creates the history of a finite world. Still, it cannot be denied that thought and intentional behavior are derived from the dealienating activity of the self, existing and developing in a finite world. And the highest expression of finite self-existence is found in the dealienating artifacts of a humanized world. Such a world is presented to the self as a product of its own powers of rationality and freedom, a product of its thought and intentional activity.

A world produced by the self reflects the self as its creator and cannot have an alien aspect, so Hegel claimed. This is found to be false in our contemporary humanized world with its problematical unintended social and environmental consequences. Therefore, a Hegelian God as master thinker creating the world from its rational intentions is naive. Moreover, a Hegelian self-knowing Spirit sublating all finite differences so that subject and object are indistinguishable extinguishes meaning itself, thereby returning the self to primitive narcissism. A humanized world emphasizes the exact opposite character. As being is revealed and meaning expanded in the process of dealienation, the self becomes richer, more complex, more differentiated within itself and from the Other(s) that once alienated its desires and aims. World and self do not become an amorphous spiritual substance reducible to abstract thought. That God or any self could by mere thought be an object to itself is impossible. For such self-consciousness is merely the negativity of thought itself presenting an indeterminate object, the abstract Other, vacuous freedom.

What or who is signified by God(s) can only be revealed and derived from the alienating finitude of self-existence. This makes one's God(s) crucially relevant to the dealienating activity of the self within its finite world. God is misconceived as a transcendent supernatural object, since such an object says nothing directly about anything encountered within self-existence. One's God(s) must signify more than the mere negativity of consciousness or thought, if God is not to remain an alien Other to the self. Theologies that do not begin with human finitude are not relevant to self-existence and so are not tenable.

The language of God is anthropocentric and anthropomorphic. *God* is spoken about with language applying to the self. Personal pronouns *he* or *she* are most frequently used. God is protecting, nurturing parent, spoken of as *father* or *mother*. Christians speak of *God the father* or *God the son*. God has purposes in mind, intending us to exist in a certain way. Religion uses a vast metaphorical language to describe who God is and what God demands of mortal selves. Emotions such as love or vengeance also describe the moods or dispositions of the divine just as they do the self. Myths and allegories present the moral teaching attributed to God.

A finite self necessarily conceives God as an object of consciousness, an abstract Other of self. However, this divine Other comes loaded with attributes and implication for the conduct of self-existence. God, to be comprehended at all, must signify some aspect of self-existence. We know about God what we know about ourselves, nothing more, nothing less. Therefore, God must signify some projected aspect of our own self-existence. The divine Other is really our self-concept constructed from alienating finitude and dealienating self-existence. The divine Other is some idealized dealienated aspect of finite self-existence as in the omni attributes of theology. God is also said to be free, rational, good, powerful, eternal, infinite, universal and so forth. Whatever is attributed to God is also attributed in some degree to us in some way. Divine attributes are inferred by negating alienating aspects of human finitude.

If God is primarily a self-projection, why then is there any need for God? The answer obviously is that an idealized self is necessary to cope with alienating conditions of self-existence. If our God is something perfect to which we can actively aspire; we have made identifications and introjected behavioral norms socializing the self. Self-projection and self-objectification conforming to divine dicta enables the self to cope in a world in which nature and society alienate it. One's God palliates human suffering and rejects evil doing. Religion deals with human sinfulness. Social control of antisocial impulses is established by requiring the self to acknowledge responsibility and be accountable for causing unnecessary suffering or evil doing.

A self persuaded of its guilt is emotionally alienated from its self-projected God. The psyche fears damnation and retribution in hell for its sinfulness. Religious dealienation or salvation lies in repentance and a whole host of religious practices such as sacrifice, confession, penance, and various purification rituals, among others. Personal dispositions may be cultivated such as asceticism. The faithful are then required to believe and worship a God whose ideals and dicta define self-projection. Introjection of God occurs in personal devotion and worship. Introjecting the divine requires a renunciation of absolute freedom and natural inclination. Nobody can do just anything they want, particularly when it harms others. In the end, God is a collective self-objectification of the faithful. This is Spirit, religiously expressed. The acting out of belief is a free expression of faith.

If God is an imaginary idealized psychological self-projection, then God is who and what we want to be like or become. God defines our dealienating response to the alienating finitude of self-existence. Divine attributes are what we believe necessary to secure the satisfaction of human desires and aims. Asserting God to signify an imaginary idealized self-projection is not equivalent to dismissing God out of hand as fictitious. For God retains enormous significance for how we exist, interpret our world and behave toward each other. Atheism either dismisses this significance or is ignorant of it. God and religion are psychic or spiritual realities to be understood. If God is described naturalistically as an imaginary idealized self-projection, there can be as many Gods as there are formally structured publicly idealized self-projections. Furthermore, God becomes instantiated in the finite objectification of religious individuals, religious institutions, attitudes, dispositions and practices. Many Gods are immanent in the world. God and religion respond to alienating self-existence by providing a social structure and mechanism for dealienation. Religion invites the self to freely convert to a creed and live by it to secure salvation.

Hegel intimated that God is an idealized Other of the self necessary to its existential construction by its free work of self-objectification. But God need not be an object independent of, or external to, the self. For to believe in God is to have certain knowledge about the self, a knowledge that enables the self to dealienate, to realize an identity of who and what it is. God, as imaginary idealized self-projection, signifies the being of the self. The sense in which this being is Other is not that it is objective, but that it is a subjective task for the exercise of freedom and rationality, those essential powers of the self necessary for releasing its potentiality for being someone and something. The Other is then an indeterminate identity; something to be realized existentially, as Hegel understood it. The Other of the self can be a self whose identity is to be constructed.

The sense in which a self-projected God is objective - something we are conscious of as Other - need not be that it is a transcendent supernatural authority or master, proscribing and prescribing self-existence. This makes God an authoritarian alien Other to the self. No! God is objective as a public socially shared idealized imaginary self-projection. Stated otherwise, God is a social self publicly shared by other selves enabling their self-objectification. God is also something publicly shared by the faithful in the collective products of religious self-objectification as in charitable works, artistic works such as the Sistine Chapel, and other artifacts glorifying one's God.

Can the self get along in life without its God(s)? Even if it could, Freudian psychoanalysis suggests the necessity of an authoritative Other, if not God, then a cultural superego providing norms of socially acceptable conduct. Either God or superego performs the same psychological and sociological function. Both socialize a self driven by natural inclinations, some of which are antisocial. Without God or superego morality and a socialized self who can sustain civilized culture disappear, leaving behind an anarchic hell of unconstrained egoism, social insecurity and instability. Such situations have been amply demonstrated throughout history. Therefore, it is necessary for the self to acquire a psychologically idealized self-projection, either through religious faith in an authoritative God or a culturally inculcated superego.

The question is not whether the self can get along without an authoritative Other. Obviously, it cannot. Rather, the question becomes what kind of authoritative Other the self must adopt for projecting itself in its dealienating endeavor. More specifically, can the self construct its own idealized self-projection which would be authoritative for itself, be a basis for socialization and trustworthy human conduct? Could a self, driven by natural desire and prone to narcissism and egoism, discipline itself so as not to threaten society? Certainly, this would seem possible. For the self can be free to act in accordance with a rational appraisal of what its alienated suffering existence teaches it.

Can the self be its own authoritative Other? Many philosophers such as Hegel answer no with the following analysis of human nature or one similar to it. The being of the self is vacuous, nothing, a mere potentiality for being something, abstract freedom. Only with the guidance of an alien authoritative Other can the self dialectically develop an identity. The authoritative Other could be anyone who nurtures: God, culture, a human collective, cultural mores, ideology, law or almost anything accepted by the self as normative. Social norms and roles embodied in authoritative Others are necessary for constructing a social identity. Every self is a work of civilization, a painstaking construction. Self-development occurs within a process of dealienation involving identification, projection and objectification resulting in an identity recognized publicly, and by the self. This self whose essential power is freedom, is defined by an authoritative Other whom it objectifies and recognizes as itself. In effect, an authoritative Other constitutes a self-concept objectively confirmed by the activity of self-existence.

There can be an alternative to an authoritarian formation of the self. It is a self that is authentic and autonomous. It is initially developed in relation to an authoritative Other who nurtures it. An authoritarian Other tempers narcissism and egocentrism. Development proceeds beyond these selves and beyond the need for an authoritarian Other to guide their development. For although its natural essence consists of all its needs and desires, they are tempered by a concurrent complementary development of its own rationality and freedom. With increasingly successful responses to alienating finitude, the self existentially discovers with its own exercise of rational freedom and in the very process of dealienation, what and whom are normative for it. What or whom it identifies with, how it projects and objectifies itself, progressively becomes a more rationally evaluated choice. A dealienation that is rational both expresses freedom and liberates the self. Stated otherwise, to be free is to be rational, and to be rational is to be free. Such elemental powers of the self need not be opposed. They are a disposition of the self toward its alienating finitude. Since neither desire nor freedom can be absolute when tempered by rationality, freedom need not be feared as self-defeating or antisocial.

Kant suggested that the self is autonomous. Existentialists suggested the self could be authentic when it understands the implications of its own mortality and freedom. Autonomy and authenticity are possible modes of self-existence. They can be painfully developed and realized, in spite of the mistakes, difficulty and suffering involved. A mature self has in fact acquired a degree of autonomy that reflects and promotes an authentic existence. Socrates' deepest wish was to acquire wisdom from a rational reflection upon self-existence. Any self developed beyond primitive narcissism and egoism must acquire some degree of wisdom that is authoritative for its conduct. Such wisdom can constitute an authentic self-projection enabling the self to cope and self-objectify. What would a Socratic authoritative Other, or God, then be? Quite simply, it would be a painful perfection of a natural self, an ideal to be projected upon the world and one's fellows. The authoritative Other would not be an alien Other coercive of the self, imposed upon it by some external source. The self would not have to capitulate to its power: would not have to renounce itself in order to adjust to its demands. An autonomous and authentic self could then replace an authoritarian self.

There can be no self and no self-projected God without the impetus of alienating finitude. A religious self and its God responds to the alienating finitude encountered within self-existence. God is of course an abstraction, but not one constructed from thought without existential significance. Attributes of God are the ideal attributes of the self. God(s) are an image of human desires and aspirations. If one's God is said to be rational and free, this is what the self aspires to become. God must then represent an imaginary projection of an idealized dealienated self. Dealienating works expressed in various self-projections and self-objectifications are an expression of the divine, which is distinctly human. Hegel intimated as much by observing that the God of a people is its highest idea of itself.[13] In addition, Hegel's own concrete representation of the divine in the person of the man-God Christ is an incarnation of dealienated humanity.

Notes

1. Hegel, G. W. F. (1830) *Hegel's Logic* Being Part One of the Encyclopedia of the Philosophical Sciences (3rd ed., 1975) (William Wallace, Trans.). London, England: Oxford University Press, 44.

2. King James Version. (1958) *The Holy Bible.* London, England: Collins' Clear-Type Press,:Deuteronomy, 6: 5-7.

3. Ibid., Leviticus, 19: 18.

4. Hegel, G. W. F. (1992) *Early Theological Writings: The Spirit of Christianity.* (T. M. Knox, Trans.). Philadelphia, PA: University of Pennsylvania Press, 238.

5. Ibid., 236.

6. Hegel, G. W. F. (1969) *Hegel's Science of Logic* (A. V. Miller, Trans.). London, England: Humanities Press, George Allen and Unwin Ltd, 129.

7. Hegel, G. W. F. (1995) *Lectures on the Philosophy of Religion: vol.1, Introduction and the Concept of Religion:1827 Introduction*, (P. G. Hodgson, Ed. & Trans.). Berkeley & Los Angeles CA: University of California Press, 149.

8. Ibid., 150, footnote 2.

9. Hobbes, Thomas. (1983) *Leviathan*. Aylesbury, Bucks, England: Penguin, 185-186.

10. *Holy Bible*. Psalm 111, 10.

11. Hegel, G. W. F. (1967) *The Phenomenology of Mind* (J. B. Baillie, Trans.). New York, NY: Harper and Row, 264.

12. Hegel, G. W. F. (1956) *The Philosophy of History* (J. Sibree, Trans.). New York, NY: Dover, 20.

13. Hegel, G. W. F. (1953) *Reason in History* (Robert S. Hartman, Trans.). New York, NY: Macmillan, 64.

Chapter Six

Cultural Alienation

Derivation of Culture

Self-existence is characterized by alienating finitude expressed by universal human needs and particular desires. Rationality and freedom respond to alienating finitude. Thus, the essential nature of the self is defined by its needs, desires, rationality and freedom. The self develops through a historical process of dealienation with a resultant realization of specific finite potentialities for being. Dealienation is a work of self-objectification. This requires socialization initially consisting of introjecting authoritative Others. Thereafter, self-identifications are formed throughout life from what culture offers as a means for the dealienating work of self-objectification. Although self-identification is usually accomplished non-rationally and sometimes irrationally, it can be consciously chosen where the self is matured by experience and in its power of rational freedom.

Culture consists of a cluster of traditional customs and attitudes expressing the ethos of a community or civilization. Embedded in every language is a cultural *Weltanschauung*. It sustains social cohesion by providing a coherent commonly shared set of values from which is derived public meaning and guidance for human conduct. Satisfaction of human needs and desires is accomplished through cultural structures. These are developed as collective responses to specific conditions of alienating finitude confronting self-existence. Culture provides socializing structures for self-development and self-realization. Universal social norms and roles are available for self-identification that enables self-projection and self-objectification. Attitudes, mores and laws of a given culture prescribe and proscribe behavior. Social institutions such as family, religious, educational, civic, commercial and governmental transmit culture. Self-objectifying works of art, science, religion and philosophy are the instantiated products of culture. Existing in such a cultural milieu, every self is for the most part a culture carrier.

Culture is historically constructed from the lives of particular individuals living together in community. The content of culture is derived from and sustained by collective dealienating endeavor. From this, social norms and roles originate. Culture exists for the sake of those whose lives create and sustain it. It cannot transcend its derivation as a collective response to the alienating finitude of self-existence. Unrelated to self-existence, culture is reduced to an insignificant abstraction. Worse still, culture is misconceived as ontologically superior to the self. Alienation then consists of an opposition of culture to self. And dealienation consists of subordinating self to culture. However, a self completely submerged and dominated by culture discovers that some of what it needs and desires cannot be satisfied. Where culture does not permit an exercise of rational freedom, the self is radically alienated by the loss of its capacity for dealienation.

Cultural alienation was first portrayed by Plato's account of what the Sophists taught to upper class politically ambitious Athenian youth. That *man is the measure of all things* expressed a deep skepticism and cynicism toward traditional cultural authority. It is not derived from any universal truth about human nature. Rather, it is an outcome of a competition between interests contending for social and political dominance. Truth is what the prevailing interest of the stronger party says it is. If *might makes right*, then truth is relative until the prevailing victorious interest proclaims it. Argument, rather than seeking universal truth, is a tool of persuasion and social domination. Rationality is thereby reduced to a rationalization of interest. Self-interest, as the sole motive for behavior, isolates the self from culture. Deviancy from established cultural norms and social roles is not merely tolerated. A permissive individualism is encouraged. An egoistic self becomes the model of success in attaining wealth, social status and power. Such a self is prized for its socially manipulative intelligence. Cunning and deceit are regarded as virtues.

Called by other names, sophism is repeated in history. Modern versions of sophism re-appear in contemporary cultural relativism, multiculturalism, postmodernism and various counter-culture protest movements. Most will fail, but some will succeed and culture will thereby be changed. The historical re-appearance of sophism is marked by apathy toward existing culture and an ascendancy of skepticism, cynicism and egoism. Although it may seem so at the time, this *anomie* is not simply social malaise. For, if one looks deeper into the cultural milieu, what is found is a vigorous individual experimentation with new attitudes and lifestyles often made inevitable with revolutionary changes, particularly in contemporary science and related technology dealing with information and biology.

Cultural alienation seems to follow a generally predictable pattern. Individuals find themselves progressively isolated from culture and its institutions. Stoically resigned, they ignore what is irrelevant to their lives. Their apathy is expressed by skeptical and cynical attitudes toward what seems irrelevant to them. They deal with what seems relevant. Thus, although skepticism, cynicism and public apathy are signs of cultural alienation, they are also signs that dealienating responses are underway. Not sustained by self-objectification, culture atrophies and social institutions eventually disintegrate; replaced by others arising from the norms and social roles originating from the actual lives and needs of individuals. Where culture is oppressive to human needs, individuals respond with rebellion, abolition or reform. No matter which course is taken, new culture and institutions replace those that have atrophied and become obsolete.

Where social norms and roles serve as successful dealienating vehicles for self-objectification, there is a reciprocal complementary relationship of culture to self. Yet, the demands of culture may oppose those of the self. The enabling structures of culture thereby become alienating. Dealienation then consists of an endeavor to restructure cultural demands to conform to the essential nature of the self. Social norms and roles then undergo change. As an objectified social product, culture continuously changes as it either succeeds or fails in its dealienating aim. Any cultural structure will be discarded when it fails to satisfy needs, desires, limits rationality and freedom, or disables self-realization. Successful culture facilitates dealienation while affirming the essential nature of the self.

Cultural role stereotypes enable self-objectification and provide a pre-established social identity acknowledged as legitimate. Stereotypical roles are guided by universally applied social norms. Behavioral rules are public. Rewards or punishments are applied to those who play a role well or poorly. Everyone knows what is expected of the role-player. He or she secures social status and a ranking in the larger social whole. Role-playing teaches and reinforces who is inferior or superior to whom. The inferior role-player works for the superior in a hierarchical ranking within and between classes. Stereotyped roles provide a socially protected and secure self-identity. This security is felt at a deep emotional level related to nurture and survival. Vigorous opposition may be expected to challenging a stereotypical role.

Every self is necessarily submerged in a culture of universally applied norms and social roles. Some roles are rigidly stereotyped with intentionally strict pre-defined limits placed upon individuality and freedom to innovate. One example would be a public official with specified duties. Another would be a job description within a bureaucracy bound by rules governing its specialized functions and the behavior of employees in carrying them out. Whatever the case, culturally prescribed norms and roles limit individuality to some degree. Selves, narrowly defined by the norms and roles of their culture build a structure of social institutions. Defined by its social function, the self is abstracted and reified by the universal predicates of interchangeability and impersonality. Although adequate for sociological purposes, such abstract descriptions of the self disregard its essential nature.

From a structuralist orientation, culture constructs the self. Philosophers such as Plato, Hegel, Marx and Freud describe and sometimes prescribe how culture provides structures for self-development. It is always accomplished by subordinating self to culture. Such social theorists consider subordinating culture to self impossible. Hegel tried to prove this with an excellent critique of personal freedom understood as egoistic license. He interpreted the historical excesses of Roman Emperors and the French revolution as evidence tending to prove that subordinating culture to self results in self-alienation. On the other hand, existentialists and some social psychologists have described the self-alienating consequences of complete cultural submersion. Ample demonstrations of this have also been provided by twentieth-century totalitarianism. It would then seem that subordinating self to culture or vice versa has alienating consequences. But why must culture and self be conceived in opposition with subordination of one to the other prescribed for dealienation? If culture is a derivative of self-existence sharing its dealienating aim, then their relationship might be better conceived as complementary and marked by reciprocity. With such a conceptual change, neither need alienate the other.

If culture is conceived as a derivative of self-existence sharing a dealienating aim, then culture is subordinate to self. Yet, subordinating culture to self was plausibly demonstrated to have alienating consequences. As Hegelian and existentialist analyses demonstrated, egoism generates self-alienation and opposition between self and culture. No cultural ethos is derivable from an egoistic freedom that merely negates what culture offers. How would a culture subordinate to self avoid such a result? Would this subordination make reciprocity between both impossible? The short answer appears to be that a self not developed beyond narcissism or egoism is a consequence of defective socialization, which does make reciprocity impossible. Not learning to temper freedom with rationality is self-alienating. Freedom, irrationally or non-rationally driven by an incompletely developed egoistic self is what Hegel criticized so effectively and existentialists erroneously glorified.

Defective Socialization

Socialization is initiated with self-identification. How it is formed determines whether self-objectification with it will alienate or dealienate. Coercive socialization is initiated with non-rational self-identifications predominant in pre-adult life. An adult, not having developed the capacity for rational freedom cannot evaluate whether what culture demands is consistent with his own demands. A product of deficient maturation, the self expresses the aims of authoritative Others; cultural elites in control of social institutions such as government, education, mass media and business. Reduced to a culture carrier, the self is socially controlled. Manipulated by culture and without its essential dealienating capacity, the self is radically alienated. It projects and objectifies a cultural Other, alien to its own essential nature. Its authentic potentiality for being remains unrealized. The criteria for successful dealienation requires that human needs and desires be satisfied by exercising the essential power of rational freedom possessed in varying degrees by every self. Defective socialization disables the development of rationality and freedom.

Freud suggested that the process of socialization and character formation end at a very early age in child development. However, this narrow view is obviously false. For socialization continues through adolescence, extending into adult life. Dealienating projects of the self aside, it is bombarded daily for its loyalty and support from diverse cultural sources, be they familial, religious, ideological, corporate or political. Their implicit requests for allegiance involve personal choices and additional socialization, minimally requiring new self-identifications, possibly with self-projected expressions of support, and maximally requiring self-objectifying work. Since every finite self creates a personal history, its identity is always an open question. What the self wants and who it is to become is answered by all kinds of attitudes and choices throughout life. A young adult must decide upon a career, marriage and family. An elderly person has to decide how to handle retired life unstructured by the previous routines of working life. Increasing longevity requires personal decisions about what attitudes to adopt toward aging, illness and death. The character forming socialization of a child does not address such choices.

Adult self-identifications formed rationally and freely, instead of non-rationally or irrationally, do not initiate defective socialization.

The chance for successful dealienating outcomes is thereby maximized. Adults constantly accept or reject what culture presents for them to choose. If what culture offers suppresses the authentic nature of the self, then defective socialization is inevitable. Culture induces alienation where the process of socialization is defective. Tragic examples end with disillusionment, regretted self-objectification and the discovery of a life of wasted human potential with unsatisfied needs and aspirations. One typical example, often artistically expressed, comes out of contemporary corporate culture. Climbing the ladder of corporate success requires a compulsive achieving character sacrificing family life to an excessively long workweek. The tragic personal realization of permanent estrangement may come in a moment when a grown child fails to acknowledge its parent too busy with career to have formed a nurturing bond. Reflecting upon the experience of corporate success may remind the compulsive achiever of certain enjoyments foregone and too late to recover.

Such revelations of alienation result from adult self-identifications with cultural norms and social roles, which misled into a self-objectification that was neither authentic nor autonomous. Lacking the application of rational freedom, the true needs and desires of the self cannot be satisfied. The adult socialization process is flawed at its inception with a non-rational culturally defined self-identification making of the self an alien Other. Dysfunctional self-projection and self-objectification can be expected where there is no personal insight into authentic needs and desires and where there is no foresight of the consequences of self-identifying choices.

Defective socialization is common in ideologies, be they collectivist, authoritarian, totalitarian, or contemporary postmodern. Each does not satisfy the criteria for dealienating socialization. Even more tragic examples of self-alienating defective socialization can be found in contemporary counter-culture ideology. It promises liberating happiness never realized from the mere rejection of existing cultural norms and social roles.

An extreme gender feminism has been found tragically alienating by many women who self-identified with its prescriptions. Prior to their self-identifying choice, they failed to critically evaluate or test the ideology presented by this subculture. Here are some relevant unasked questions. Is it true that there are no genetically determined differences between males and females? Or, if there are, can they be disregarded? Should traditional femininity be shunned and replaced by gender neutral unisex mores? Is it true that females are dominated by an oppressive male culture, and that the solution is to successfully compete and dominate males in corporate and political life? Are male genitals weapons and is heterosexual intercourse equivalent to rape? Are masturbation and lesbianism preferable substitutes for heterosexual satisfaction? Should traditional heterosexual marriage be replaced by instituting homosexual marriage? Political and legal sanction has been sought to legitimize homosexual marriage. Whether a single unmarried female or cohabiting lesbians can bear and nurture children better than the traditional heterosexual married couple can be doubted. Public information and discussion of such contentions tends to be suppressed by the public controversy surrounding the deviant family lifestyle.

Some negating consequences of gender feminist belief and practice are already manifest in contemporary culture. A mixed sex military is discovered to be problematical as sexuality interferes with discipline and morale. Efforts to assert social equality are opposed by genetically determined differences relating to physical reproduction, physical strength, spatial versus language aptitude and aggressive temperament, among others. That women nurture and men destroy does not seem to be purely culturally determined. Thus, to socially engineer a unisex soldier, equal in every respect as a human being, would appear doomed to failure. That a gender feminist counter-culture ideology liberates women to realize their true potential is doubtful. Contradicting the biological needs and sexual desires related to their satisfaction can only alienate the self while creating tragically destructive gender warfare. Socially coercive practices cannot liberate or enhance the realization of human potential.

Masculinization of females has more profoundly alienating consequences than the loss of femininity. Self-identifying as a career woman often leads to a total sacrifice of the joys of nurturing parenthood and family life. Wanting to be both career woman and nurturer places a staggering burden upon an individual, made even worse by single parenthood. Super Moms are stretched so thin that neither role is satisfying. One may be sacrificed to the other in the attempt to do and have it all at the same time. This lifestyle choice results in stress and guilt about what goes undone. Of course, it is possible to correctly assess one's own capabilities and take career woman and nurturer in a successful sequence. Still, many women make an either-or choice. When it is to be an ambitious career woman hostile toward competing males, the sacrifice may be found not be worth the reward. Isolated and without the love of family, more than one woman past menopause, has regretted her sacrifice of maternity and family.

Re-treading the path of the self-alienated corporate male is found even less satisfying to a woman whose biological nature creates, nurtures and renews life. Competitive domination of males or establishing a gender-neutral unisex social environment may permit neither liberation nor self-realization of the human potential possessed by a woman. Hard choices entailing sacrifice confirms the finitude of sexuality. However, sexuality need not be alienating, when approached with the freedom to make choices based upon personal insight and rational foresight.

The demand for authenticity and autonomy finds cultural expression in historic feminist advocacy from suffrage to equal treatment in the workplace. Yet, liberation of women is not without alienating social consequences. Substituting a single working or welfare-dependent parent for the traditional family is problematical. For it denies children the opportunity to self-identify with traditional family role models to develop moral attitudes and conscience. Absent parental and religious socialization, entertained by a popular culture of violent fantasy, and subjected to peer group pressure, children are defectively socialized. Accustomed to the violence of television entertainment, video games and gangster rap music, an unsupervised child may murder without remorse or empathy for the victim. Government has not been able to compensate for defective socialization with public education, programs providing day care for working mothers or public assistance to unwed teenage mothers. Usurping the socializing functions performed by traditional institutions of family and religion has not ameliorated the defective socialization of children.

Self-identification with counter-culture ideologies requires personal choices, often painful and sacrificial. This is true even when ideology is not an issue, as when one must choose between career and family, or when contemplating divorce. The agonizing question is which comes first, self or family? More accurately formulated, who is the self? Which self-identification predominates for self-projection and the creation of a self-objectified identity? Times of personal crisis often provide the answers. Contemplating a prospective divorce, someone will answer questions indicating a self-identity acquired through socialization. The following might be asked. Am I without fault to the spouse I find fault with? Is it reasonable to demand perfection in a mate, particularly when I recognize my own imperfections? What obligation do I feel toward those who love and depend upon me? Is my conscience willing to tolerate the suffering of spouse and children caused by divorce? Answers are self-defining. Loath to divorce, a nurturing parent will seek a compromise, sacrifice something desired and tolerate some degree of marital incompatibility. A narcissist or egoist would be expected to find divorce easier, or abandon family without regret.

Objects of identification are widely variant: parent, peer group, religious, cultural, ideological, political, governmental, to name a few. Of itself, identification is insufficient to achieve successful dealienation. Socially coerced irrational or non-rational self-identifications establish an opposition of self to culture. A cultural demand for obedience without reason disregards what the every self demands; a capacity to reason and behave freely in order to satisfy its authentic needs and desires. When socialization is coercive, something demanded by the self is negated. What is negated is replaced with a substitute. An effective substitute satisfies what was originally negated and provides something socially advantageous to the self. However, socialization may also be dysfunctional where there is no substitute or it is inadequate. This condition is marked by psychological and sociological conflict. If the self had no needs and desires of its own, then it would be infinitely malleable by culture. Personality would then only be a product of socialization by culture. Yet, the self is not infinitely malleable as witnessed by the fact of dysfunctional socialization.

Dealienation always involves an interaction with some object of desire. It can be related to the self in myriad ways as in being consumed, destroyed, possessed, dominated, used, transformed or created. Dealienation not only changes the world by self-objectifying work, it also creates self-identity. The very process of socialization continuously transforms the self. The first self-identifying step of this process is critical to achieving a dealienating outcome. Simply introjecting an authoritative Other in an irrationally or non-rationally coercive manner makes of the self an alien Other, since its own rationality and freedom are not operative in its subsequent self-projection and self-objectification. Culturally dictated socialization normally follows this path and so subjects the self to social demands often contrary to its own. The self is then resigned to the dominant power of culture, which may thwart the realization of its authentic potentiality for being. In this way, culture can alienate the self.

Nevertheless, there are rational responses to alienating cultural demands. They may be disregarded by accepting the burden of social opprobrium. Alternatively, attempts may be made to change what the culture demands. This is the course of moral or social activism. More often than not, the self will attempt a compromise of conflicting demands to neutralize the harshness of the culture and effect a modicum of satisfaction for itself. This course effects a change in the self as well as culture. Short of abandoning a prohibited desired object, a substitute may be found which effects an acceptable compromise with self-satisfaction less than complete, but optimized within the prevailing cultural circumstances. Yet, compromise does not eliminate the alienating opposition between culture and self. Neither does it completely satisfy all the criteria for successful dealienation.

A self subordinated to and dominated by an alien Other(s) in ways that negate or neglect its own demands and natural capacities is alienated in a most fundamental manner. Socialization, wrongly intended or applied, has alienating consequences with various psychological and sociological descriptions. The self may become neurotic with eccentric behaviors and beliefs that are hysterical, phobic, obsessive or compulsive. Even worse, it may withdraw from the social into a delusional world of psychoses such as paranoia, schizophrenia, melancholia or mania.

Normal responses to an alienating socialization range widely from the aggressively destructive to apathy. Hateful or hostile attitudes are commonly expressed. However alienation is specifically manifested, the being of the self is dissociated from its thought and behavior. Its being is not authentic and the truth of its being is repressed. An improperly socialized self must deceive itself about its true nature. This self-deceiving inauthentic being, a coercively socialized alien Other, must then be projected onto the world and its fellows through the work of self-objectification. In order to disguise and control the truth of itself, its character must be disingenuous. The inner psychic conflict of an improperly socialized self will always require a deception of others and self. Behavior and belief will not coincide. Dissociation and deception will predominate. An inauthentic self remains hidden with an unconscious psychic life. Whenever subconscious, that authentic self must become deceitful, hypocritical, disingenuous, cynically manipulative or even socially exploitative to satisfy its culturally prohibited wants. An egoistic self masters various behavioral artifices to achieve its secret aims. Existing in Sartrean *bad faith*, the self is aware that it is something other and more than can be expressed by playing a culturally provided social role.

Subordinating Self to Culture

Culture is a historical product of collective dealienation. However, culture may be differently conceived. For example, the structure of a given society might be abstractly analyzed as composed of classes of people and institutions performing specified functions relative to each other. Whether the organizing principle is organismic, teleological, hierarchical or structural, the self is subordinated to culture. Reduced to a social function, the self is a replaceable, interchangeable universal part of a social structure described by certain universal social norms and roles. Individuality or deviancy is then confined to the limits defined by the functional requirements of the social structure.

Traditional customs, attitudes, and social conventions are observed. The self exercises its freedom only in being a good father, mother, businessman, citizen, soldier and so forth. Deviant individuality, dysfunctional to the social structure, threatens it with disintegration. Authoritarian or totalitarian cultures attempt to control or suppress deviancy. Personal freedom is not permitted to be a factor in the creation of social norms and roles. Rather, freedom is confined to sustaining culture by applying existing social norms and roles to self-existence. Freedom is limited to doing the self-objectifying work of a pre-established culture considered an authoritative Other for the self.

Plato's formulation of justice in the *Republic* suggests a complementary and reciprocal relationship between self and culture. Justice is that natural condition where the self *does what it can do best* with society gaining maximum benefit from its contribution. A perfectly proportioned social whole would utilize individual differences of temperament and natural talent. The implication is that alienation would not exist in a social structure where culture and self are placed in a complementary and reciprocal relationship. Each gives to the maximum of its capability and each receives the full measure of what it deserves. Social contribution and personal satisfaction would thereby be maximized. Such a view is indeed appealing. Nevertheless, Plato's prescription for achieving a utopian society fails by replacing reciprocity of self to culture with subordination of self to culture. The Republic would use an educational institution to place individuals into a rigidly class structured society designed to perform the functions believed necessary for the social whole. Hierarchically organized, it would be governed by an elite class of wise men.

Hegel also conceived of society hierarchically structured into social institutions controlled by elite state bureaucrats and religious authority. Marx demanded reciprocity by asking, *from each according to his abilities and to each according to his needs.* Again, Marx's prescription requires subordinating the self to a revolutionary culture dictated by an elite proletarian ruling class replacing a capitalist one. Understanding that a self subordinate to culture places the former into a permanent condition of unreconcileable alienation, Freud offered no utopian prescription. The presumption common to such diverse social thinkers is that coercive socialization is necessary for creating and sustaining civilization. However, coercive socialization negates the authenticity and autonomy essential for dealienation and self-realization. For this reason, any social structure coercively subordinating of self to culture must fail. This defect is shared by authoritarianism, totalitarianism and collectivism, elements present in Platonic, Hegelian and Marxist social perspectives.

Consciousness is an act of negation, a presentation of an Other alien to self. Reduced to negativity, the self is vacuous, not an object, mere negating freedom without aim. Since it cannot take itself as an object, the self must identify with an Other alien to itself. Self-identifications with alien Other(s) provide freedom with an aim enabling self-objectification that creates a historical identity. Without essence and with negating freedom, there is no alternative to a self-identification with culture. Yet, cultural submersion, or complete subordination of self to culture is problematical. Where domination by culture is coercively established, the self is discovered to suffer alienation. Its demand for authenticity, autonomy, and certain other important needs and desires cannot be satisfied. Hence, mere self-identification with culture fails as a prescription for dealienation. The failure of coercive socialization and submersion in culture implies the inadequacy of abstractly conceiving the self to be negating freedom without essence or inner direction. Yet, the fact that the demands of culture can alienate those of the self implies that it has an essential nature. How culture responds to it determines whether it will suffer alienation or develop a capacity for dealienation.

War presents the most extreme example of a coerced subordination of self to culture. The common rationale of war is the preservation of culture. This may or may not be true or believed by any soldier whose life is at risk in battle. The alienating consequences of a coerced subordination of self to culture are amply demonstrated by the wartime requirement for the stereotypical soldier, the conscript. By the threat of incarceration, he is coerced to become a soldier. He must relinquish a civilian lifestyle and aspirations, at least for the duration of the war. In addition, he is aware of the possibility of death in battle. Dedicated to the purpose of war, his life is expendable. It does not matter that he understands or agrees with the purpose of war. Autonomy is not only irrelevant to playing the role of the soldier; it is suppressed in a training that conditions him to immediately obey without question any order issued by a superior authority. Individuality is strictly confined within the norms defining the soldier's role. Military culture prescribes and proscribes a soldier's behavior.

The self-identification necessary for the self-objectification of a conscript is effected by social coercion. Non-rational rewards and punishments are applied in training recruits to conform to military culture. The conscript will be rewarded with promotion and decorations conferring social status and esteem. Or, he may be punished for disobedience with demotion, removal, fines, imprisonment or even death in extreme cases. Questioning or acting outside the limits set by the soldier's role while on duty is considered lawless. Some degree of autonomy may be recovered after training, but it is always limited to carrying out orders. Self-objectification with a soldier's role is to live within a highly socially controlled culture. Self-existence confined to the conscript role stereotype replaces the satisfactions of certain needs and desires authentic to the self with those of the authoritative Other, military culture. Role-playing carries out the aims of authoritative Others. Socially coerced to play a stereotyped role, the authenticity and autonomy of the self is sacrificed to the demands of culture. Alienation is here an inescapable consequence of socially coerced subordination of self to culture. Of itself, subordination of self to culture does not establish alienation. Nevertheless, subordination, coercively effected does, thus confirming an opposition between the demands of culture and those of self.

Popular culture presents an image of a self dominated by the Other(s). Television continuously sends this subliminal message with its commercial advertising and entertainment. Survival by high show ratings has turned programming into entertainment. From talk shows to politics, television makes subjects for serious thought into adversarial entertainment. Viewers watch, passively enjoying the entertainment, whether provided by political pandering or tales of personal woe. The appeal of the celebrity or ordinary person is his or her entertainment value. Passive viewers, treated to short adversarial confrontations, are invited to take sides emotionally rather than rationally. They must *feel the others' pain* rather than deliberate upon it, since commercials permit no time for that. Most viewers are educatively unprepared to think seriously, since this requires solitude and privacy. Mass public education leaves the ordinary TV viewer *dumbed down*, shallow, passive, and a part of the crowd. Ideologically propagandized and ready to be entertained, the TV viewer is easily deceived and manipulated by alien Others. Thought is cleverly controlled linguistically through redefining the usage of words and subliminally loading them with emotional connotations. College youth are exhorted to speak in a *politically correct* manner, ostensibly from respect for diversity, but really to effect thought control for ideological purposes.

Transmitted by Hollywood movies, television and musical entertainment, the thrust of popular culture is to replace a private self with a public self. It is OK to let it *all hang out* for everyone to see. This pervasive attitude, reinforced by education and entertainment, sends a subliminal message that individuality can only be legitimized by a test of approval from a public authoritative Other. A self so formed is passive, taught to obey popular tastes and emotionally decide perplexing questions. Rational freedom is de-emphasized, thereby diminishing a personal capacity for dealienation. When privacy and solitude become suspect, the self is fully prepared for social control by subliminal messages from impersonal anonymous authoritative Others who remain unrecognized and concealed.

The effect of the mass media and thought control has been recognized by philosophers such as Carl Jaspers and Hannah Arendt, as well as literary figures such as George Orwell and Aldous Huxley. Before mid-twentieth century, such thinkers were alarmed by a modern totalitarian stripping away of a private self and its replacement with a public self controlled by the mass media. Socialist ideology denigrates individuality, insultingly referring to a person as merely one of the *masses*. There is no human dignity to the *masses*. Individuals need to be *dumbed down* to be socially controlled by elites claiming to know what is best for everyone. This process continues with public education dominated by a socialist counter-culture ideological agenda reinforced by a popular culture transmitted through the entertaining mass media. Its thrust is to replace the private with a public self: one who is passive, emotionally driven, dependent, fully prepared to be manipulated and duped by those who do not respect personal dignity. However, individuality is not so easily suppressed by the authoritative Others of popular culture. For rational freedom, the basis of human dignity, is a potentiality demanding self-expression in response to alienating finitude.

Subordinating and submerging the self in culture is carried out in the bureaucratic organization of industrial society. Vast government bureaucracies supported by public income taxation are controlled by an elite class of career professional politicians. Their power is maintained through a vast *zero sum* game of income redistribution to politically active and dependent minority groups competing for special privilege. They claim discrimination, are politically declared victims and legislatively awarded special public subsidies. Within this political process, both victims and victimizers alike are subjected to a labyrinthine morass of government laws and regulations. A paternalistic government progressively usurps the functions of traditional institutions of civil society such as the family, religion and education. Micromanaging the lives of citizens progressively eliminates their autonomy in favor of dependency upon authoritative Others falsely presumed to act on their behalf. As this process advances, liberty is progressively eroded.

Continuous exposes of government corruption and scandal incrementally portray contemporary political culture alienating the citizenry from its government. The threat of government regulation imposed or withheld translates campaign contributions into retaining political power. And this is achieved by expenditure on media and political consultants, pollsters, public relations and marketing experts who package and sell the politician much like a commodity. Public opinion is manipulated with subliminal advertising, polling and use of political focus groups. Cynically deceptive propaganda and slanderous television sound bites make politically persuasive emotional appeals. Special interest voting minority groups are courted with promises and favors proffered by the candidates. Elections become auctions where competing candidates bid for power with promises of spending general income tax revenues on behalf of voting blocks seeking favors, privilege, advantage and regulatory tax relief.

At best, the political process is considered benign, irrelevant and ignored by the unrepresented. Recognized as merely representative of special interests and responsive to campaign money, apathy and distrust of government increase. Well under half of the American citizenry bother to vote. Exposed as deceptive, manipulative and corrupt; skepticism and cynicism toward government express an alienation of the political process. Without commitment to the general public welfare or public service, politics is reduced to a game of self-aggrandizement without redeeming social value.

Scarcity signifies the alienating finitude of self-existence expressed by human needs and desires. Whatever is scarce has value by the very fact that it is necessary to satisfy needs and desires. Poverty, when signifying a scarcity of the necessities of life, is alienating. Those afflicted with poverty are alienated from material and spiritual goods. The inscrutable forces of a free marketplace sometimes truly victimize some individuals or classes of them. Capitalist economies are well known for cyclical recessions, or even depressions. There are also, occasions where the self-interest of politically powerful dominating socio-economic elites victimize individuals or classes of them. Socialist ideology focuses upon such cases demonizing wealthy individuals or corporate entities. Capitalists are called exploiters of the laboring poor and producers of grinding poverty from which there is no escape. Wealth and the wealthy are suspect: being made to feel guilty for their accomplishment although their wealth is used as the investment engine of economic prosperity, employment and public charity. By the demonization of the rich, the poorer classes are tempted by envy and greed to accept schemes that legally rob the wealthy of what has been acquired by intelligence and merit. Such political and legal scams are common. Responding to the widespread alienation created by poverty and excessive scarcity are regulatory institutions, religious, civil and governmental.

There are various solutions to alienating poverty. Age-old remedies involve simple charity, corporate beneficence and paternalism.

The modern welfare state driven by socialist ideology has attempted to eradicate poverty. The predominant governmental remedy has been a coercive redistribution of wealth by means of income taxation. This zero sum game has been largely successful. A Dickensian described nineteenth century English poverty no longer exists where crime and prostitution responded to an absence of the physical necessities of life. Notwithstanding governmental coercion, poverty remains an ineradicable perennial problem. Where the lowest income level of a given social system defines poverty, it is by definition ineradicable. For an income defined poverty level is subject not only to the level of economic prosperity prevailing at any given time, but also to re-definition for political advantage. This so-called poverty level can be arbitrarily established. Furthermore, any socio-economic system, particularly one based upon free self-seeking, is continuously altering and characterized by inequality of every description. Excess and shortage always exist. The distribution of wealth is never equal. The value or price of anything is established by the economic law of supply and demand. Individuals are constantly becoming rich as well as poor, moving up and down the rungs of the socio-economic ladder.

Poverty is not of itself evil, although it would be if someone were to deliberately inflict it on someone else. Yet, poverty is alienating without question. For it deprives those who suffer it. They lack opportunity, since poverty limits the range of choices available to them. They cannot be what they could otherwise become. In order to realize their potential, material resources are necessary. Without it, freedom of choice and action is limited. Eliminating poverty has an obvious appeal and moral rationale. When not socially addressed by welfare state programs, religion or other civic institutions, the challenge of poverty lies in a personal response to its alienating condition. Coping with poverty can be character building, since certain virtues are required such as intelligence thrift, courage and perseverance. One who has met this test acquires a true knowledge of self, things and other persons. Thus although poverty is alienating and undesirable both personally and socially, it presents an opportunity for self-development and self-realization. Those who have met the test of overcoming poverty can be admired for the noble virtues of character they have displayed. They rightfully take pride in having met and overcome poverty. Their demand that others suffering poverty do the same as themselves is not beside the point, where poverty is not an evil deliberately inflicted by another person or class.

The state always poses a potential danger to personal liberty, particularly when it provides a benevolent socialism with a paternalistic bureaucracy. To be legitimate, the state must demonstrate itself worthy of respect and trust by citizens who have the capacity to pass judgment upon its actions and control it by appropriate representation. The state exists for the sake of the individual, to protect and promote freedom and rationality, comprising his power to dealienate and realize his complete potential. A worthy state is composed of citizens whose lives demonstrate their autonomy and authenticity.

Subordinating Culture to Self

Arguing for the primacy of self-existence, existentialists subordinated culture to self. Kierkegaard elevated the religious above the ethical, the individual above a sterile Christian conformism. Sartre viewed role-playing as a loss of freedom and reification of the self. Heidegger thought of the *they-self* as inauthentic, failing to reveal who it is. No doubt, Hegel was right in asserting that role-playing make the self a *somebody*, socially recognized and commanding some degree of public respect. But a social role may be a veneer, disguising a self despairing over its identity, over the loss of its own capacity to be what it truly is, to realize its full potential and aspirations. Adopting the norms set by the authoritative Other(s) and playing their prescribed social roles may well result in lives of quiet desperation. Hegel's abstract logical view of the universal transcending the particular, and of a larger social whole ontologically superior to the individual, disregards the primacy of self-existence in establishing and sustaining culture. What is universal and transcendent is not cultural Others, be they social institutions or a creator God. Rather, what is universal and transcendent is the essential power of rational freedom defining self-existence as a spiritual process of dealienation.

Contemporary American culture asserts the subordination of culture to self. It demands the authenticity and autonomy asserted by existentialism. There is a broad tolerance of deviancy from prevailing social norms and stereotyped roles. The boundary between tolerance and permissiveness is often indistinct. Lifestyle experimentation among young adults is rampant. Cultural tolerance provides the possibility of legitimizing deviancy obtainable from acceptance and practice by the majority. Organized advocacy attempts to gain public acceptance by portraying deviancy as normal, or just another lifestyle choice to be respected. Cast under the umbrella of respect for individuality and human rights, efforts are put forth to legitimize deviant lifestyles. Counter-culture groups organize around their claim of discrimination and human rights violations. Portrayed as victims of discrimination, political alliances are formed. Acceptance of deviancy is also carried on by ideological indoctrination in educational institutions. Mass media publicize the case for deviancy with editorial propaganda and subliminal messages. Controversial deviancy has popular entertainment value. An entertainment industry using popular culture art forms makes the emotional appeal favoring deviancy.

The social struggle over deviancy has been characterized as a *culture war* carried on with argumentation between advocates of counterculture and those of traditional culture. The culture war is fought in America primarily among special interest groups or lobbyists seeking favorable legislation and legal precedents from expensive court cases. However, the winner will ultimately be determined from the collective result of lifestyle choices by the populace. Where culture is subordinate to a self free to experiment, evaluate and choose its lifestyle, deviancy might be considered a relative concept. Deviancy accepted becomes the norm and changes culture. However, with respect to its alienating or dealienating consequences for self-existence, deviancy is not at all relative. The prospective consequences of choosing different lifestyles are always subject to debate. The actual consequences of deviancy determine whether it is preferable.

Contemporary life increasingly subordinates culture to self. Priority is given to the demands of the self for authenticity and autonomy. This has resulted in substantial changes to traditional social roles and institutions. Their promise of personal satisfaction is skeptically regarded. Understood contractually, they are treated experimentally. Fearing the prospect of personal unhappiness ending in divorce, experimental cohabitation is widely practiced instead of, or before marriage. It is no longer considered essential or even desirable for social renewal. Single parent families are common. Advances in reproductive medical technology challenge the social necessity of the traditional family as does the changed roles of women in the workforce. Families are possible without heterosexuality. The sacrament of marriage and sanction of the welfare state is being extended to homosexuals. Abortion has achieved legal sanction for the sake of maternal health. The traditional role of physician is challenged by attempts to legalize euthanasia for the elderly whose life has been prolonged by advances in medical technology. Although such trends may cause anxiety, their effects cannot be fully judged in advance of experimenting with deviancy.

If a prescription for a dealienated society is to be viable, the overlooked requirement seems to be to allow individuality a far greater degree of autonomy than most social thinkers would tolerate. Confusing license with personal freedom and disregarding its relationship to rationality results in a distrust of freedom and an overemphasis upon its potentially destructive social consequences. However, rational freedom is creative rather than destructive. A self, having developed this capacity, can modify, replace and even create novel cultural norms and social roles. This in fact happens continuously and is the engine of cultural change. A culture trusting and encouraging personal liberty avoids coercive socialization. The self is prized for daring to be different and for exercising its unique creative capacity. Tolerance of deviancy allows culture the flexibility to change and respond to alienating conditions encountered by self-existence. That the self could create culture was not believed possible in principle by Plato, Hegel, Marx and Freud. Even where they proclaimed the power of rationality or freedom, they did not fully comprehend its integrated power to effect dealienation. Building trust in rational freedom was left to later generations of western civilization that created freer societies than previous thinkers dreamed possible.

Without developing the capacity for rational freedom, dealienation is impossible in principle. However, what if adults were not subject to coercive socialization with non-rational or irrational self-identifications? Instead, what if the self-identifications were formed deliberatively? Not only would the dealienating capacity of the self be preserved, but also the alienating consequences of culturally provided norms and social roles would be minimized. And, if what culture offers is found deficient, it could be modified or replaced with norms and roles created from the dealienating process of self-existence

Satisfying the needs and desires of others is prerequisite to satisfying those of oneself. You give and you get. Reciprocity is a universal social demand. Something of value is voluntarily exchanged, usually with money that is fungible. However, quite often reciprocity is absent. One may work in a bureaucratic organization and be paid without acceptance of one's work product. Personal satisfaction with work demands a self-confirming exchange. What one does must make a difference, be accepted, used and valued by those it was intended to benefit. An absence of social reciprocity is dysfunctional and typical of bureaucracy. It will only accept what it has pre-established as conforming to its rules and so innovative individuals are rarely rewarded. Non-conformists are at best tolerated, but more often punished. However, no culture, bureaucratic or otherwise can survive without reciprocity. The demand for it persists. Thus, the crucial question for cultural survival is whether genuine products of individuality will be accepted and acknowledged. Where this is not the case, cultural alienation persists. The alternative is for culture to permit authentic expressions of autonomous individuals. Where culture encourages self-realization, the self will bond with it. Reciprocity provides satisfaction of the deepest human aspirations. None of this is possible where individuality is not encouraged.

Correctly conceived, culture originates from self-existence and collective dealienating endeavor. Every self is identical, similar and distinct in some respect from every other. Each makes claim upon the other to the demands presented by its needs, desires and the freedom required for realizing its authentic human potentiality. The essential nature shared by every self implies a relationship of reciprocity rather than subordination: each contributing its particular strength in co-operative endeavor and exchange for mutual benefit and survival. Human dignity resides in a respect for the equal claim made by every self. This claim is asserted by the demand for equal opportunity and personal liberty commonly recognized as a basis for human rights, justice and constitutional democracy.

A coercive subordination of self to culture is prevalent in non-democratic cultures. Their social structure is hierarchical. The dealienating claim of one self is not equal to others of a different social class. Laws accord unequal treatment to individuals depending upon their social function or membership in a class. One is born a peasant to labor or a nobleman to enjoy leisure. A slave has no legal rights. Rank has its privileges as where only property owners can vote. Class mobility, where permitted, is limited. Reciprocity between social functions and classes is strictly regulated. Contrast this sketch with one based upon subordinating culture to self. This principle is more prevalent in democratic culture, particularly in the institutions of representative government and information age commercial corporations. Their social structure is horizontal rather than hierarchical and bureaucratic. Organizations and selves supporting their social function make equal claim upon each other. Treated as equals, tend to maximize reciprocity. Rewards and social status is determined by personal achievement and merit rather than by any accident of birth. Equal opportunity provides upward class mobility.

If individuality is allowed the freedom imputed to it, then spontaneity and creativity flourish. A free individuality is socially transformative. There is room to think and act *outside the box*, so to speak. Individuality is not bound to universal norms and stereotyped social roles prescribed for it by some alien Other, be it an elite, the state or God. Abstracted from their dealienating existential origin, cultural norms and social roles lose the factual basis for their authority. Inhibited by stereotypical roles, self-existence is distorted by being confined to inflexible social structures where behavior is entirely predictable and socially controlled. This describes a bureaucracy or totalitarian state in which human needs, desires and mechanisms for their satisfaction are pre-planned. A self coercively subordinated to such a culture will be bored, depressed and apathetic; emotions signifying alienation. If submersion in such cultures provided an identity sought by the self, then bureaucratic life would be successful and satisfactory. However, this is not the case. Many are unwilling to accept the norms and roles of a bureaucratic culture. Their demand for autonomy struggles against inducements to conform. And non-conformity persists even where opposition is acknowledged futile.

Adopting a role deviating from the stereotype, when not understood, lacks a self-confirming socially acknowledged legitimacy. Deviant roles challenging stereotypical ones are often greeted with opprobrium censure, ostracism or punishment. Any expression of individuality outside the cultural norms governing role-playing is suspect by its non-conformity, possibly even considered unlawful. Deviant roles challenge culture by competing with stereotypes. Neither can be condemned without trying both. Their respective dealienating claims are judged by their results to determine which is preferable. Successfully competing deviant roles often become the norm replacing less successful cultural stereotypes. The process continuously responds to alienating conditions of self-existence.

Whole social structures have been built from a hierarchy of stereotyped roles. The boundaries of individuality are thereby clearly established. Nevertheless, this rigid perspective also has disadvantages. Non-conformity to stereotypical roles may be suppressed thereby disallowing experimentation with deviancy that might promote successful dealienation. Cultural intolerance of deviancy is then undesirable. Inflexible role stereotyping without toleration of deviancy or experimentation invariably creates tragic suffering by individuals who are different from what culture prescribes.

Role reversal and experimental arrangements utilizing the relative actual capacities of individuals can be beneficial. But this would be lost when, for example, a mother who could earn twice the family income of her husband would not be permitted to work while the father cared for their children. Individual differences do not always fit some universal stereotyped role, since such differences are matters of discovered fact. A healthy culture requires toleration of individual differences and the flexibility to discover and utilize them effectively. Disallowing spontaneity and creativity in establishing or changing roles alienates both the self and its culture. Cultural tolerance of deviancy - the freedom of individuals to be different - promotes the realization of unique human potentialities while facilitating the replacement of alienating role stereotypes. Rather than a cultural intolerance of deviancy, tolerance of it can function much like a safety valve promoting collective social health.

Identification with Cultural Authority

Hegel understood alienation and dealienation metaphorically as circular loss and recovery. Mythology postulated an idyllic life of ignorance and innocence. Its loss defines alienation with subsequent history consisting of attempts to recover it. Hegel interpreted the drama of history with this metaphor. The ancient Greek *polis* illustrated an original innocent unity of self with the divine. However, this unity was shattered by a conflict of human and divine duty between Antigone and King Creon as artistically portrayed in the Sophoclean tragedy *Antigone*.

When Greek civilization was replaced by the Roman, the self discovered its freedom residing within its capacity to react only in thought to the tyranny of Emperors and their corruption of culture. This abstract vacuous freedom is embodied in the legal rights of the Roman citizen supported by the absolute power of the Emperor. Stoically resigned to its fate, the self is free in its own thoughts, but not in its actions. It is cynical of its civilization, and its newfound capacity to think for itself merely ends in skepticism. For its own reasoning capacity leads it only to contradictory conclusions, equally plausible and arguable. Its freedom can only negate traditional authority and its reasoning capacity cannot reach any truth that could guide its conduct.

Replacing Roman civilization, Hegel characterized the medieval with the self-concept of an *Unhappy Consciousness* in despair of its finitude and its own capacity to overcome its alienation. Its transcendent perfect God and heaven are beyond its reach. However, Christianity humanizes the divine in the person of Christ thereby making salvation within the reach of every self. With the Protestant Reformation, Hegel believed religious alienation to be historically terminated. A lost relationship of self to the divine was finally recovered through a reformed Christianity. A self-identification and self-projection of Christ's example is accomplished by a free self-objectification conforming to his divine revelation and promise of personal salvation. Hegel's Christian prescription for dealienation is to renounce egoistic self-seeking and place a self-alienating freedom and rationality in service to the authority and dicta of the divine.

The biblical myth of expulsion from paradise and Antigone's tragic conflict of religious with civil law portrays a loss of symbiosis, an initial negation distinguishing a self alienated from its authoritative Other. From this follows a dealienating historical process of recovery. The lost innocence and ignorance of an original narcissistic symbiosis cannot be recovered. Instead, a Hegelian dialectical process of historical dealienation presents different figures of alienation accompanied by the development of a self-conscious freedom. That lost narcissistic symbiosis is replaced by a dialectical process of self-development, self-realization and self-discovery.

Hegel interpreted the history of western civilization as developing from a loss and recovery of *Sittlichkeit*, that original unconscious narcissistic symbiosis of self submerged in a culture completely authoritative for it. Alienation is a loss of *Sittlichkeit* in a cataclysmic historical event as portrayed in religious mythology and art. Dealienation is a recovery of *Sittlichkeit* through a collective work of history wherein the self reconciles its own demand for personal freedom with those of culture, represented by authoritative Others embedded in social institutions of family, civil society, state and religion. A dialectical recovery of *Sittlichkeit* reveals personal freedom to be self-alienating, except when subordinated to culture. As recovery historically progresses, freedom moves away from primitive narcissism and egoistic self-assertion. As freedom expands, its implications are revealed. In service exclusively to egoism, freedom can be counterproductive leading into eddies which dead-end in perversion, sadism and masochism. However, when these are understood and avoided, freedom can broaden its horizons and expand constructively toward sustaining culture, community and larger social structures transcending the self. So aimed, complete development and recovery of *Sittlichkeit* can occur within a context of self-realization expressing the social and spiritual nature of the self.

The dissolution of classical Athenian culture occurred with the Sophists who made the individual self-conscious by requiring him to think for himself, to reflect upon traditional authority and question its legitimacy from his own perspective. The self is the locus of truth and value replacing the dicta of traditional cultural authoritative Others. Hegel believed that such subjectivism, although an advance in self-conscious freedom, is also self-alienating. For extreme individuality and relativism threaten social cohesion provided by cultural institutions and law, human and divine. The sophist viewpoint introduces an alienation taking millennia to work through. Nevertheless, this sophistic relativism is inevitable and even necessary for freedom to develop and alienated *Sittlichkeit* to be recovered. Ensuing history is a long dealienating process of human suffering whereby traditional cultural authority is re-introjected by recognition of its rationality and a free self-identification with it.

In the context of Roman life, the Emperor and destiny are the masters of self-existence. They are alien Others, external, threatening and hostile to the freeborn citizen. They make him self-conscious of the nullity of his existence. Yet, he recognizes his own subjective will and its claims. It demands freedom of expression, objectification in property and a law guaranteeing them both. Just as society recognizes but contradicts and frustrates these demands, so the individual internalizes this social alienation becoming self-consciousness of a bifurcated nature. His life, beset by absolute power, a destiny beyond control, an insecurity and contingency of existence, generates a melancholy sense of isolation, helplessness and nullity. How is this world of alienating finitude to be overcome? The individual makes no attempt to change the culturally alienating conditions that appear immutable and overwhelming. Accepting them as authoritative for himself, he tries instead to change himself. He identifies with the oppressive alienating Other, a deified Emperor, conceiving him as an omnipotent and perfect God. The escape from the alienating finitude of the times takes the form of Christian religious longing, a desire for symbiosis with the creator. Salvation from a sinful world is sought through identifying with God and doing his will. Self-consciousness now aims for the perfection of a universal being sorely missing from its world. This is the otherworldly Christian response to the alienation of the Roman empire.

The alienated soul of the Roman citizen is in pain and longing after the realization of its own true potential and aim; to freely express what is rational and perfect. His misery and nullity of existence is in contrast to a being that is all-powerful and perfect. His emotional response is a world weary melancholy with a life of alienating finitude, a life dominated by the vagaries and contingencies of nature, a life of insecurity, subservience to external authority and irrevocable destiny. Spiritually, the freeborn Roman citizen lives in wretched isolation from community and God. His existence is in contradiction to a higher perfection of a God and realization of his own essential nature, which he thinks about, but which is alien, denied, beyond him, frustratingly out of reach.

In order to understand any particular historical form of alienation, one must ascertain the true nature of the Other. It is the whim of an absolute monarch for the medieval courtier, a transcendent God beyond the reach of the miserable sinner, an Enlightenment self unable to recognize its identity when reduced to mere useful object or, a Romantic self glorified by an absolute negating freedom lacking transcendent purpose. Freedom lost, alienates the self as much as freedom lacking guidance. Both contributed to the failure of the French Revolution. It assumed the individual to be a lawgiver. Then it alienated the freedom of individuals to a political body and finally to a tyrant. Historically developed tradition and social institutions were discarded by political fiat. Freedom proved unable to provide the laws governing its use. So, what it destroyed was not replaced. *Equality*, *fraternity, liberty* turned out to be vacuous slogans, not intentionally created norms necessary for reconstructing society. Alienating individual freedom to the state and dictator deprived the community of what creates and sustains it. Conformity imposed by coercive totalitarian authority could only produce a facade of universality among those calling each other *citizen* but unfree and isolated by suspicion and terror.

For Hegel, to be alienated meant to be an isolated individual, neither participating nor contributing to community or fulfilling divine intentions. The prescription for dealienation is very simple: identify with norms divine and communal, and play a role in sustaining them. Abandon natural self-seeking desire. Discipline personal freedom by placing it in service to culture and Geist. Conform to the prescriptions of traditional authority universally applicable to individuals. Submerge individuality in the prevailing culture. Become a culture carrier. Objectify oneself in conformity to the dicta of traditional authority and receive in return an identity, which is universal and related to the larger social whole, even to the cosmos. Then, the particular life of an individual expresses a universal Idea and is a vehicle for Geist, actualizing its larger transcendent purpose.

A prevalent cultural formula for dealienation is to renounce, identify with traditional norms and social roles and self-project them. In return, the self is rewarded with a socially created identity, status and prestige. These nurture the ego as it carries the culture. The self is said to belong or be at home in its culture. Reciprocity is secured as self and culture complement each other. Although appealing, this formula is problematical. Renouncing certain demands authentic to the self may not be possible or replaceable by identification with a cultural substitute. Then the process of renunciation and substitution is self-alienating. Freudian repression explained the psychic dynamics of a dysfunctional cultural substitution. An ego not able to get what it wants adopts non-rational or irrational unconscious defenses. The demands of the repressed return with the symptoms of neurosis. Here, alienation is culturally induced. The self becomes inauthentic by conforming to culturally prescribed norms and social roles suppressing its own essential nature. Dominated by a repressive cultural authoritative Other, autonomy is sacrificed. The very capacity for dealienation is compromised. An authentic potentiality for being remains unrealized.

Existing in ignorance and innocence is to be in an unconscious symbiosis with an authoritative Other. This condition characterizes a narcissistic self with undeveloped potential; dependent upon and dominated by an alien Other; and lacking a capacity for dealienation. Such an undeveloped self is a mere product of a culture that nurtures and so is authoritative for it. Culture is its destiny. Moreover, culture is sustained in no small measure by that original unconscious narcissistic symbiosis and the natural tendency to maintain it. Continued nurture by culture is conditional upon conformity with its demands. Yet, these very demands eliminate symbiosis, forcing the self to develop beyond narcissism to egoism. Symbiotic dependency is replaced by self-directed behavior with some degree of freedom and rationality. Boundaries are set by cultural norms and social roles that structure egoistic behavior. Culture prescribes how the self is to satisfy its needs and desires.

Hegel's implied view of identification would require it to be rational as opposed to irrational or non-rational, freely chosen as opposed to coerced. Thus to make a cultural identification is to freely choose based upon a knowledge of one's duty. But cultural identification consists of coercive non-rational or even irrational socialization processes unrelated to freedom or rationality. The self must be indoctrinated to doing its duty. Acknowledging one's duty is not equivalent to knowing the truth of what is good for oneself and everyone else. Duty is not knowledge. Rather, knowing and doing one's duty expresses the cultural demands of authoritative Others alien to the self. Certainly, a self existing in ignorance and innocence is in narcissistic symbiosis with its authoritative Others and has no need of freedom. A self submerged in culture is not free. Neither is a self necessarily free when duty bound and deliberately subordinated to culture.

Freedom is entirely ambiguous until it is given an aim. Shall freedom be directed by the self or by the Other(s)? Hegel argued that freedom egoistically directed and devoted to self-seeking desire alienates the self. He advocated placing freedom in service to the Other(s) with the prospect of a dealienating result. What or who are these Others? They are God and the institutions of society, which prescribe norms of conduct, or law. They also prescribe social roles for the self to play. In short, they structure life with prescriptions and proscriptions for conduct. They are the source establishing a basis for human rights that govern the exercise of freedom. No self can realize who or what it is, its complete human potential, without recognizing its duty to obey these authoritative Others. They provide an ethical order to guide the exercise of freedom in the work of self-objectification.

The result of harnessing freedom to duty toward authoritative Others is to instantiate their dicta, to create what Hegel referred to as *ethical substance*. He analyzed its components as family, civil society and the state, built into a hierarchical structure crowned by religion and God. Each sustains the other in one organic whole. The subordinate sustains itself and supports the superior. In turn, the superior guides the subordinate. Every living self participates, contributes and sustains the whole with a freedom devoted to doing its duty. In the performance of duty, the individual recognizes the culture as a reflection of himself, as a product of his own work. The result is that the culture loses its alien character. Freedom structured by duty enables the self to realize who and what it is in every dimension of its being within the larger whole of being transcending itself.

Hegel considered individual freedom dangerously destructive if not exercised within the limits established by civilizing cultural structures. These are the traditional authorities found within a civilization in the form of custom, duty, community, family, civil society, the state, religion and God. The norms established by such entities proscribe or prescribe the conduct of individuals and uses of their freedom. Unbridled individualism attacks those restraining civilizing structures cultivated by centuries of human struggle and carefully transmitted by indoctrinating young energetic individuals. This view persisted into the twentieth century with other notable thinkers such as Freud who also distrusted as antisocial individual freedom in the form of unfettered instinctual gratification. Civilization protects itself from the threat posed by freedom of individuals with psychological repression and sublimation of instinctual gratification. However, unlike Hegel, Freud recognized the alienating price to be paid by the individual in the form of neurosis.

For Hegel, the structures of social control cannot be alienating. Rather alienation finds its source within the rebellious individual misdirecting the use of his freedom without regard to civilizing social structures. Those norms, pre-established by traditional authority and universally true for everyone without exception, are disregarded by individuals driven by their own desires and aims. Self-objectification must then be subordinated to norms designed to socially control the threat personal freedom poses to culture. Hegel believed cultural norms and social roles, universal in scope and prescribed by traditional cultural authoritative Others, transcend individuality, which must remain subordinate to them, if dealienation is to proceed successfully. Given this view, self-objectification is not equivalent to authentic self-realization. For the normative source and aims of what the individual realizes are alien to himself. The question Hegelian self-objectification always raises is for what and for whom is the self acting. The answer is always for an alien Other presumed ontologically superior to the self.

Natural self-seeking directed by duty allows authoritative Others to control the life of the self. However, the dicta of those authoritative Others can also alienate the self. When it does, the self can only escape it by its own power to think and act independently of authority. It is then compelled to critically evaluate what the authoritative Others mandate. Alienating dicta can be rejected, reformed or replaced. With this, the authoritative Other either compromises or faces a challenge to its legitimacy. Whatever the result on any given occasion, the source of authority must shift to the self with an appeal to its conscience and its power of rational freedom to cope with alienation. This conflict of self with an alienating culture demonstrates that the source of authority must ultimately reside in an autonomous self and not in the authoritative Other(s). Hegel could not admit that the cultural authoritative Other(s) could alienate the self. He conceived alienation to be a result of freedom egoistically directed and unconstrained by duty to cultural authoritative Other(s). The question then arises as to whether freedom so hobbled by duty can remain freedom at all. While it is true that egoistic freedom can alienate and do evil, it is also true that freedom and rationality driven by self-seeking desire is the basis for dealienation. This compelling fact makes an autonomous self the ultimate source of authority.

Where personal freedom is irrational license, its evil consequences can be alienating. Cultural taboos inhibit the licentious misuse of freedom. Licentious freedom is dangerous and can be understood to be a product of defective socialization wherein the self has not developed beyond narcissism or egoism. What lurks in the unconscious psyches of defectively socialized selves are alien sado-masochistic desires. They provoke anxiety when unknown; fear and punishment when known or acted upon. Defectively socialized selves require social control exerted by cultural means. However, culture can also unnecessarily inhibit personal freedom to such a degree that the autonomy and authenticity of the self is sacrificed. This culturally induced loss of dealienating capacity radically alienates self-existence. This is what ancient mythological accounts of alienation did not comprehend. A recovery of lost *Sittlichkeit* by obedience to cultural authority is not a solution to the problem of radical self-alienated freedom.

Applying the metaphor of loss and recovery does not provide an adequate understanding of alienation. For what was lost is a fictitious mythological self-existence. Since alienation is an expression of an ontological condition of finitude, it can neither be initiated nor terminated by any single historical event or series of them. Alienation is not a mere stage in either the development of the individual or of world history. Religious alienation did not terminate with the Protestant Reformation. Neither was alienation terminated with the historical ascendancy of the nation state. Emphasizing negative freedom as self-alienating disregards its positive dealienating aim. Alienation can be culturally induced and is most often found in social institutions that are not ontologically superior to the individual by virtue to their mere universality. Finally, to be a vehicle of Hegelian Geist or uncritically submerged in culture is not to have overcome alienation, but to exist self-alienated without autonomy or authenticity.

Totalitarian Culture

Authoritarian and totalitarian cultures have much in common. Both coercively subordinate self to culture. Both defectively socialize the self by unnecessarily restricting the development and expression of rational freedom. Both compel the self to think and act as alien authoritative Others dictate. Deviancy from established norms and social roles is carefully controlled, if not altogether suppressed. Human needs, desires and mechanisms for their satisfaction are preplanned by a governing elite.

Totalitarian culture is authoritarian, but authoritarian culture is not necessarily totalitarian. The principal difference between them lies in the degree of suppression of rationality and freedom. Some historical versions of political and religious authoritarianism limit the scope of restrictions upon freedom and thought control. Historically, the domain of religious authority has been limited to spiritual as distinguished from secular life. Where the dicta of religious authority does not apply, decision is left for individual conscience or secular authority. This historical trend is so pervasive that religion has been progressively excluded from the domain of secular governance and public education. Both authoritarian and totalitarian cultures sometimes permit a limited exercise of rational freedom carefully contained in some domain not threatening to established authority and acting as a social safety valve. Instances of economic freedom amidst repressive religious or political regimes are not uncommon. Totalitarian states have flourished with capitalist economic freedom. So-called mixed economies blend capitalist economic freedom with socialist political regimes.

Generally, authoritarianism permits a greater degree of individual autonomy than totalitarianism. The modern totalitarian state exhibits the most egregious restrictions upon rationality and freedom seen in human history. Abortive attempts have been made to strip away a private self and replace it with a public self. Rewards and punishments are used to inculcate norms dictated by the controlling authoritative Others. Stereotypical roles are idealized making youth ready for a culturally directed self-identification and self-projection. Although such non-rational processes of socialization are universal, irrational means are more often used by totalitarian culture to force certain self-identifications intended by those in authority. Techniques used have ranged from subliminal suggestibility to outright intimidation and physical torture. Such techniques are deliberately deceptive, manipulative and without respect for human dignity. The result sought is a dehumanized self bereft of rational freedom, cynically manipulated by propaganda, appeals to self-interest, envy and greed—an automaton possessing an inauthentic identity controlled by the covert intentions of alien authoritative Others. Totalitarian techniques of coerced socialization are profoundly immoral. Authoritarian culture does not generally use such severe and obvious immoral techniques to establish or maintain social control. Self-identifications are not as irrational. Persuasion is more prevalent than terror.

Given his veneration for rationality and freedom expressed by Spirit, Hegelian philosophy had no totalitarian intent as understood today. However, his authoritarian view of the state relative to the individual implies a justification of a totalitarian attitude. This follows from the ontological superiority of the state to the individual. Here are some statements lending support to the contention that Hegelian philosophy supports totalitarianism.

> All the value man has, all spiritual reality, he has only through the state. ... Only the will that obeys the law is free, for it obeys itself and, being in itself, is free. ... We are free when we recognize it (the state) as law and follow it as the substance of our own being. ... The true and antique morality is rooted in the principle that everybody stands in his place of duty.[1]

Hegel's discussion of the State begins by idsentifying it with Morality by virtue of the fact that the state is an actual uniting of the universal, essential and rational with the subjective will of individuals. This identification of State with Morality is *a priori* - theoretically stipulated by definition - rather than empirical, since some states are obviously immoral by their behavior. The state is then said to embody the laws of ethics, which are inherently rational rather than accidental.[2] Finally, divine rationality is presumed to be the source of ethical laws and morality, thereby justifying secular authority.

> The State is thus the embodiment of rational freedom, realizing and recognizing itself in an objective form. For its objectivity consists in this - that its successive stages are not merely ideal, but are present in an appropriate reality; and that in their separate and several working, they are absolutely merged in that agency by which the totality - the soul - the individuate unity - is produced, and of which it is the

> result. The State is the Idea of Spirit in the external manifestation of human Will and its Freedom.[3]

This conception of the state differs substantially from the modern that considers it from the viewpoint of non-rational or even irrational interest. But why does Hegel say that the state embodies rational freedom? No doubt, we can all agree that it ought to be so, that this conception is an ideal for any state. But how is it a reality in every historical state? First, what is real is ideal for Hegel. The State is real: as a product of intentional and purposive collective human activity throughout the millennia; as a whole complex of historically developed component social institutions; as universal or applicable to everyone; as a concrete product of human will and freedom in general; as an embodiment of the spiritual progress of mankind; as an objectification of human ideals of self-regulative law; as a strictly human product whereby humanity recognize its rational free essence; and finally is real as Idea of the divine mind.

The state is certainly a spiritual entity as a complex of ideas, but it is not an abstraction. Rather, it is a concrete collective product of the thought and deeds of a people sharing the same cultural history. The state provides the rational guidance and mechanism whereby the individual citizen satisfies his particular needs by exercising his freedom. He thereby secures an identity and recognizes himself in the free and rational exercise of his duty toward the state. He is what and who he is through the state and his participative contribution to it reflects back his own rational freedom.

Hegel considered history to be driven by a dialectical progression of thought whereby the potential ideal essence of something is made actual through the spiritually free activity of individuals, peoples, nations and civilizations.

> Spirit is essentially the result of its own activity: its activity is the transcending of immediate, simple, unreflected existence - the negation of that existence, and the returning into itself. ...Spirit is immortal; with it there is no past, no future, but an essential *now*. ... Spirit comprehends within it all earlier steps. ...what Spirit is it has always been essentially; distinctions are only the development of this essential nature.[4]

A mature civilization expresses its particular idea or principle in the culture of its people and their institutions - Hegel called it the *Spirit of a Nation.* When its culture and institutions are developed to maturity, their realized actuality is reflected in the ideals that give them expression. Thought about, the realized expression of the *Spirit of a Nation* then follows a course driven by a dialectic of negation.

Hegel saw stoic resignation as a stagnation of Spirit in an ordinary life of custom, a life of tedium culminating in the death of the individual, nation or civilization.

> The nation lives the same kind of life as the individual when passing from maturity to old age - in the enjoyment of itself - in the satisfaction of being exactly what it desired and was able to attain. Although its imagination might have transcended that limit, it nevertheless abandoned any such aspirations as objects of *actual endeavor*, if the real world was less than favorable to their attainment - and restricted its aim by the conditions thus imposed.[5]

An attitude of resignation is evident here. As the youthful vitality of self or nation ebbs and it proceeds toward death, resignation replaces aspiration. Challenging limits are accepted as permanent limitations. Frustrated desires are no longer actively dealt with. Rather they are accepted with resignation to things the way they are, which one could not change. The war with alienation is over, even if only half won or completely lost.

Stoic resignation is a philosophical response to alienation. Its wisdom in effect says aspire only to what is within your power to attain or change and resign yourself to the rest of the world as it is. Avoid the frustration and the wasted efforts of a *no win* situation. Resignation allows one to retain sanity and balanced perspective. Unpleasant realities are tolerated. Is such resignation really wisdom? Possibly, if expectations are impossible or unrealistically high and need to be lowered. Yet, such resignation is the acceptance of alienation as our irrevocable destiny. Moreover, if a particular form of alienation were intolerable, we would tolerate it, resign ourselves to it, and rationalize it. Yet, some forms of alienation such as enslavement are in fact intolerable, as witnessed by a risking of life itself to oppose it. With such cases, resignation is not an option. Something is so alienating that it cannot be tolerated or rationalized. There is an uplifting nobility of spirit in fighting the good fight, particularly when we know the odds of winning are long or we know the struggle to be hopelessly lost. In such situations, there is always dignity and respect even in the loss, as there was for Don Quixote. The impossible dream may in fact we worth fighting for when it bespeaks the nobility of the human spirit.

The Hegelian tendency is to rationalize alienation as a mere moment within a historical dialectic. Alienating evil is explained away as necessary to knowing and doing what is good. Dialectic rationalizes whatever happens as being what it ought to be in a cosmic order inaccessible to the individual. Where you don't understand it, just let it alone and it will eventually go away. *This too shall pass* and so it always does, as does the life of the sufferer. This orientation accepts alienation and tempts the self to succumb to it by stoical resignation. The dialectical necessity of alienation justifies a deeply conservative mentality. Human destiny is not of our own making, beyond our human capacity to comprehend and so cannot be altered, no matter what we think or do.

Hegel accepted the prophetic Judaic interpretation of human suffering as divine retribution for sinful disobedience to authority. When one suffers an alienation of freedom and doesn't know why, the fault must lie in the sinner. This religious interpretation rationalizes alienation and palliates somewhat, but does not permit dealienation. Recognizing this, Marx called religion an *opiate of the people*. The psychological dynamics of rationalizing interpretations warrants scrutiny. An effect of believing it is to load the psyche with guilt, which is itself a punishment. When guilty, punishment from an authoritative Other is merited and anticipated. Hence, the response of resignation to suffering alienation. The proper religious response is a piety which reinforces the authoritative Others whose dicta socially control the self. In fairness to religion, it must be said that the same kind of interpretive rationalization is employed by secular politics, totalitarianism, and parental discipline. Rationalized interpretation and resignation promote a tendency to accept traditional authority, even if it is oppressive. Any philosophical rationalization of alienation promoting an attitude of resignation disallows the dealienating response of rational freedom.

The Hegelian ontological hierarchy coupled with a rationalization of authoritarianism made the more universal social structures such as the state superior to the individual, who is thereby subordinated and culturally submerged. Consequently, Hegel overlooked social forms of alienation so important in subsequent history. Particularly in the twentieth century, alienation flourished in social institutions exhibiting a highly rationalized structure, such as the vertically structured bureaucracies of the industrial age, which extend even today into the information age. A Hegelian State was preconceived as an absolutely rational social structure, notwithstanding factual evidence to the contrary. Such glorification of the state provides a rationalization of totalitarianism, although not intended as such by Hegel. In principle, however, any actual social structure is rationalized as what ought to be resulting from its development within a Hegelian conceived historical dialectic. This promotes an attitude making any critical evaluation of institutions theoretically impossible. Everything that is ought to be as it is, thereby making stoical resignation a primary virtue. This is how traditional authority, conservatism and prevailing establishment ideology can be theoretically rationalized by philosophy.

The limitations of the actual are sought, recognized and given expression in a skepticism of current authority, cultural beliefs and practices. Reasons are demanded for tradition, and when not found, that very tradition and duty toward it are attacked and undermined. The result of this skeptical dialectical dialogue is to isolate individuals from the Spirit of their Nation - their culture with its norms and practices. This result is also tantamount to isolating individuals from each other. Such isolation is manifested in the rise of unfettered individual self-seeking taking immoral forms such as selfishness, unbound passions, vanity and all manner of corruption. Public interest and public service virtually disappear as do personal integrity, trust and honor among citizens at all levels of society. Such isolation among individuals and between them and the State bespeaks a pervasive social alienation in which the current culture, State and possibly a civilization disintegrates before one's very eyes.

In this condition of alienation Hegel's Spirit of a Nation is no longer a realized reflection of Thought, is no longer compelling and felt as obligatory upon citizens to sustain it. Hegel considered this situation to set the stage for another synthesis of Thought through another historical exercise of human freedom. The dialectic proceeds from this point to further actualize the potential inhering in the current alienating situation; to reveal and express a new essence within it; to retain and add something concrete to an expanding concrete universal enriched by degrees and by the inclusion of finite particulars contributed by the human exercise of freedom. What emerges is an evolution of thought, a new culture, civilization or Spirit of a Nation as Hegel called it. When this is fully mature, there is a flowering in which Spirit again recognizes itself as a reflection of the Thought of its time. History is a process of alienation and dealienation, which is continuous but not interminable for Hegel. Its aim and termination reside in expressing the divine mind, its will, purpose and plan for the cosmos.

The Hegelian State is the actual *world-historical* representation of national spirit instantiated in its particular form of religion, art, science and philosophy. A state is formally structured by its constitution and laws. Social institutions such as the family and civil society give the state life through the free self-expression of citizens. Hegel gives enormous importance to the State as a universal Idea including all the above mentioned components. When he speaks of the State, he is referring to a complete culture of a people or a civilization. Therefore, the State is a high order generalization loaded with all the ontological content of its components. That its components are hierarchically arranged is mere logical convention, but that they are arranged in a peculiar Hegelian ontological hierarchy is debatable. For example, making religion the basis of the state is not a mere logical convention, but rather a true or false interpretation of historical facts.

A Hegelian type of individual who knows and does his duty makes his subjective freedom an expression of the divine rationality, ethical laws and morality presumably embodied in the State. Duty consists of using personal freedom to obey laws of the State. Dealienation is then a subordination of personal freedom to conformity with laws, divine and human, presumed rational and expressed by a secular state. Conformity and obedience to law reconciles personal freedom with an objective cosmic order. Free will is hereby reduced to obedience and conformity.

A willing contributor to a cosmic order, the self fits in, belongs, finds a home, and is reconciled with the totality of being. Now, this is all well and good. But, notice the presumptions. First, law, divine and human is rational. But, by what warrant? Undoubtedly, by a Hegelian rationality consisting of abstract universality deductively ordering the components of a totality with the self placed at the bottom of an ontological hierarchy of God, state and social institutions. However, notice that this hierarchy is maintained not by its inherent rationality, but by obedience of the self to authority. The ontological hierarchy is upheld by a self whose freedom resides in obedience. This suggests that the Hegelian ontological hierarchy with its abstract rationality is really a rationalization of authority. Moreover, Hegel's philosophical endeavor served the purpose of reconciling the conflicting claims of the religious and secular authorities of his time. The warrant for law, human and divine, then are not rationality, but rather obedience to authority pre-existent and definitive for self-existence.

Hegelian philosophy was clearly intended to justify traditional authority. Yet, it also rationalized authoritarian culture. In so far as totalitarian culture is also authoritarian, Hegelian philosophy inadvertently rationalized a totalitarian culture which, however, he deplored in the brutal excesses of the French Revolution. Yet, relative to the state, the self is subordinate, not autonomous. Self exists for the sake of the state, not the reverse. Personal freedom consists of obedience to what is ontologically superior, among which are laws of the state with divine sanction. Where personal freedom is reduced to cultural obedience, the self is not really free to dissent from whatever is presumed superior to itself. Consent is secured not through autonomy, but through obedience and cultural conformity. Autonomy is replaced by a blind conformity to the higher authority of the state and God. Hegel said as much by presuming world history to be driven by the covert intentions of Geist, manipulating self-seeking individuals who are ignorant and unconscious of its influence upon them. Individual autonomy was claimed irrelevant to the unfolding of history. Unknown purposes of God, state and culture govern self-existence and there is no recourse. Hegel was uncomfortable defending this interpretation of history precisely because he sensed its inconsistency with personal freedom, which he esteemed.

His criticism of Rousseau's social contract theory again illustrates Hegel's commitment to an authoritarian culture, thereby indirectly lending support to totalitarianism. The purpose of the social contract is to secure the liberty of individuals to promote self-seeking. Nevertheless, Hegel considered such liberty capricious, licentious and destructive of a larger social order, the interests of community and the rationality of the State. Placing individual above community reverses Hegel's presumably correct conception of an ontological hierarchy. The less universal lower order individual is falsely placed above the more universal higher orders of being. Self-seeking, serving no higher purpose of culture, community, State or God cannot sustain Hegel's ontological architectonic.

Of itself, and located strictly within an autonomous self, self-seeking without telos is irrational, wasted freedom. Personal desire finds complete satisfaction when conforming to universal *Reason* and the purposes of Spirit. Therefore, the individual must completely identify with those universal norms prescribed for him by morality, community ethos, the state, religion and God. He must then place his free will in service to them. This view is, in effect, a deep conservatism, a justification, or more truly, a rationalization of the so-called establishment status quo. By Hegelian logic, such a view is correct on two counts. First, the established social order is a result of a dialectical development in history and so the very fact of its being presents normative imperatives necessary for civilization itself. Second, it relates the individual to the larger social whole as a contributing participant in the divine plan of history. The significance and value of the individual is thus secured and ensured. Moreover, to have such cosmic significance is very appealing both rationally and emotionally. We mere mortals are still central players on the stage of history, and we have our place, know what it is and how to fulfill it to our deep satisfaction.

Cultural Dealienation

A self, existing with appropriate norms and roles, functions in socially successful ways. It is not narcissistic, egoistic, nor a conformist submerged in the collective lacking the rational freedom necessary for dealienation. Presuming culture to supply the tools by which the self is enabled in its dealienating endeavor, a foundation is provided for understanding culture by answering two questions. First, under what conditions does culture become alienating? Secondly, under what conditions does culture promote successful dealienation? Satisfactory answers consider what previous social thinkers have said against the backdrop of recent history and contemporary culture.

Culture is a collective product of the dealienating endeavor of individuals living in a community. The dealienating process of satisfying their needs and desires historically forms cultural norms, social roles and institutions. They serve as models for the socialization of the self. When these models are defective, culturally induced alienation results. Self-identification with culture is not possible where its demands contradict those of the self. Opposition between the demands of culture and those of the self is expressed by apathy toward a culture that is irrelevant to personal living. Reciprocity between self and culture is missing. An isolated self adopts skeptical if not cynical attitudes toward its culture as it self-projects and self-objectifies in ways unrelated to traditional cultural norms and social roles. If not tolerated, this deviancy is viewed as a threatening competitor to be suppressed. A self is then placed into the position of being dominated by a cultural Other, alien to its essential nature.

Cultural alienation can be induced by defective socialization. This occurs when self-identifications with cultural demands are coercive, employing non-rational or irrational means. Coercive self-identifications fixate the self in narcissism and egoism, denying the completed development of a social self with rational freedom, its dealienating power. Dissociated from cultural channels for their expression, the authentic needs and desires of the self are displaced into sadomasochistic perversions. Then, to gain any satisfaction of what is repressed, various forms of deception from calculated hypocrisy to unconscious psychic defense mechanisms are employed. As Freud explained, a self whose demands are opposed by culture becomes neurotic. Unstable compromises may be found, but the authentic demands of the self continuously threaten cultural disintegration. Trapped in the institutions of an alien culture, the self will emotionally suffer depression and boredom. Alternatively, the self may even respond irrationally with a psychotic withdrawal into a self-delusional world.

There is a broad range of responses to cultural alienation. Various responses are found in Epicureanism and forms of Hedonism. Hegel imaginatively described a stoic response to the cultural alienation of the late Roman Empire. A version of Stoicism remains in contemporary culture with its tolerant and often permissive attitude toward deviant individual lifestyles. The stoic resignation of non-voters defines contemporary political alienation. Apathetic toward an alien political culture, citizens consider it irrelevant and benign, uninteresting, worthy only of being ignored.

However, where an alien political culture is believed to diminish liberty, other rationally directed activist responses are forthcoming. A self with liberty threatened will become hostile to its alien cultural Other, demanding reform to alleviate its burden. This response utilizes the capacity to formulate strategies and employ tactics against an alienating culture. Organizations are formed around an interest in changing culture. Sophisticated means, in reinforcing combination, are used to persuade the public. News events are created for the mass media to *get the message out.* Political alliances are formed. Judicial activism is used to provoke favorable court decisions defining the law. Educational institutions indoctrinate youth with ideology disguised as knowledge. Advocacy can be purchased by employing political lobbyists, pollsters, public relations experts and various types of consultants to make the public case for cultural change.

Cultural alienation can be minimized where culture reinforces dealienation. The norms and social roles offered by culture for self-identification, self-projection and self-objectification must respect the essential nature of the self, defined by its authentic needs, desires, rationality and freedom. Socialization cannot be established coercively. Culture, which enables complete self-development, avoids alienating fixations in narcissism or egoism. A social self developed to effectively utilize rationality and freedom has maximized its dealienating capacity. Trusting the consequences of this capacity justifies tolerating experimentation with culturally deviant norms and social roles. Since culture changes in response to science, technology and new lifestyles, anxiety over the accelerated pace of cultural change is pointless.

A dealienating relationship of culture to self is one of reciprocity. A relationship of self subordinate to culture invariably results in unnecessary alienation. A dominating culture opposes the authentic nature of the self—its needs, desires, and demand for rational freedom. Therefore, instead of self meeting the demands of culture, the trend is for culture to meet the demands of the self. Now it is true that culture subordinate to the self can be alienating, as previous thinkers have pointed out so well. However, this is only true when that self is defectively socialized, or egoistic, with freedom misconstrued as license to negate the benefits of culture. However, culture can be safely subordinated to a social self who has learned to use its freedom rationally. The essential nature of the self demands that culture respect and promotes its autonomy and authenticity. The historic trend toward personal liberty and democracy confirms the fact that culture is responding with toleration of deviancy, even permissiveness of it. The prospect is of a culture promoting self-realization rather than suppressing human potential.

Notes

1. Hegel, G. W. F. (1953) *Reason in History* (Robert S. Hartman, Trans.). New York, NY: Macmillan, 52-53.
2. Ibid., 50.
3. Hegel, G. W. F. (1956) *The Philosophy of History* (J. Sibree, Trans.). New York, NY: Dover, 47.
4. Ibid., 78-79.
5. Ibid., 74.

Chapter Seven

Dealienation

Defining Dealienation

Alienation and dealienation has been understood by various metaphors: of loss and recovery; emptying and filling; odyssey of departure and return. Where alienation is conceived as loss and dealienation as recovery, then with recovery, alienation is overcome. Recovery then is an event where something is found, with the loss made good. However, this metaphor of loss and recovery is too simplistic. For the significance of the lost object and the being of the searcher remains unchanged. However, the very process of recovery may transform the significance and value of what is lost as well as the being of the searcher. This is the point of Hegelian sublation. A Hegelian process of dealienation is circular, beginning with abstract being and returning to it with an enriched determinate significance resulting from the mediating activity of the self. It appropriates its being by becoming the Other of itself, thereby affirming its being through a dialectical process based upon ontological negativity.

There is an alternative to understanding alienation and dealienation by metaphors of circularity. Alienation may be conceived as a deficiency in being with dealienation as a negation of the deficiency. As with the former simpler metaphorical concepts, this one involves a historical process to overcome the specific deficiency encountered, but with somewhat different implications. Alienating finitude is an ontological condition defining self-existence. Dealienation is then a response with intentional self-activity. Conceived as a temporal process, alienation is overcome incrementally, but never with finality. Thus, the process of alienation and dealienation is infinitely continuous in principle. Historical events can neither initiate nor terminate this ontologically based process. Although specific forms of alienation are overcome, others are always encountered. The essential nature of the self is to confront any limit to its needs and desires by responding with rationality and freedom, its dealienating powers. Negating intentional self-activity realizes all possibilities of being. By so doing, the meaning of being is revealed as self-realization temporally proceeds.

Dealienation is a response to alienating finitude. This rudimentary definition implies that whatever the specific dealienating response, it always occurs within an existential context. No matter how complex are the means for dealienation, it is a process of self-existence. Dealienation may be overlaid with additional speculative interpretations not essential to its existential significance. For example, it could be said that dealienation has a telos moving the alienated being from the part toward a perfect completed whole. This could be conceived as an actualization of a potentiality for being pre-established by divine or cultural authoritative Others. Whether the process has a telos, a terminus, or is an infinite temporal progression; or makes explicit what is implicit in a postulated undifferentiated whole; or presents being with enriched sublated meaning; or presents an expanding whole of being: all this is irrelevant to the functioning of the process itself.

No doubt being is further differentiated as dealienation progresses with successive negations over time. History bears witness to this fact by the explosion of knowledge, technology and increasingly humanized environments. With regard to being, dealienation discovers it, even creates it. Its meaning is revealed within existential processes. Conceived as process, dealienation implies nothing more than what it does. But what does its result signify? It may be interpreted as merely confirming what the Other(s) have pre-established as true of being and normative for human conduct. Alternatively, the result itself may create what is true of being and normative for human conduct. Certainly, the latter view is simpler, eliminating any alien aspect in the result of dealienation.

Meaning originates from the fact of ontological negativity. Its expression is found in the alienating finitude of self-existence. An alien Other signifies a deficiency in being, a limit of some kind, something that frustrates the needs and desires of the self. To think is to negate the alien Other(s) in some way. So, meaning is thought and self-activity responding to the limits set by the alien Other(s). Dealienation is precisely this whole process taken from within an existential context. Moreover, true meaning is a product of successful dealienation. More specifically, true meaning is a product of self-existence, of encountering alienating finitude and responding to it freely with thought and intentional activity.

Dealienation is then an existential process of self-identification, self-projection, self-objectification, and self-realization. The process is a finite temporal actualization of the potentiality for being something or anything. Within this process, being is revealed, and even created. What is true meaning and normative is a continuous result of revealing being with an indeterminate horizon. A finite world and self is comprehended by degrees as being is revealed and its meaning expands. What is absolute is what endures the test of dealienation over time, which is to say that there certainly is accumulative knowledge and wisdom, but nothing absolute standing apart from self-existence. A self-existence resulting from confronting alienating finitude with rational freedom describes a process of dealienation establishing the true meaning of being and what is normative for human conduct. Human existence so described is authentic and self-validating. Anything less does not dealienate and so is false and inauthentic to the power of rational freedom constituting the essential nature of the self.

Alienation elicits a dealienating response from the self with an aim, which may or may not be achieved in varying degrees. Dealienation is a complex temporal process. It involves self-identification with something other than the self. A capacity for rationality and freedom permits the self to intentionally project itself as need and desire into a world offering possibilities of satisfaction. Self-objectifying work accomplishes dealienation. The result is an altered condition of being, a potential realized in a finite temporal world. Since alienating finitude is a necessary and inescapable condition of self-existence, a completely dealienated self is impossible. Nevertheless, a self with maximum dealienating capacity is attainable. It can be described as one that has maximized its power of rational freedom. This results from a process of self-development beyond narcissism and egoism. Thus, a fully socialized self with a highly developed power of rational freedom has maximized its capacity to dealienate. It can proceed with dealienation which is also self-realization of its own complete range of potentialities.

Dealienation can be authentic self-realization rather than reconciliation with authority. Conceiving the self to be the locus of truth and value approaches dealienation existentially in that the very process of dealienation creates whatever is true and normative. Self-existence not strictly bound by authoritative Others then has an entirely different significance. Alienating Other(s) would provide the impetus for dealienation with self-existence creating what is true and right. Freedom and rationality then assume their appropriate role in the process of dealienation. This existential approach to dealienation is experimental and inductive. Universality is an existential product of dealienation built consensually from particular instances of dealienating self-existence.

Overcoming Alienation

Can alienation be overcome? Contradictory answers to this fundamental question follow from how alienation is initially conceived. Where alienation is conceived as a specific kind of undesirable separation of self from something, possibly God or culture, successful dealienation is possible and in fact occurs. However, where alienation is conceived as a result of ontological negativity, any final overcoming of alienation is impossible. This view, defended herein, does not imply that dealienation cannot occur. In fact, dealienation occurs continuously as alienating conditions are successfully dealt with by a human capacity for rational freedom. Dealienation is thus an incremental historical process. Since the specific historical conditions of alienation are infinite in principle for human beings, achieving some utopian condition of human existence is not possible. How and when utopia is attainable then becomes a superfluous question. More relevant is the question of how to maximize the capacity for dealienation. The conditions for maximizing the capacity for dealienation must be specified.

Conceived as an ontologically based process, alienation cannot be overcome. As long as life and history continues, there would always be some form of undesirable separation, an alien Other(s) to be confronted, limits presented, obstacles to the satisfaction of needs and desires. So, dealienation would be a perpetual aim with no termination, no finally achievable goal. Existentialists as widely divergent as Kierkegaard and Sartre believed this. For Sartre, no final goal is achievable in principle due to the irrational demands made by a freedom placing human desires in absolute contradiction within an interpersonal setting. For the Christian Kierkegaard, that alienation could be overcome in this life is impossible, and that it could be overcome by the promise of an afterlife is an absurd belief. Nevertheless, the alienating absurdity of this life calls for an absurd faith in the promise of alienation overcome between self and its creator God. So, a Kierkegaardian Christian would conclude alienation can be overcome in principle through an absurd faith, but not in fact in a life cursed by sin. Contemporary secular philosophy seems to have abandoned hope of overcoming alienation in any final sense. Marxists and utopian socialists believed alienation of socially oppressed classes of people could be overcome by social engineering experiments of one kind or another. This hope has been shattered by the persistence of war and concomitant loss of faith in the dealienating effect of applied science.

Conceived as a continuous process responding to the alienating finitude of self-existence, dealienation is interminable. Thus, a completely dealienated utopian civilization is not possible in principle. Utopias are then wishful fantasies. Moreover, western social philosophers from Plato to Marx believed that self-alienating behavior and instinctual repression are required to sustain civilization. That human history is moving toward a dealienated civilization would indeed seem dubious. Utopian socialists advocated a revolutionary social restructuring to create a dealienated civilization. However, by the end of the twentieth century, the predictions of an activist Marxism were defeated by global free market capitalism. Moreover, a socially engineered American welfare state, creating a parasitic underclass, proved no more successful. Although utopian dreams are not achievable, this does not mean that the conditions for maximizing the potential for dealienation cannot be specified. A subordination of culture to self and experimentation with deviant lifestyles is undergoing a serious trial in contemporary western culture. The limits of personal freedom are being tested and expanded. In order to check its possible abuses, a personal freedom rejecting the guidance of culture and traditional authoritative Others is forced to rely upon conscience and a nurturing self-giving love.

Hegel thought alienation could be overcome both in principle and in fact. His discussion of the *spurious infinite* rejected interminable sublation, which implies that alienation cannot be permanent, or dealienation interminable. However, this conclusion is contradicted by his ontological analysis of alienating finitude and his conception of dealienation as a continuous developmental process. True enough that the aim of Hegel's dialectical progression is the overcoming of alienation. Philosophical closure is attained and alienation is overcome with a comprehension of the absolute Idea wherein humanity serves as the vehicle for expressing the intention of Geist. Phenomenologically and historically, alienation is overcome in principle and in fact when the universal self-conscious Spirit terminates its odyssey with a self-objectification so humanizing the world that it loses its character as alien Other and becomes a reflection of a transforming self. The once alien Other(s) are converted by a historical dialectic process into a reflection of those Notions and Ideas constituting the being of a self who thinks and acts. Thus is its self-expression simultaneously the comprehension of an infinite whole, of a totality of being.

Within the historical odyssey of developing Spirit, Hegel generally characterized alienation as the second *moment* of Spirit becoming self-conscious. This moment requires that the individual distinguish himself through an opposition of his demands to those of his culture. To him, the culture then appears as alien Other. Its being is for-another as opposed to his being which is for-itself. But, the individual introjecting the demands of an alien culture dialectically sublates this moment of alienation. The individual, presumed lacking an essential being of his own, must become substantial; an actual instantiation of Spirit. In the Hegelian vernacular, a being, which is *for-itself*, must become a being, which is *in-itself*. When alienation is conceived as a moment in a dialectical process of fully realizing Spirit as social substance, the sublation of this moment terminates its alienating condition. As a moment of dialectical progression, of the actualization of Spirit, alienation is viewed as a mere temporary state of the human condition. This optimistic view appears to rest upon the classical Greek spirit of human perfectibility as well as the Christian promise of historic redemption, so influential with Hegel's philosophizing. Such roots would mold Hegel's philosophical purpose to demonstrate how alienation would be historically overcome through achieving perfect community in a final revelation of self-conscious Spirit with the absolute Idea.

From a strictly phenomenological and historical Hegelian perspective, alienation abides with a continuously changing form. As one form is overcome, a new level of spiritual self-consciousness arises, again presenting alienation in a new form within a new life situation. In this way, dealienation is a continuous process wherein the Hegelian Spirit moves from a lower stage of primitive consciousness to a higher stage of self-consciousness and then through additional sub-stages of incomplete self-consciousness. These correspond to moving from undeveloped freedom of an incompletely socialized individual to a completely socialized individual whose freedom is in service to duty, to a larger social whole, to universal Ideas which guide higher spiritual development. The crown and termination of this dealienating process is the absolute Idea in which each partial stage of alienation is contained and transcended; a final sublation, if you will, wherein the infinite or whole of reality is philosophically comprehended. With the absolute Idea, the philosophical comprehension of history terminates. For even as history continues, there would be nothing more to be comprehended about it, nothing Other or alien to be further encountered. The philosophical comprehension of an infinite whole is at once the termination of alienation. What we fully comprehend can no longer be alien.

If dealienation is a continuous ontological process, then alienation is only overcome if it terminates with the end of history, or with a philosophical comprehension of the absolute Idea wherein there can no longer be any alien Other(s) in opposition to the knowing, acting subject. A self completely objectified and the world completely humanized represent alienation overcome. Hegel surely would have been convinced he overcame alienation with a philosophical comprehension expressed through his systematized Logic. The absolute Idea presumably signifies a concrete actuality. A grand vision, or grandiose nonsense! Nevertheless, alienation is not an illusion to be rectified by abstract philosophical speculation. For the comprehension of it does not effect the existential condition of it which humanity must continuously endure.

Hegel's philosophical comprehension of the infinite would therefore seem to be a final intellectual victory of dealienation, yet still an abstraction for the rest of us. The absolute Idea, of itself, seems a sterile theoretical abstraction rather than a concrete actuality resolving the condition of alienating finitude. Mere thinking the absolute Idea does not change who and what we essentially are as finite beings living in a finite world. No doubt, Hegel would have agreed. How can it be that a finite human being who must always sublate an alien Other could overcome alienation with finality? This would seem impossible. Humanity, conceived in the Hegelian mode as dealienating spiritual process, continuously develops an infinite whole, but without final closure. This is what is implied in the notion of process. Even if, as Hegel assumed, infinity is the aim of dealienation, infinity conceived as a process remains an ever-expanding whole, a product of finite historical struggle, only approaching finality asymptotically, if at all.

Any telos expressed in the world by subjective will and action is beset by finitude. For achieved human ends are mutable and contingent upon the conditions that brought them about. More often than not an achieved end has unintended meanings and consequences. Someone else may make something else of an achieved end. And in time, the achieved end may itself pose a limit for someone else. Hegel observed, "the End achieved consequently is only an object, which again becomes a Means or material for other Ends, and so on for ever."[1] Such a consideration implies that dealienation, as a process of self-objectification, can itself generate further alienation thus forming an interminable sequence, infinite in principle. Therefore, we see alienating finitude to be inescapable when considered in a means-end context of contingent and mutable human meanings and outcomes. Such a process lacks the satisfaction or enjoyment of any final consummation. The ultimate aim of overcoming all possible forms of alienation is never secured within the context of finitude. Hegel implies as much when he says, "Within the range of the finite we can never see or experience that the End has been really secured."[2] Nevertheless, in the same breath he asserts that the infinite End is already actual in the implicit being of the whole although we don't see it before our very noses, so to speak. "The consummation of the infinite End, therefore, consists merely in removing the illusion which makes it seem yet unaccomplished."[3]

Hegel's ontology implies alienation and dealienation is continuous and interminable in human history. This follows from his analysis of finitude. Human beings, as finite and subject to nature, must always encounter alienation as a basic feature of their existence. Made infinite by a self-determining Spirit characterized by rationality and freedom, human beings are always involved in a process of dealienation. This implies alienation cannot in principle be overcome with finality. Contrary to his ontology, but consistent with his religious commitment, Hegel interpreted the historical Reformation to be the end of religious alienation and thought of the Prussian Nation State as terminating secular alienation of self from culture and community.

When historically developing Spirit ascends to the ontologically higher social realm, Hegel gave the impression that alienation had been overcome by no longer speaking about it. Yet, nation states are retrogressively treated on the model of egoistic individuals alienated from each other to the degree that war is the necessary catharsis, a dealienating process establishing social cohesion, among other beneficial social effects. Apparently, alienation reappears at the social level as war and poverty, which Hegel rationalized, but did not recognize as alienating conditions. Was Hegel inconsistent in his view of alienation or just confused about it? His ontological hierarchy from the individual to the social implies alienation can be overcome and left behind as a relic of past development. Yet, his view of the State as an organism akin to the individual implies a reintroduction of alienation at the social level.

In the *Phenomenology of Spirit,* Hegel associated overcoming alienation with a self-consciousness transcending individuality. Alienation is restricted conceptually to an opposition of Other to self, including oppositions within a self-conscious individual. However, this restrictive view has disadvantages for dealing with alienation at the social level. For if alienation is essentially a phenomenon of individual self-consciousness, then it tends to be overlooked or dismissed at the social level. However, it is crucially important to recognize the social dimension of alienation. This is not possible if it is restricted to a stage of developing self-consciousness and then dismissed with the further development of a socially determined self. For the alienating dynamics of this socially determined self warrants critical examination. If alienation is implicit in the dialectical dynamics of life, then we would again expect to greet other forms of alienation at levels of being superior to the individual, namely, cultural, community, state and world history. Yet, after Hegel's discussion of culture, we do not find further discussion of it applied to other socially higher forms of being. Whereas, Hegelian ontology implies alienation cannot be overcome, his exposition of the development of self-consciousness terminates it at the point where introjecting culture to form a social self transcends individuality.

It would seem as if Hegel relegated alienation to a stage in the development of the individual and to a stage of historical development. For the former, alienation is a feature of the negative freedom of the individual—that freedom which refuses and says *no*. When the individual develops to a fully socialized being, the alienation of individual negative freedom disappears and is replaced by identifying with an ontologically superior culture and social organization more universal than the self. The individual's life projects are then given structure and aim through introjecting the culture, its values, ideals and so forth. This is how society has a life of its own i.e., through the free agency of individuals who become culture carriers, or in Hegel's terminology, vehicles of Geist. Thus, when Hegel discusses social institutions, nation states and world history, he appears to have left alienation behind as a relic of some prior historical stage of development.

Alienation would appear to have been overcome when the individual's rationality and freedom are harnessed by his duty to larger social structures transcending him. Where Hegel speaks of duty, he is also implying in our more modern way of viewing it, an identification with and introjection of traditional authority. Where in history alienation is a feature of Christian religious organization, as with medieval Catholicism, the Lutheran Reformation historically overcomes it, thus presumably liberating individuals to personally carry out the divine plan through their life projects.

Since Hegel's ontology provides the foundational conception of alienation, it cannot simply be a stage of dialectical development in the individual or in world history. For alienation is the condition which generates every variety of dialectical progression. Considered a mere stage in a historical dialectic trivializes alienation, robing it of ontological import. When Hegel considered it in this way, his thinking was inconsistent. For alienation cannot be both an ontological process and a historical event of that process.

This ambiguity in Hegelian thought presents a philosophical choice. Is alienation a stage in a dialectical progression, or is it the driver of dialectical process? An optimistic attitude toward it would incline one to view it as a transient feature of the dialectical development of Spirit. A pessimistic or tragic attitude toward it would incline one to view it as the ontological basis for any dialectical development whatsoever, and thus indicative of a permanent necessary feature of being. The alien Other, as derived from ontological negativity, implies alienation is an essential aspect of being and the process from which is derived every determinate form of being, so expressed in Hegelian terminology. This is the deeper view of alienation making it an ontological foundation for his whole Logic of being. Of necessity, it must be preferred and cannot be sacrificed to the lesser view of alienation as a mere stage of dialectical progression. Also, the deeper ontological view is preferable for the explanatory power it provides for understanding post-Hegelian world history as well as social forms of alienation he did not consider, but which we painfully confront in the contemporary conditions of life.

Clearly Hegel's ontology is fundamental to his whole philosophy and implies an explanation of alienation. His interpretation of history follows from his ontology and is therefore subordinated to it. History, Hegel theorized, is moved by great heroic figures, beguiled by the *cunning of reason*, unaware of the true import of their deeds and the larger purpose of the World Historical Spirit, or Geist. Lacking autonomy, the hero is himself dominated by an alien Other, Ideas of Geist alien to his intellect and will. He falsely believes that his behavior serves his own desires and aims, not realizing that the historic import of his deeds is not a product of his own choice and will.

This theory implies that as long as history continues to be driven by alienated heroic figures, there can be no termination of alienation. In fact, alienation is required for the continuance of history. Hegel's giving special significance to the Reformation for ending religious alienation rationalized his religious commitment to justifying Protestant Christianity. For, after the Reformation, there occurs the French Revolution in which alienation reappears with a vengeance. Subsequent history of the nineteenth and twentieth centuries is rife with tragic human suffering and alienation in myriad forms. The more plausible Hegelian answer to the question of whether alienation can be overcome with finality is no. It is a permanent feature of the human condition, even as various forms of it are overcome. Alienation would appear to be a perennial task for human freedom; offering a perpetual challenge to the human spirit to continue the process of dealienation through its infinite capacity to be rational and free. This interpretation of how Hegel would have answered the question is consistent with his description of personal self-development and the historical development of Spirit.

Ontological negativity revealing being is the basis of consciousness and self-consciousness, and drives a dialectical progression of human history. The essential characteristic of consciousness is its *objective intentionality*, meaning that the object the self is aware of is always distinct from itself, external or objective. In the Hegelian vernacular, consciousness always *posits* its object as *other than itself*. This positing of its object as *other* is an expression of ontological negativity definitive of the Ego and human freedom. A capacity to negate is implied in the presentation of any object whatsoever, be it the world, culture, self or any spiritual product. Alienation is an expression of ontological negativity, a structuring principle of perceiving, thinking, feeling, and intentional self-activity. An alien Other defines whatever is considered real. The true significance of alienation is then as the first moment of negation in a process of dealienation, a process of revealing reality through humanizing the finite world. Without life and history terminating, the process of dealienation does not terminate. Neither does alienation, which is ontologically necessary. As the process of dealienation cannot terminate in principle or in fact, so alienation, as an essential part of it cannot terminate either.

The aim of the process of dealienation is to overcome alienation and this aim is continuously being fulfilled, but never with finality. For, if this were possible, then the ontological process, of which alienation is always a necessary initial part, would itself cease. However, this is impossible. For an ontological process is just a principle of being, and so without beginning or end. Therefore, to demand the final termination of alienation is to demand the impossible termination of an ontological process. Nevertheless, let us assume the absurd is possible here. The final moment would not culminate in a consummation or affirmation of being, Rather, the final moment, if one were possible, would be a destructive negation of being. Finally overcoming alienation is certainly impossible in fact and not even desirable in principle. For without challenge, obstacles and struggle, neither the finitude of self-existence nor the dealienating capacity of rational freedom would have meaning, and nothing could be signified.

As ontologically based, alienation is a permanent feature of finitude and so cannot be overcome with finality. Nor should it be. For as perpetually permanent condition of human existence, alienation provides life with meaning and purpose. Moreover, alienation drives the development of rational freedom, thereby providing it with enormous significance for self-existence. An integration of rationality and freedom is the true and successful response to alienating finitude; the means whereby being is revealed. Alienation in its infinite variety prompts dealienation, the perennial task for humanity. Ironically then, alienation, although constituted by negation, has a positive effect. With it, an affirmation of being is not only possible, but also necessitated. Without it, no affirmative revelation of being would be possible. Alienation provides that limiting obstacle calling forth human endeavor that establishes the value of anything and everything. Suffering alienation in one form or another is necessary and to be accepted as such along with its positive effects. An alienating finitude makes human beings reach for and realize the infinite potential within themselves.

Authoritarian Dealienation

Hegel thought of the Other as rationally comprehended in opposition to the self, dealt with by a dialectical process of thought and intentional activity and finally incorporated as a part of the being and meaning of the self. Hegelian philosophy described dealienation as a dialectical ontological process. The self is strictly speaking *nothing*, possessing no being without an alien Other opposed to it. This Other is rationally cognized, appropriated, assimilated and incorporated to express a being of the self. There can be no self without dialectical confrontations with alien Others. It is they, which define the self and provide its identity.

A Hegelian process of dealienation is the self becoming Other in being in a very literal way. For example, taking nature as the alien Other, the self uses it for sustenance. Nature is exploited and artificially transformed to satisfy human needs and aims. In the social or religious dimension of human existence, dealienation would consist of a dialectical process of identifying with the alien Other, introjecting it and then expressing its being and meaning in finite self-projections and self-objectifications. In this case the self becomes and incarnation of the Other, possibly God, who thereby no longer remains alien to the being of the self. The disposition of the self is to surrender its vacuous willfulness, and in submissive obedience acquire an identity provided by the authoritative Other. Self-projection and self-objectification then express objective standards of being and conduct established solely by the authoritative Other(s). Conforming to the demands initially imposed by an alien authoritative Other is effected by introjecting it and self-identifying with its dicta. When so defined by an authoritative Other(s), the self is presumed to have overcome self-alienation resulting from its egoistic freedom. With all this, Hegel provided an authoritarian prescription for dealienation.

Alienation is experienced as need and desire. Something is lacking in being and so ought to be other than it is. A limit is confronted and must be overcome. That which is an alien Other to self is what it is not and must become in being. Alien Others frustrate the self, serving as a foil for its development and realization of its finite potentialities. An alien Other, whatever or whomever it may be, is an initial negation of self which it responds to with a second or subsequent negations. Where the alien Other is a parent or culture, its prescriptions and proscriptions are authoritative for a self whose capacity for rationality and freedom are undeveloped. Hegel suggested that dealienation consists of simply introjecting such authoritative Others. This dialectical process might be called *authoritarian dealienation.* It presumes that existing traditional authority is legitimated by the mere fact of its existence. Whatever exists ought to be as it is, since it is a product of a historical dialectic of a rational Spirit - Geist or God - with certain preordained intentions dictating historical outcomes and human destiny, generally.

Hegel implied that the illusion of subjectivity as creator of being and meaning lies in a misplaced and mistaken egoism, in not recognizing that the world is as it ought to be. Platonic Idealism asserted that the world does not depend upon subjectivity to be what it ought to be. In other words, the world already is as it ought to be in the realm of universal Ideas (sometimes called Forms) without reference to the subjective striving of any given individual. Who and what I am is predefined by the Hegelian universal Notion whether or not it is realized as my identity. Where the Notion is kept Platonic, it loses the absolute idealist merit of linking it to subjectivity thereby making the finite continuous with the infinite. When Hegel asserted that the world is as it ought to be, he contradicted his distinctive rendering of the significance of universals. On the one hand, the Notion is actual and so ought to be as it is. On the other hand, our response to alienating finitude signifies that what ought to be is not, and must be made so by our own power of rationality, freedom and transformative activity upon the world.

Hegel wanted to keep the Notion strictly objective and universal. Yet he recognized the Notion we have is subjectively determined by our own negation of something that ought to be other than it is found. Self-objectification seems to be a trivial result if we take subjectivity as a mere vehicle for actualizing universal objective Notions. Yet, Hegel maintained self-objectification is central to the continuity and unity of the finite and infinite. Hegelian ontology asserts that the world is not found to be as it ought to be. Notions are universal. However, they cannot be objective per se. Rather they must originate in the being that thinks them, responds to them and uses them to seek its own ends, thereby transforming the world and itself.

By claiming that the world is as it ought to be, Hegel contradicted his ontology and explained away negativity, alienation and dealienation. This attitude trivializes subjectivity, not allowing a process of self-objectification to resolve the contradictory bifurcation of subject and object. Thought and being become discontinuous and disunited. In addition, the continuity of finite and infinite is destroyed. Man is not reconciled to an imperfect finite world by claiming that things are as they ought to be, by making the Notion independently real, beyond and external to the powers of human subjectivity, by denying the Notion its subjective origin and objective effect. Why did Hegel make this blunder? It was a facile reconciliation. It keeps God as the source of the Notion. It controls the fallible human propensity for egoism and hubris. The world simply does not get better and better without human aspiration and struggle against that which alienates. In fact without the subjective human component, the world is an abstract nullity. Objectivity is the recognition of the alienating Other(s). Subjectivity is the dealienating response. Notions originate as subjective responses to alienating finitude. The action of subjectivity is neither illusory nor trivial, nor subordinate to Notions whose origin is external to subjectivity.

Hegel strongly believed that the world is, as it ought to be. The effect of this conviction is to suppress dealienating endeavor and reinforce the power of authoritative Others. Hegel was committed to justifying traditional authority expressed in social institutions and orthodox Christian theology. Evil is not attributable to the divine, but rather to the human misuse of the divine gift of personal freedom. A divinely created world must be as it ought to be, even if mortals cannot understand at any particular time why this is so. Believing that somehow the world is as it ought to be rationalizes a deeply apathetic otherworldly conservative mind-set. Alienating social conditions are philosophically explained away. For example, the world is a mixture of good and evil complementing each other. In fact, corruption and evil are necessary to a historical dialectic revealing goodness. This being so, vice cannot be condemned absolutely and rejected by the virtuous individual. The world is to be left as it is in the hands of an inscrutable God. Humanity tragically tolerates its suffering. The individual must adjust to this harsh world without rebelling with heroic romantic virtue or revolutionary activism. The Hegelian message is stoically resign, adapt to the world as it is and get along as best you can by obeying the dictates of traditional authority. Have faith that in the end a divine plan will make it come out all right.

Rationalizing the *is* as the *ought* tends to maintain the status quo. It can be called at least conservative and at most, reactionary where it hearkens back to those ancient norms and foundations of community challenged by the enlightenment and romanticism. The effect of these philosophical movements was to change the locus of truth and value from traditional authority to an individuality that evaluated everything and attempted to transform what it found wanting. The effect, if not the intent, of the Hegelian defense of traditional authority was to place the individual within the collective, justifying it as normative for him. One must know one's place and accept it. Knowing one's place is socially conforming and doing ones duty as prescribed by traditional authority. If this entails suffering, believe that you serve some higher and worthier good than yourself. Such rationalization belies the secret purpose of denigrating personal freedom, which is to assert social control over the individual.

Authoritarian dealienation is problematical in many respects. The mere introjection of the authoritative Other(s) may further alienate the self. For their dicta can frustrate the satisfaction of human needs and desires. The dictates of traditional authority can stunt self-development and thwart a realization of authentic human potentiality. Exclusive reliance upon the dicta of authoritative Others prevents the development and exercise of rational freedom, a human capacity essential for dealienation. Self-existence exclusively pre-determined by the norms and social roles presented by authoritative Others lacks autonomy and so cannot be authentic.

A self lacking rational freedom and dominated by the dicta of authoritative Others cannot existentially validate its guidance for self-existence. Without an existential and personal test of legitimacy, traditional authority must be accepted as a postulate of faith. Whether it is rational or satisfactory for self-existence is doubtful. Hegel was right in recognizing Reason as establishing the legitimacy of authority. However, he was wrong in presuming those traditional sources of authority, or the law itself, to be inherently rational. Neither may be rational and so their legitimacy always remains subject to the test of self-existence. Assent to authority or law can only be secured after rational examination of their intent, consequences and merit. Authority and law need questioning about their rationale, who is subject to them and whose interests are served by them. The universal validity of authority and law resides not in any Hegelian abstraction of their meaning or in any ontological status presumed superior to the individual. Legitimacy is a self-imposed obligation created by the rational judgment of everyone concerned.

Hegel begins and ends his philosophy with the religious conviction that divine intentions irrevocably govern human destiny. This absolutist conviction presumes that divine Ideas governing man are eternally true, not subject to any modification by anything mere mortals can think or do. The historical dialectic of human freedom in no way effects what is pre-established for self-existence by divine authority. An exercise of human freedom merely discovers and expresses divine intentions. Rebellion only places the individual in an alienating isolation from community and God. Dealienation then, must be a rediscovery and reaffirmation of divinely originated truth through the historical suffering of humanity. What is true for human beings is recovered by a re-introjection of traditional authority. No matter how freedom and rationality is used, they can be none other than vehicles of Geist, carriers of the traditional cultural values and beliefs Hegel presumed eternally true and therefore universally obligatory.

To prize subjective freedom is hubris, wasteful abstract negativity without transcending purpose. Alternatively, re-introjecting traditional authority changes the self-concept of the individual and ethos of a whole people. What then is freedom in this authoritarian cultural context? Is it a means for realizing eternal truths ultimately mandated by divine thought? Most certainly, this is the Hegelian absolute idealist interpretation of the significance of human freedom. However, it is also clear that this interpretation is a rationalization of traditional authority. By reducing human freedom to a mere means for God's purpose, Hegel reintroduces a determination by destiny contradicting freedom. Still, treating man as mere means also bothered Hegel with good reason. For this deprives man of the dignity and moral autonomy Hegel wished to uphold. If in the end man has a destiny not guided by his own rationality and freedom, he remains profoundly alienated. His alienation is not overcome by a re-introjection of traditional cultural authority. Moreover, the significance of his freedom as a generic response to alienation is sacrificed.

Hegel was not completely comfortable with the authoritarian dealienation he proposed and was committed to by his religious faith. While recognizing extraordinary heroic individuals to be the creators of world history, they remain vehicles of the *Zeitgeist*. Of himself, the hero is possessed as if by a demon. An alien Other manipulates him. It is a power external to him, unconsciously possessing him and bending his behavior and desires to its purposes without his knowledge or consent. He is reduced to a mere foot soldier, executor of an alien will. The *cunning of reason* deceives him about its alien purpose; keeping him ignorant of whom or what he serves. In thought and behavior, he is not autonomous. History, as impersonal and dominated by *Geist*, makes the self a pathetically alienated figure. The historic hero is merely a player unconsciously acting from a script and author alien to his own desires. He is not autonomous, remaining in alienated subjugation to unconscious spiritual forces. A dominating alien authoritative Other can also be the force of culture residing in a Freudian repressed psyche, keeping its antisocial impulses from destroying civilization. Freud also advocated authoritarian dealienation by his presumptions about antisocial human instincts found in his analysis of the psychological dynamics maintaining civilization.

Human history reflects varying degrees of the realization of moral, ethical and religious principles, the origin of which lies in the Idea or Reason which Hegel equated with divine wisdom. The moral worth of the individual consists of the rational apprehension of his duty based upon moral, ethical and religious principles. Conforming to their divine source, they are infinite and eternal, uneffected by contingent historical circumstance.[4] Any individual can participate in these principles and in so far as they are part of his soul, imperfect as this may be in any historical epoch, they constitute an inviolate sacred core of individuality. Moral autonomy, wherein moral worth is independent of circumstance, consists of a rational apprehension of one's duty with its divine source external to the individual. The individual is alienated from the divine source of being, and history is a chronicle of his faltering attempts to overcome this alienation and realize divine rational purposes. Subjective freedom characterized by volition, resolution and action is also the sacred core of individuality to be respected as the essence of human nature and basis of human rights.

Even conscience, although imperfectly originating with a particular individual in particular circumstances, is also included in that inviolate sacred core of individuality. But individuality, of itself, is not autonomous as is demonstrated in cases where conscience justifies evildoing. The true significance and value of subjective freedom does not lie with an inviolate sacred core of individuality. Rather the truth and value of subjective freedom is instrumental or a mere means for carrying out the divine purpose in world history. Therefore, the individual maintains an ontological position subordinate to moral, ethical and religious principles with their divine source. Hegel steadfastly refused to upset this ontological apple cart by placing individuality above any of them. Doing so would be hubris, ontological sin, which might invite philosophical chaos.

Hegel believed it impossible to judge history from a moral point of view:

> For the history of the world moves on a higher level than that proper to morality. ...The demands and accomplishments of the absolute and final aim of Spirit, the working of Providence, lie above the obligations, responsibilities, and liabilities which are incumbent on the in-

> dividuals in regard to their morality. ...They (world-historical acts) stand outside of morality.[5]

This appears to be an amoral view of history subordinating the individual to an inscrutable divine purpose, the moral value of which transcends that which is human. Yet, it takes human deeds to express the historical actuality and value of the divine purpose. A world-historical criminal could bring about the purpose of Geist just as well if not better than can a martyr to a lost moral cause. Any means used by Geist, be it good or evil justifies its end. This is not an amoral point of view. It is an immoral point of view that rationalizes evil and impugns the very purpose of Geist. If Geist uses immoral means to achieve its historical purpose, isn't Geist somehow immoral? In being manipulated by Geist, man confronts an Other which alienates him by denying him autonomy in the process of making history. Moreover, he is alienated from himself, his fellows and God by his evil deeds done in the service of realizing the divine purpose. How can God demand morality of man and sanction immorality by his agent in realizing the divine purpose? Nevertheless, Hegel insisted that evil means could bring about a good end.

Hegel believed that the foundation of moral conduct is held to reside in treating human beings as ends, not as means. A divine authoritative Other mandates this principle of moral conduct. Yet, divine intentions are actualized historically by means of immoral human conduct. Immorality on a world historical scale is thereby rationalized. By rejecting the relevancy of moral conduct to historic outcomes, Hegel denied continuity between the self and the divine authoritative Other it must obey. Most perplexing is how the truth, goodness and beauty of divine purpose can become actual through immoral heroic deeds.

An authoritative Other, namely Geist, whose inscrutable purposes not understood by the players, is required to rescue chaotic human history from its obvious existential absurdity. Yet, it did not escape Hegel's notice that making Geist the puppeteer of history degrades human dignity by denying it the autonomy that Hegel elsewhere asserted was its essential nature and right. Furthermore, unconsciously being used to fulfill Geist's inscrutable purpose profoundly alienates the self from an authentic existence necessitated by its own capacity for rationality and freedom. If the individual cannot know in what way his existence contributes to human history and destiny, how can a philosopher assert that history exhibits its rational purpose of any kind, as opposed to mere sound and fury signifying nothing?

Still, it is demonstably clear that although history is not specifically predictable, human destiny can be understood in broad outline. It is a progressive development; an existential self-realization based upon those twin pillars of western civilization, rationality and freedom, powers essential to humanity itself. So human history then becomes a finite continuous process of alienation and dealienation progressively revealing being and its true meaning. Humanity did not make the irrational choice of nuclear annihilation in the twentieth century, thereby affirming that existence is not absurd and without purpose. Thus, the destiny of every individual is to contribute to this continuous process of self-realization, to spontaneously create, develop and further express the potentiality for rational freedom, universal to human nature.

Alienation is multifaceted depending upon the specific nature of an undesirable separation or loss. Human beings can be alienated by nature, by destiny, by other human beings. Authority can also be the cause of alienation. The source of authority, be it parent, Emperor, God, State or culture is no guarantee of its legitimacy. It can only be maintained by being perpetually open to question and a testing of the consequences of its application. What is critical is how authority is internalized. If internalized by a non-rational or even irrational process of socialization, authority will invariably alienate individuals subject to it. If however, authority is internalized through a process involving freedom and rationality, then it will promote successful dealienation.

The correct response to alienation is rational freedom. This much Hegel suggests. To locate freedom within the individual is obviously correct. However, Hegel's refusal to so locate rationality is a mistake. Humanity has been alienated by nature and by the arbitrary subjective will of individuals as Hegel correctly claims. Nevertheless, humanity has been equally alienated by the traditional authority of community, State and God. The correct response to these sources of alienation lies in the complete rational freedom of the individual to test and change them whenever necessary. The marks of dealienation are individual authenticity and autonomy. In this context, the obligation to authority and law is not alien to the individual. Knowledge and duty are not simply instruments of obedience to alien higher authority. Rather, knowing one's duty is a product of the rationality inherent to every individual. The law is independently tested by the rationality of each individual and its obligation is naturally self-given. In such a circumstance, obligation is not felt as obedience, but as inner need, as natural desire.

Authoritarian dealienation is ultimately made unsuccessful by the interposition of an alien Other between the self and a realization of its authentic potentiality for being. Yet, there remains another sense of dealienation. It confronts the same conditions of self-existence and alienating finitude. Here again, an alien Other frustrates the desires and aims of the self that responds with its capacity for rationality and freedom. The response can be described as a dialectical process between self and alien Other. But, the Other(s) does not strictly define the self. It makes no attempt to replicate anything pre-established for its destiny. Rather, the self is allowed to define itself with the alien Other serving as its foil, as impetus for self-development. Self-transformation is from nothing to something, from unknown potentiality to actuality via interaction with alien Others. What the self is to become and express is not pre-established by an authoritative Other or known in advance. Its destiny is its own rather then dictated by the Other(s).

The being and meaning of self and Other is revealed as a product of an interactive process described as self-realization. It displays novelty in dealienating outcomes. What makes it authentic is that the self exercises its own powers of rationality and freedom to realize its identity rather than taking that identity strictly from an authoritative Other. Non-authoritarian dealienation then does not literally replicate what the Other is or demands of the self. Rather, the self realizes its own potentiality for being through its own powers. Its freedom is not placed in service to the Other, but rather in service to its own existential potentiality for being residing within its own essential capacity for rationality and freedom. Self-sufficiency and independence are maintained with respect to the alien Other serving to stimulate self-development. Where the self must replicate the being and demands of the authoritative Other(s), authenticity and autonomy are unavailable and cannot be developed. However, where the self can use its inherent powers for dealienation, authenticity and autonomy is expressed. These are the marks of successful dealienation.

Conscience Guiding Freedom

Circumstances of alienation provoke a personal discovery of conscience. It becomes operative under conditions of personal distress. For example, the self might confront a dilemma posed by a conflict between different duties with equal claim. Which is to be chosen and acted upon? When there are limited resources at one's disposal, who is to be helped and who neglected? Alienating finitude often poses such dilemmas. Where authoritative Others provide no guidance, the self must decide without assistance from any external source. Conscience, an authoritative voice of the self, is then invoked. It senses the authentic needs and desires of the self as personally felt obligations to behave in certain ways appropriate to the situation as determined by an exercise of rational freedom. From this dealienation proceeds.

Conscience is also discovered where cultural disintegration is in progress. A self alienated by the demands of culture has no recourse but to rely upon its conscience and its own dealienating capacity. Socrates sought wisdom by reasoning about what was perplexing in the culture of his time. Stoics resigned themselves to prevailing circumstances, lowered expectations, and attended only to a private domain within which they could enjoy personal freedom. Christians turned away from this world toward God and a world to come. Ideologists called for social reform and revolution. Contemporary society has its counter-culture movement, its collapse of the family, increase of crime, drug addiction, political apathy, mass media techniques manipulating public opinion, cynically deceptive propaganda and unscrupulous public servants, among others. Government policies and programs are filled with anomalies and unintended consequences. Skepticism and cynicism prevail.

Regardless of the historical circumstances of cultural alienation, turmoil or disintegration, the self is always forced to turn inward to its own conscience and creative capacities for salvation. The self listens to that voice of conscience emanating from itself to guide its conduct. Conscience is invoked to replace norms, mores and social roles found oppressive, irrelevant or obsolete. The product of what conscience dictates then becomes a new archetype for identification, projection and objectification. Virtuous examples of courageous individuals acting from conscience continuously move culture from disintegration to renewal.

Conscience is regarded as having an authoritative voice. But whose authoritative voice is it? Interpretations diverge. Conscience has been said to be the voice of God. If not God, yet still an Other, the authoritative voice of culture consisting of many human voices such as parents, popular role models, ideology and so forth. Whether the voice of conscience is God or human, it is from an authoritative Other and so identical in concept. An inner authoritative voice of conscience commanding personal conduct is presumed right by virtue of its source. Conscience is called upon to provide guidance for personal freedom in unguided distressing situations. Heidegger made the radical suggestion that the authoritative voice of conscience originates from the self. It could be a source of authority for itself. This prospect evokes dread, anxiety, and anguish over the prospect of exercising personal freedom to realize authentic human potentialities.

Even where conscience is considered the voice of God, it still emanates from within the self. Lacking divine guidance, the voice of conscience is heard by the anguishing religious question, "What would

God have me do?" The answer must come from the depths of the soul, from its own human capacity for dealienation. Unguided by any authoritative Other, but by a conscience guided freedom - and rationality it might be added - an authentic, autonomous self can create itself, its own culture and express the divine in terms of human ideals. What is this divine, if not a human ideal or the best within us? It is what the voice of conscience calls the self to realize in finite situations. And this, above all, requires an exercise of rational freedom rather than simple obedience to what an authoritative Other(s) pre-establishes for self-existence and dealienation. A self, heeding the voice of its conscience is a witness to the divine within the human, to the authenticity and autonomy of a creative self.

Conscience is identified by that inner voice heard by the self. As conscience *calls*, it is heard as if from an Other. The reason for this is that consciousness, including self-consciousness, is objectively intentional, always presenting itself as an Other by means of negation. The crucial question of conscience is what or who is this Other speaking to the self? Stated otherwise, what kind of self is spoken to? No doubt, it is a self that develops through and by means of the Other(s). It is also a self that exists with limits, with a future, with freedom, with rationality, with a potential for developing in certain directions, thereby realizing its being. So, when conscience calls, its calls the self to its own capacity for autonomy and authenticity. But, this is far different from the call understood as a command to obey the authority of an alien authoritative Other.

Conscience is a curious phenomenon with widely divergent interpretations of what it signifies. On the one hand conscience is interpreted as the authoritative voice of the Other(s) controlling and commanding self-conduct, denying the self absolute freedom to satisfy its desires any way it pleases. On the other hand, the self acknowledges its freedom with its conscience. For in suffering *pangs of conscience*, feeling remorseful or acknowledging its guilt, it knows itself to be a doer who can choose. It also knows this when hearing its own voice of conscience prompting it to act courageously, alone and contrary to cultural authoritative Others. But, whether conscience is guided by that authoritative inner voice of the self or outer voice of the Other(s), the self is presumed to be a moral agent with freedom to choose and act to some degree: either to act for itself according to its own rational determination or for the Other(s) in accordance with its dicta.

Conscience is the voice of freedom. Regardless of the source of its voice, conscience is a universal acknowledgment of personal freedom. If this presumption were false, there would be no reason for praise or blame, reward or punishment, indoctrination, propaganda and any of the other practices which pre-determine the conduct of the self coercing it toward social conformity. Although basing conscience upon freedom or upon socialization appear contrary to one another, both are not necessarily contradictory. For the self must first know how the Other(s) wish it to behave in order to discover how it would choose to behave. Normal moral development from childhood to maturity begins with the authority of the Other(s) and progresses toward autonomy. Freedom and morality develop concurrently until the self is able to act from conscience recognizing its autonomy, its intentions, and the possible consequences of its behavior. Herein, conscience bespeaks a high degree of freedom, an autonomous self with a heightened moral sensibility. This is not to say that conscience cannot be perverted into an excuse for evil doing; or, that it cannot become sick imprisoning the self in the proscriptions of the Other(s) suppressing its desires and attempts at dealienation; or, that it may fail to realize its own potential by donning the straight jacket prescribed for it by the Other(s). All of this, tragic as it is, happens too frequently.

When viewed psychologically, conscience consists of moral ideals introjected by the self. These ideals, as mandated by an Other(s), have an origin external to the self. They may even contradict the desires or aims of the self. Yet, they are effectively normative for its conduct. When violated, self-punishment is inflicted and felt as pangs of conscience or remorse. The process of creating a conscience and experiencing its operation is a result of a more general developmental process of socialization.

Then there is a second sense of conscience in which the individual is not bound by some rule of conduct and so must be guided by conscience. This implies an agent responsible for its actions, an agent free from external restrictions and free to decide for itself. This sense of conscience is of freedom unguided by the Other(s). What then is left to guide one's conscience? Obviously, desire and rationality. The individual must, by thinking the situation through form a conclusion upon which conduct can be based. Regardless of outcome, the individual is held responsible and accountable.

Following from a conscience expressing radical freedom, one is *guilty*, no matter what the outcome. This sensing of existential guilt does not lie in giving moral offense. Rather, it expresses an ontological basis for moral guilt implicit in the necessity of alienating finitude and the consequences of intentionally dealienating behavior. The self is bereft of any excuse for what it does. It cannot excuse itself from accountability by citing the norms and authority of the Other(s). *They* made me do it is insufficient. The self cannot hide from its freedom behind the Heideggerian *they*. So, conscience is felt as the agony of radical freedom. It has a sobering and salutary effect upon the self, bringing into sharp relief what it means to exist authentically and to fully bear the heavy burden of suffering that radical freedom entails. To escape this is to embrace a conscience in the former sense, one provided by the Other(s). Clearly then, one has a choice of conscience which at least in part determines how one shall exist in the world with others.

Conscience recognizes duty. The self feels an obligation. However, the critical question is whether the obligation originates with the Other(s) or from within the self. In the former case, the obligation is a result of a natural process of socialization. Duty is a cultural mold into which self-existence is cast. However, in the latter case, obligation results from the very process of self-existence. Therefore, it has existentially embedded reasons. Self-existence or historical human experience rationally persuades as opposed to the non-rational or even irrational persuasiveness of the authority of an Other(s). What is felt to be right can therefore be explained or argued, if necessary.

Conscience can be thought of as the self apprehending its duty. But, if duty is an apprehension of the demands coercively imposed by cultural authoritative Others, then conscience is not operative. For, conscience imposes an obligation upon the individual to act from personal conviction, particularly when it violates a commonly acknowledged duty. Therefore, obligations of conscience, often fraught with risk of censure or worse, express autonomy and authenticity in an exercise of personal freedom. Conscience can be right where duty is wrong. A stand taken from conscience can only be judged according to the merits of a situation requiring its exercise. When an appeal is made to conscience, it must have reasons to override the demands of duty. It is then that conscience is judged right and superior to duty. That conscience is right is confirmable by any self who thinks about the reasons for what it commands. This is why conscience is publicly respected as a sacred domain of the self. Obeying one's conscience in defiance of duty commands public respect. Law acknowledges conscience, for example, by exempting conscientious objectors from military service or providing non-combatant alternatives. The autonomy and authenticity that acts of conscience demonstrate acknowledges the inherent dignity of a self capable of courageously thinking and acting for itself, even if alone.

The voice of conscience is dramatically evident in acts of civil disobedience. While acknowledging a respect for law by a willingness to pay its penalty, the self nevertheless heeds the commanding voice of its conscience. Such an act of conscience commands public respect for two reasons. First, the disobedient self demonstrates a general respect for the origin and purpose of law. Second, the authenticity of its conviction cannot be doubted. Sometimes the act of conscience is protest against a commonly acknowledged duty rejected by the disobedient self. Or, disobedience may follow from a conflict of duties as, for example, between state and God. No matter the reason for being disobedient, the self must decide what is obligatory for it under the circumstances. Disobedient conduct often affirms a higher obligation sensed by conscience, superseding that which is violated. Conscience, regardless of its source in authoritative Others or a free self can function to preserve liberty from tyranny, particularly that of the state. For, if an individual citizen is religious, God is cited as an authority higher than the state. By obeying its conscience, whether believed to be an inner divine voice or the voice of personal freedom, a citizen can justify disobedience to the state. Regardless of its source, a respect for and appeal to conscience protects liberty.

Hegelian Critique of Conscience

Hegel derived conscience from a subjective will attempting to reconcile opposed duties. Confronted by this dilemma, an appeal is made to conscience.

> Conscience, then, in its majestic sublimity above any specific law and every content of duty, puts whatever content it pleases into its knowledge and willing. It is moral genius and originality, which knows the inner voice of its immediate knowledge to be a voice divine; and since in such knowledge it directly knows existence as well, it is divine creative power, which contains living force in its very conception.[6]

Listening to the divine voice within the self, Hegel would only permit locating the source of conscience in a divine cultural authoritative Other. Since subjective freedom cannot to be trusted and conscience is an expression of it, it follows that conscience cannot be trusted. "To have a conscience, if conscience is only formal subjectivity, is simply to be on the verge of slipping into evil; in independent self-certainty, with its independence of knowledge and decision, both morality and evil have their common root."[7] Egoistic motives and evil intentions may lurk behind hypocritical avowals of conscience. Evil deeds can be rationalized by the claim that they emanate from the dictates of a presumably *good conscience.*

Hegel considered a conflict of duties tragically irreconcilable between Antigone and King Creon as artistically portrayed in the Sophoclean tragedy *Antigone.* Both religious and civic duties are valid obligations of the self toward different authoritative Others with equal claims to obedience. Each party does evil in disobeying a legitimate authority, and each has no recourse. Regardless of Hegel's belief that conscience had not been developed in classical Greek culture, an appeal to conscience might be made to reconcile conflicting duties. However, conscience expresses only what a particular subjective will intends to be universal, not what is actually universal according to Hegel. Individuals acting from their inner voice of conscience merely reassert their isolation from community. Private conscience cannot generate universally obligatory norms serving as an ethos for community. Lacking this, what the self considers its duty does not rationally compel assent or obligate anyone else. Conscience demonstrates the deeply held Hegelian conviction that self-objectifying behavior can realize universal norms but not create them. Conscience cannot be a basis for law, since Hegel believed it couldn't be socially universalized. Only what is pre-established by legitimate authoritative Others can create that absolute universality Hegel required for social cohesion.

Hegel thought conscience insufficient to establish a moral foundation for society. The primary reason is that conscience is based upon a self free to judge what shall be normative for itself and its fellows. This self would determine what is good, bad, right or wrong. In other words, the self would replace the moral authority of the Other(s). This, Hegel believed, would be dangerous in several respects. Conscience could be used to justify disobedience to authority, which for Hegel was tantamount to rationalizing evil doing. The self could, by an appeal to conscience, falsely convince itself and its fellows that its deed is right, since it originates from a conscience presumed to have good intentions; something commanding public respect. But what the self wants and does is indicative of its own interest and can be contrary to that of others or to the common good. Under the guise of conscience, evil could masquerade as good based merely upon either the presumed or avowed good will of the perpetrator. Self-aggrandizing desire could falsely parade as social good. For conscience allows a complete justification of personal desire without social constraint.

Since conscience expresses the freedom of the self to establish its own norms, and that very self is a creature of desire, the temptation is overwhelming for conscience to rationalize narcissistic or egoistic behavior. A Hegelian *bad conscience* - one doing evil by violating the dicta of authority - can convince itself and its fellows that what it wants is good or right, since emanating from its conscience. The deed following such a bad conscience misrepresents the intentions of the doer as being noble rather than motivated by self-seeking desire defying authority. A conscience disguising the true intent of the self allows it to deceive and cynically manipulate its fellows for some purpose they would not agree with.

If the self is convinced that its deed is right and good due to originating within its conscience, it can even deceive itself as to the import of its motives or the consequences of its deeds. If one's motives were pure, and they would have to be when derived from conscience, then social consequences and personal accountability for them could be dismissed. The question of guilt cannot be broached. Moreover, shame cannot apply when motives are pure. An appeal to conscience allows the self to hide its guilt and shame. Thus, conscience eliminates the usual moral constraints of guilt and shame associated with violating the dicta of a cultural authoritative Other(s). A self-deceptive or socially deceptive conscience eroding personal honesty and trustworthiness is indicative of social disintegration, in fact one of its causes.

Conscience allows feeling, imagination and capricious individual preference to morally govern.

> But if a good heart, a good intention, a subjective conviction are set forth as the sources from which conduct derives its worth, then there is no longer any hypocrisy or immorality at all; for whatever a man does, he can always justify by the reflection on it of good intentions and motives, and by the influence of that conviction it is good. ... My good intention in my action and my conviction of its goodness make it good.[8]

This is moral anarchy. With a good conscience, anything goes: standards of conduct collapse into a moral relativism dictated by the conscience of each individual; evil can be rationalized as mere error; the end can justify the means. When two consciences are opposed, there is no basis to judge which is right by any appeal to conscience.

Conscience can be used to undermine law and one's duty to respect and obey it. For the obligation of law is not imposed by the law itself, but is located within a self whose sense of obligation is derived from the autonomy of its conscience. But without an obligation imposed by law with sanctions for violating it, the conduct of an autonomous self can only be driven by egoistic desire. Hegel believed conscience rationalizes egoistic desire thereby providing an excuse for disregarding an obligation to obey the law and consider the welfare of others. Conscience gives the self license to behave in a capricious and socially irresponsible manner. This is social dynamite leading to anarchy and misery. That the self can be the source of its social obligations is a monstrous self-conceit. Claiming a good conscience, evil can be trivialized, explained away as mere error, unintended and somehow produced by agencies external to and uncontrolled by a self who cannot be held accountable.

The preceding Hegelian critique of conscience is based upon psychological insight about its social use. Admittedly, false appeals to conscience can be used to socially deceive and manipulate for self-interested motives. However, this is an abuse preying upon the public respect for conscience, not an authentic exercise of conscience. Abuses of conscience can be detected when what it commands is subject to evaluation within the situation to which it applies. The fact that conscience can be abused does not invalidate its authentic use in personal moral decision making.

It would seem true that different voices of conscience can be contradictory on some moral issues such as the contemporary American dispute over abortion. Without resolution, contradictory voices may just be tolerated to maintain civility. Yet, where different consciences publicly collide, the issue is evaluated. Reasons are sought and provided to support either voice. Although different individuals may assign different priorities to conflicting values involved in a difficult moral situation, resolution is possible. For every self shares common needs and desires. Moreover, the value of something and its obligatory force can be influenced by rational considerations. The universality, which Hegel demanded for morality and believed not attainable from the voice of conscience, is in fact attainable. For determinations of conscience rest with rational freedom, a universally shared human capacity for dealienation.

Whereas Hegel sensed that conscience is a derivative of personal freedom, his unnecessary distrust of the latter was extended to the former. However, a conscience based upon rational freedom meets the Hegelian demand for universality. For rational freedom partially defines an essential and universal nature shared be every self. Conscience need not be dismissed if rationality is located within dealienating self-existence rather than the dicta of cultural authoritative Others. Rationality need not be confused with authority. Conscience is not invalidated by Hegel's reduction of personal freedom to the mere negativity of an egoistic subjective will. More correctly conceived, conscience is an expression of personal freedom integrated with rationality.

Freedom guided by conscience is a basis for moral conduct. There is no authoritative Other who can guarantee the rightness of a personal decision formed by conscience. Assurance must be sought in applying rationality to the situation that conscience addresses. Even if an anguishing burden, there is no alternative but to develop and exercise rational freedom. This is the ethos and historic task creating the destiny of western civilization. From a faith in the spontaneity and creativity of a flourishing rational freedom shall emerge a self-realizing humanity, which is good, right, and just. The religious sense of western civilization resides in its ethos of rational freedom. Although Hegel distrusted a personal freedom guided by conscience, he sensed this ethos calling it Spirit and describing its dialectical development throughout human history.

Dealienating Love

Love is well recognized to have dealienating power. Salvation through love is an age-old religious message. Hegel understood divine love to be the essence of Christianity. Love is a feeling, infinite in power, unifying all oppositions, and transcending understanding. Spontaneous loving between selves is reciprocated. Lover and beloved are simultaneously enriched. A youthful Hegel thought of love as the primary means of dealienation. Later, even before writing the *Phenomenology of Spirit*, Hegel had abandoned the influence of Kantian philosophy, strictly distinguishing *Understanding* from *Reason*. The unifying power of love was replaced with Reason. *Agape* then became mere emotional feeling, an infinite yearning widening the gulf between the self and its object of love. The role of love is then reversed. From a dealienating power, it becomes a confirmation of alienation.

A youthful Hegel believed love to be the crowning virtue that replaces all the restrictions and dilemmas encountered in living by many separately prescribed virtues. "To complete subjection under law of an alien Lord, Jesus opposed not a partial subjection under a law of one's own, the self-coercion of Kantian virtue, but virtues without lordship and without submission, i.e., virtues as modifications of love."[9] Agape requires no domination by the Other, no submission of self to an external authority. For agape is infinite in its scope, not a measurable quantity of something, not commanded by an intimidating authoritative Other(s). Love, "... is this feeling of unity of life, a feeling in which all oppositions, as pure enmities, and also rights, as unifications of still subsisting oppositions, are annulled."[10] A youthful Hegel was impressed with the emotion of love, sensing its intimate connection with the rationality and freedom of the self. Yet a more sober older Hegel later dismissed the power of emotion, distrusted freedom and relocated rationality from the self to authoritative Others.

Hegel's early theological thinking suggests the possibility of God, the authoritative Other, becoming a deep expression of humanity, of love, freedom and rationality even though it would be left to other philosophers such as Feuerbach to further develop a humanized God. Hegel saw early Christianity making love a self-transcending expression of divine intention: so much so, that law and duty become superfluous. Particular natural inclinations given impetus by love rather than a self-opposing duty or God's moral law is then a spontaneous expression of autonomy. Love is a natural expression of the inner spontaneity of the self, which is whole and unfettered by social constraints. Deeds done from love rather than fear, anxiety or duty to law express the full potency of the self and are therefore the most satisfying. Authentic self-expressions of agape immediately express the divine that is within humanity itself. Christ, believed to be the incarnation of divinity, set the example of love as that selfless purity of heart which is a divine virtue. Through a self imbued with agape, divine law loses those alienating qualities of an *ought* in opposition to natural inclination, and of coercion by an Other external to the self.

When duty is replaced by love, divine law loses its alien character. For a loving self fully engages its dealienating capacity. The result of loving is not a sterile formality of customary religious practice. Neither is it mere conformity to duty. Loving objectifies the natural inclinations of the self while expressing divine law. This Christian view prevailed in Hegel's philosophy although the emotion of love was later dismissed as capriciously dependent upon the individual and therefore socially unreliable. Yet, Hegel's earlier viewpoint subordinating duty to a freely offered love is compelling, since it proffers answers to Kantian deontological formalism, to accepting God as inaccessible, to the necessity for moral coercion, and to the hypocrisy of religion.

Love is too abstract a principle to secure the social cohesion of the Christian religion. "The need to unite subject with object, to unite feeling, and feeling's demand for objects, with the intellect, to unite them in something beautiful, in a god, by means of fancy, is the supreme need of the human spirit and the urge to religion."[11] Therefore, God was objectified into the man-God Christ: an actual historical person who lived, died and was resurrected. Believers could identify with a concrete object of worship attached to images, emotional feelings and a creed. Christ is their common master and teacher. Their relationship is more one of subordination than love. A youthful Hegel considered this tragic. For then *positive religion* - organized church and clergy - replaced that agape foundation with authoritative Others providing ritual practices and prescriptions for salvation. A dependence upon these impoverished the spirit of Christianity with heresies, political conflict and religious wars. Christ was to be affirmed not by agape, but as master by force when necessary. Thus, does positive religion alienate the self from its fellows and from God, suppressing agape practiced by an autonomous and authentic religious self.

Love dealienates when it is authentically self-giving. For then love is an expression of not only rationality and freedom, but of talent, knowledge and skills acquired by the self. Self-giving love is always intensely focused upon the welfare of what or whom it is bestowed upon. Such love expresses deep motivations and natural inclinations. Human beings need to be loved and to love in return. The need to love is undoubtedly instinctually based with roots to be found in biological survival and narcissism. The welfare and flourishing of the beloved provides deep satisfaction, even joy to the giver. This is experienced both with the exercise of human powers in acts of loving and in a return of the flourishing welfare of the beloved, if not in expressions of appreciation. The self-giving lover takes pride in what has been contributed to the beloved and in what has been thereby accomplished by the beloved.

Self-giving love is a work of self-objectification focused upon the welfare of the Other. Thus, the product of self-giving love affirms the being and powers of the giver. The return of love is anticipated with pleasure, since it affirms the powers of the lover whose identity is secured by their application. What the beloved returns is recognition of self, which, as objectified, is authentic and undeniable. Self-giving love is then narcissism redirected upon the Other and returned. Moreover, in the process, narcissism is transformed. Yet, the objectified return of self-giving love and expressions of appreciation by the beloved do provide narcissistic satisfaction to the lover and more. For, the satisfaction in the giving itself, in exercising one's powers for another cannot be overlooked. Just as a work of art can be appreciated by everyone including its creator, so, also, is there enormous satisfaction in creating the work itself.

A complete satisfaction of self-giving love moves the adult well beyond narcissism. The social product of self-giving love is a bonding of self with its fellows in their mutual desires and aims. Through the Other(s), the self realizes who and what it is. Socially, the unification is a bonding achieved by reciprocity consisting of an authentic exchange of something of value, which is appreciated. Clearly then, self-giving love gives impetus to and at least partially describes a process of dealienation wherein self and Other(s) are unified through self-objectifying behavior in which there is a self-realization of human powers, the creation of self-identity and public acknowledgment of it.

Obviously, love of any kind is a deeply felt emotion. However, although love is emotional, it is not a particular identifiable emotion. When so considered, it is misconstrued. Rather, loving is a complex activity of evaluated meanings set in attitudes and behavioral dispositions. The self is enthusiastically devoted to what it loves. There are a great many emotional feelings associated with loving such as pleasure, pride, joy, jealousy, worry, grief and consolation, among others. In loving, the self can experience upon memorable occasions a euphoric feeling of happiness. This can be experienced sexually, but has a less physical and more spiritual aspect as one ages in a caring and sharing relationship with the beloved. Then there is an ecstatic feeling associated with doing for the beloved, exercising ones powers on behalf of the beloved, bringing comfort, pleasure, and joy in being recognized and prized by the beloved. Also, doing for the beloved can create an ecstatic feeling of self-transcendence in a union wherein the very different contributions of both create something more than either could separately, absent reciprocity.

To be loved is to gain self-esteem from the esteem returned by the beloved. Thus, parental love is required for a child to flourish and develop into an adult with a secure a sense of self-worth and potency. Without this, the capacity to love dies, but with it, this capacity blooms and is reinforced into adult self-potency. Pride is another emotion resulting from acts of love and a witnessing of their beneficial effects upon the beloved. Then, of course, love has its price in any sacrifice required to express it. This only adds worth and merit to loving. Witnessing the demise of the beloved brings emotional pain, a dreaded destiny, and anguish over being helpless to prevent an impending loss. Natural forces and mortality are humbling, reducing the self to impotence and resignation to the finitude of an inescapable destiny. One cries in grief and mourns the loss of the beloved, meeting permanent absence with wishful dreams, even temporary hallucinations. Death ends the possibility of expressing love, but not the memory of what loving meant when it was expressed.

Loving deeply is an encounter with finitude and a response to its alienating dimension. Loving is also a celebration of life's potency, a temporary tragic defiance of mortality. Immortality is not to be gained by speculative fantasy. If it can be achieved at all, it resides, at least for a time, in the lives of beloved survivors, in their memory of a bygone gift of love that lingers in the present extending into the future. While love must be expressed in finite human actions, its power bespeaks a transcendence of finitude within the living potency of the finite. Loving describes and expresses, at least in part, the continuous living process of dealienation.

Self-giving love is neither narcissistic nor egoistic. Rather, it is offered by a completely socialized self who expresses it's most deeply felt needs and desires. Moreover, self-giving love also expresses a self-acquired capacity for rational freedom. Any exercise of self-giving love provides an experience that is exhilarating, self-enhancing and liberating. A work of self-giving love engenders an enjoyment of life wherein the self soars and transcends its isolation from the world and its fellows.

Character and Virtue

An alienated self suffers unresolved opposition between itself and the Other(s). The opposition is created by something or someone posing a limit to satisfaction of human needs and expression of human desires. Alienation can have an external and internal source. *It* or *they* alienate me. In turn, I am alienated from realizing some authentic potentiality for being. An alienated self can neither be nor do what it wants. Rather, it is and does what the Other demands of it. With its authentic needs and related desires frustrated, self-existence demonstrates only what an alien Other prescribes. A projection and objectification of authoritative alien Others, both reifies and bifurcates the self. In effect, it recognizes itself to be an alien object, which it cannot acknowledge, and so it is not self-possessed. What and who it really is lies unrealized, suppressed, unknown, unconsciously concealed and expressed only in disguise. Rational freedom, its inherent dealienating capacity, is neither exercised nor developed. Thus, an alienated self-existence can be described as inauthentic and non-autonomous.

Social psychologists such a David Reisman describes a contemporary alienated self as an *other-directed personality*. It is whoever its fellows want it to be. In being all things to all people, such a self is really nothing; without personal content, lacking in convictions and what would be called character. Such a self is uncertain about itself, what it does, and how it should relate to its fellows. Everything, particularly its own self, is valued instrumentally. Anonymity conceals its authenticity. Authoritative Others conceal its autonomy.

A corporate conformist described by William H. White as the *organization man* of the mid-twentieth century presented a modern characterless person; an empty suit, passive, dependent, ambitious and inured to bureaucracy. Contemporary American political culture further portrays that same character as a slick politician: highly educated but without integrity, shrewd, unscrupulous, deceitful, untrustworthy, dishonest, driven by egoistic ambition, always pandering to voting constituencies and co-opting the opposition. Uninformed by principle, conviction is contingent upon the moment. Hired marketing consultants package the candidate's personality from popularity profiles constructed by public polls, and focus groups. The candidate's identity is fictitious, a projected image of popular culture solely aimed at attaining or maintaining political power. Such a personality, strictly defined by cultural authoritative Others, is found disappointingly unable to govern those Others who govern him. For those who obey only the Heideggerian *they*, whose Sartrean existence is merely *for-another*, and who follow the Nietzschean herd, are radically alienated.

Lacking authenticity and autonomy makes this so, even where there is no awareness of it, except in those strange moments of angst.

Socialization enables the establishment of self-identity or personality. A byproduct of socialization is *character* expressed by a set of attitudes and behavioral predispositions. Character traits are commonly understood as a subset of a whole package of personality traits, particularly those that are considered to establish moral life. Although not commonly recognized, socialization and character formation are continuous throughout life. Incomplete socialization arrested in narcissism and/or egoism results in defective character. Adult socialization initiated by non-rational or irrational self-identifications also results in defective character. It is signified by a self alienated from its needs, desires, rationality, and freedom: a flawed self also lacking the capacity for dealienation and self-realization. A character that is narcissistic, egoistic, or misdirected by faulty self-identifications will cause unnecessary suffering. Socialization arrested in narcissism, egoism, or defective adult socialization, presents a naturalistic description of an alienated self. Even more significant, defective socialization implies the formation of defective character commonly described as immoral; a self lacking empathy, indifferent to causing suffering and thus prone to evil.

Defective socialization forms defective character. A self with defective character is alienated from realizing its inherent potentiality for being human. Defective character, whether reflecting narcissism, egoism or misdirected adult self-identifications, propagates alienation by dysfunctional self-projection and self-objectification. Moreover, to the extent that such behavior causes unnecessary suffering, defective character is accountable for propagating evil. A self whose existence is neither autonomous nor authentic is dominated by alien authoritative Others. Rational freedom, its fundamental dealienating capacity, is undeveloped and inoperative in either its motivation or behavior. So described, defective character is the structural nexus of authoritarianism, totalitarianism, collectivism and certain counterculture ideologies such as postmodernism.

Virtuous character can be acquired by cultural habituation and the arduous work of self-discipline as Aristotle observed. Yet, an expression of cultural ethos is only one aspect of virtuous character. Undoubtedly, virtuous character is esteemed in so far as it sustains the ethos of a culture. Yet, a virtuous character guided by conscience can also creatively transform culture. This occurs when alienating traditional mores are opposed by courageous exemplars of virtue. Responding to cultural alienation with an exercise of virtue, outstanding individuals advance cultural dealienation. Hegel believed the imitative attraction of virtuous conduct insufficient to establish social cohesion. For most individuals cannot be relied upon to possess sufficient courage and self-discipline to universalize virtue. Its practice, established by noble example is only voluntary, and so not universally obligatory. While this viewpoint is plausible enough, a self of virtuous character has developed the capacity to identify, project and objectify itself intelligently. It is this, which provides virtue with its compelling universal public appeal. Virtuous character formation signifies a self free of developmental fixations; one correctly socialized beyond narcissism and egoism. Formed to be authentic and autonomous, virtuous character maximizes the capacity for dealienation and self-realization.

Virtuous character and example respond to alienation, particularly its cultural variety. If the world were as it ought to be, then dealienation would be impossible and virtue would be absurd. However, neither the self nor its world is as they ought to be. The fact of alienating finitude always signifies something that ought to be otherwise. Finitude presents the Hegelian *ought,* meaning that alienation with its infinite variety is necessary to the human condition and calls forth from individuals free to think and act various dealienating responses such as virtuous conduct aimed at transforming a degenerate culture.

That a virtuous character does not transform the world does not prove that personal freedom is untrustworthy, for the world can be intransigent. Yet, the nobility of virtuous conduct remains evident. Sometimes, the practice and example of virtue works in a rather startling if not spectacular way. Hegel would have been the first to admit that Christ's example of love certainly had enormous transformative power upon the wicked ways of the world. Therefore, the failure of virtue is not inevitable, as Hegel wanted to argue. The success of virtue lies more in the persuasive power of its ideals and in its noble example, rather than in its failure to eradicate vice, or in Hegel's demand for its universal applicability.

By denigrating the individualism of the romantic rebel and virtuous hero, Hegel meant to demonstrate that individualism and freedom are normatively inadequate. Closing the door on individualism opens the door to the possibility of returning to traditional authority. Individualism freely pursuing its own desires and purposes Hegel considered capricious, undisciplined, uncontrolled, negative, socially dangerous if not overtly destructive. The Hegelian result of denigrating it was to harness any potential misuse of personal freedom to traditional authority. Contrary to Hegel's suspicion of personal freedom, it is not now considered dangerous or destructive. Rather, it is viewed in a more positive light as a transformative power of self: an inherently trustworthy, spontaneously creative response to all forms of alienation. To be alienated means to be dominated by and in bondage to an Other of some kind: unable to choose and be oneself; unable to effect one's destiny. Dealienation then consists in a faith and trust placed in those individual gifts, powers and capacities Hegel claimed to be misused and wasted when solely in the hands of a completely free and rational individual. Hegel's distrust of a personal freedom capable of establishing valid norms outside traditional authority gets in the way of a deeper trustful understanding of personal freedom implicit in his ontology.

Prescription for Dealienation

The specific conditions of alienating finitude are infinite in principle, not pre-established or known in advance. Neither is the result of responding with the essential human capacity for rationality and freedom. Therefore, the Other need not strictly define the self, but by limiting and frustrating its desires and aims, allows a self-realization of unforeseen human potential. Rationality and freedom are authentic dealienating powers of the self rather than restrictive gifts of authoritative Others. These twin powers inhere essentially to the self as its infinite potential for dealienation, for realizing meaning in general and any potentiality for being an authentic self. Self-realization is at once a transformation of self and world rather than a simple incorporation of the being of the Other by a self whose vacuous threatening freedom requires strict social control. Freedom can be trusted when guided by rationality and self-discipline. Self-development is then not simply conformity to what the Other demands, but occurs by means of an opposition of the Other to the essential powers of the self and its authentic potentiality for being.

The perennial question about human freedom is how it can be trusted. Human history demonstrates that freedom can be misused and so result in evil and alienation. Yet, freedom is necessary for dealienation and so must be trusted. Certain conditions justify a faith placed in personal freedom. Rational freedom develops as the self learns to evaluate circumstances, contemplate possibilities and anticipate the consequences of behavior. This mitigates the misuse of personal freedom by a defectively socialized narcissistic or egoistic personality. A properly developed social self respects the demand for dealienation by its fellows to be equal to its own. Conscience, reflecting authenticity and autonomy of the self, informs it of its obligations toward its fellows and itself. Certainly, conscience can restrain the misuse of personal freedom. Directed by a nurturing self-giving love, the exercise of personal freedom is emotionally satisfying while enabling complete self-realization of human potential.

The alienating finitude of self-existence poses a perennial and universal question for humanity. Who and what ought it to become? What should self-existence project as the content of character? And what shall be the legacy of its self-objectifying work? Rationality and freedom are the human powers necessary for dealienation. Therefore, a continuous development of rational freedom is the essential way of dealienation as western civilization has prescribed since classical Greek culture flowered in Athens over two millennia ago.

Mistrusting freedom has been a major obstacle to the development of rational freedom. Hence, the historical responses of authoritarianism, totalitarianism and collective submersion in culture. However, these always alienate the self from its capacity for dealienation. Still, freedom can be trusted if the self is properly socialized beyond narcissism and egoism. This is accomplished by family, religion and cultural institutions, ever creating and transmitting the mores and morality of a civilization. If these institutions flourish without governmental subversion, then a self will maximize its capacity for dealienation. Self-existence will be marked by autonomy and authenticity, not by a psycho-sociological pathology of domination by alien Others. In addition, self-existence will be marked by a conscience related to freedom, not one censoring the natural desires and aspirations of each self. Human needs will be more easily satisfied without fear of consequences, without the coercion of any repressive authority. Self-existence would then be a kind of utopia, but not one in which alienation is absent, but rather one in which it is dealt with most effectively, allowing the human spirit to flower and soar in its all too brief individual moment of finitude. This is possible and will come to pass, if the forgoing philosophical analysis is correct.

Alienation cannot be eradicated, since it has an ontological basis humanly expressed by the alienating finitude of self-existence. However, the self continuously overcomes alienation by satisfying its needs and desires. This is accomplished by rational freedom, a capacity it has, and can develop, to effect dealienation. The capacity for dealienation can be maximized where self-existence and culture meet certain conditions. Rationality and freedom must be integrated and developed concurrently. Socialization cannot fixate in narcissism or egoism, but must be completed to the point where a responsible social self emerges. Self-identifications initiating the process, particularly in adult life, must be formed rationally rather then non-rationally or irrationally. This enables self-projection and self-objectification to be authentic. Self-realization can thereby express an authentic potentiality for being.

Not dominated by alien authoritative Others, authentic needs and desires can be acknowledged and satisfied by an autonomous self. Acknowledging its obligation to satisfy its own demands, a correctly socialized self universalizes its own claim. This results in acknowledging the claims of its fellows to be equal to its own. A socialized self has learned to postpone its gratification by sharing, queuing up and taking turns. Acknowledging the universality of equal claim for satisfying needs and desires forms the basis for social reciprocity. From this follows human rights, respect for human dignity and democracy. Civility and social cohesion based upon acknowledging human equality makes superfluous a submergence in culture and any coercive subordination to its norms, social roles and institutions. When subordinated to self rather than cultural authoritative Others, dealienation can be enabled and reinforced. Cultural coercion and domination is thereby replaced by a toleration of personal experimentation with deviant lifestyles. And when found better, these replace what traditional culture has provided without creating an opposition between the demands of culture and those of the self.

What does a *dealienating-self* look like? Properly socialized beyond narcissism and egoism, it avoids being the cause of unnecessary suffering, or evil. Rational freedom, its capacity to dealienate, has been maximized. Religious, political or cultural authority does not suppress its needs, desires, rationality and freedom. It is integrated with authority and community to realize its complete human potentiality. It is not dominated or controlled by alien authoritative Others. Its self-existence is authentic and autonomous. Its behavior is subject to a sense of obligation arising from the demands of its own needs and desires as well as its conscience. Self-giving love expresses its own power of rational freedom used to satisfy its natural needs and desires. Acknowledging this essential nature of the self implies a whole panoply of human rights universally extending equal opportunity for self-realization. Pursuing self-realization by voluntary participation creates and sustains democratic culture. Within this process of personal dealienation, the general welfare is secured by individual merit correctly associated to social esteem and human dignity.

Since the conditions of self-existence are indeterminate with respect to the future, so human desires in a finite world are infinite in principle. Freedom and rationality are the means employed by every self for satisfaction of its desire. Desire is legitimated to begin with by the mere fact of being human. The same is true of freedom and rationality, the essential powers of every self. Yet, these powers require discipline and socialization to become fully developed and effective in the process of dealienation. Progressive socialization broadens desire beyond narcissism and egoism. Wealth, power and fame give way to an altruism, which transforms self-seeking into a cultural contribution transcending self. It takes little thought to recognize that each self makes equal natural claim to the satisfaction of its own desires and aims. Shrewd thinking reveals what is in the common interest. The general welfare is served most effectively when every self, equal in virtue of its desires and powers of rationality and freedom, cooperates by providing mutual support. In fact, the self cannot survive without developing in this way. Reciprocity between selves of need and desire establish social cohesion.

A self, unable to acknowledge who it is cannot behave rationally and freely to get what it wants or to express its authentic identity. Its authentic potentiality for being remain unrealized, concealed by a disguise wrought by defective socialization. The meaning of being in general and its own being in particular cannot be revealed. Possibilities of being cannot be discovered or created by a self alienated from rationality and freedom. Personality is ossified. Self-existence affirms an alien authoritative Other in coercive obedience and drab conformity to universal stereotypical norms and social roles. Crippled by defective socialization, the self exists in relative isolation from community. But, if socialization is correctly undertaken, self-existence need not be alienated unnecessarily beyond that which it must encounter by its own finitude.

What then are the conditions of a dealienating socialization? First, it must not be psychologically or sociologically coercive. Every component of socialization requires rationality and freedom. The initiating self-identification must be rational and freely accepted in conformance with the essential nature and potential dealienating capacity of the self. Non-rational or irrational identifications are to be avoided. Then, ensuing self-projection and self-objectification will be free of unresolvable opposition between the demands of culture and those of the self. Socialization, while necessary for the suppression of evil, need not suppress the essential demand of the self for authenticity and autonomy. Socialization can proceed through narcissistic and egoistic development without abnormal fixations of unresolved conflict between self and culture. A social self having developed a dealienating capacity has integrated rationality and freedom. The equality of human needs and desires among selves who form community is acknowledged. Reciprocity exists between self and culture with each complementing the other.

A self expressing what authoritative Others prescribe is not necessarily authentic. In fact, more often than not, such a self is inauthentic. Therefore, self-expression must be qualified to become authentic. For authenticity is a product of fully operative powers possessed by the self. These are developed in a process wherein rationality and freedom are brought to bear upon something alienating the self. In other words, dealienation by an exercise of rational freedom is required for authenticity. Alternatively stated, authenticity is autonomous self-expression. In normal circumstances, authenticity is a product of personal experience in which the self works through a process of dealienation. Now, it is possible for self-expression to be authentic and still express what the authoritative Others prescribe. However, for this to be the case, the self cannot be coerced. Rather, it must be capable of thinking freely about what authoritative Others prescribe, relating it to its own personal experience, evaluating it within some specific existential context and concluding that it is worthy of being personally subscribed to and acted upon. It is how the self deals with what is presented to it that is crucial for dealienation characterized by autonomy and authenticity.

A self, fully prepared for dealienation and self-realization, is one whose self-existence is both authentic and autonomous. An alien Other, although always driving dealienation, does not dominate a dealienating self. It is not irrationally or non-rationally submerged in its culture or controlled by alien authorities. Its aspirations and deeds respond to the voice of its conscience. Its character is virtuous. It relates to its fellows with a store of acquired wisdom and self-giving love. Its needs and desires are satisfied and integrated in complementary ways with its fellows. Most importantly, a dealienating self is one who has socially developed and maximized its rational freedom to a degree permitting a complete realization of all its potentialities, thereby revealing the very meaning of being.

Notes

1. Hegel, G. W. F. (1830) *Hegel's Logic*: Being Part One of the Encyclopedia of the Philosophical Sciences (3rd ed., 1975) (William Wallace, Trans.). London, England: Oxford University Press, 273.
2. Ibid., 274.
3. Ibid.
4. Hegel, G. W. F. (1956) *The Philosophy of History* (J. Sibree, Trans.). New York, NY: Dover, 36-37. Also see *Reason in History*, 48.
5. Hegel, G. W. F. (1953) *Reason in History* (Robert S. Hartman, Trans.). New York, NY: Macmillan, 82-83.
6. Hegel, G. W. F. (1967) *The Phenomenology of Mind* (J. B. Baillie, Trans.). New York, NY: Harper and Row, 663.

7. Hegel, G. W. F. (1977) *Hegel's Philosophy of Right* (T. M. Knox, Trans.). New York, NY: Oxford University Press, 92.

8. Ibid., 99.

9. Hegel, G. W. F. (1992) *Early Theological Writings: The Spirit of Christianity* (T. M. Knox, Trans.). Philadelphia, PA: University of Pennsylvania Press, 244.

10. Ibid., 278.

11. Ibid., 289.

Chapter Eight

Argument Recapitulation

Negativity

Descriptions of alienation whether literary or scientific very often lack coherence, which has led analytical philosophers such as Richard Schacht to dismiss the subject as nonsensical. Yet, discussions of alienation continuously recur in literature, religion, ethics, psychology, social psychology, sociology and political science. Such discussions always employ a language of negativity. Western philosophy dating back to Parmenides has developed a tradition centered upon an ontological conception of negativity. It provides a theoretical foundation for a coherent and general philosophical understanding of alienation. Negativity was recognized early in western philosophy by Socrates as a basis for seeking wisdom through dialectical discourse. Later, Hegel reinterpreted and extended the dialectical method to serve as an ontological principle driving both thought and being.

Considered an ontological principle, negativity is a ubiquitous driver of any kind of process occurring in the cosmos at any level of being. The power of this principle is evident in its universal applicability. It takes on various forms depending on the context of being under consideration. In logic, it appears as implication, formal or material, a principle necessary to thought and knowledge. Understanding temporal sequence and mathematics is based upon negativity. Within nature, negativity is expressed as temporal change of state, as physical or chemical processes which when regular, repetitive and predictable is deemed causal. In astrophysics, it appears as anti-matter, cosmological black holes, other worlds. In theology, it appears as God creating the world from nothing. In psychology it appears as ego defenses and pathology. In sociology, it appears as cultural conflict. It is equally applicable to an expression of human desires and ideal human aspiration in the realm of moral behavior. Its universal applicability ranges over the human, non-human, the finite and infinite alike.

Ontological negativity provides a theoretical principle for the thought of being and being of thought. The universals of thought presume negativity: a negativity of distinction creating meaning; a negativity presenting an alien Other(s) as the signified; a negativity implying complex meanings, suggesting possibilities of meaning, being, experience and action to be explored. Meaning is constructed by the negative implication of thought; by a difference which distinguishes something from something else. In fact, negativity is displayed as contradiction in the process of thought. Rather than terminating thought, contradiction is necessary for it to proceed. The meaning of anything presumes a whole and some form of negativity to distinguish and relate its parts. Contradiction provides a stimulus for thought to seek the truth and overcome limiting obstacles. The very act of thinking requires simultaneously holding in mind something and its negating Other. Implicit contradiction is necessary for thought to occur. Being is, by the operation of negativity, a temporal presentation of an alien Other. That which alienates provides an impetus for thought to proceed by successive differentiation and intentional self-activity creating a unified structure of meaning revealing being and occasionally even creating it.

Although negativity is common to signifier and signified alike, it is a mistake to equate their meaning. The thought of being and being of thought are distinct. Universals signify by implying finite differences without enumerating them. Thinking the universal is unable to provide meaning although Hegelian logic falsely presumed this to be true. Meaning can only be revealed by an existential encounter with alienating finitude. Encountering alien Others poses the ontological question, "Who or what is the Other?" This question applies to world and self alike as it experiences the alienating finitude of its own existence, and so discovers the world and itself through its own interactive capability. Finitude is defined by an encounter with a negating Other, whether it is what is not but potentially could be, or something which poses a limit to be transcended. Consciousness and self-consciousness always encounters something Other, an objective presentation of a determinate being. Self-existence is marked by need and desire. Frustration of either expresses negativity in painful ways.

Alienation is implied by negativity experienced through the needs and desires of self-existence. Responses define dealienation as a process of intentional interaction with the environment. In effect, negativity forms a seamless whole whether it limits, differentiates, contradicts, denies, refuses, opposes, struggles, suffers, comes into being or ceases to be. The root of human alienation lies in the presentation of an Other alien to a self who exists, perceives, thinks and acts in a finite world. Ontological negativity provides a structure for thinking about alienation and dealienation. With this fundamental principle driving any process, alienation and dealienation are built into the very structure of being. Since negativity describes any natural process, alienation and dealienation acquire universal cosmic significance. Finitude and human existence is generally explained by ontological negativity. Conceived as existential process driven by ontological negativity, alienation and dealienation is ubiquitous. Regarding the self, a negating process of dealienation implies radical freedom and rationality, both innate and developable by human beings.

Was the ancient philosophical attitude correct in not separating truth from value? The answer appears to be that the ancients were correct, although the answer offered herein is somewhat different from theirs. First, consider the implications of ontological negativity. Encountering an alien Other is to encounter a limit from within or without; a limit that implies a negation of whatever is limiting. Finitude is the presentation of a deficiency in being or a limit to being something. Deficiency and limitation is experienced as something which is not present but ought to be in the future. An expression of this general ontology is an experience of finitude, of something needed or desired. Value is this sensing of need and desire: something that ought to be the case, thereby providing impetus for intentional goal seeking activity. Human beings respond to this sensing of needs and desires with their peculiar intelligent capacity for dealienation, namely rational freedom.

Suffering the alienating finitude of self-existence establishes the value of anything. Thus, in effect the fact of need or desire is already value-laden. That self-activity is motivated by need and desire provides indubitable proof of this. The satisfaction of need or desire is a consummation both in the fact of something achieved and in the enjoyment of its value, emotionally and otherwise. Dealienating endeavor further enhances value-laden facts. Negative value resides in what alienates and positive value resides in the result of successful dealienation. Value is determined in degree by the extent of dealienating endeavor. The greater the degrees of suffering, sacrifice and work required, the greater the value of something. The converse is also true. A scarcity of what is needed or desired also determines its value. Thus, value is an attribute of dealienating endeavor. It is measured by what is involved in satisfying the motivating need or desire to acquire something. The measure of value is usually stated by the price paid to get it, whether the price is expressed as money, an expenditure of labor, or in terms of some other aspect of dealienating endeavor.

Hegelian sublation suggests a general explanation of alienation and dealienation. Encountering the Other as a limit to or deficiency in being is the initial negating moment of alienation. The Other signifies that the being in question is finite and alienated from what it can be. Its being is a possibility for it, a potentiality for being something, which it has never been and is not at the present moment. This alienating finitude fundamentally characterizes a world of finite beings. It is the impetus for alteration, transformation, and development in being. Everything finite is altered with time, comes to be, develops, is transformed, and ceases to be.

Hegel is a seminal thinker on the subject of alienation and dealienation. Thought requires a thinker, negativity and an alien Other. With these, its movement occurs as a finite process Hegel conceived as sublation. In terms of process, all the infinite can be is an incremental movement of the finite, an expanding horizon. Since thought must be of the finite to be about being, its work is continuous and interminable. Hegel's analysis of the Ego, as a negating encounter with an Other of itself, as freedom and rationality, suggests that its being is an infinite potentiality for being, but not that it can ever comprehend being with finality merely by thinking the universal. What rationality and freedom -that infinite essence of the self - allow is an interminable process of sublation wherein finitude is continuously transcended incrementally, if never with finality. Within this process the self develops and realizes its finite potentiality for being.

Heidegger posed the fundamental ontological question, "What is the meaning of Being?" Hegel suggested that negativity define not only being as such, but also finite beings that exist. Existentially rephrased in terms of Hegelian negativity, the Heideggerian question of the meaning of being becomes "Who or what is the Other?" The self, a finite being, exists only in relation to Others, alien to itself. Of itself, it is nothing and must become something Other than it is. It acquires an identity from its dialectical relationship to alien Others. The being of this self is always in question and a question for itself, as Heidegger observed.

Hegel earlier observed the negativity of the self implies that freedom is its being. Finite beings, especially the self, are a potentiality for being Other than they are at any given moment. Their being is a process of development. Ontological negativity, existentially expressed, is a developmental process of alienation and dealienation. The truth about being is revealed existentially in the whole process of dealienation, self-development and self-realization. Forced by the negativity of human need, desire, frustration and human suffering, truth is revealed in outcomes of alienation and successful dealienation. Although an alien Other always provides the impetus to know the truth, authoritative Others cannot pre-establish or dictate what shall be true of being. Rather, the truth must be learned through an agony of coping with the alienating finitude of self-existence.

The question, "Who or what is the Other?" arises existentially as an Other, alien to the self, is encountered. However, the self is not a privileged being: encountering itself likewise as an alien Other. Initially, the self is uncomprehended, strange, hidden, lacking coherence, unstructured by most human needs, desires and aims. Through a negating existential interaction of self with alien Other(s), the question of being acquires an answer. The being of the self, initially an alien Other, is a potentiality for being which is realized by a process of negativity with respect to the alien Other. As self-realization progresses, alien Others are dealt with interactively. Being, thought about and acted upon, progressively acquires a coherent structure of meaning. As selves develop, every potentiality for being is realized and the meaning of being is revealed. The process is continuous and interminable. Answering what the Other is simultaneously answers who the self is. So the question of being is always being asked and answered by a potentially infinite number of human experiences in a world driven by negativity, characterized by finitude and temporal sequences of alteration in being.

Self-Development

Hegel claimed the self to be a finite being who develops in relation to Others alien to itself. Existentialism claimed the being of the self to be a perpetual question answerable by its freedom. Granting both claims, the self is more than negating freedom and blind self-assertive conatus. For it is also a being who has the capacity for rationality. Moreover, it does have an essential nature consisting of universal biological needs imperative for its survival. These needs are to be satisfied by its desires and intentional self-activity in relation to the alien Other(s) and to a community of its fellows. Thus, the self is not merely a nullity. Its essential nature consists of needs, desires, rationality and freedom. These are integrated into a singular social being whose existence is an encounter with and response to alienating finitude.

Intentional self-active beings become something Other over time in response to sensing some deficiency in themselves or the environment. Desire is an experience of something that is not the case, but ought to be the case: or, something that is the case, but ought to be different. Sensing some deficiency and responding with intentional activity may be associatively induced, hypothetically imagined, or thought through by conceiving complex means-ends relationships toward and within the environment. The sensing of whatever is wanted may make of desire a drive, aim or goal. A seeking and transforming to satisfy desire implies some degree of intelligence along with some degree of freedom. Desires often issue from deliberation and planning. Complex social imperatives and ratiocination can create a desire and a sense of obligation to fulfill it.

The self is a being who develops and so realizes its potentiality for being. Its identity is acquired through how it responds to alien Others as it develops. Self-development begins in narcissism. Its primary form is symbiotic union with a nurturer. A primitive narcissistic self is a helpless bundle of biological needs completely dependent upon nurturing Others. Cognition and motility are undeveloped. Satisfaction of need is only constrained by what nurturing Others may refuse to provide. A narcissistic self is unconstrained by any internalization of social demands, since it has insufficiently developed cognitive skills necessary to satisfy its own needs. Narcissistic self-existence is exhausted by demands made upon nurturing Others and dependency upon them for fulfillment. Narcissistic desire disregards finitude. Nevertheless, this is impossible as finitude intrudes casting narcissistic desire aside in favor of higher socialized forms. Without symbiosis, narcissism cannot be maintained. However, a developmental fixation in a narcissistic posture may persist into adult life even after securing a modicum of rationality and freedom by a normal process of socialization.

As the self develops its natural capacity for rationality and freedom, narcissism is replaced by egoism. Still, an egoistic self is socially alienating. For its fellows are valued only instrumentally for the satisfaction of narcissistic desire. They exist to be manipulated, exploited and discarded like any common object when found no longer useful. Herein, the egoistic self enters the realm of the immoral. There, the desires of other selves go unacknowledged. If their desires do not count, then they may be considered radically different, possibly subhuman, although human. Thus, they cannot make equal claim to the satisfaction of desire. Immorality and evil has its source in narcissistic egoism, in an absence of acknowledging the natural equality of the desires and claims of other selves.

Acknowledging the universality of every individual with respect to the satisfaction of needs and desires forms the basis of morality and civilized society. Egoism founders upon conflict between selves whose relationship can only consist of dominance and submission rather than genuine reciprocity. A socialized self painfully learns to acknowledge and satisfy the desires of his fellows in exchange for their satisfying some of his own. Customs, norms, roles, practices and laws regulate the reciprocal satisfaction human needs and desires. Since these are universal to human nature, they make an equal claim among individuals. To acknowledge this provides a foundation for morality, social justice, law and institutions supporting them. In fact, to make and acknowledge equal claim with other individuals to the satisfaction of desire is the social cornerstone of western civilization. From this flows recognition of the dignity of each individual, as well as his personal liberty, his rights and obligations as a citizen, his equality under the law, and equality of opportunity.

Replacing an egoistic with a social self occurs through an interpersonal dialectic. Both selves appear opposed, requiring a compromising reconciliation in which the substitute satisfies some of the desires of what it replaces while satisfying social requirements. Dealienation requires the self to want and in fact become what the community demands. When complete socialization is achieved, a narcissistic and egoistic self is renounced and transformed into a socially sustaining contributor with a predefined social role. Narcissistic and egoistic desire is channeled and controlled in service to the social unit of which the self is a member and from which it gets social rewards and personal satisfaction. When the self wants to be and has in fact become what the community wants it to be, socialization is nearly complete. Until then, the self is presumed alienated in its social dimension. However, the question remains as to whether or not dealienation is successfully effected only by processes of socialization.

Psychoanalysis and existentialism describe an over-socialized self. Alienated from the satisfaction of its own desires, the self becomes neurotic and inauthentic. It is not free to express its desires. Outlets for self-expression are blocked by its bondage to a social self, which is an alien Other. Being so defined and controlled, the alienated self is not free to realize its own potentiality for being. Its social bondage is maintained coercively by means that are non-rational or irrational. An over-socialized self is alienated from its powers of rationality and freedom and from any authentic potentiality for realizing its being.

Just as an under-socialized narcissistic or egoistic self is socially alienated, so too is an over-socialized repressed self alienated from realizing its authentic potentiality. With the contemporary decline of family and religion - those primary socializers of children and youth - a permissive popular culture under-socializes the self. Attitudes such as, *anything goes* and *if it feels good, its OK* predominates. Alienation reappears in the guise of drug addiction and violent criminality. Both under-socialization and over-socialization in fact alienate the self that each one creates. This demonstrates that socialization is not equivalent to dealienation as many philosophers such as Hegel presumed. A social self, although more developed than its narcissistic and egoistic predecessors, is not necessarily a dealienated self; or one who has attained a capacity for successful dealienation.

Rationality and freedom are essential powers allowing the self to cope with alienating finitude. Thus, realizing its identity is to some degree a product of exercising these powers. When they are suppressed, a specifiable profile of an alienated self emerges. Its being remains deficient with unrealized potentiality. Its being also remains limited, by the world, its fellows and itself. What or who is alien to itself solely determines its destiny. In fact, such a self is not a *who*, but a *what* or an *it*. Its being is reified, as Sartre understood it, a Heideggerian *theyself*, a Freudian repressed self. It remains unconscious of what or who it is, and its desires conform to the demands of what or who controls it. Since it does not think or act for itself, it can be easily deceived, cynically manipulated and emotionally controlled. It is victimized and dependent upon an alien Other to satisfy its needs and desires. Its being is constructed for it by the Other as, for example, by public opinion, polling, focus groups, or media image spin.

Reified into an object of social utility, apathy and isolation from community involvement are common outcomes. With respect to intellect, alienation is a world not making sense, standing as Other in opposition to the self. As strictly determined by the Other, an alienated self is not authentic. Without the power to think and act for itself, the alienated self is not autonomous. No doubt the self is an alien Other in so far as it is undeveloped in being and meaning. No doubt, the self requires the Other for it to develop and realize who it is. But the self can never discover who it is, if it mistakes itself to be nothing but the Other.

While an alien Other is necessary for the self to develop, it is not entirely defined by the Other(s). For the self develops itself through its own needs, desires, rationality and freedom. The latter two are intrinsic powers of every self. Yet, they are also a potentiality that can develop or atrophy depending upon whether they are exercised. When exercised, the self becomes to a greater degree something of its own making, a being existing autonomously and authentically. Then, alien Other(s) do not dominate the self, but rather serve as a foil for self-development. The self does not simply obey the dicta of powerful authoritative Others and so become merely what they require. Rather, the self can respond to overcome the limit they impose. The means adopted can be in principle infinitely variable depending upon the circumstances encountered. Clearly, intelligence is indispensable for success. The crucial question is whether the self has within its powers of rationality and freedom a guide sufficient for the task of dealienation. While this is not obviously true, if it were, then autonomy and authenticity would be marks of character necessary for dealienation.

It has often been philosophically proclaimed that natural inclination can enslave the self. Narcissistic or egoistic desires often do this. Yet, neither natural inclination nor desires are, of themselves, alienating. Rather, they are an initial response to alienating finitude. The complete and successful response that satisfies desire requires the self develops and applies rationality and freedom. These powers define its spirituality, which is only expressed partially and negatively by the suppression of natural inclination and desire. Rational freedom is more completely and positively expressed when serving as a means for dealienation by meeting the demands posed by natural inclination and desire within a social context. One's behavior must factor in the Other(s). This requires the prohibition of unlimited self-seeking, postponement of gratification, and substituted objects of desire. The needs and desires defining self-existence cannot be suppressed. If severely inhibited or psychologically repressed by non-rational or irrational means, they re-appear in disguise as neurosis or psychosis, which are dysfunctional to self and community.

"Why evil?" is a baffling question for humanity. A gestalt approach to understanding evil can be helpful. An evildoer is the integration in being of physical, biological, psychological and sociological aspects of a whole. In addition to a moral consideration of the question of evil, it bears analysis from psychological and sociological perspectives. The question is clarified when cast in terms of unresolved psychic conflicts and defective socialization. Such explanations of the dynamics governing evil do not excuse it. For even when we understand how an evil self is formed, we still recognize moral degeneracy and demand its removal. Moral responsibility is still required of every self possessing some capacity for freedom and rationality. No self can be permitted an unlimited satisfaction of desire which causes unnecessary suffering. Such behavior alienates every self.

Narcissism is the root of evil. Unable to acknowledge the needs and desires of his fellows, the narcissist is so self-absorbed as to be oblivious to anything they need, want or suffer. Without any real consciousness of one's fellows, there is also no conscience regarding anything or anyone that may cause their suffering. When their suffering does not matter, the potentiality for evil doing becomes enormous and the actuality of it inevitable. The narcissist does evil without even caring about it. Where there is no social reciprocity of needs and desires among selves, community becomes impossible. The narcissistic self, if it can be said to be one, exists in social isolation, parasitically through symbiosis, or by the altruistic compassion of its fellows. For without acknowledged social dependency and reciprocity there can be no mutual satisfaction of most needs and desires of any self that would ensure its survival. Thus, narcissism is self-limiting and self-alienating.

Although it is a normal advance beyond narcissism to a higher level of social self-development, egoism has a potential for causing evil. Egoistic conduct is a product of socialization, including a partial development of rationality and freedom. The social consequences of conduct are calculated prior to its execution in words and deeds. Social reciprocity is understood and practiced as well as the art of psychological manipulation by the skilled egoist. Yet, although the needs and desires of one's fellows are acknowledged, they are always subordinated to self-seeking interest. When self-seeking causes evil, it is usually deliberate. The consciousness and conscience of the egoist are fully operative. Evil doing is blameworthy, since the egoistic self knows that it is responsible for the suffering it causes.

The narcissist who lacks consciousness of his fellows and a conscience from his own sense of agency is blameless for causing suffering. Not so for the egoist who is developed enough to know better. Whereas the narcissist has no friends, the egoist only calls a friend anyone useful to satisfying his interests. With limited social reciprocity, the egoist is less self-alienated than the narcissist. Although advanced beyond narcissism, egoistic socialization remains incomplete. For when the suffering caused by self-interest does not matter to the egoist, he will invariably suffer social sanctions. Refusing to acknowledge the equal claim of the needs, desires and suffering of one's fellows reaps the same in some measure from them. Socialization, arrested in narcissism or egoism, explains the psycho-sociological basis of evil.

The preferred definition of evil - causing unnecessary suffering - is an operational one that tests any experience. Beyond this, evil is herein viewed as a special case of alienating self-existence. Moreover, evil is more comprehensively understood in terms of socialization dynamics. Fixated or perverted self-development explains how evil is humanly created. Socialization arrested in narcissistic or egoistic self-seeking behavior causes evil. So do the common perversions of sadism and masochism. Both inflict unnecessary suffering and so can be considered species of evil. Both separately or together, involve the suffering of guilt and punishment, psychologically and sociologically inflicted. The dominance and submission required by either, or both together, leave opposing demands of self and community unresolved.

Suffering continues with obsessive or compulsive sado-masochistic behavior without satisfactory consummation.

Neuroses and psychoses scientifically describe evil and a profoundly alienated self-existence. The emotions and behavior of the self do not express its authentic needs and desires. Rather, the desires of a presumed authoritative Other(s) alien to its own desires dominate self-existence. An alien Other(s) maintains social control by teaching the self to feel guilty. Notwithstanding the theological doctrine of original sin, an innocent secular self is persuaded of its culpability toward those presumed victimized by its society or history. Convinced of its guilt, of not measuring up to an alien standard imposed upon it, and filled with low self-esteem, the self is made ready to be socially controlled.

The penance or restitution prescribed by the alien authoritative Other(s) presumably assuages guilt. Instead, the self is made to suffer punishment and inflict it. Such unnecessary suffering is evil. The ensuing sado-masochistic behavior then becomes a demonstration of social control usually exercised by a governing elite. Guilt is maintained, not assuaged. Those repressed needs and desires definitive of authentic self-existence are ignored and this is what truly alienates the self. Thus, the behavior of such a socially alienated self is dysfunctional to itself and its community. Satisfactory self-seeking is perverted into evil doing not only by earlier narcissistic and egoistic phases of self-development, but also by a later more socialized sado-masochism. All these represent a dysfunctional, fixated, perverted and incomplete socialization process. Without rationality and freedom brought to bear, the opposing demands of self and community cannot be resolved. Alienation and evil inevitably result.

Evil doing teaches us to discern what is good and what is normative for human conduct and development. Wisdom is acquired in learning from the historical experience of a suffering humanity. Such wisdom must be culturally transmitted so that we recognize it when we see it. Narcissism, egoism and sado-masochism psychologically and sociologically describe the roots of evil. A self, so disposed, disregards rationality and so cannot be free to realize its true potentiality. Its behavior is counterproductive. Dealienation and self-realization cannot proceed with a self opposed to itself and its fellows. Invariably, social opposition blocks any self-objectification that is narcissistic, egoistic or sado-masochistic. In turn, social opposition blocks the formation of a complete relationship of self with any larger social whole, be it community or humanity, not to mention its own God.

Socialization

Dealienation is a process of responding to the alienating finitude of self-existence. The result of dealienation is an objectified self composing a humanized world. It is a continuous historical product of self-objectification as Hegel claimed. Self-objectification is the product of a fundamental process of dealienation accomplished by human work. Alienating finitude makes work an ontological necessity. Thus, work has a far deeper significance than is commonly recognized by simply holding a job to earn a living. From the perspective of its originator, it would seem then that the work of self-objectification is intended to achieve the aim of dealienation. However, from a more universal perspective, the result of self-objectifying work enters into a complex social dialectic with the needs, interests and purposes of other persons. Hence, the work of one person may become the condition of alienation for another person, and when that work loses its original significance, it may even become alien to its originator.

Self-objectifying work has a profound ontological significance. Working and work product reveal the meaning of being, if not occasionally creating it. The dealienating work endeavor also reveals the being of the self. What and who it is, is what it does with the alien Other(s). It, or they, does not define the self. Rather, the self discovers who and what it is by the work it does with them. They are the vehicles for self-discovery. Working and work product present reality in both its subjective and objective aspects as Hegel might have put it. Just as work is a fundamental response to alienation, a dealienating process with subjective aim, so work when completely objectified in a public social context, may again present alienation. The dialectic of working is a continuous process of alienation and dealienation.

The ideal case of dealienating work occurs when there is perfect knowledge of intention underlying human action, the circumstances surrounding it, and a perfect correspondence of outcome with intention. All the impediments to dealienation point toward the condition of its success, a will free to act upon its intentions and subordinated to rationality. However, given the finitude of self and its world, the ideal rarely occurs and only in the simplest circumstances. Most often, the alien Other(s) intrudes in unexpected ways that make a self-objectifying work product itself an alien Other. In the work product, something of the self is abstracted and reduced to something external. With the reification, comes a loss of control over what the work product signifies. Its meaning invariably changes with time, place, unintended consequences, chance, accidental circumstances, misinterpretation, re-interpretation, and various uses other persons attach to it. When the social feedback from self-objectifying work negates its purpose, the significance of the work is distorted into something unexpected, unintended and possibly unwanted. If the social feedback is lacking or disinterested, the identity-establishing aim of self-objectification is thwarted. Without its originating significance, work simply exists as mere impersonal fact, as mere object for somebody else, as not one's own, and so incomplete in meaning and being.

Self-objectification through work can be problematical and even alienating. Marx viewed it this way by pointing out how alienating the work product can become when it is neither owned nor enjoyed by the worker whose labor produced it. Once my work is public, it is no longer strictly mine, no longer bears only the significance I gave it when produced. In fact, its significance can even change for me personally as I change my views and circumstances relating to it. Therefore, self-objectifying work is partially definitive of myself, but never completely so. It is who I was or am now, but not who I may become tomorrow. Work is an exercise in finitude through which we become aware of our own limitations and those set for us by nature, culture and historical circumstance. The work we are compelled to do represents a potentially infinite variety of human responses to a potentially infinite variety of alienating circumstances confronted by life itself. Being an outcome of an interminable process of dealienation, no work product escapes alienating finitude. Work defines human destiny.

Within any group working for a common cause is found disagreement among individuals, attempts to influence others in the group by praise or condemnation. The attempts by individuals to influence the common work among themselves produces a trans-personal outcome effected by strong self-assertiveness and interpersonal compromise. Collective work, always a socially dynamic interaction of individuals, is a gestalt—greater than the sum of constituent interests, motives and intentions, but created by them. In effect, what is signified by the individual as the common cause is not what is signified by its realization. A collective social work product expresses something substantially different from that of an involved individual or collection of them. The social resultant is something unexpected, unintended, unpredictable, novel in character, previously unknown, mysterious and strange. The impression is that in common work, we are flying blind, so to speak, unaware of what is really driving us to do what we do. It is as if the outcome is pre-ordained by some force or power other than our own and outside us. So, at a social level, the interactive dialectic reveals an alienation of its own, an alienation even more profound than that experienced by any single individual.

Self-objectifying work, be it individual or collective, is infected by negativity of one kind or another. In a contemporary world of bureaucratic institutions, the law of unintended consequences often prevails in executing social policy and government programs. The original intent of a law or regulation is frequently circumvented by what special interest groups or individuals make out of it to satisfy their own purposes. Good intentions seem to generate contradictory results. As is often said, "The road to hell is paved with good intentions." A confluence of diverse social interests by groups as well as individuals creates a degree of complex social interaction with consequences impossible to predict or even understand in advance of policy implementation. The alienating outcome of collective work can be explained by the indeterminacy of self-existence, the fact of human freedom and incomplete knowledge of the social dialectic. This is certainly a simpler explanation and less problematical than supposing individuals personally engaged in collective work to be the mere dupes of a Hegelian Geist.

Socialization is the work of developing a self-concept enabling dealienating self-objectification. Socially driven negating processes progressively develop a self-concept from narcissism to a completely socialized self. Socialization transforms primitive desires by creating substitutes. Antisocial desires and behavior is prohibited by saying *no* and coercively by a variety of punishments. The process continues until renunciation of certain self-seeking desires is internalized. Overt social prohibition is then no longer necessary as the self punishes itself with guilt for a violation of its *ego ideal*.

Both Hegel and Freud understood the process of socialization to be dialectical. In addition, both understood that no desire could be completely renounced. A substitute is always found for desires that are socially prohibited and self-renounced. The substitutes define a social self-concept. The desires of a socialized self are expanded in number and complexity. Such a self is often called sophisticated in tastes and lifestyle. A socialized self has identified with cultural norms and social roles provided by various social institutions. A rational identification has explicitly expressible reasons why it is worthy that are derived from personal experience of alternatives. These have been worked through and thought over. When one identification is seen as better than another for good reasons, the mechanism for sustaining it is free of unconscious unresolved oppositions. Then the social product of identification is not unstable and liable to disintegration. Rationally based identification is not a fiction, but a fact for both youths and adults alike.

Desire is a constant in the process of dealienation. It never changes its alienating impetus or dealienating aim, but its object can change. Desire can be transformed in two ways. It can remain the same with a substitution of its object. Freud thought of repression in this way. Instinctual drives always remain the same, but are sublimated with substitute objects. However, it may be possible for desire to change with a substitute object. Certainly, the significance of a particular desire changes with a substitute object. With this, the quality of desire cannot remain the same. It is experienced as something transcending its original meaning. This is what Hegelian sublation implies. When sublated, the being and meaning of something is transformed. It incorporates the original with an additional difference. It is more differentiated, richer in meaning, significance, value and quality of experience. Might it not be possible for desire with a substitute object to be a transformed desire, which possesses only traces of its original meaning? When primitive desire is sublated, it is literally transformed with a socially constructive aim. Primitive desire then gets its universal transcendent significance different from its original form. Socialization of desire does more than overlay it with a social aim providing its original primitive expression with a thin social veneer.

Culture is created and sustained by the lives of individuals. In order to receive the benefits of culture, the individual must sacrifice unlimited satisfaction of personal desires and unlimited self-seeking. The renunciation or alienation of these aspects of individuality is a necessary first negation in a process of forming culture. The process of finding an adequate substitute is a work of identification by the individual. This work can be non-rational, coerced by rewards and punishments provided within the family or through other social institutions of such as religion or the state. Educative institutions also provide indoctrination and training necessary for an identification of individual with culture. Of course, there are always customs, traditions, and laws. Identification can also be non-coercive as when one is convinced of the value of one's culture upon rational grounds. In this case, reasons can be provided to support cultural beliefs and practices. This is a sophisticated way of making a cultural identification. However, whether the identification is made non-rationally or rationally, once made, the individual has found the necessary substitute social self, replacing a narcissism and egoism that do not sustain culture.

Socialization is a continuous process of self-identification. What or who the self identifies with determines its self-concept which, when self-projected by self-objectifying work, has alienating or dealienating consequences. What the self identifies with are cultural norms. Who the self identifies with are social roles. Both cultural norms and social roles provide the self with an identity. This is obviously true. But, the question Hegelian philosophy raises is whether identity can only be secured by identifying with norms and social roles established by authoritative Others such as parents, peer group, popular culture, community, educative, religious, economic, civic and governmental social institutions. Yet, cultural norms and social roles do not appear to be pre-established by authoritative Others as Hegel believed. Both continuously change as witnessed by an older generation unable to understand the lifestyle of its youth. If cultural norms and social roles were pre-established, then there could be no new lifestyles. However, the evidence is overwhelmingly to the contrary.

It may be believed that total identification and participation in social life signifies an absence of alienation. This belief is plausible, but false. Complete unconscious submersion in the group, or Hegelian *Sittlichkeit*, can be alienating as witnessed by totalitarian societies. Hegel understood that self-consciousness is compelled to dialectically develop beyond *Sittlichkeit*. When culture or community poses alienating conditions, an unconscious identification and participation is tantamount to being manipulated and coerced by an Other alien to oneself. The suppression of anything beyond the norms and social roles prescribed for the self by traditional authoritative Others often denies certain needs and desires vital to self-realization. Such repression may end in neurosis with unnecessary and unacceptable loss to the self and community.

The psychic product of self-identification with a cultural norm or social role has been variously called identity, self-consciousness, self-concept, ego ideal, or social self. Whatever called, it is formed by the negation of desire by an authoritative Other(s). Its demands and prohibitions are alien to the self who is forced to accommodate with a substitute satisfying its desire. Although the self is initially given an identity from the interpersonal dynamics of a dialectical opposition between its own desires and those of the alien authoritative Other(s), its identity is not reducible to what the Other says it is or acknowledges it to be. For the self is a work in progress meeting its own needs and desires in a social context. Thus, self-identity continuously changes with the particular conditions of alienating finitude and self-objectifying work.

The source of changing norms and roles is to be found in needs and desires not predictable in advance of self-existence. This implies that the very process of dealienating self-existence generates novel cultural norms and social roles. From an existential perspective, the self has a far greater degree of autonomy and authenticity than either Hegel or Freud suspected. Its being encompasses far more than any pre-established definition of it by an Other, no matter what or who the Other might be. Since the self must existentially create its own identity, its being is far more than any particular social definition imposed upon it. Thus, it is not necessary to have authoritative Others alien to the self completely define and determine what or who it shall be. Doing so has alienating consequences.

A process of negation between self and Other generally describes appropriation. The self temporally alters in being, becoming Other than what it once was. An appropriation of the alien Other is a good Hegelian beginning for understanding dealienation. However, this definition is incomplete. For, it could mean that the self merely appropriates something alien to itself. Consequently, its being would consist of unreconciled oppositions or a bifurcated self, acknowledged by Hegel and Freud, even if differently described. Therefore, it must be the nature of the appropriation that would determine whether alienation remains or dealienation is successful.

Appropriating the Other, when understood as a process of identification has several aspects: identification with *what* or *whom*, the manner in which it is carried out, and its consequences. If *what* or *who* remains alien to the self, then self-identification does not permit successful dealienation. A self that renounces its own desires by identifying with a substitute provided by an authoritative Other may remain alienated from what it renounced and alienated by the consequences for self-existence of the dicta of the authoritative Other. Identifications are always tested by their consequences, which are found to be alienating or dealienating for self-existence. If the identification, which is a substitute for an antisocial desire, fails, then alienation may well be compounded. For neither the substitute nor the prohibited desire can be satisfied. Moreover, the consequences of repressing desire with an alienating substitute are devastating to the self. It becomes disabled, neurotic, as described by Freudian repression.

The essential meaning of authenticity is to make something an expression of oneself. One way of being authentic is to identify with a social norm or role, projecting it with self-objectifying work. Hegel thought God's laws and pre-established social roles require self-identification and are the necessary bases of self-objectification giving freedom its legitimate purpose. From such a view, it might be thought that any successful identification is sufficient to establish authenticity. However, this is false when the Other with which the self identifies remains alien to its essential nature, or produces alienating consequences when self-projected and objectified. Whether the Other alienates in these ways is determined by the very process of self-identification. When it proceeds irrationally, or is non-rationally coerced by natural rewards and punishments, what or whom the self has identified with remains an alien Other opposed to some aspect of its nature, be it rationality, freedom, need or desire. Without satisfying all of these, the self is dominated in some way by an alien Other. Authentic self-expression and self-realization are then not possible.

An Other appropriated by rational self-identification cannot be alien to the self, since it is a product of its own essential nature and dealienating capacity. The result of rational self-identification is then necessarily an authentic self-realization of potentialities for being residing in the very nature of the self, not in the nature of an alien Other. A rational self-identification with the Other is then both successful dealienation and authentic self-realization.

True, the Other often initiates a process of dealienation by a sometimes painful socialization process. However, the Other need not serve as a pre-established and fixed norm or role model simply to be uncritically or slavishly imitated. Rather, the Other is suggested to the self with the purpose of assisting it to maximize its needs and desires within a structured social context. What or whom it suggests the self become, enables it to realize its authentic hidden potentiality for being. So, when the self accepts the suggestion from the Other, it is not suppressing or repressing its essential nature. Neither is it simply obeying a law or the dicta of an unquestioned authoritative Other. For it is free to change the norm or role it has identified with to comport with the conditions of self-existence. This happens continuously as dealienation proceeds with a projected self-concept and self-objectifying work. The Other, then, does not dictate, but enables self-development and self-realization. The result is sometimes quite novel and not entirely predictable. It reflects the nature of the self as need, desire, rationality and freedom.

How role-playing effects the authenticity or autonomy of the self determines the extent of its dealienating capability. If the self behaves only as *they* prescribe and not from its own choice and conviction, its character loses both autonomy and authenticity. It may not itself be free, but live merely a shadow life dictated by the Other(s). Such considerations indicate that role-playing can cut both ways. By contributing to the larger social whole, role-playing dealienates. But, if not expressing the autonomy and authenticity of the self, role playing can just as well alienate the self from realizing its own desires and unique potentiality. Contemporary examples abound of how oppressive and restrictive social role stereotypes can be. Every woman is destined to be nurturing wife and mother and not much else, like it or not; and, every man cannot nurture, but is destined to be the breadwinner, like it or not.

Freedom

Ontological negativity is necessary to think, to be, and to become. Taking the form of intentional self-activity, ontological negativity signifies freedom. It is a capacity to intentionally become or change something. To be conscious of the world or self, and to think, is to intend an Other distinct from self. Thought is an activity, which intends the Other, representing it with symbols possessing implication. Just as thought is a negating activity of symbolic signification, so also is freedom a negating activity with conative intention directing self-existence in the world. From the perspective of ontological negativity, thought and being are continuous. Freedom creates this continuity, extending it in either direction. Thought, even at the highest level of logical abstraction is translatable to being by existentially directed intentional self-activity. Human freedom is commonly manifested by self-activity following thought. The reverse also occurs. Just as thinking makes one free, so freedom makes one think.

That freedom resides in rationality has been asserted through the ages from ancient philosophy to contemporary psychology. Without thought, freedom is not possible. Freedom is encountered in the very activity of thinking, which represents reality of the Other(s) through a public language, and with abstract symbolic codes. Imaginary models of reality can be constructed by thinking which contemplates logical possibilities, and anticipates future events and behavioral consequences. Strategies relating chosen mean1s to resulting ends can be formulated to secure human purposes. The ability to think secures freedom in both its negative and positive aspects. Reasoning allows the self to obtain or avoid consequences, satisfy desires, achieve aims, and successfully deal with the Other(s). Thinking can liberate the self from the alienating Other thus allowing it to transform its world and even itself to correspond with its desires and satisfy its needs. Moreover, reasoning provides the freedom to behave in ways not pre-determined by natural inclination or emotional impulse. Gratification can be postponed, given a different priority, or even suppressed to secure certain advantages.

Rationality and freedom are correlative concepts, coextensive in signification. One cannot be rational without being free and one cannot be free without being rational. Without either, self-development and self-realization are blocked. Intentional self-activity, self-objectifying work, overcoming obstacles, satisfaction of human needs and desires display the relatedness of rationality and freedom, or *rational freedom*, more truly named. With both properly conceived and operative, self-existence is autonomous and authentic. Herein lies an adequate response to every possible kind of alienation.

Freedom and rationality are the twin pillars of western civilization. Both express the spiritual essence of being human. Together they define intelligent behavior and constitute the human power necessary for dealienation. The negativity of being in general and alienating finitude of self-existence in particular provides the impetus for their development within the individual and throughout history. Even if we do not know their precise relationship, we intuitively sense their connection. Taken singly, either can alienate the self. Without rationality, freedom is impossible. Without freedom, rationality is severely restricted, if not entirely sacrificed to irrational impulse or non-rational social forces.

Of great concern, then, is to precisely understand how freedom and rationality are related - their common signification. Understood as a whole, a concept of rational freedom enables the self and has far-reaching dealienating potency. The importance of rational freedom cannot be overemphasized. Authentic self-realization becomes possible with it. Without it, alienation persists and the self becomes sick and atrophies. Any loss of freedom is not often tolerated, and its complete loss is intolerable. An essential power, it is both something needed and deeply desired, not very different from basic physiological needs. It could even be said that freedom is a human drive with dealienating aim. Beyond this primitive characterization, freedom and rationality require cultivation much like any human discipline.

Whereas negative freedom is a primitive response, as in just saying *no*, positive freedom requiring rationality must be developed by degrees as a power of the self to cope with alienating finitude. Rationality, conceived as a developed ability to consider and evaluate all possibilities, both expresses freedom and enables it. The philosophical habit of thinking about something in multiple perspectives, or *outside the box* so to speak, is to be free. Restricted conceptions of rationality make of it some kind of logic or some set of propositions presumed authoritative or lawful. However, rationality is better conceived as a power of the self establishing freedom and maximizing its exercise. Failure to comprehend the intimate relationship between rationality and freedom can only lead to alienating misunderstandings. Without rationality, the self loses its dealienating capacity and sinks into an alienating abyss of domination by irrational antisocial impulse, by non-rational forces of social conformity or destiny.

Rationality provides the possibility of liberation from alienating conditions. When rationality is translated into intentional activity, dealienation is underway. Freedom driven by rationality tends to dealienate whereas, freedom driven by the irrational or non-rational tends to alienate. An initial experience of freedom is through a self-consciousness negatively expressed by denial, refusal and rebellion. This negative freedom rejecting the limiting Other, while necessary to dealienation, is only its first step. Just saying *no* acknowledges some kind of alienation, but is insufficient to dealienate.

A self cannot develop without in some way transcending *no*. Further negation is required by thought and its extension with intentional self-activity. This is rationality in its most general signification wherein alternatives to the limiting Other are revealed, possibilities of being then actualized as the self realizes what and who it is. Hegel drew attention to a self who does not transcend the first negating response signifying alienation, therefore remaining trapped in it. Without rationality, primitive freedom becomes an absolute, a capricious negativity with destructive outcome never affirming anything of the self or world. Emotionally, the self is left with anxiety, melancholy and despair reflected in attitudes of skepticism, cynicism and nihilism. Hegel's analysis of negative freedom and its alienating consequences are valuable and instructive, notwithstanding his limited conception of rationality as universality and confusion of rationality with the dicta of traditional authority.

Any successful exercise of freedom requires a fairly high degree of rationality. In fact without rationality, freedom is liable to failure. Considered as mere means without rational direction, freedom is ambiguous. It can be used to secure anything and so is a potentiality for either good or evil. Therefore, the critical question about freedom always concerns the purpose of its use. In fact, the value of freedom is determined by the purposes it serves and the consequences of its application. These can in large part be determined by character or personality. A narcissistic or egoistic self will use freedom in counterproductive ways that stunt self-development, prevent self-realization and result in social isolation or worse. A completely dependent narcissistic self cannot be free. Neither can an independent egoistic self, pursuing its desires without regard to social consequences. In fact freedom is maximized and guaranteed by certain restrictions placed upon self-seeking that would cause unnecessary suffering and social disintegration. A misdirection of freedom is most easily observed with defectively socialized selves whose behavior is psychologically compulsive, obsessive or sado-masochistic. In such cases, among others, the self is enslaved to non-rational or irrational forces that fixate development in dysfunctional patterns of behavior.

A self completely unconstrained has no freedom. For the alienating existential conditions generating it would be absent. Nobody ever had it or could possibly have it. Thus, *absolute freedom* is a theoretical fiction. Conceived as non-rational or irrational conatus, freedom becomes self-contradictory resulting in bondage. Freedom untempered by rationality isolates the self from culture and community. According to Hegel and even existentialists such as Sartre, a demand for absolute freedom is irrational and self-alienating. Unlimited freedom can only lead to a narcissism and egoism disregarding the dealienating claims of other selves.

Placed in the hands of a single individual, unlimited freedom permits the creation of evil and perversion. Hegel believed that historical periods such as the late Roman Empire and French Revolution bore witness to the egoistic excesses of tyrants whose will became law. The dictators and totalitarianism of first half of the twentieth century also confirm this. Given the historically alienating abuses of freedom and its future potential for evil, a distrust of personal freedom would seem justified. Its threatening aspect and dangerous exercise warrants social control. Yet, contemporary western culture promotes a permissive personal freedom. Can this expansion of freedom be trusted to produce a dealienating result? Or, would increasing personal freedom only lead to social disintegration, as notable social thinkers have feared?

Narrowly defined as license or unlimited self-seeking power, freedom presents the possibility of lawlessness and antisocial behavior with evil consequences. Of course, freedom then becomes potentially dangerous and destructive of self and society. Hence, from Plato onward, many philosophers have distrusted freedom and proposed to socially control it with rationality located in an authoritative Other. However, such a proposal also results in too narrowly defining rationality. Separated and placed in opposition, freedom and rationality are misconstrued with unfortunate alienating consequences. The dicta of an Other, whatever or whoever it might be, cannot be presumed either rational or authoritative. For nothing can be authoritative or presumed so for self-existence that is not critically evaluated, tested by experience and freely accepted with personal conviction.

The dicta of authoritative Others can only be validated by the power of a self, free to think and act upon what that dicta signifies for self-existence. A self both rational and free in the broadest sense listens to what the Other prescribes, evaluates it relative to existence, and tests the consequences of operating with it. A more broadly defined and integrated rational freedom relating to self-existence is required to establish the rationality and authoritativeness of anything prescribed for the self. Authoritative Others such as culture, custom, community, law or God may in fact alienate self-existence. If they do, they can be neither rational nor authoritative. How often have authoritative Others alienated the self by denying its needs, desires, and freedom to think and act for itself? That the dicta of an Other are neither rational nor authoritative is also proved when non-rational coercive means such as natural rewards and punishments are required for enforcement. Respect for authority compelled by assiduous indoctrination can create a disciplined self with repressed antisocial desires. However, they are liable to resurface out of control upon occasion.

Freedom is not adequately understood in the thinking of Hegel, Marx, Freud and existentialism or in the mind-set of a rationalized bureaucracy. For all these, the deficiency lies in an inability to integrate rationality with freedom. Either freedom or rationality is sacrificed. Hegelian freedom is reduced to obedience to traditional authority with rationality falsely located in its abstract dicta pre-established for self-existence. Marx sacrificed freedom to the presumed rationality of an economic pseudo-science and ideology. Freudian psychoanalysis dismissed rationality, subordinating it to irrational impulse and non-rational social forces resulting in neurosis. The existentialist glorification of irrational freedom makes it the source of alienation. Rationality is so completely overlooked that freedom cannot cope with an absurd existence, which the self must face with resignation. Bureaucracy completely replaces freedom with rule-bound rationality prohibiting innovative thought and action. These considerations indicate that rationality and freedom are complementary and must be integrated to achieve successful dealienation. Singly, either tends toward alienation and is insufficient for dealienation.

Freedom, considered as a power of the self, has dealienation as its aim. Thus, freedom is itself of inestimable value. But is freedom normative? Considered as a means to achieving any end, freedom is ambiguous and value-neutral. It cannot establish the end for which it is exercised. If freedom is mere means, it is not normative. The question then becomes what or who determines the end for which the self exercises it? Hegel made freedom a vehicle for the purposes of Geist, social institutions and traditional authority held to be ontologically superior to the self. The problem with this perspective on the question is that an Other, presumed authoritative for the self, establishes the aim of its freedom. However, authoritarianism, totalitarianism and collectivism alienate freedom of thought and action essential for dealienation. If neither freedom nor an authoritative Other can be normative for self-existence, then the question is what can be? Recasting the question in terms of alienation may be more fruitful.

What is true or right is normative for the self. Norms have to be universal in the sense of applying equally to everyone. If norms are not an outcome of dealienation, then their actual universality can be taken as evidence of their validity. However, this reduces what ought to exist to an empirical actuality, to what generally prevails, even with some exceptions. What ought to be the case is just what is and what the self should be or do is merely what everyone else is or does. Universality is here not absolute and the exceptions to the norm require explanations. Classical Greek and Christian explanations are that the exception results from an ignorance of what is truly good for us, or a perverse free will.

Considering norms to be validated by their actuality is problematical. For why should the self believe or do what everyone else believes or does? The mere fact of something actual does not make it normative. By such logic, anything can be justified. If what *they* do is immoral, so is what I do. Mere conformity is taken as establishing and validating the norm. Thought and choice are not required; just obedience to what everyone else thinks and does. Intellectual indolence and ignorance prevail. The hard process of experience testing and rational evaluation is avoided. Without this, normative significance vanishes. When not revealed existentially and by the power of rational freedom, the acceptance and promotion of a norm is inauthentic, abstract and alien to the self. Rather than a demand placed upon self-existence and determining it, what is true or right is an existential result of a dealienating process.

The acceptance of externally imposed norms, although providing the self with an identity, does not allow authentic self-realization. Norms governing self-existence must result from confronting alienating finitude with the power of rational freedom. Dealienating self-existence discovers and creates its norms. The history of humanity is a discovery of what it means to be human through suffering alienation and responding with dealienating activity. In this process, the self discovers who it is and what is normative for it. The history of western civilization has been a progressive discovery that every human being is rational and free. Human suffering and dealienation has been a working through in specific detail of the implications of rationality and freedom.

Whereas freedom cannot obligate one self to agree with another, rationality can do so. Free selves guided by rationality can arrive at consensus, even universal consensus at times when the reasons for a belief or course of action are overwhelming. Therefore, it would seem that a self who is both free and rational could be not only the locus of universal truth and value, but also its originator. The Sophists were right to say that *man is the measure of all things*, that humanity is the locus of truth and value. Culture, community, law and God are human creations and not the repositories of a rationality alien to the self.

A self merely reflective of the Other is not free, is not necessarily rational, is not authentic and has a destiny not of its own making. If dealienation is reduced to an identification and introjection of authority, then rational freedom is not operative in providing the self with an identity. The resulting identity is neither rational nor free. It is an identity established by an Other, alien to the self and its essential powers. Therefore, identification and introjection, although describing a natural process of maturation, may not signify dealienation. Rather, identification and introjection signify a non-rational psychological process, an immature commitment of faith without reasons, a blind trust in a controlling authority. Self-identity is constructed coercively by natural rewards and punishments. Moreover, a self-existence, confronted by coercive authority, is alienated not only from its own natural inclination, but also from the exercise of its own powers. Authentic self-realization is not possible. Natural processes of self-identification and introjection of authority may very well alienate the self from its authentic potentiality for being. The least that can be said is that successful dealienation requires something more than what is offered by the natural processes of socialization and maturation. An autonomous self can challenge and reject any authority not consistent with its own needs.

Alienated freedom is self-alienation in its most radical form. For what is lost is a general capacity for dealienation. Without freedom, there is no possible response to alienating finitude. Therefore, alienated freedom has a peculiar and special ontological status as an archetypal form of alienation, its worst case. Every self is condemned to be free by the fact of its finitude, the necessity of choosing with attendant consequences. The burden of freedom is to be responsible and accountable for personal behavior. A free self accepts the prospect of being wrong, making mistakes and being penalized. Punishments for failure or error can be severe, are always painful, and can be self-inflicted by remorse. As existentialists and various religious philosophers have claimed, being free brings with it a deep sense of guilt. For there are consequences regardless of whether the self chooses to act or not to act. Nobody enjoys being castigated, censured, criticized or ridiculed. Humiliation is never pleasant. The natural tendency is to avoid a public or private loss of respect, honor, status and esteem. Just as there is no escape from freedom, so there is no escape from its burden.

The way to escape the burden of freedom is to displace authority from the self to the Other, whatever or whomever it might be. When the stakes are high, the temptation can be overwhelming. Moreover, the self may not even be aware of displacing its freedom onto an authoritative Other. Or, it may rationalize doing so by presuming the authoritative Other to have wisdom superior to its own. The mere fact of authority and its power does not warrant allegiance. When misconceived as mere obedience to authority, freedom is dismissed.

Authoritarian control of freedom disconnects it from rationality. When this occurs, freedom loses its dealienating power. Freedom placed exclusively in service to authority invariably results in a loss of freedom. For simply being and doing what authority prescribes, may not be an exercise of freedom. Refusal of authority may not in fact be the path of error and loss of freedom as is often claimed. Only a trial of self-existence can prove such a claim. In fact, refusal may be the better choice. For refusal may well be the initial response to alienation and therefore a first step in a dealienating process.

The social consequences of freedom, in its primitive licentious form make morality and law necessary. Repression of primitive licentious freedom is socially necessary and justifiable. However, carried beyond this, such repression becomes counterproductive by interfering with the dealienating power of freedom. Since its aim is to satisfy basic human needs and desires arising from the alienating finitude of self-existence, freedom demands the maximum possible scope and minimum possible restriction. Exceptions are only justifiable and desirable when responding to specific human actions, which cause unnecessary human suffering, have antisocial consequences and promote social disintegration. Licentiousness and anarchy are enemies of freedom in so far as they subvert a structure of law intended to guarantee personal security and protect personal freedom from abuse.

Human rights follow an acknowledgment of rational freedom being the essential nature of every self. Just as that nature cannot be falsified, so rights cannot be surrendered voluntarily or by coercion. For a right is an expression of freedom with a specific content. Freedom is protected by specific rights with universal equal applicability to every individual. Each is obligated to acknowledge its universality. Rights signify a public respect for the autonomy and dignity of every individual. Essential kinds of freedom are made inviolate by rights, implicit in law or explicitly stated in a constitution upon which law is based. Just as freedom is an inalienable fact of being human, so are the rights guaranteeing an expression of that freedom.

Freedom for every self is maximized in a democratic organization of social life. A democratic culture is therefor worthy of acceptance and support by every self interested in liberty. The collective life of selves exercising their freedom creates a dynamic social fabric continuously responding to the circumstances of alienation encountered at any given historical moment. There is nothing sacrosanct about any social organization within which one lives. In fact, social organization other than democracy tends to diminish or even eliminate personal liberty, and this loss of freedom has been profoundly alienating to everyone. For this reason, totalitarianism has been found wanting and unworthy of self-identification and self-objectification.

In a free society, the individual may or may not choose to identify with or project cultural mores which tend to alienate him in some way. He may respond by ignoring them or experimenting with substitutes. Alternatively, he may rebel and change them through public advocacy or political activism. If successful, alienating mores or laws can be abandoned, changed, or replaced along with those social institutions that promote them. Responding in this manner allows individuals to make a difference and transforms culture within a social structure permitting rational freedom to flourish. Social institutions sustain norms established by the freedom of individuals.

The self-projection and self-objectification of each individual member of any group concretely defines how it exists and what it is. Free selves behaving rationally can create community. Rational freedom, whether potential or actual, is of the highest value to every individual. From this, and the fact that it creates community, follows a whole democratic civilization, which respects individual dignity demands personal liberty, equal rights and equal opportunity for everyone. Narcissistic or egoistic selves cannot create stable communities. Only a fully socialized self who is autonomous and authentic can do so. Both anarchic self-seeking and absolute power of authoritative Others generate similar alienating consequences. The history of western civilization is plausibly a progressive realization of the dealienating power of rational freedom, a potentiality of every self. The terrible human suffering of twentieth century wars was a working through of rational freedom. There was a worldwide rejection of totalitarianism. Freedom was asserted by the triumph of democracy. It has become a real worldwide possibility for the twenty-first century. The refusal of self-destructive nuclear war was a triumph of rationality currently undergoing near exponential growth with advances of scientific knowledge and technology.

Religion

Every religion is concerned with alienation, particularly with its manifestation in human suffering and mortality. These are religiously interpreted and ameliorated with general prescriptions for dealienation known as ways of salvation. Generally described, salvation is achieved by faith in, love of, and obedience to the dicta of an authoritative Other of the self, be it a prophet, God, or however defined. Salvation is promised or earned by a self-objectification of the faithful conforming to certain prescriptions involving love, prayerful contemplation and ritual observances. Religious moral prescriptions socialize the self and create a community of the faithful with all its attendant spiritual and practical benefits.

Religious socialization assists the family generally, by reinforcing the self-development of its youth, transmitting mores, and providing a sense of empathy with and compassion for the plight of others through charitable works. Historically, religion has provided a moral foundation for law and government effecting every social institution. Religious ritual celebrates significant life transitions with sacraments for birth, adulthood, marriage and death. Religion has actively confronted various alienating conditions of life and offered various palliative responses to human suffering which are more than resignation or mere opiates. Any adequate understanding of religion must consider its response to alienation from psychological and sociological perspectives. Without such an analysis, religion can be easily overlooked or dismissed as ignorance and superstition, an unfortunate conclusion indeed.

The alienating finitude of self-existence prompts a religious attitude and religious questions such as, "Who or what is God?" Or, in critically important and perplexing life situations lacking self-guidance, "What would God have me do?" Any chosen way of salvation answers such questions and provides self-identity. A religious orientation defines the self through its authoritative Other, its God. The self is alienated from its fellows and its God by a natural self-seeking disregarding the evil consequences of its behavior. An incompletely socialized self, be it narcissistic or egoistic, with unconstrained freedom, is by its very nature an evildoer. Freedom is problematical in its potentiality for evil doing and sin. Moreover, unconstrained freedom invariably results in sin, which disobeys one's own nature and God. Since the self is a blind conatus toward unlimited self-seeking desire, an authoritative Other is necessary to constrain the evil consequences of freedom. Fear of punishment and obedience to the commands of an authoritative Other socializes a primitive self, whose freedom is otherwise undisciplined and dangerous. A religious self fears its God, humbles itself, self-identifies with an identity pre-established by its God, and projects itself in the world with others in conformity therewith.

Religion presents an authoritarian conception of evil excellently depicted by the biblical myth of the fall. Evil doing is held to be disobedience of the self to its true definition as prescribed by the dicta of an authoritative Other. However, disobedience to authority is too narrow and problematical a conception of evil. What it presumes true of human nature is dubious at best. That it presumes self-existence can be pre-established by an authoritative Other is falsified by a being who is free, rational and self-realizing. An authoritarian conception of evil is inadequate.

The paradigmatic case of authoritarian defined evil is a self choosing to act upon its own natural desires in opposition to the dicta of authority. In doing so, the lesser is mistakenly placed above the greater, the particular above the universal, which Hegel presumed absurd. The root of evil is then a personal exercise of freedom, which is irrational by virtue of defying the true nature of the self as pre-established by an authoritative Other(s). Rationality would here consist of using freedom to establish self-existence conforming to a universal definition of it. Traditional authority establishes the truth of human nature from which follows whatever is normative for self-conduct. Thus, in order to avoid evil doing, every self must be carefully taught to know what traditional authority prescribes for its existence and, that its duty is to obey the customs, behavioral norms and laws established by authoritative Others.

Since whatever traditional authority prescribes is presumed universally true of and for self-existence, any rational self is obligated to obey and instantiate it. Not only is disobedience to authority evil doing, but it is also a falsification of the true being of the self, self-contradiction, an alienation of self from itself as well as its authoritative Other. Self-identity is not possible without self-objectification proceeding from a conception of self mandated by authoritative Others. Freedom, conceived negatively, has no content except that provided by an authoritative Other. Thus, freedom is unable to establish self-identity, and is a mere means for self-objectification. Self-realization is limited to instantiating the prescriptive ideas of authoritative Others. Life in every dimension, personal or social, is then structured in an authoritarian mode.

Historical religions illustrate in varying degrees alienating doctrines and practices. Holy wars, inquisitions and pogroms have caused enormous suffering. The innocents have been hunted down, persecuted as heretics, convicted of witchcraft and burned at the stake. Galileo's forced recantation attacked intellectual freedom. Books have been placed upon the Index Expurgatorius or destroyed. That ignorance, superstition and prejudice have been promoted by religion at various times is well known. However, to disregard or deny religion or religious institutions a place in modern society risks overlooking their primary socializing and educative functions. Institutions such as the state, not formed for such purposes, have failed as substitutes for family and religion, which together, perform these vital social functions.

The hallmark of both Judaism and Christianity is a self-concept of the sinner. A self, feeling guilty of sin, is subject to social control by its nurturing authoritative Other. The sinner acknowledges his guilt by placing the blame for his alienated condition upon himself rather than projecting it upon the world or his fellows. This is an appealing alternative for a self, fearful of public reprisal, overwhelmed and made helpless in a hostile oppressive world, as were the persecuted Christians of the Roman Empire. The subjective focus of a sinful self-concept attempts to overcome its alienating condition through changing itself, particularly when it cannot change the conditions of its existence. Changing oneself by atonement sets a proselytizing example, which may be hoped, or may in fact, change the world in time. Convincing someone of their guilt opens their behavior to social control, or even deceptive manipulation. Christianity, at least in part, subverted the Roman Empire by converting the psyches of the oppressors to a sin-consciousness needing to atone for guilt feelings. The oppressed ascended to power by using a psychology appropriate to socialization in an authoritarian culture.

Any religious creed requires acknowledging its God as ultimate substance and ground of being including self. Nevertheless, any authentic affirmation of creed requires the work of self-identification and self-objectification. The self must strive to negate its pride, humble itself, surrender its natural self-seeking propensity and discipline its own freedom to objectify itself in conformity to the dicta of its religious authoritative Other, usually prescribed by traditional ecclesiastical authorities and institutions. Every religion requires some degree of self-renunciation in preparation for religious self-objectification. God must be loved before self. Religious devotion or worship reinforces self-identification with a divine Other that enables religious self-objectification. A self fully identified with its creator and objectifying itself accordingly acquires an identity pre-established for it by its authoritative Other.

Religious self-identification and self-objectification does permit some degree of self-realization along with the formation of community. Still, it must not be forgotten that religion can also alienate the self from realizing its potentiality for being resulting from its own powers of rationality and freedom. With religion, the question remains of how the individual directed by any authority external to himself, rational or otherwise, can be authentic and autonomous. Dealienation requires both. They are denied the self by any religion presenting an authoritarian Other for self-identification and self-objectification. A self-realization that expresses both will also express the divine, if human beings are courageous enough not to fear the means they have to effect dealienation, and if they are not coerced by an authoritative Other in their self-objectifying life work. Successful dealienation teaches the self what and whom it is. A culturally transmitted self is a continuous product of historical dealienation. Such a self serves as an authoritative Other necessary for the self-development of future generations. A well-socialized self learns to respect the desires, freedom and rationality of its fellows. Such respect promises the possibility of developing culture beyond authoritarianism toward one respecting human dignity and law.

History is replete with all kinds of religions and Gods. An answer to the question, "Who is your God?" also answers the question, "Who are you?" In other words, the identity of the self is an expression of whom or what it believes its God to be. God as alien master defines the self as obedient subordinate. Or, God as agape, defines the self as autonomous nurturer. To know oneself at the deepest level is to express the being of one's God. What does this historically based observation say about what God really is? Better posed, "Who is God?" Feuerbach suggested that God is the self writ large, a projection of the self with its powers, and its foibles. This makes sense of the historical variety of religions.

Hegel's God is a philosophical self who by thinking and willing creates its own world. God's thinking transcends the finite while its instantiation by free agents, namely ourselves, creates the history of a finite world. Still, it cannot be denied that thought and intentional behavior are derived from the dealienating activity of the self, existing and developing in a finite world. The highest expression of finite self-existence is found in the dealienating artifacts of a humanized world. Such a world is presented to the self as a product of its own powers of rationality and freedom, a product of its thought and intentional activity.

A world produced by the self reflects the self as its creator and cannot have an alien aspect, so Hegel claimed. However, this is found to be false in our contemporary humanized world with its problematical unintended social and environmental consequences. Therefore, a Hegelian God as master thinker creating the world from its rational intentions is naive. Moreover, a Hegelian self-knowing Spirit, sublating all finite differences so that subject and object are indistinguishable, extinguishes meaning itself, thereby returning the self to primitive narcissism. A humanized world emphasizes the exact opposite character. As being is revealed and meaning expanded in the process of dealienation, the self becomes richer, more complex, more differentiated within itself and from the Other(s) that once alienated its desires and aims. World and self do not become an amorphous spiritual substance reducible to abstract thought. That God or any self could by mere thought be an object to itself is impossible. For such self-consciousness is merely the negativity of thought itself presenting an indeterminate object, the abstract Other, vacuous freedom.

The language of God is anthropocentric and anthropomorphic. *God* is spoken about with language applying to the self. Personal pronouns *he* or *she* are most frequently used. God is protecting, nurturing parent, spoken of as *father* or *mother*. Christians speak of *God the father* or *God the son*. God has purposes in mind, intending us to exist in a certain way. Religion uses a vast metaphorical language to describe who God is and what God demands of mortal selves. Emotions such as love or vengeance also describe the moods or dispositions of the divine just as they do the self. Myths and allegories present the moral teaching attributed to God.

A finite self necessarily conceives God as an object of consciousness, an abstract Other of self. However, this divine Other comes loaded with attributes and implication for the conduct of self-existence. God, to be comprehended at all, must signify some aspect of self-existence. We know about God what we know about ourselves, nothing more, nothing less. Therefore, God must signify some projected aspect of our own self-existence. The divine Other is really our self-concept constructed from alienating finitude and dealienating self-existence. The divine Other is some idealized dealienated aspect of finite self-existence as in the omni attributes of theology. God is also said to be free, rational, good, powerful, eternal, infinite, universal and so forth. Whatever is attributed to God is also attributed in some degree to us in some way. Divine attributes are inferred by negating alienating aspects of human finitude.

If God is primarily a self-projection, why then is there any need for God? The answer obviously is that an idealized self is necessary to cope with alienating conditions of self-existence. If our God is something perfect to which we can actively aspire; we have made identifications and introjected behavioral norms socializing the self. Self-projection and self-objectification conforming to divine dicta enables the self to cope in a world in which nature and society alienate it. One's God palliates human suffering and rejects evil doing.

Religion deals with human sinfulness. Social control of antisocial impulses is established by requiring the self to acknowledge responsibility and be accountable for causing unnecessary suffering or evil doing. A self, persuaded of its guilt, is emotionally alienated from its self-projected God. The psyche fears damnation and retribution in hell for its sinfulness. Religious dealienation or salvation lies in repentance and a whole host of religious practices such as sacrifice, confession, penance, and various purification rituals, among others. Personal dispositions may be cultivated such as asceticism. The faithful are then required to believe and worship a God whose ideals and dicta define self-projection. Introjection of God occurs in personal devotion and worship. Introjecting the divine requires a renunciation of natural inclination and unlimited freedom. Nobody can do just anything they want, particularly when it harms others. In the end, God is a collective self-objectification of the faithful. This is Spirit, religiously expressed. The acting out of belief is a free expression of faith.

If God is an imaginary idealized psychological self-projection, then God is who and what we want to be like or become. God defines our dealienating response to the alienating finitude of self-existence. Divine attributes are what we believe necessary to secure the satisfaction of human desires and aims. Asserting God to signify an imaginary idealized self-projection is not equivalent to dismissing God out of hand as fictitious. For God retains enormous significance for how we exist, interpret our world and behave toward each other. Atheism either dismisses this significance or is ignorant of it. God and religion are psychic or spiritual realities to be understood. Moreover, if God is described naturalistically as an imaginary idealized self-projection, there can be as many Gods as there are formally structured publicly idealized self-projections. Furthermore, God becomes instantiated in the finite objectification of religious individuals, religious institutions, attitudes, dispositions and practices. Many Gods are immanent in the world. God and religion respond to alienating self-existence by providing a social structure and mechanism for dealienation. Religion invites the self to freely convert to a creed and live by it to secure salvation.

Can the self get along in life without its God(s)? Even if it could, Freudian psychoanalysis suggests the necessity of an authoritative Other, if not God, then a cultural superego providing norms of socially acceptable conduct. Either God or superego performs the same psychological and sociological function. Both socialize a self, driven by natural inclinations, some of which are antisocial. Without God or superego, morality and a socialized self who can sustain civilized culture disappear, leaving behind an anarchic hell, unconstrained egoism, social insecurity and instability. Such situations have been amply demonstrated throughout history. Therefore, it is necessary for the self to acquire a psychologically idealized self-projection, either through religious faith in an authoritative God or a culturally inculcated superego.

The question is not whether the self can get along without an authoritative Other. Obviously, it cannot. Therefore, the question becomes, "What kind of authoritative Other the self must adopt for projecting itself in its dealienating endeavor?" More specifically, can the self construct its own idealized self-projection which would be authoritative for itself, be a basis for socialization and trustworthy human conduct? Could a self, driven by natural desire and prone to narcissism and egoism, discipline itself so as not to threaten society? Certainly, this would seem possible. For the self can be free to act in accordance with a rational appraisal of what its alienated suffering existence teaches it.

Culture

Existing in ignorance and innocence is to be in an unconscious symbiosis with an authoritative Other. This condition characterizes a narcissistic self with undeveloped potential; dependent upon and dominated by an alien Other; lacking a capacity for dealienation. Such an undeveloped self is a mere product of a culture that nurtures and so is authoritative for it. Culture is its destiny. Moreover, culture is sustained in no small measure by that original unconscious narcissistic symbiosis and the natural tendency to maintain it. Continued nurture by culture is conditional upon conformity with its demands. Yet, these very demands eliminate symbiosis, forcing the self to develop beyond narcissism to egoism. Symbiotic dependency is replaced by self-directed behavior with some degree of freedom and rationality. Boundaries are set by cultural norms and social roles that structure egoistic behavior. Culture prescribes how the self is to satisfy its needs and desires.

Satisfaction of human needs and desires is accomplished through cultural structures. These are developed as collective responses to specific conditions of alienating finitude confronting self-existence. Culture provides socializing structures for self-development and self-realization. Universal social norms and roles are available for self-identifications that enable self-projection and self-objectification. Attitudes, mores and laws of a given culture prescribe and proscribe behavior. Social institutions such as family, religious, educational, civic, commercial and governmental transmit culture. Self-objectifying works of art, science, religion and philosophy are the instantiated products of culture. Existing in such a cultural milieu, every self is for the most part a culture carrier.

Culture is historically constructed from the lives of particular individuals living together in community. The content of culture is derived from and sustained by collective dealienating endeavor. From this, social norms and roles originate. Culture exists for the sake of those whose lives create and sustain it. It cannot transcend its derivation as a collective response to the alienating finitude of self-existence. Unrelated to self-existence, culture is reduced to an insignificant abstraction. Worse still, culture is misconceived as ontologically superior to the self. Alienation then consists of an opposition of culture to self and dealienation consists of subordinating self to culture. However, a self completely submerged and dominated by culture discovers that some of what it needs and desires cannot be satisfied. Where culture does not permit an exercise of rational freedom, the self is radically alienated by the loss of its capacity for dealienation.

Where social norms and roles serve as successful dealienating vehicles for self-objectification, there is a reciprocal complementary relationship of culture to self. Nevertheless, the demands of culture may oppose those of the self. The enabling structures of culture thereby become alienating. Dealienation then consists of an endeavor to restructure cultural demands to conform to the essential nature of the self. Social norms and roles then undergo change. As an objectified social product, culture continuously changes as it either succeeds or fails in its dealienating aim. Any cultural structure will be discarded when it fails to satisfy needs, desires, limits rationality and freedom, or disables self-realization. Successful culture facilitates dealienation while affirming the essential nature of the self.

The social struggle over deviancy has been characterized as a *culture war* carried on with argumentation between advocates of counterculture and those of traditional culture .The culture war is fought in America primarily among special interest groups or lobbyists seeking favorable legislation and legal precedents from expensive court cases. However, the winner will ultimately be determined from the collective result of lifestyle choices by the populace. Where culture is subordinate to a self free to experiment, evaluate and choose its lifestyle, deviancy might be considered a relative concept. Deviancy accepted becomes the norm and changes culture. However, with respect to its alienating or dealienating consequences for self-existence, deviancy is not at all relative. The prospective consequences of choosing different lifestyles are always subject to debate. The actual consequences of deviancy determine whether it is preferable.

Cultural alienation seems to follow a generally predictable pattern. Individuals find themselves progressively isolated from culture and its institutions. Stoically resigned, they ignore what is irrelevant to their lives. Their apathy is expressed by skeptical and cynical attitudes toward what seems irrelevant to them. They deal with what seems relevant. Thus, although skepticism, cynicism and public apathy are signs of cultural alienation, they are also signs that dealienating responses are underway. Not sustained by self-objectification, culture atrophies and social institutions eventually disintegrate; replaced by others arising from the norms and social roles originating from the actual lives and needs of individuals. Where culture is oppressive to human needs, individuals respond with rebellion, abolition or reform.

No matter which course is taken, new culture and institutions replace those that have atrophied and become obsolete.

Socialization is initiated with self-identification. How it is formed determines whether self-objectification with it will alienate or dealienate. Defective socialization alienates the self by disabling the integrated development of rationality and freedom. Defective socialization is initiated coercively with non-rational self-identifications predominant in pre-adult life. An adult, not having developed the capacity for rational freedom cannot evaluate whether what culture demands is consistent with its own demands. A product of deficient maturation, the self expresses the aims of authoritative Others: cultural elites in control of social institutions such as government, education, mass media and business. Reduced to a culture carrier, the self is socially controlled. Manipulated by culture and without its essential dealienating capacity, the self is radically alienated. It projects and objectifies a cultural Other, alien to its own essential nature. Its authentic potentiality for being remains unrealized. Lacking the application of rational freedom, the true needs and desires of the self cannot be satisfied. The adult socialization process is flawed at its inception with a non-rational culturally defined self-identification. Dysfunctional self-projection and self-objectification can be expected where there is no personal insight into authentic needs and desires; and where there is no foresight of the consequences of self-identifying choices.

Freud suggested that the process of socialization and character formation end at a very early age in child development. However, this narrow view is obviously false. For socialization continues through adolescence, extending into adult life. Dealienating projects of the self aside, it is bombarded daily for its loyalty and support from diverse cultural sources, be they familial, religious, ideological, corporate or political. Their implicit requests for allegiance involve personal choices and additional socialization, minimally requiring new self-identifications, possibly with self-projected expressions of support, and maximally requiring self-objectifying work. Since every finite self creates a personal history, its identity is always an open question. What the self wants and who it is to become is answered by all kinds of attitudes and choices throughout life. A young adult must decide upon a career, marriage and family. An elderly person has to decide how to handle retired life unstructured by the previous routines or working life. Increasing longevity requires personal decisions about what attitudes to adopt toward aging, illness and death. The character forming socialization of a child does not address such choices.

Plato's formulation of justice in the *Republic* suggests a complementary and reciprocal relationship between self and culture. Justice is that natural condition where the self *does what it can do best* with society gaining maximum benefit from its contribution. A perfectly proportioned social whole would utilize individual differences of temperament and natural talent. The implication is that alienation would not exist in a social structure where culture and self are placed in a complementary and reciprocal relationship. Each gives to the maximum of its capability and each receives the full measure of what it deserves. Social contribution and personal satisfaction would thereby be maximized. Such a view is indeed appealing. Nevertheless, Plato's prescription for achieving a utopian society fails by replacing reciprocity of self to culture with subordination of self to culture. The Republic would use an educational institution to place individuals into a rigidly class structured society designed to perform the functions believed necessary for the social whole. Hierarchically organized, it would be governed by an elite class of wise men.

Hegel also conceived of society hierarchically structured into social institutions controlled by elite state bureaucrats and religious authority. Marx demanded reciprocity by asking *from each according to his abilities and to each according to his needs.* Again, Marx's prescription requires subordinating the self to a revolutionary culture dictated by an elite proletarian ruling class replacing a capitalist one. Understanding that a self subordinated to culture places the former into a permanent condition of unreconcileable alienation, Freud offered no utopian prescription. The presumption common to such diverse social thinkers is that coercive socialization is necessary for creating and sustaining civilization. However, coercive socialization negates the authenticity and autonomy essential for dealienation and self-realization. For this reason, any social structure coercively subordinating of self to culture must fail. This defect is shared by authoritarianism, totalitarianism and collectivism; elements present in Platonic, Hegelian and Marxist social perspectives.

A prevalent cultural formula for dealienation is to renounce, identify with traditional norms and social roles and self-project them. In return, the self is rewarded with a socially created identity, status and prestige. These nurture the ego as it carries the culture. The self is said to belong or be at home in its culture. Reciprocity is secured as self and culture complements each other. Although appealing, this formula is problematical. Renouncing certain demands authentic to the self may not be possible or replaceable by identification with a cultural substitute. Then the process of renunciation and substitution is self-alienating. Freudian repression explained the psychic dynamics of a dysfunctional cultural substitution. An ego not able to get what it wants adopts non-rational or irrational unconscious defenses.

The demands of the repressed return with the symptoms of neurosis. Here, alienation is culturally induced. The self becomes inauthentic by conforming to culturally prescribed norms and social roles suppressing its essential nature. Dominated by a repressive cultural authoritative Other, autonomy is sacrificed. The very capacity for dealienation is compromised. An authentic potentiality for being remains unrealized.

Authoritarian and totalitarian cultures have much in common. Both coercively subordinate self to culture. Both defectively socialize the self by unnecessarily restricting the development and expression of rational freedom. Both compel the self to think and act as alien authoritative Others dictate. Deviancy from established norms and social roles is carefully controlled, if not altogether suppressed. Human needs, desires and mechanisms for their satisfaction are preplanned by a governing elite. Totalitarian culture is authoritarian, but authoritarian culture is not necessarily totalitarian. The principal difference between them lies in the degree of suppression of rationality and freedom.

Some historical versions of political and religious authoritarianism limit the scope of restrictions upon freedom and thought control. Historically, the domain of religious authority has been limited to spiritual as distinguished from secular life. Where the dicta of religious authority does not apply, decision is left for individual conscience or secular authority. This historical trend is so pervasive that religion has been progressively excluded from the domain of secular governance and public education. Both authoritarian and totalitarian cultures sometimes permit a limited exercise of rational freedom carefully contained in some domain not threatening to established authority and acting as a social safety valve. Instances of economic freedom amidst repressive religious or political regimes are common. Totalitarian states have flourished with capitalist economic freedom. So-called mixed economies blend capitalist economic freedom with socialist political regimes.

Satisfying the needs and desires of others is prerequisite to satisfying those of oneself. You give and you get. Reciprocity is a universal social demand. Something of value is voluntarily exchanged usually with money, which is fungible. However, quite often reciprocity is absent. One may work in a bureaucratic organization and be paid without acceptance of one's work product. Personal satisfaction with work demands a self-confirming exchange. What one does must make a difference, be accepted, used and valued by those it was intended to benefit.

An absence of social reciprocity is dysfunctional and typical of bureaucracy. It will only accept what it has pre-established as conforming to its rules and so innovative individuals are rarely rewarded. Non-conformists are at best tolerated, but more often punished. However, no culture, bureaucratic or otherwise can survive without reciprocity. The demand for it persists. Thus, the crucial question for cultural survival is whether genuine products of individuality will be accepted and acknowledged. Where this is not the case, cultural alienation persists. The alternative is for culture to permit authentic expressions of autonomous individuals. Where culture encourages self-realization, the self will bond with it. Reciprocity provides the satisfaction of the deepest human aspirations. None of this is possible where individuality is not encouraged.

Contemporary American culture asserts the subordination of culture to self. It demands the authenticity and autonomy asserted by existentialism. There is a broad tolerance of deviancy from prevailing social norms and stereotyped roles. The boundary between tolerance and permissiveness is often indistinct. Lifestyle experimentation among young adults is rampant. Cultural tolerance provides the possibility of legitimizing deviancy obtainable from acceptance and practice by the majority. Organized advocacy attempts to gain public acceptance by portraying deviancy as normal, or just another lifestyle choice to be respected. Cast under the umbrella of respect for individuality and human rights, efforts are put forth to legitimize deviant lifestyles. Counter-culture groups organize around their claim of discrimination and human rights violations. Portrayed as victims of discrimination, political alliances are formed. Acceptance of deviancy is also carried on by ideological indoctrination in educational institutions. Mass media publicize the case for deviancy with editorial propaganda and subliminal messages. Controversial deviancy has popular entertainment value. An entertainment industry using popular culture art forms makes the emotional appeal favoring deviancy.

If a prescription for a dealienated society is to be viable, the overlooked requirement seems to be to allow individuality a far greater degree of autonomy than most social thinkers would tolerate. Confusing license with personal freedom and disregarding its relationship to rationality results in a distrust of freedom and an overemphasis upon its potentially destructive social consequences. However, rational freedom is creative rather than destructive. A self, having developed this capacity, can modify, replace and even create novel cultural norms and social roles. This in fact happens continuously and is the engine of cultural change. A culture trusting and encouraging personal liberty avoids coercive socialization. The self is prized for daring to be different and for exercising its unique creative capacity. Tolerance of deviancy allows culture the flexibility to change and respond to alienating conditions encountered by self-existence. That the self could create culture was not believed possible in principle by Plato, Hegel, Marx and Freud. Even where they proclaimed the power of rationality or freedom, they did not fully comprehend its integrated power to effect dealienation. Building trust in rational freedom was left to later generations of western civilization that created freer societies than previous thinkers dreamed possible.

If individuality is allowed the freedom imputed to it, then spontaneity and creativity flourish. A free individuality is socially transformative. There is room to think and act *outside the box*, so to speak. Individuality is not bound to universal norms and stereotyped social roles prescribed for it by some alien Other, be it an elite, the state or God. Abstracted from their dealienating existential origin, cultural norms and social roles lose the factual basis for their authority. Inhibited by stereotypical roles, self-existence is distorted by being confined to inflexible social structures where behavior is entirely predictable and socially controlled. This describes a bureaucracy or totalitarian state in which human needs, desires and mechanisms for their satisfaction are pre-planned. A self coercively subordinated to such a culture will be bored, depressed and apathetic, emotions signifying alienation. If submersion in such cultures provided an identity sought by the self, then bureaucratic life would be successful and satisfactory. But this is not the case. Many are unwilling to accept the norms and roles of a bureaucratic culture. Their demand for autonomy struggles against inducements to conform. Non-conformity persists even where opposition is acknowledged futile.

Whole social structures have been built from a hierarchy of stereotyped roles. The boundaries of individuality are thereby clearly established. This rigid perspective also has disadvantages. Non-conformity to stereotypical roles may be suppressed thereby disallowing experimentation with deviancy, which might promote successful dealienation. Cultural intolerance of deviancy is then undesirable. Inflexible role stereotyping without toleration of deviancy or experimentation invariably creates tragic suffering by individuals who are different from what culture prescribes.

Role reversal and experimental arrangements utilizing the relative actual capacities of individuals can be beneficial. But this would be lost when, for example, a mother who could earn twice the family income of her husband would not be permitted to work while the father cared for their children. Individual differences do not always fit some universal stereotyped role, since such differences are matters of discovered fact. A healthy culture requires toleration of individual differences and the flexibility to discover and utilize them effectively.

Disallowing spontaneity and creativity in establishing or changing roles alienates both the self and its culture. Cultural tolerance of deviancy - the freedom of individuals to be different - promotes the realization of unique human potentialities while facilitating the replacement of alienating role stereotypes. Rather than a cultural intolerance of deviancy, tolerance of it can function much like a safety valve promoting collective social health.

A dealienating relationship of culture to self is one of reciprocity. A relationship of self subordinate to culture invariably results in unnecessary alienation. A dominating culture opposes the authentic nature of the self, its needs, desires, and demand for rational freedom. Therefore, instead of self meeting the demands of culture, the trend is for culture to meet the demands of the self. Now it is true that culture subordinate to the self can be alienating, as previous thinkers have pointed out so well. However, this is only true where that self is defectively socialized, or egoistic, with freedom misconstrued as license to negate the benefits of culture. However, culture can be safely subordinated to a social self who has learned to use its freedom rationally. The essential nature of the self demands that culture respect and promotes its autonomy and authenticity. The historic trend toward personal liberty and democracy confirms the fact that culture is responding with toleration of deviancy, even permissiveness of it. The prospect is of a culture promoting self-realization rather than suppressing human potential.

Dealienation

Meaning originates from the fact of ontological negativity. Its expression is found in the alienating finitude of self-existence. An alien Other signifies a deficiency in being, a limit of some kind, something that frustrates the needs and desires of the self. To think is to negate the alien Other(s) in some way. So, meaning is thought and self-activity responding to the limits set by the alien Other(s). Dealienation is precisely this whole process taken from within an existential context. And true meaning is a product of successful dealienation. More specifically, true meaning is a product of self-existence, of encountering alienating finitude and responding to it freely with thought and intentional activity.

Dealienation is then an existential process of self-identification, self-projection, self-objectfication, and self-realization. The process is a finite temporal actualization of the potentiality for being something or anything. Within this process, being is revealed, and even created. What is true meaning and normative is a continuous result of revealing being with an indeterminate horizon. A finite world and self is comprehended by degrees as being is revealed and its meaning expands. What are absolute are what endures the test of dealienation over time, which is to say that there certainly is accumulative knowledge and wisdom, but nothing absolute, standing apart from self-existence. A self-existence resulting from confronting alienating finitude with rational freedom describes a process of dealienation establishing the true meaning of being and what is normative for human conduct. Human existence so described is authentic and self-validating. Anything less does not dealienate and so is false and inauthentic to the power of rational freedom constituting, along with human needs and desires, the essential nature of the self.

Conscience is a curious phenomenon with widely divergent interpretations of what it signifies. On the one hand conscience is interpreted as the authoritative voice of the Other(s) controlling and commanding self-conduct, denying the self absolute freedom to satisfy its desires any way it pleases. On the other hand, the self acknowledges its freedom with its conscience. For in suffering *pangs of conscience*, feeling remorseful or acknowledging its guilt, it knows itself to be a doer who can choose. It also knows this when hearing its own voice of conscience prompting it to act courageously, alone and contrary to cultural authoritative Others. But, whether conscience is guided by that authoritative inner voice of the self or outer voice of the Other(s), the self is presumed to be a moral agent with freedom to choose and act to some degree: either to act for itself according to its own rational determination or for the Other(s) in accordance with their dicta.

Conscience is the voice of freedom. Regardless of the source of its voice, conscience is a universal acknowledgment of personal freedom. If this presumption were false, there would be no reason for praise or blame, reward or punishment, indoctrination, propaganda and any of the other practices which pre-determine the conduct of the self coercing it toward social conformity. Although basing conscience upon freedom or upon socialization appear contrary to one another, both are not necessarily contradictory. For the self must first know how the Other(s) wish it to behave in order to discover how it would choose to behave. Normal moral development from childhood to maturity begins with the authority of the Other(s) and progresses toward autonomy.

Freedom and morality develop concurrently until the self is able to act from conscience recognizing its autonomy, its intentions, and the possible consequences of its behavior. Therefore, conscience bespeaks a high degree of freedom, an autonomous self with a heightened moral sensibility. This is not to say that conscience cannot be perverted into an excuse for evil doing; or, that it cannot become sick, imprisoning the self in the proscriptions of the Other(s) suppressing its desires and attempts at dealienation; or, that it may fail to realize its own potential by donning the straight jacket prescribed for it by the Other(s). All of this, tragic as it is, happens too frequently.

Conscience can be thought of as the self apprehending its duty. However, if duty is an apprehension of the demands coercively imposed by cultural authoritative Others, then conscience is not operative. For, conscience imposes an obligation upon the individual to act from personal conviction, particularly when it violates a commonly acknowledged duty. Therefore, obligations of conscience, often fraught with risk of censure or worse, express autonomy and authenticity in an exercise of personal freedom. Conscience can be right where duty is wrong.

A stand taken from conscience can only be judged according to the merits of a situation requiring its exercise. When an appeal is made to conscience, it must have reasons to override the demands of duty. It is then that conscience is judged right and superior to duty. That conscience is right is confirmable by any self who thinks about the reasons for what it commands. This is why conscience is publicly respected as a sacred domain of the self. Obeying one's conscience in defiance of duty commands public respect. Law acknowledges conscience, for example, by exempting conscientious objectors from military service or providing non-combatant alternatives. The autonomy and authenticity that acts of conscience demonstrate acknowledges the inherent dignity of a self capable of courageously thinking and acting for itself, even if alone.

Love dealienates when it is authentically self-giving. For then love is an expression of not only rationality and freedom, but of talent, knowledge and skills acquired by the self. Self-giving love is always intensely focused upon the welfare of what or whom it is bestowed upon. Such love expresses deep motivations and natural inclinations. Human beings need to be loved and to love in return. The need to love is undoubtedly instinctually based with roots to be found in biological survival and narcissism. The welfare and flourishing of the beloved provides deep satisfaction, even joy to the giver. This is experienced both with the exercise of human powers in acts of loving and in a return of the flourishing welfare of the beloved, if not in expressions of appreciation. The self-giving lover takes pride in what has been contributed to the beloved and in what has been thereby accomplished by the beloved.

Self-giving love is a work of self-objectification focused upon the welfare of the Other. Thus, the product of self-giving love affirms the being and powers of the giver. The return of love is anticipated with pleasure, since it affirms the powers of the lover whose identity is secured by their application. What the beloved returns is recognition of self, which, as objectified, is authentic and undeniable. Self-giving love is then narcissism redirected upon the Other and returned. Moreover, in the process, narcissism is transformed. Yet, the objectified return of self-giving love and expressions of appreciation by the beloved do provide narcissistic satisfaction to the lover and more. For, the satisfaction in the giving itself, in exercising one's powers for another cannot be overlooked. Just as everyone including its creator can appreciate a work of art, so, also, is there enormous satisfaction in creating the work itself.

A complete satisfaction of self-giving love moves the adult well beyond narcissism. The social product of self-giving love is a bonding of self with its fellows in their mutual desires and aims. Through the Other(s), the self realizes who and what it is. Socially, the unification is a bonding achieved by reciprocity consisting of authentic exchange of something of value, which is appreciated. Clearly then, self-giving love gives impetus to and at least partially describes a process of dealienation wherein self and Other(s) are unified through self-objectifying behavior in which there is a self-realization of human powers, the creation of self-identity and public acknowledgment of it.

Socialization enables the establishment of self-identity or personality. A byproduct of socialization is *character* expressed by a set of attitudes and behavioral predispositions. Character traits are commonly understood as a subset of a whole package of personality traits, particularly those that are considered to establish moral life. Although not commonly recognized, socialization and character formation are continuous throughout life. Incomplete socialization arrested in narcissism and/or egoism results in defective character. Adult socialization initiated by non-rational or irrational self-identifications also results in defective character. It is signified by a self, alienated from its needs, desires, rationality, and freedom: a flawed self also lacking the capacity for dealienation and self-realization. A character that is narcissistic, egoistic, or misdirected by faulty self-identifications will cause unnecessary suffering. Socialization arrested in narcissism, egoism, or defective adult socialization, presents a naturalistic description of an alienated self. Even more significant, defective socialization implies the formation of defective character commonly described as immoral: a self lacking empathy, indifferent to causing suffering and thus prone to evil.

Defective socialization forms defective character. A self with defective character is alienated from realizing its inherent potentiality for being human. Defective character, whether reflecting narcissism, egoism or misdirected adult self-identifications, propagates alienation by dysfunctional self-projection and self-objectification. Moreover, to the extent that such behavior causes unnecessary suffering, defective character is also accountable for propagating evil. A self whose existence is neither autonomous nor authentic is dominated by alien authoritative Others. Rational freedom, its fundamental dealienating capacity, is undeveloped and inoperative in either its motivation or behavior. So described, defective character is the structural nexus of authoritarianism, totalitarianism, collectivism and certain counterculture ideologies such as postmodernism.

The alienating finitude of self-existence poses a perennial and universal question for humanity. Who and what ought it to become? What should self-existence project as the content of its character? What shall be the legacy of its self-objectifying work? Rationality and freedom are the human powers necessary for dealienation. Therefore, a continuous development of rational freedom is the essential way of dealienation as western civilization has prescribed since classical Greek culture flowered in Athens over two millennia ago.

Mistrusting freedom has been a major obstacle to the development of rational freedom. Hence, the historical responses of authoritarianism, totalitarianism and collective submersion in culture. However, these always alienate the self from its capacity for dealienation. Still, freedom can be trusted if the self is properly socialized beyond narcissism and egoism. This is accomplished by family, religion, and cultural institutions ever creating and transmitting the mores and morality of a civilization. If these institutions flourish without governmental subversion, then a self will maximize its capacity for dealienation. Self-existence will be marked by autonomy and authenticity, not by a psycho-sociological pathology of domination by alien Others. In addition, self-existence will be marked by a conscience related to freedom, not one censoring the natural desires and aspirations of each self. Human needs will be more easily satisfied without fear of consequences, without the coercion of any repressive authority. Self-existence would then be a kind of utopia, but not one in which alienation is absent, but rather one in which it is dealt with most effectively, allowing the human spirit to flower and soar in its all too brief individual moment of finitude. This is possible and will come to pass, if the forgoing philosophical analysis is correct.

Alienation cannot be eradicated, since it has an ontological basis humanly expressed by the alienating finitude of self-existence. However, the self continuously overcomes alienation by satisfying its needs and desires. This is accomplished by rational freedom, a capacity it has, and can develop, to effect dealienation. The capacity for dealienation can be maximized where self-existence and culture meet certain conditions. Rationality and freedom must be integrated and developed concurrently. Socialization cannot fixate in narcissism or egoism, but must be completed to the point where a responsible social self emerges. Self-identifications initiating the process, particularly in adult life, must be formed rationally rather then non-rationally or irrationally. This enables self-projection and self-objectification to be authentic. Self-realization can thereby express an authentic potentiality for being.

Not dominated by alien authoritative Others, authentic needs and desires can be acknowledged and satisfied by an autonomous self. Acknowledging its obligation to satisfy its own demands, a correctly socialized self universalizes its own claim. This results in acknowledging the claims of its fellows to be equal to its own. A socialized self has learned to postpone its gratification by sharing, queuing up and taking turns. Acknowledging the universality of an equal claim for satisfying needs and desires forms the basis for social reciprocity. From this follows human rights, respect for human dignity and democracy. Civility and social cohesion based upon acknowledging human equality makes superfluous a submergence in culture, a coercive subordination to its norms, social roles and institutions. When subordinated to self rather than cultural authoritative Others, dealienation can be enabled and reinforced. Cultural coercion and domination is thereby replaced by a toleration of personal experimentation with deviant lifestyles. And when found better, these replace what traditional culture has provided without creating an opposition between the demands of culture and those of the self.

What does a *dealienating self* look like? Properly socialized beyond narcissism and egoism, it avoids being the cause of unnecessary suffering, or evil. Rational freedom, its capacity to dealienate has been maximized. Religious, political or cultural authority does not suppress its needs, desires, rationality and freedom. It is integrated with authority and community to realize its complete human potentiality. It is not dominated or controlled by alien authoritative Others. Its self-existence is authentic and autonomous. Its behavior is subject to a sense of obligation arising from the demands of its own needs and desires as well as its conscience. Self-giving love expresses its own power of rational freedom used to satisfy its natural needs and desires. Acknowledging this essential nature of the self implies a whole panoply of human rights universally extending equal opportunity for self-realization. Pursuing self-realization by voluntary participation creates and sustains democratic culture. Within this process of personal dealienation, the general welfare is secured by individual merit correctly associated to social esteem and human dignity.

A self, unable to acknowledge who it is, cannot behave rationally and freely to get what it wants or expresses its authentic identity. Its authentic potentiality for being remain unrealized, concealed by a disguise wrought by defective socialization. The meaning of being in general and its own being in particular cannot be revealed. Possibilities of being cannot be discovered or created by a self alienated from rationality and freedom. Personality is ossified. Self-existence affirms an alien authoritative Other in coercive obedience and drab conformity to universal stereotypical norms and social roles. Crippled by defective socialization, the self exists in relative isolation from community.

If socialization is correctly undertaken, self-existence need not be alienated unnecessarily beyond that which it must encounter by its own finitude. What then are the conditions of a dealienating socialization? First, it must not be psychologically or sociologically coercive. Every component of socialization requires rationality and freedom. The initiating self-identification must be rational and freely accepted in conformance with the essential nature and potential dealienating capacity of the self. Non-rational or irrational identifications are to be avoided. Then, ensuing self-projection and self-objectification will be free of unresolvable opposition between the demands of culture and those of the self. Socialization, while necessary for the suppression of evil, need not suppress the essential demand of the self for authenticity and autonomy. Socialization can proceed through narcissistic and egoistic development without abnormal fixations of unresolved conflict between self and culture. A social self having developed a dealienating capacity has integrated rationality and freedom. The equality of human needs and desires among selves who form community is acknowledged. Reciprocity exists between self and culture with each complementing the other.

A self, fully prepared for dealienation and self-realization, is one whose self-existence is both authentic and autonomous. An alien Other, although always driving dealienation, does not dominate a dealienating self. It is not irrationally or non-rationally submerged in its culture or controlled by alien authorities. Its aspirations and deeds respond to the voice of its conscience. Its character is virtuous. It relates to its fellows with a store of acquired wisdom and self-giving love. Its needs and desires are satisfied and integrated in complementary ways with its fellows. Most importantly, a dealienating self is one who has socially developed and maximized its rational freedom to a degree permitting a complete realization of all its potentialities, thereby revealing the very meaning of being.

Glossary

A priori (Kantian terminology). A two-word phrase signifying anything known prior to experience and never derived from it or any aspect of it such as sensuous intuition.

Absolute Idealism. Hegelian philosophy equating being with thought making reality spiritual as opposed to material.

Absolute Idea (Hegelian terminology). A culminating Idea resulting from a dialectical developing of rationality and freedom - Spirit - which returns to Being by traversing finitude, terminating alienation from the Other(s), and reaching the infinite.

Agape (Judaeo-Christian terminology). Unconditional nurturing love without expectation of return bestowed upon a sinner by a perfect God. This kind of love is an indiscriminate, unmotivated, spontaneous expression of divine creative power. Christianity believes agape, the supreme virtue, is necessary for salvation.

Alienation (author's terminology). Ontologically defined as a deficiency in being or limit established by negation. Also, humanly experienced through the finitude of self-existence as need, desire, the frustration thereof, and a negating encounter with the Other(s).

Angst (existential terminology). Variously translated as anguish, anxiety or dread. These terms all signify an emotional feeling akin to fear, except without a definite object. Existentialism provides a special significance to this experience, claiming it to signify personal freedom wherein the self confronts the necessity to choose from among possibilities without guidance from an authoritative Other. This recognition of personal responsibility is an agonizing burden of freedom.

Anomie (Durkheim sociology). A now common word signifying a social pathology or malaise in which individuals do not identify with, project or objectify prevalent social norms and roles thereby leading to their disintegration or transformation. This concept originated with French sociologist Emile Durkheim's attempt to explain suicide rates related to divorce and widowhood; also social conflict between labor and capital.

Antinomy (Kantian terminology). Antinomies are contradictory principles or assertions that can be argued with equal plausibility, since no fact determines which is true. Kant maintained that this feature of the mental faculty of Reason invalidates speculative metaphysics. One example of an antinomy would be that some events in nature occur without a cause versus every event in nature occurs with a cause. This antinomy is reflected in the prolonged dispute between advocates of free will versus advocates of determinism.

Archetypal Images (Jungian psychoanalysis). Also called *archetypes* which are metaphorical symbols and themes found in art, mythology, religious culture and dreams that have deep psychological and spiritual significance for life.

Authenticity (existentialist terminology). Attribute of a self whose needs, desires, rationality and freedom govern its existence rather than domination by the dicta of authoritative Others.

Authoritative Other(s) (author's terminology). Those whom the self identifies with, self-projects and objectifies. They can be norms of conduct and social roles provided by parents, culture, social institutions and religious faith in a God.

Autonomy (Kantian terminology). An attribute describing a rationally self-determining human being.

Becoming (Hegelian terminology). Temporal alteration by negation wherein something finite or an aspect of it comes into existence and then ceases to exist.

Being The ultimate abstract signifier of an undifferentiated infinite whole, exhausting all possibilities of finite existence.

Being-for-other (Hegelian terminology.) A being negatively defined merely by relation to an Other alien to itself.

Being-for-another (Hegelian or Sartrean terminology). A being not defined by its own capacity, but by Others alien to itself. Primary Sartrean examples are blind social conformity or, playing a social role preventing the realization of authentic potentialities for being human.

Being-for-itself (Hegelian or Sartrean terminology). Any being seeking satisfaction of desires without regard to any social demands. Freedom is blind conatus and the self is not developed beyond narcissism or egoism.

Being-in-itself or ***being-within-self*** (Hegelian terminology). An undifferentiated being, equivalent to non-being, without identity defined by difference from any other being.

Being-in-and-for-itself (Hegelian or Sartrean terminology). A product of an ontological process: a being which is what it has become: a being expressed by a final product of a self-objectifying process.

Cartesian. A philosophical orientation expressed by seventeenth century philosopher René Descartes, a rationalist and subjective idealist who famously proclaimed, *"I think, therefor I am."* A Cartesian Cogito proclaims the existence of the self by a logically irrefutable intuition of an ego that thinks.

Categorical Imperative (Kantian terminology). A rule based upon logical consistency, for determining whether an action is right or wrong. The right action can be universalized without any contradictory exception. A religious expression is the Christian golden rule proclaiming, *"Do unto others as you would have them do to you."* A Kantian social corollary is to always treat persons as ends, never as means.

Category. Universal concepts, exhaustive of thought and every mode of being. Aristotle's ten categories were substance, quality, quantity, relation, place, time, position, state, action and passion. Kant offered twelve a priori categories of mind exhaustive of predication; necessary for synthesizing the phenomena of experience; and making knowledge of anything finite possible.

Cathect (Freudian terminology). Emotional energy or affect associated with an idea, object or cluster of them.

Catharsis (Aristotelian or Freudian terminology). A purification by purging something. The process discharges emotion in the audience of an ancient Greek Sophoclean tragedy. Emotionally, affects of certain ideas are discharged by Freudian therapeutic hypnosis or by free association of repressed thoughts.

Ceasing-to-be (Hegelian terminology). A finite negating temporal process leaving behind a historical being which is no longer and never again will be in fact. Hyphens between words signify an existential sense of immediacy.

Collective Unconscious (Jungian psychoanalysis). A psychic reservoir of inherited tendencies, or archetypes, such as a feminine or masculine nature determining thought and behavior and brought to consciousness in dream and fantasy life.

Conscience. A guide for human conduct provided by an authoritative Other or solely by the self. The former is supplied by internalized cultural norms - Freud's censoring superego - or, religiously by hearing the command of a divine voice. The latter senses an obligation originating from the authentic needs and desires of the self. Whatever its source or whatever it dictates, it signifies authenticity and autonomy. Most importantly, it can provide guidance for exercising freedom.

Culture (author's terminology). A historically developing ethos derived from collective dealienating endeavor expressed in social institutions, knowledge and artifacts presenting norms and social roles enabling socialization of the self.

Dasein (existentialist terminology). A German word variously translated as *being-there*, *being-there-and-then*, or *being-present-to.* The hyphens signify an existential sense or unmediated, immediate experience of being. The nuanced meanings depend upon which philosopher - Heidegger, Sartre or Jaspers - employed the term.

Dealienation (author's terminology). A process whereby some deficiency in being or limit posed by an alien Other is overcome. Also, humanly experienced by a process of intentional interaction with the alien Other involving the capacity for rationality and freedom developed by the self.

Defective Socialization (author's terminology). A process of establishing a self-concept by non-rational or irrational coercive means: consequently fixating self-development in narcissism and/or egoism, minimizing social reciprocity, the development of rational freedom, and consequently a generalized capacity for dealienation.

Deontological (Kantian terminology). An ethical orientation claiming that what obligates conduct resides in an intuition of what is right, not from any motive derived from the needs or desires of the self or any consequences of behavior. Kant sought an *a priori* basis for ethical conduct, demanding that guidance must reside in a rationality, which makes moral rules necessary and universally applicable, without exception. Rationality was held to form the objective basis of self-given laws. From an autonomous self -both rational and free - flows moral worth, a good will and respect for law. The apprehension of duty is an autonomous self respecting laws emanating from its own rationality. The *categorical imperative*, cited above, was Kant's famous expression of locating moral conduct in the rationality of the self.

Desire (author's terminology). A drive or aim of an intentional self-active being to become something Other than it presently is in response to sensing some deficiency in itself or its environment.

Dialectic. A process of opposition driven by negativity operative in thought, dialogue or activity.

Diremption (Hegelian terminology). The opposite of sublation. Any process driven by disunifying negativity whereby the meaning or being of something is separated from something else to which it was previously united in some way.

Displacement (Freudian terminology). A dissociation of a socially prohibited desire from an idea expressing it; associatively replaced with a substitute disguising the original. Formulated by mechanistic analogy, psychic energy associatively attaches and detaches from ideas thereby generally explaining dreams, psychoneurotic symptoms and unconscious mental processes.

Ego (Hegelian terminology). An abstract being which is nothing, deficient or limited in some way and implied by sensing, thinking or becoming Other.

Ego Ideal (Freudian terminology). An internalized norm governing personal behavior and obtained by identifying with authoritative Others.

Egoism (author's terminology). A phase of normal self-development following narcissism. An egoist uses rationality and freedom to socially manipulate or exploit as a means to satisfy personal desires.

Emotive Theory. The analytical claim that aesthetic or ethical statements convey emotion, but not the truth about anything. Paradigmatic examples of emotive statements are exclamations or commands.

Empiricism. A British philosophical tradition claiming that experience is the sole source of knowledge derived from sense perception, observation and inductive generalization.

Enlightenment. A period of western intellectual history extending from early seventeenth to early nineteenth century applying the test of reason to understanding anything. The German philosopher Immanual Kant was the most notable exponent of this philosophical attitude by his metaphysical and ethical critiques.

Epistemology. Any philosophical theory explaining the origin, content, object, structure and limits of knowledge understood to be truth as opposed to falsity or doubtful belief.

Essence (existentialist terminology). That defined nature of something or someone pre-established by authoritative Others such as God, culture, or nature.

Eros (Platonic terminology). A drive toward perfection in being manifested in the love of or desire for something. Imperfect finite beings are attracted by universal ideals of perfection in being; namely, truth, beauty and goodness. Through aspiring toward and imitating them, finite beings can partake of and partially participate in their perfection.

Equality (author's terminology). Acknowledging the universal demand for the satisfaction of needs, desires and self-realization without selective social restriction of any self.

Evil (author's terminology). An alienation existentially manifested by unnecessary suffering. This definition is herein preferred to its authoritarian definition: namely, disobeying the proscriptions or prescriptions of authoritative Others.

Existence (existentialist terminology). That which appears to a conscious or self-conscious being without mediation. A pure perceptive experience with the sense of being *here and now* or just *being there*; unstructured by concepts and unconditioned by any cultural bias.

Existentialism. A philosophy denying the self an essential nature: instead, defining it strictly in terms of its conscious existence and freedom. Prominent existentialists are Kierkegaard, Nietzsche, Heidegger and Sartre.

Facticity (existential terminology). The condition of finitude wherein the self confronts Others not of its own choosing or doing.

Finitude (quasi-Hegelian terminology). An essential attribute of existence described by alteration driven by a temporal process of negativity whereby what exists is potentially Other than it is, or is limited by an Other opposed to it in some way.

Fixation (Freudian terminology). A phase of self-development that is not transcended and so becomes dysfunctional to the demands presented by the current environment. Examples are found in irrational emotional attachments and obsessions.

Freedom (author's terminology). A basic developable capacity for dealienation exercised by a being who thinks, chooses, acts intentionally, is responsible and accountable for what it does in the world and with its fellows.

Frustration. Alienation from the satisfaction of need, desire or thwarting the achievement of some aim.

Geist (Hegelian terminology). An infinite self-conscious Spirit, expressing itself by means of Notions and Ideas constituting reality. Also see Zeitgeist, defined below.

General Will (Rousseau's terminology). An expression of a collective wisdom and moral force in social action. The true interest of the individual is expressed by a collective social gestalt. Public deliberation and democratic consensus is presumed to create a collective wisdom and interest superior to that of any individual. By obeying it, the individual presumably expresses his universal social nature.

Gestalt (German psychological terminology). Something considered as a whole being without abstracting any physical, psychological, sociological or moral aspect of it.

God (Feuerbachian terminology). That ideal possibility of being, or ego ideal, projected by the self into the world as the best that it could become.

Guilt (psychoanalytic and existentialist terminology). Psychological guilt signifies an emotion of unworthiness and regret resulting from violating an internalized culturally defined norm. This guilt is a painful internalized punishment. Existential guilt signifies unavoidable responsibility and accountability of a self who is at once free, although burdened by finitude.

Hedonism. A doctrine that pleasure, either psychologically compelling or ethically obligatory, is the sole source of value and is to be maximized to secure happiness

Homeostatic (biological terminology). The tendency to maintain a steady state or equilibrium in functioning of an organism.

Hubris (religious terminology). A sin of pride committed by an individual placing his opinions or actions above those prescribed by established authoritative Others, be they ecclesiastical or divine.

Idea (Hegelian terminology). The thought product, or Notion actualized by a spiritual being that thinks and acts intentionally.

Idea (Platonic terminology). A universal concept expressing an eternal essential nature from which any particular finite thing obtains its rational identity. Platonic Ideas are ideal in the sense of perfection, serving as a model to understand an ever-changing finite world. Mold is to casting as the Idea is to those imperfect finite things imitating or partaking of it. Platonic Ideas are objects of thought: nontemporal, nonspatial, nonphysical existing in a supersensible realm. Examples are triangulatity and goodness among many others often called Forms in English translation.

Index Expurgatorius. A list of books prohibited from being read by the faithful of the medieval Roman Catholic Church. This practice has been discontinued.

Infinite (author's terminology). An unbounded continuously expanding whole of being and the meaning thereof. Hegel thought of it as a totality of being with indeterminate specificity, achieved with the complete termination of finite processes in which all potentiality is actualized.

Instantiate. A concrete example or public fact originating with a conception made actual.

Introjection (psychoanalytic terminology). A process whereby an authoritative Other is incorporated into the being of the self which identifies either non-rationally or irrationally. The opposite of introjection is projection.

Intuitionism. Any philosophical theory claiming to acquire knowledge of something by an unmediated direct apprehension which can be sensuous, ethical or logical.

Meaning (author's terminology). Anything signified or intended by the use of signs. Negativity, in the form of distinguishing something from an Other, is prerequisite.

Mediation. A process of finite transition in meaning or being wherein a compromise formation is effected from previously opposed differences.

Metaphysics. A philosophy initiated by Aristotle establishing first principles describing being in general.

Moment(s) (Hegelian terminology). A particular difference in a finite being temporally altering such that it is not presently what it was previously or will become in the future. Also, a temporal aspect of an ontological process whereby identity is maintained through a temporal sequence of differences. Acorn and oak tree are different moments of an identical being.

Narcissism (Freudian terminology). Self-existence exclusively focused upon immediate gratification without reference to the needs and desires of other selves. Pleasure is secured in social isolation or provided by a primitive symbiotic union with a nurturer. Self-love is the connotation of common parlance.

Naturalism. A philosophical orientation toward explaining self and world in terms of the physical and social sciences.

Necessity. An aspect of implication wherein something is compelled to be the case, or without which something cannot be the case. Founded by ontological negativity, major examples are alienating finitude, natural forces, destiny and a sense of obligation. Freedom becomes meaningful and given impetus by necessity.

Need (author's terminology). A deficiency in being which is felt as an obligation to rectify. Something lacking which ought to exist and is achievable by intentional self-activity within an environment.

Negative freedom (author's terminology). Negativity, existentially expressed by a reactive, non-creative self with the capacity to refuse, say no, or deny. Hegel thought of freedom as essentially negative self-activity lacking social control and thus socially threatening, if not actually destructive. Negative freedom requires law and authoritative Others to channel its use and prevent its abuse.

Negativity (author's terminology). A ubiquitous attribute of thought, being and process. Signifier of difference in thought or being and basis for implication, formal or material, as well as any process.

Neurosis (Freudian terminology). Abnormal behavior, beliefs or attitudes resulting from a psychic compromise between instinctual demands and socially prohibited behavior. The substitute replacement for the prohibited desire is irrational and unstable.

Non-being or ***Nothing*** (Parmenidean or Hegelian terminology). The obverse of Being. An abstract signifier of a negation of Being or a potentiality for any finite being.

Notion (Hegelian terminology). Categories or concepts implicit to thought applicable to finite beings with implications expressed by a progressive dialectical process of sublation making explicit a whole structure of thought encompassing being.

Nuomena (Kantian terminology). The presumed being of something, not constructed by subjective mental processes applied to sensuous intuitions, and so unknowable.

Objective Intentionality (Husserlian terminology). A concept of phenomenology and fundamental attribute of consciousness or self-consciousness reflective of subjective negativity wherein the content of thought is always *other* than the subject.

Obligation (author's terminology). A sensing of need or desire by a free and rational subject who can think of something that is not, but ought to become actual through intentionally directed behavior.

One and Many (Parmenidean or Platonic terminology). The *One* signifies a being with an identity without a distinguishing difference. The *Many* signifies a being with an identity solely formed by distinguishing differences. How the *One* could be *Many*, or the converse, is enigmatic.

Ontological Negativity (author's terminology). A principle governing the being of thought and the thought of being; providing the meaning of anything and its identity while undergoing a temporal process of finite alteration.

Ontology. Any philosophical theory explicating the meaning of being.

Other(s) (author's terminology). Something whose being and meaning consists of what it is not, and so always signified negatively by distinction from something else or opposition to it. This term is capitalized and has (s) added to indicate both singular and plural senses applicable within the context of the sentence.

Particular. Something finite, the meaning of which is determined negatively by differences from others related to it.

Perversion (psychoanalytic terminology). Deviation from a norm and choice of object to obtain pleasure by a fixation upon objects dissociated from an instinctual aim. Examples are homosexuality, paedophilia, bestiality, pederasty, fetishism, transvestitism, voyeurism, exhibitionism, sado-masochism, bulimia, anorexia, dipsomania, drug addiction, prostitution and delinquency.

Philosophical Anthropology (author's perspective). An answer to the question of what it means to be human from the combined perspectives of naturalism, pragmatism, existentialism, psychoanalysis and social psychology.

Phenonena (Kantian terminology). Something finite that appears, signified by the application of subjective mental categories and an imaginative schema providing space-time order synthesizing sensuous intuitions.

Phenomenology. A method of knowing something immediately according to its conscious appearance without interpretation or mediation by any given structure of thought or influence of concepts acquired from past experience. One suspends judgment about what appears and simply describes it as it appears. Edmund Husserl invented the method and it was applied by twentieth century existentialists who attempted to know being simply as it appears to a conscious subject.

Positivism. An empiricist and analytic philosophical tradition eschewing ontological or metaphysical presuppositions, attempting to be purely descriptive and value neutral according to an ideal of eliminating bias in scientific procedure.

Positive freedom (Hegel's or Ricoeur's terminology). A dealienating response resulting from dual moments of negativity in which a limit is confronted and transcended by deliberation and intentional self-directed behavior.

Postmodernism. A late twentieth century contemporary philosophical relativism and counter-culture movement claiming the individual to be strictly a product of dominant contending interests, historical and cultural forces embedded in language forming beliefs and attitudes without alternatives. Originating as a method of literary and social criticism, major exponents are Derrida and Foucault, also an advocate of structuralism.

Pragmatism. An American philosophy claiming that the meaning of a concept is constituted by the consequences of its use. Meaning is hypothetical activity: if one does this, then something observable and predictable will follow. Prominent exponents were Pierce, Dewey, and James, who follow in the philosophical tradition of British empiricism and utilitarianism.

Psychoanalysis. A Freudian method of exploring psychic conflicts by uninhibited talking, associating thoughts and providing therapeutic relief by working-through psychological and behavioral suffering. Theories associated with the method imply a general philosophical worldview applicable to understanding self and culture.

Psychosis (psychoanalytic terminology). The psychological negation of reality so traumatic that the self withdraws into a delusional or hallucinatory world of its own construction.

Rational Freedom (author's terminology). An integration of thought with intentional self-activity developed through a process of socialization defining a capacity for dealienation expressive of the spiritual essence of being human.

Rationalism. A philosophical tradition asserting the identity of reality with rationality such that the real is rational and vice versa. Plato and Descartes are the most famous exponents.

Rationalization (psychoanalytic terminology). Providing reasons to evade censure for a belief or action unconsciously or subconsciously motivated. The reasons disguise motives and so are not really intended to justify as much as to dismiss objections to the belief or action in question.

Realism. A metaphysical doctrine asserting that objects are entirely distinct from the self who can sense and know something about them.

Reason (Hegelian terminology). A capacity of thought to absolutely comprehend that being which is infinite and unconditioned as opposed to understanding finite objects contingent upon an experience of their relationship to each other. Reason is a speculative synthesis dealing with Ideas resulting from a dialectical process of sublation and self-active intention or free will. Reason comprehends Ideas such as God and Hegel's absolute Idea.

Reification. A process of self-objectification whereby the original intentions of an objectified work product are contradicted by its subsequent social uses. A reified self is one transformed into an alien Other: lacking freedom; unable to know who or what it is; an object of social use manipulated by intentions alien to the aims of its original nature.

Repression (Freudian terminology). A psychic process of negativity whereby some instinctual desire is censored, excluded from consciousness, and prohibited from expression. Instinct and idea are dissociated and displaced by unconscious non-rational psychic defenses in obedience to what authoritative Others proscribe.

Romanticism. A late eighteenth and early nineteenth century philosophical and cultural critique of rationalism: emphasizing subjectivity, intuition, emotional passion, natural process and spirituality as the basis for establishing truth and value.

Sado-masochism (Freudian terminology). A behavior in which pain, suffering or humiliation is inflicted on oneself or someone else. The enjoyment of such suffering is a perversion of some authentic instinctual aim, also evil, and so alienating to both perpetrator and victim, even when the same person.

Self (author's terminology). A human being with needs and desires who develops and realizes its potentiality for being by responding to alienating finitude with its capacity for rationality, freedom and goal seeking behavior.

Self-existence (author's terminology). An existential condition of being human by confronting alienating finitude and responding with dealienating intentional activity.

Self-concept (author's perspective). The beliefs, attitudes and dispositions defining personality and enabling self-projection and self-objectification.

Self-giving Love (author's terminology). An expression of the dealienating power of rationality and freedom in nurturing behavior. Reciprocity between lover and beloved form intense emotional bonds sustaining social cohesion.

Self-identification (author's terminology). A psychological process initiating socialization, whereby a self-concept is acquired from an authoritative Other, coercively by non-rational or irrational means, or non-coercively by rational means. Incorporating attitudes, beliefs and dispositions of authoritative Others serves as a model for developing personality to cope with environmental conditions.

Self-identity (author's terminology). An objectified self corresponding to a self-concept that is true and achieved by completing the process of socialization.

Self-objectification (Hegelian terminology). A process through which the self secures an objective identity by projecting its beliefs, attitudes and values into the world through intentional self-activity, or work. The work product is an instantiated self and legacy of work remaining in the world.

Self-projection (quasi-psychoanalytic). Expressing beliefs, attitudes or values indicative of personality through behavior of an individual.

Self-realization (author's terminology). Actualizing the human potentiality for being in the world and with its fellows by dealienating intentional self-activity responding to need and desire.

Signified (linguistic terminology). Whatever is represented by a signifier in a language system. Being is the most abstract general representation with a linguistic sign. Unrelated to existence, nothing other than the logical capacity for thought can be represented. Signified and signifier are correlative concepts.

Signifier (linguistic terminology). A sign within a logical system of signs. What is represented is either the thought of being or the being of thought. Signifier and signified are correlative concepts.

Socialization (author's perspective). A process of dealienation consisting of the formation of a self-concept by a self-identification with authoritative Others, a self-projection of their prescriptions and proscriptions, and self-objectification with them.

Social Psychology. An explanation of character formation by psychological and sociological influences. Prominent thinkers such as Fromm, Reisman and White offer valuable critiques of contemporary culture.

Social Self (author's terminology). A final phase of socialization and self-development marked by complete social integration directed by a highly developed capacity for rational freedom.

Spirit (quasi-Hegelian author's terminology). A being with attributes of rationality and freedom forming an infinite potentiality for being.

Spurious Infinite (Hegelian terminology). Interminable negating succession of something finite not to be confused with a perfect infinite whole of being.

Structuralism. A European originated positivist methodology for scientifically describing language as a logical system of associative signifiers abstracted from existential context, disregarding the nature of what is signified. The methodology eschews hidden philosophical presuppositions, suspends any search for truth or telos and so is historically allied with ancient Sophism, Cultural Relativism and contemporary Postmodernism. Originating in the linguistic science of Saussure, the methodology was extended by Foucault and Lacan to show how language is employed for socialization. Levi-Strauss applied the methodology to interpret culture.

Sublation (Hegelian terminology). A mediating dialectical process driven by negativity whereby the meaning and being of something is enriched and transformed to effect a compromise, incorporating originating oppositions, but with an added difference and new significance.

Sublimation (Freudian terminology). A substitution of one desire and object for another which redirects an instinctual aim away from antisocial behavior.

Subjective Idealism. A metaphysical perspective defining objects of the world in terms of the constitution of the mind. Bishop Berkeley enunciated the position by claiming that *to be is only to be perceived.* Kant elaborated mental structures required for the possibility of a world and knowledge of it.

Superego (Freudian terminology). A psychic mechanism for social control of individual behavior. Introjected Others, namely parental and cultural authority, create an ideal self-concept that censors its own behavior, provides the reward of self-esteem and punishment of guilt for either the projection or violation of internalized norms. This Freudian psycho-sociological concept is a naturalistic explanation of conscience.

Tautology (logical terminology). A proposition in which the predicate is identical to the subject in meaning, although employing different linguistic signs. The signified literally repeats the signifier as in, *Baldheaded men are hairless men.*

Telos (Aristotelian terminology). The aim of something or goal toward which something develops.

They-self (Heideggerian terminology). A self whose potentiality is unrealized and obscured by the domination of authoritative Others; also characterized by public anonymity and impersonality, and most importantly lacking authenticity and autonomy.

Thought (author's terminology). A process of symbolic signification of being with formal logical and material implication and generating intentional self-activity.

Totality. That which is absolutely inclusive, exhausting every potential or actual aspect of being or meaning.

Truth (author's terminology). The meaning of being driven by ontological negativity and existentially revealed by a process of dealienation responding to the alienating finitude of self-existence.

Universals. Class concepts with signifying intention and meaning expressed by implication, either formal or material. Since the universal is an abstract signifier including unenumerated implicit differences among the many signified, it also implies complex relationships among them.

Utilitarianism. British ethical philosophy initiated by Jeremy Bentham, inventor of a hedonistic calculus, socially defining right conduct in terms of *the greatest happiness for the greatest number* of persons. The value of something is judged by its usefulness in securing a preponderance of pleasure over pain according to John Stuart Mill's exposition of the doctrine.

Via Negativa. (negative theology). A method of knowing an infinite God by negating the specific attributes of finite beings. Jewish philosopher Maimonides claimed that human beings could only know what God is not, but not what God is. No positive knowledge of the divine is possible.

Weltanschauung. A German word connoting comprehensive perspective or world-view. Any synoptic philosophy or comprehensive cultural interpretation embedded in a public language providing coherence to experience, and from which is derived meaning, value and guidance for human conduct.

Work (author's terminology). Self-activity and self-projection in the world and with one's fellows intended to overcome some form of alienation by satisfying specific needs and desires while leaving behind a humanized world of self-objectified products.

Zeitgeist (Hegelian terminology). A German word translated as *World Historical Spirit* signifying a spiritual force of predominant ideas or cultural ethos in historical epochs expressed through the agency of heroic individuals.

Bibliography

Cited Works of Georg Wilhelm Friedrich Hegel:

Hegel, G. W. F. (1992) *Early Theological Writings* (T. M. Knox, Trans.). Philadelphia, PA: University of Pennsylvania Press.

Hegel, G. W. F. (1995) *Lectures on the Philosophy of Religion*: vol.1, Introduction and the Concept of Religion (P. G. Hodgson, Ed. & Trans.). Berkeley & Los Angeles CA: University of California Press.

Hegel, G. W. F. (1830) *Hegel's Logic*: Being Part One of the Encyclopedia of the Philosophical Sciences (3rd ed., 1975) (William Wallace, Trans.). London, England: Oxford University Press.

Hegel, G. W. F. (1969) *Hegel's Science of Logic* (A. V. Miller, Trans.). London, England: Humanities Press, George Allen and Unwin Ltd.

Hegel, G. W. F. (1967) *The Phenomenology of Mind* (J. B. Baillie, Trans.). New York, NY: Harper and Row.

Hegel, G. W. F. (1977) *Hegel's Philosophy of Right* (T. M. Knox, Trans.). New York, NY: Oxford University Press.

Hegel, G. W. F. (1956) *The Philosophy of History* (J. Sibree, Trans.). New York, NY: Dover.

Hegel, G. W. F. (1953) *Reason in History* (Robert S. Hartman, Trans.). New York, NY: Macmillan.

Other citations:

King James Version. (1958) *The Holy Bible*. London, England: Collins' Clear-Type Press

Hobbes, Thomas. (1983) *Leviathan*. Aylesbury, Bucks, England: Penguin

Index

N

O

P